Study Guide

J. L. GILLES LEVASSEUR
UNIVERSITY OF OTTAWA

The Law and Business Administration in Canada

Ninth Edition

J.E. Smyth
Late Professor of Commerce, University of Toronto
D.A. Soberman
Professor of Law, Queen's University
A.J. Easson
Professor of Law, Queen's University

Toronto

Vice President, Editorial Director: Michael Young
Developmental Editor: Maurice Esses
Production Editor: Jennifer Therriault
Production Coordinator: Deborah Starks

2 3 4 5 05 04 03 02

Printed and bound in Canada

To my parents, the best parents.

Preface

Business law has changed greatly in the last ten years, especially with advent of electronic commerce. We are dealing with new legal rules that are still, in several cases, to be defined and elaborated by the courts and governmental authorities.

Nevertheless, the bulk of the legal principles to be applied in business law and electronic commerce still resides in the basic concepts of contract law and related fields including intellectual property and negotiable instruments. Consequently, it's important to fully understand the basic legal elements affecting businesses today in order to deal with the business ventures provided by the Internet and electronic commerce.

The purpose of this Study Guide is to help students better understand the ramifications, complexity, and applications of business law. The Study Guide is composed of sections including essay, multiple choice, and true/false questions. Answers are provided in each section to facilitate the learning of business law.

I hope that the Study Guide for the ninth edition of *The Law and Business Administration in Canada* will be a valuable supplement for your business law course. Any suggestions that you have for improving it would be most welcome. Please send them to me care of the Acquisitions Editor, Business Law, Pearson Education Canada, 26 Prince Andrew Place, Don Mills, Ontario M3C 2T8.

J.L. Gilles LeVasseur

1

Law and Society

Purpose and Significance

This chapter provides us with a background against which the workings of our legal system can be seen more clearly. The chapter begins by considering law from a philosophical point of view. What is law and what is its significance in the business environment? How do we distinguish between the "laws of nature" and the "laws of human conduct"? What is the relationship between the law and business ethics?

After considering how law is defined, we will discuss how the courts decide whether the legislation is valid under the Canadian Constitution. We must understand how stakeholders determine the effects of legislation, particularly the effects of the *Canadian Charter of Rights and Freedoms* and the protection of civil liberties.

Finally, we must understand how the courts, when settling disputes, interpret legislation originating from both the federal Parliament and provincial legislatures.

Learning Objectives

A. Discuss the nature and source of law.

B. Outline the purposes of a legal system.

C. Describe the role of the courts.

D. Define the characteristics of the *Canadian Charter of Rights and Freedoms*.

E. Explain how courts interpret legislation.

Content Outline

I. Nature and source of law
  - A. Definition of law
  - B. Natural law theory
  - C. Legal positivism

II. Purposes of a legal system
  - A. Law and morals
  - B. Law and business ethics

III. Legislation and the courts
  - A. Two challenges to the validity of a statute
  - B. Meanings of civil liberties

IV. *Canadian Charter of Rights and Freedoms*
  - A. Justification under Section 1
  - B. Burden of proof
  - C. Rights and freedoms protected by the *Charter*

V. Interpretation of legislation by the courts
  - A. Process and limitations of statutory interpretation adopted by the English courts
  - B. Consideration of a piece of legislation's history

Questions on Learning Objectives

Objective A: Discuss the nature and source of law.

A.1 How is law defined? (pp. 2–3)

A.2 When, if ever, is it right to break the law? (p. 4)

A.3 What are the two mainstreams of natural law theory? (p. 4)

A.4 Who are the legal positivists? (p. 5)

A.5 Describe Hume's distinction between "is" and "ought". How does this relate to positive law? (pp. 5–6)

Objective B: Outline the purposes of a legal system.

B.1 Is a legal system necessary for a harmonious society? (pp. 6–8)

Objective C: Describe the role of the courts.

C.1 What do courts do? (p. 8)

C.2 Why does the role of courts differ between federal states and unitary states? (pp. 9–10)

C.3 What are the two challenges to the validity of a statute? (pp. 10–11)

C.4 What are the various meanings of civil liberties? (pp. 11–12)

C.5 Explain how a Canadian court can declare a statute passed by the Canadian Parliament unconstitutional. (pp. 10–12)

C.6 What can the Canadian Parliament do if the court curbs a piece of legislation? (pp. 10–12)

Objective D: **Define the characteristics of the *Canadian Charter of Rights and Freedoms*.**

D.1 What does "entrenchment" mean? (p. 12)

D.2 How does the *Constitution Act, 1982*, differ from other statutes passed by the Canadian Parliament? (pp. 12–13)

D.3 Must provincial legislation comply with the *Charter*? (pp. 13–14)

D.4 Explain the justification under Section 1 of the *Charter*? (p. 13)

D.5 What is the burden of proof under the *Charter*? (p. 13)

D.6 What fundamental freedoms are recognised by the *Charter*? (p. 14)

D.7 List the categories of rights that are dealt with by the *Charter*. (pp. 14–16)

D.8 Freedom of expression is one of the fundamental freedoms assured by the *Canadian Charter of Rights and Freedoms*. Does this mean that people can say or broadcast whatever they want? (pp. 12–16)

Objective E: **Explain how courts interpret legislation.**

E.1 Describe the process and limitations of statutory interpretation adopted by the English courts. (p. 16)

E.2 Will Canadian courts consider the history of a piece of legislation when they are attempting to interpret it? (p. 17)

Answers to Questions on Learning Objectives

A.1 A simple definition of law would be misleading because law is so diverse and complex. Law provides rules of conduct that are enforceable by the courts in order to protect and predict the behaviour of people.

A.2 A legal system can be confronted with extremely difficult moral questions. No solution is entirely satisfactory, and reasonable people can strongly disagree about the appropriate disposition of a difficult case. We must always respect the principle that when breaking the law, necessity must present in the decision process but also, the consequences of breaking the law must never exceed the initial reasons for breaking the law.

A.3 The more traditional mainstream of natural law is based on religious belief. It accepts that law is premised on religious precepts and values. The second mainstream assumes that rational people applying reason and logic can arrive at an understanding of the ultimate principles of justice. These truths, according to the Dutch philosopher Grotius, would exist independently of God or a divine source.

A.4 Legal positivism is concerned with ascertaining the body of law that "is" with describing those criteria or tools that can be used to distinguish positive law from all other rules. Legal positivists are those who insist upon a clear distinction between law and morals.

A.5 Hume distinguished between physical laws (e.g., the law of gravity) and normative laws (e.g., the law against drunk driving). In Hume's analysis, some normative rules have sanctions that authoritatively compel compliance. This "is" the law. Some normative rules are merely suggestions of appropriate conduct without authoritative compulsion (e.g., giving a holiday bonus to your employees). There are things that people "ought" to observe that are not law. The legal positivist

(John Austin, for example) would say that law is created only by those who hold power to punish law-breakers and "command" obedience.

B.1 The premise that a legal system is necessary for a harmonious society has been examined and challenged throughout history. Of course, current economic and social conditions influence our answers to this question. Attempts have been made to examine this question by imagining what life in society might be like without law.

C.1 Courts determine the validity of legislation, interpret legislation, protect civil liberties, and resolve disputes between private parties.

C.2 In a federal state, legislative and governmental powers are allocated between the central government and the governments of the federal units (such as provinces). This allocation of power often requires an adjudicator—a role courts are usually called on to perform. In addition, the specifics of allocation often require a written constitution. The enforcement and interpretation of the constitution is a task well suited to courts.

In a unitary state, such as England, this role of supervising allocated powers and interpreting a carefully drafted constitution is not as likely to be required. The role of the courts is, therefore, more likely to be limited to construing and enforcing the statutes of a supreme legislation.

C.3 First, the courts may challenge a statute if it is ruled unconstitutional. The statute will be void and no change in the law will occur. Second, the courts may interpret statutes narrowly to avoid interfering with existing private rights. Such interpretations may, in large measure, frustrate an intended reform.

C.4 The term civil liberties is difficult to define because it comprises a number of quite separate ideas related only by a general concern for the well being of the individual citizen. Two other terms, civil rights and human rights, are often used as synonyms. The latter terms are older and refer primarily to freedom of the individual in politics and religion. The freedoms include freedom of expression (both of speech and of the press), freedom of association and assembly, freedom to practice and preach one's religion, freedom from arbitrary arrest and detention, and the right to a fair trial.

C.5 A court can decide that a statute is unconstitutional because it purports to deal with an area that is exclusively within the jurisdiction of the provinces under the *Constitution Act, 1867*. Additionally, it can decide that even if the law is within federal jurisdiction under the constitution, the government as prosecuting authority has placed an unreasonable interpretation on the statute and has applied it beyond its competence.

C.6 A constitutional defeat is more serious than a narrow interpretation. A constitutional amendment would be the only way of changing the result of a court ruling that a statute is unconstitutional. However, if the problem is simply one of interpretation, the government can subsequently introduce an amendment to preclude similar, future arguments.

D.1 The entitlement of individuals to certain civil rights is an integral part of the Canadian legal system. However, our legal system originally relied on tradition and custom to assure that courts and legislatures would assert these rights. The *Constitution Act, 1982* introduced the *Canadian Charter of Rights and Freedoms*. With this, certain civil rights were entrenched, or given legal recognition and form beyond convention and tradition.

D.2 The *Constitution Act, 1982* differs from other statutes in two substantial respects. First, it cannot be repealed or amended like other legislation. It can be amended only under the terms of an amending formula contained in the act, which requires the participation of the provinces. Second, no statute can be passed or enforced which offends the provisions of the *Constitution Act, 1867*.

D.3 At the insistence of several provinces, the *Charter* includes Section 33, which permits a provincial legislature to override the *Charter*. The statute must state expressly that it "shall operate notwithstanding" specified sections of the *Charter*. The years overriding section expires five years after coming into force unless it is re-enacted by the provincial legislature.

D.4 None of the rights set out in the *Charter* is absolute. Section 1 states that rights are subject "to such reasonable limits prescribed by law as can be demonstrably justified in a free and democratic society". First, the object to be served by the limit must be "of sufficient importance to warrant overriding a constitutionally protected right or freedom". That is, the object must not be trivial but "pressing and substantial". Second, the means chosen must be proportional to the importance of the objective and must impair the *Charter* right as little as reasonably possible in achieving the objective. Third, on an overview, when the effects of the infringement on rights are compared with the object that has been achieved, that object must on balance justify the infringement.

D.5 In general, a statute is presumed to be valid (i.e., within the power of a legislature passing it) and a person attacking it must show why it is invalid. However, a person needs show only that one of his constitutionally guaranteed rights has been infringed by a provision in a statute. The provision would then be presumed invalid unless the government could persuade the court that the infringement was "demonstrably justified". Thus, the burden is on the government to establish that the section of a statute that interferes with constitutional rights is justified.

D.6 The following fundamental freedoms are recognised by the *Charter*: freedom of conscience and religion; freedom of thought, belief, opinion and expression, including freedom of the press and other media of communication; freedom of peaceful assembly; and freedom of association.

D.7 The categories of rights dealt with by the *Charter* are as follows: legal rights; equality rights; democratic rights; and mobility rights.

D.8 Obviously limits will be imposed on an individual's rights to freedom of expression. There will undoubtedly be long and continuing debates about the extent to which the restrictions to freedom should fetter the right of expression. The issue of censorship is one that is unlikely to find a community consensus. In discussing the issue of freedom of expression, we should bear in mind the important public interest in open and free discussion, as well as the private interest in free expression.

E.1 The English position is that a statute should be interpreted on its face. That is, a person reading the statute should be able to rely on the words alone without looking outside the statute. The problem is that words and phrases don't always have exact meanings. A word or phrase might even have multiple meanings. A dictionary does not always reveal the intended meaning. It may emerge from an understanding of legislative purpose.

E.2 Until 1976 Canadian courts followed the English approach to public debate of a social problem. In the Reference re Anti-Inflation Act case, the Supreme Court of Canada made a substantial change in its position. The court referred to both a government White Paper and the House of Commons debates in arriving at its decision.

Multiple-Choice Questions

1. What is the definition of law?

a) Law provides a framework that gives people broader freedom of choice.
b) Law provides rules of conduct that are enforceable by, or with the help of, government.
c) Law prohibits conduct that society believes to be harmful to others.
d) Law prescribes simple, but vital, rules that allow people to function in their everyday lives.
e) All of the above.

2. What is the distinction between physical laws and normative laws?

a) Physical laws are laws of government established to regulate human conduct whereas normative laws are laws of nature that cannot be broken.
b) Physical laws are laws of conduct connected to the physical interaction of humans whereas normative laws are laws that establish the norms for human interaction.
c) Physical laws are laws of nature that cannot be broken whereas normative laws are laws of government established to regulate human conduct.
d) Physical laws are laws of conduct connected to the physical interaction of humans whereas normative laws are laws of God.
e) Physical laws are laws of nature that cannot be broken whereas normative laws are laws that establish the norms for human interaction.

3. What is the distinction between moral rules and positive laws?

a) Moral rules cannot be broken whereas failure to observe positive laws results in sanctions.
b) Failure to observe moral rules creates annoyance in others and a bad conscience in the wrongdoer whereas failure to observe positive laws results in sanctions.

c) Failure to observe moral rules results in sanctions whereas positive laws cannot be broken.
d) Failure to observe moral rules creates annoyance in others and a bad conscience in the wrongdoer whereas positive laws cannot be broken.
e) Failure to observe moral rules results in sanctions whereas failure to observe positive laws creates annoyance in others and a bad conscience in the wrongdoer.

4. How can natural law be used for contradictory purposes?

a) Natural law can be used to punish offenders and to compensate victims.
b) Natural law can be based on religious beliefs and on the notion that people are rational.
c) Natural law can be used to support reforms and revolutions and to maintain the status quo.
d) Natural law is self-evident and is hidden in religious doctrine.
e) Natural law can be based on religious beliefs and used to compensate victims.

5. What is the basic element that the different theories of natural law share?

a) All theories of natural law are based on religion.
b) All theories of natural law are based on fundamental, immutable moral principles.
c) All theories of natural law are based on the laws of nature.
d) All theories of natural law are based on human laws.
e) All theories of natural law are based on the physical laws of the earth.

6. What is a Brandeis Brief?

a) Evidence of the legislative history of a statute.
b) Evidence of a constitutional nature.
c) Evidence of the circumstances surrounding the case.
d) Evidence of a socio-economic nature, scientific studies and technological advances.
e) Evidence of the harm caused by the statute.

7.The federal Parliament passes a new law prohibiting the use of cartoon characters in advertising aimed at adults. A national association objects to the new restrictions and wants to have the law declared unconstitutional. Who has the final word on whether a law is constitutional?

a) The Supreme Court of Canada because judges are always lawyers while only some members of Parliament are lawyers.
b) Parliament because it represents the elected will of the people.
c) The Supreme Court of Canada because it is an independent arm of the government that strives to decide matters impartially and fairly.
d) Parliament because it is the top authority according to the constitution.
e) Parliament because the Supreme Court of Canada is nine elderly lawyers, neither elected nor representative of the people, defeating the wishes of a democratically elected legislature.

8. Which is more serious — a constitutional defeat in the courts or a narrow interpretation?

a) Interpretation because this determines what the statute actually means.
b) Constitutional defeat in the courts because the result could be that the statute would have no effect.
c) Interpretation because a very narrow interpretation could result in the statute not applying to any situation.
d) Constitutional defeat in the courts because Parliament would have to re-enact the statute to correct the problem.
e) Interpretation because a narrow interpretation could frustrate the will of Parliament.

9. A radical supremacist group plans a parade and rally downtown. The group's principles say that they are better than any other group. The city council wants to prohibit the parade and rally, but is afraid of being seen to deny the group its *Charter* right to freedom of expression. Does the council have an argument to prohibit the parade and rally?

a) Yes, because the group's expressions defame other people.
b) No, because nothing can infringe on a *Charter* right.
c) Yes, because the group's principles are immoral.
d) No, because the freedom of expression is the highest right in the *Charter*.
e) Yes, because the group promotes hate and advocates infringing the rights of others.

10. The Constitution gives both the federal and provincial governments powers in sections 91 and 92. How may those powers be characterised?

a) Inclusive powers and overlapping powers.
b) Exclusive powers, concurrent powers, and residual powers.
c) Inclusive powers, compatible powers, and residual powers.
d) Exclusive powers, overlapping powers, and compatible powers.
e) Inclusive powers, overlapping powers, and residual powers.

11. How may the *Charter* allow an activity or law to infringe a right in the *Charter*?

a) By having section one of the *Charter* apply to the law.
b) By having the activity done by a nongovernmental person or organisation.
c) By having Parliament pass the law using section 33 of the *Charter*.
d) By having the activity completed prior to the date the *Charter* came into force.
e) All of the above.

12. Jamal, an immigrant from Europe, arrived in Canada. He is fluent in English and has qualifications as a doctor from his home country. After receiving landed immigrant status, Jamal looks for employment as a doctor in Toronto and Vancouver. He is repeatedly told that he is not qualified as a doctor in Canada and he would have to return to school for three years before being allowed to take the medical qualification exams. Jamal thinks this policy is discriminatory so decides to challenge it. What section of the *Charter* could this policy infringe?

a) Section 6 — the mobility right to pursue the gaining of a livelihood.
b) Section 7 — the right to life, liberty and security of the person.
c) Section 2 — freedom of association.
d) Section 15 — discrimination based on national origin.
e) None of the above.

13. The police are investigating a series of murders and suspect Harold. The police want to question him at the police station. Under section 10 of the *Charter*, what information do the police need to give Harold before they begin questioning?

a) That he has the right to counsel, the right to be informed promptly of the reason for the questioning, and the right not to say anything.
b) That he has the right to counsel and if he cannot afford counsel, he has the right to have counsel appointed for him.
c) That he has the right to confess without the police being able to use the information against him in court.
d) That he has the right to a trial within one month of the questioning.
e) No information has to be provided to the accused by the police prior to questioning.

14. The federal government passes a statute that makes possession of one or more kilograms of a prohibited drug an offence of trafficking unless the accused proves otherwise. The first person charged under this new offence challenges it as being contrary to the *Charter*. What argument should the government consider in support of the new offence?

a) The offence was passed by a lawfully elected Parliament following the proper procedures.
b) The offence is criminal law, which overrides the *Charter*.
c) The offence can be re-enacted using section 33 to override the *Charter* for a period of ten years.
d) The offence is a reasonable limit prescribed by law that can be demonstrably justified in a free and democratic society.
e) The offence is not contrary to the *Charter* right of an accused being considered innocent until proven guilty.

Answers to Multiple-Choice Questions

1. e)
See pages 2–3 for more information.

2. c)
See page 5 for more information.

3. b)
See pages 5–7 for more information.

4. c)

See pages 4–5 for more information.

5. b)

See pages 4–5 for more information

6. d)

See page 18 for more information.

7. a)

See page 9 for more information.

8. b)

See pages 10–11 for more information.

9. e)

See page 14 for more information.

10. b)

See pages 9–10 for more information.

11. e)

See pages 12–14 for more information.

12. e)

See pages 12–14 for more information.

13. a)

See pages 12–14 for more information.

14. d)

See pages 12–14 for more information.

True/False Questions

1. The rule of law is a code of conduct established by the governments to regulate private business.

2. Normative law is physical laws of nature.

3. In a federal country such as Canada or the United States, the federal government cannot alter the structure of provincial governments without a proper constitutional amendment.

4. The *Charter* clearly applies to governments (federal, provincial and territorial) and to governmental activities.

5. The Brandeis Brief is an oral argument presented by the court.

6. In a federal state, legislative and governmental powers are allocated between the central government and the governments of the federal units (such as provinces).

Answers to True/False Questions

1. False. The rule of law is established legal principles that treat all persons equally and that government itself obeys.

2. False. Normative law is law made by government establishing standards of behaviour and regulating human conduct.

3. True

4. True.

5. False. A Brandeis Brief is a written argument presented to the court.

6. True.

2

The Machinery of Justice

Purpose and Significance

The purpose of this chapter is to give a clear understanding of the Canadian legal system and the tasks courts are called upon to perform. We first discuss the various ways in which law is classified. Then we examine the sources of law; judge-made, legislation, administrative rulings, and the Canadian court system. Finally, we explore concepts that underlie the processes of the legal system.

Courts perform a wide variety of functions that are often complex and have very different roles and functions. For example, we examine specific elements that distinguish trial courts from appeal courts and provincial courts from the Supreme Court of Canada.

Learning Objectives

A. Describe the classifications of law.

B. Examine the need for certainty.

C. Outline the sources of law.

D. Discuss the system of courts in Canada.

E. Examine basic concepts necessary to use the courts.

F. Discuss alternative methods of resolving disputes.

G. Examine the legal aid system.

Content Outline

I. Classifications of Law

II. Substantive and procedure law

III. Public and private law

IV. Civil law and common law

V. The need for certainty
      A. Theory of precedent

VI. Sources of law
      A. Variety of sources
      B. Law made by judges
            1. common law
            2. equity
            3. mergers of the courts
      C. Statutes
      D. Subordinate legislation

VII. System of courts in England

VIII. System of courts in Canada
      A. Courts of first instance
      B. Appellate courts
      C. Federal courts

IX. System of courts in the United States

X. Using the courts
    A. Who may sue?
    B. Standing to sue
    C. Class actions
    D. Procedure law
    E. Settlement out of court
    F. Procedure before trial
    G. The trial
    H. Appeals
    I. Costs
    J. Contingent fees

XI. Alternate dispute resolution

XII. Legal aid

XIII. Legal profession

Questions on Learning Objectives

Objective A: Describe the classifications of law.

A.1   Distinguish between substantive law and procedural law. (p. 22)

A.2   Explain the difference between public law and private law. (p. 22)

A.3   What is common law? In what provinces does it apply? (pp. 22–24)

A.4   What is civil law? What province in Canada operates under a civil law system? (p. 23)

Objective B: Examine the need for certainty.

B.1   What is the meaning of *stare decisis*? (p. 24)

B.2 What limitations to the doctrine of *stare decisis* exist and why?
(p. 24)

Objective C: Examine the sources of law.

C.1 List the sources of law and how each is created. (pp. 25–28)

C.2 What source of law is related to *stare decisis*? (pp. 24)

C.3 What is subordinate legislation and what role does it play? (p. 25)

C.4 Distinguish awards available from common law courts with those available in equity. Are the distinctions still relevant today? (pp. 26–27)

C.5 What purposes do statutes serve? (p. 27)

Objective D: Discuss the system of courts in Canada.

D.1 List and describe the three levels of courts in Canada. (pp. 30–32)

D.2 Describe the jurisdiction of courts of first instance and intermediate appellate courts. (pp. 30–32)

Objective E: Examine basic concepts necessary to use the courts.

E.1 Who may sue in Canadian courts? (p. 33)

E.2   What is standing to sue? Who has it? (p. 33–34)

Objective F: **Discuss alternative methods of resolving disputes.**

F.1   What advantages does an out-of-court settlement have? (pp. 35–36)

F.2   Define entering an appearance, statement of claim, statement of defence, and counterclaim. (p. 36–37)

F.3   Who pays the costs of a lawsuit and on what basis? (pp. 38–39)

F.4   What is a contingency fee? Do you think that such arrangements should be permitted? (pp. 40–41)

Objective G: **Examine the legal aid system.**

G.1   What is legal aid? Do you think it should be extended? If so, into what areas of law? (pp. 42–44)

Answers to Questions on Learning Objectives

A.1   Substantive law is the law that lays down the rights and duties, protected by the law, of each person. For example, both the right to own property and to move about safely within the country are rights you have that the law will protect.

Procedural law is the law by which substantive law rights are enforced. Procedural law encompasses the different levels of court, the documentation that must be produced for the courts and the actual step-by-step proceeding in any lawsuit.

A.2   Public law is the law that deals with relations between the State and persons. It encompasses constitutional law, criminal law, and administrative law. Private law is the law regulating relations between persons. The private law domain encompasses contracts, torts, property, and trusts.

A.3   Common law has a number of meanings. Normally, we use it to mean the body of precedents originally established in Common law courts in England allowing persons to predict future court decisions in which similar facts are present. All cases that are heard in the courts are recorded. To decide the outcome of a new case, judges look back at how similar, previous cases were decided. All the provinces and territories in Canada except Québec follow the common law system.

A.4   Civil law has more than one meaning. Its most common meaning and the one that we will use is that the law is contained in a code that deals with private and properties rights and obligations. When you want to know what your rights or obligations are, you simply refer to the code. Québec operates under a civil law system.

B.1   *Stare decisis* is a Latin term meaning courts are to follow precedent (i.e., previous decisions of a similar nature.).

B.2   The doctrine of *stare decisis* is inappropriate when significant changes in society occur. Its application is also limited by the fact that no two situations are identical. As well, ambiguous language used in previous decisions can make it difficult for it to be strictly followed.

C.1   Case law, statutes, orders-in-council, by-laws and regulations are all sources of law. The courts create case law while the legislatures and Parliament pass statutes. The cabinet issues orders-in-council and municipalities and other delegated authorities are empowered to pass by-laws and regulations.

C.2   *Stare decisis* is the doctrine of following previous cases. The body of these cases becomes a source of law. Both common law decisions and the decisions of the courts of equity are followed so both are sources of law.

C.3   Parliament and the legislatures delegate their authority to certain administrative agencies. When those administrative agencies exercise their powers and create law, it is termed subordinate legislation.

C.4   The approach to legal problems and the remedies given in common law courts are different from those in equity. In common law, the usual remedy is damages. In equity, specific performance, the injunction, and rescission are available. In the past, the remedies were different and were granted as a right of common law whereas they were discretionary in equity. In the late 19th century, there was a "merger" of the common law and equity courts. While administration of the two is now merged, (a single court can dispense either common law or equitable remedies) the two systems of law are still separate. It is therefore important to remember that, when we are dealing with a particular head of liability or a kind of remedy, we have to know whether it comes from the common law or from equity.

C.5 Statutes can either codify or reform the common law. They can also authorise government activity. If a statute codifies existing common law, all it does is restate the common law. This is done so that it is easier to discover what the law is. If the purpose of a statute is to reform the common law, it will depart from the existing case law. The statute explains how the law is to be changed from what previously existed. Enabling legislation authorises the government to carry out programs.

D.1 The three levels of court are courts of first instance where a matter is initially heard, intermediate courts of appeal where appeals from decisions of the courts of first instance are first heard, and the Supreme Court of Canada — the ultimate appellate body.

D.2 Provincial courts hear all criminal cases except the very serious offences such as murder. Appellate courts will hear appeals from courts of first instance.

E.1 Any adult citizen in Canada, of full mental capacity, has the right to sue in Canadian courts. Infants who are Canadian citizens must sue through appropriate adults (e.g., parents). Sometimes non-Canadians are given the right to sue in Canadian courts.

E.2 Individuals affected by a particular wrong normally have the right to "stand" before the court. That is, they have the right to be heard by a court. The courts have had to restrict the class of people with standing in any particular matter to those who are directly affected by the wrong.

F.1 Settling a legal dispute out of court is normally faster and less expensive than actually taking it to court. It has less risk because the result in any court action is uncertain. It also saves emotional energy as it is very trying to go through a trial.

F.2 Entering an appearance is the notice a defendant gives to show that he intends to contest a lawsuit. A statement of claim is a document in which the plaintiff details the allegations he has against the defendant. A statement of defence is the defendant's response to a plaintiff's allegations in which he outlines the facts he disputes and introduces those he will use to support his position. A counterclaim is a claim by the defendant for compensation for an alleged wrong.

F.3   The parties to a lawsuit pay whatever costs they incur. However, the party who loses at trial must pay a certain portion of the successful litigant's costs, usually on a party and party basis. Party and party costs are a scale of costs and are usually less than the full legal costs involved (solicitor and client costs).

F.4   When a lawyer agrees to charge a proportion of whatever he recovers on behalf of his client instead of being paid on an hourly basis, he has accepted payment on a contingency fee basis.

G.1   Legal aid is a program arranged and paid for by the State so that persons with low incomes have access to legal services without having to pay.

Multiple-Choice Questions

1. David is charged with counterfeiting $20 bills. In what court would he be tried?

a) Provincial Court
b) Federal Court, Trial Division
c) Federal Court, Appeal Division
d) Superior Court
e) Supreme Court of Canada

2. A bar owner refuses to pay the Blue Trees Band for a gig. In what court can the band try to collect the $2000?

a) Supreme Court of Canada
b) Superior Court
c) Federal Court, Trial Division
d) Provincial Court
e) Small Claims Court

3. Greg is charged with aggravated assault and he elects to be tried by jury. In what court would he be tried?

a) Small Claims Court
b) Provincial Court
c) Youth Court
d) Superior Court
e) Federal Court, Trial Division

4. Mr. Jones contracts to buy a house for $200 000 from Mr. Smith who refuses to complete the deal. In what court would Mr. Jones sue to have the sale completed?

a) Small Claims Court
b) Provincial Court
c) Youth Court
d) Superior Court
e) Federal Court, Trial Division

5. The federal government wants to find out if a law it passed last year is within its constitutional jurisdiction. In what court should the government ask its question?

a) Provincial Court
b) Superior Court
c) Court of Appeals
d) Federal Court, Trial Division
e) Supreme Court of Canada

6. Alvin and Harry have entered into a contract whereby Alvin has agreed to sell Harry his house, car, and sailboat for $150 000. The sale is to close on April 1. If the deal does not close and a lawsuit results, what category of law is, or categories of law are, relevant to the case?

a) Public law for the sale of the house and private law for the sale of the car and sailboat
b) Substantive law for the right to sell the items and procedural law for the process of the court hearing
c) Civil law for the process of the court hearing and common law for the right to sell the items
d) Roman law for the sale of the house and civil law for the sale of the car and sailboat
e) Substantive law for the entire case

7. Both civil and common law exist in Canada. Which province or provinces have civil law?

a) Newfoundland, Québec and Saskatchewan
b) New Brunswick and Québec
c) Ontario, British Columbia and the Yukon
d) Manitoba
e) Québec

8. Construct Co. agrees to build a house for Gavin, but does not carry out the agreement. Gavin sues Construct Co. and collects money damages. Bigger Limited makes an identical contract with Elvira, but fails to carry out the contract. Relying on the earlier case, Elvira sues Bigger Limited for damages in the same court, but the lawsuit is dismissed. Are these two decisions a problem for a system of justice?

a) No, because each case must be decided independently on its own facts without reference to other decided cases.
b) Yes, because there is a need for consistency, predictability, and fairness in a system of justice.
c) No, because if cases are always decided the same way, there is no need for a system of justice.
d) Yes, because it does not tell builders what they must do to terminate a contract.
e) No, because there would be no justice if cases were always decided the same way.

9. Which of the following is a source of law?

a) Statutes
b) Regulations
c) Prior judicial decisions
d) Administrative decisions
e) All of the above

10. The courts in England, Canada, and the United States are all based on a similar structure, which means that any particular court case can be considered by how many levels of court?

a) 1
b) 2
c) 3
d) 5
e) Infinite

11. American motion pictures and television programs are responsible for a misconception about the way in which trials proceed. What is this misconception?

a) Opening and closing statements are permissible.
b) Surprise witnesses are permissible or surprise confessions are common.
c) Oral decisions from the bench are permissible.
d) Objections to the questioning style of the other counsel are permissible.
e) Not all types of evidence are permissible.

12. How does a judge decide a case when there is no precedent available?

a) The judge's personal preference based on the facts
b) By applying the existing precedents applicable to the circumstances
c) The judge's own values applicable to the facts and parties
d) By applying general legal principles and reason by analogy from other cases
e) By applying the doctrine of *stare decisis* to the case

13. "I was never ruined but twice; once when I won a lawsuit and once when I lost one." How can a successful litigant lose?

a) Costs do not usually cover the full bill of a successful litigant's lawyer and the time and effort required of the litigant.
b) Publicity of the dispute cannot affect the reputation of even a successful litigant.
c) Having to go to court is a personal defeat as the parties have to say that they are unable to settle their own disputes.
d) The extremely short time period typical for a court case makes any successful litigant a loser.
e) None of the above.

14. What are the advantages of alternative dispute resolution?

a) Speed
b) Confidentiality
c) Preserving on-going relations
d) Less costly
e) All of the above

15. Does the Canadian system of awarding costs encourage or discourage litigation?

a) Discourages, because the entire case has to be paid for before the court reaches a decision.
b) Encourages, because the successful litigant gets all his legal costs covered by the loser.
c) Discourages, because an award of costs rarely covers all the legal costs of the successful litigant.
d) Encourages, because the government pays all the costs associated with a court case.
e) Encourages, because there is no incentive to settle the dispute before the court trial.

16. Which of the following is (are) sources of law?
I. Previously decided cases
II. Legislation
III. Substantive law

a) I only
b) II only
c) III only
d) I, II and III
e) I and II only

17. Which of the following is not an advantage of a settlement?

a) Speed
b) Less expense
c) More public exposure
d) Less emotionally taxing
e) Less risk

18. Standing to sue is

a) the capacity of an adult person in Canada to bring an action in Canadian court.
b) those persons who are so directly affected by a wrong that the courts recognise them as being capable of bringing a lawsuit in relation to that wrong.
c) a group of people affected by the same wrong who launch a single court action instead of a series of individual actions.
d) the right of a child to be represented in a lawsuit by an adult person.
e) the right of an insane person to sue through a court-appointed representative.

Answers to Multiple-Choice Questions

1. a)
See pages 30–31 for more information.

2. e)
See page 30 for more information.

3. d)
See page 31 for more information.

4. d)
See page 31 for more information.

5. e)
See page 32 for more information.

6. b)
See page 22 for more information.

7. e)
See page 23 for more information.

8. b)
See pages 23–24 for more information.

9. e)
See pages 25–28 for more information.

10. c)
See pages 29–32 for more information.

11. b)
See page 37 for more information.

12. d)
See pages 24–28 for more information.

13. a)
See pages 38–39 for more information.

14. e)
See page 42 for more information.

15. c)
See pages 38–39 for more information.

16. e)
See page 23 for more information.

17. c)
See page 35 for more information.

18. b)
See pages 33–34 for more information.

True/False Questions

1. The most common meaning of civil law is that the law is contained in a code.

2. *Stare decisis* is the Latin term for the rule that courts are not obliged to follow precedent.

3. Both common law decisions and the decisions of the courts of equity are sources of law.

4. The two levels of court are: courts of first instance where a matter is initially heard and the intermediate courts of appeal where appeals from decisions of the courts of first instance are first heard.

5. When a lawyer agrees to charge a proportion of whatever he recovers on behalf of his client instead of being paid on an hourly basis, he has accepted payment on a contingency fee basis.

6. Legal aid is a program arranged and paid for by the government so that people with low incomes may have access to legal services without having to pay for them.

Answers to True/False Questions

1. True.

2. False. *Stare decisis* is the Latin term for the rule that courts are to follow precedent (i.e., previous decisions of a similar nature).

3. True.

4. False. The three levels of court are: courts of first instance where a matter is initially heard, intermediate courts of appeal where appeals from decisions of the courts of first instance are first heard, and the Supreme Court of Canada, the ultimate appellate body.

5. True.

6. True.

3

The Law of Torts

Purpose and Significance

A tort is a wrong, recognised as compensable by the law, that a person suffers at the hands of another. This definition may seem unsatisfactory because it is not concrete. Unfortunately, no better definition can be given because the kinds of harm for which the law compensates change. Slander, defamation, assault, battery, trespass, negligence and deceit are examples of torts. We are all familiar with such wrongs and know that we cannot commit them without having to compensate the victims of our actions.

In this chapter, we explore tort law by explaining what wrongs are considered torts and when compensation may be recovered. We also discuss the nature and purposes of tort law. Finally, we examine the tort of negligence in detail, as negligence has become a broad head of liability.

Learning Objectives

A.   Discuss the basis for tort liability.

B.   Outline the tort of negligence.

C.   Describe occupier's liability.

D.   Examine several torts other than negligence.

Content Outline

I. Scope of tort law

II. Development of the tort concept

III. Basis for liability
      A. Fault
      B. Strict liability
      C. Social policy
      D. Vicarious liability

IV. Negligence
      A. Elements of a negligence action
      B. Duty of care
      C. Standard of care
      D. Causation
      E. Remoteness of damage
      F. Economic loss
      G. Burden of proof
      H. Plaintiff's own conduct
      I. Relevance of insurance

V. Special aspects of negligence
      A. Hazardous activities
      B. Product liability

VI. Occupier's Liability

VII. Nuisance
      A. Public nuisance
      B. Private nuisance
      C. Environmental protection

VIII. Other torts
    A. Trespass
    B. Assault and battery
    C. False imprisonment and malicious prosecution
    D. Defamation
    E. Economic torts

IX. Remedies

Questions on Learning Objectives

Objective A: Discuss the basis for tort liability.

A.1 What is the primary purpose of tort law? (pp. 48–49)

A.2 Describe the bases for liability in tort law. (pp. 49–51)

A.3 List some of the defects of a compensation system based on fault and describe alternatives to such a system. (p. 50)

A.4 What is vicarious liability? (p. 51)

Objective B: Examine the tort of negligence.

B.1 What three elements must be proven in any tort action? (p. 52)

B.2 To whom do we owe a duty of care? (pp. 52–53)

B.3 What standard of care do we owe to those persons to whom you owe a duty of care? (pp. 53–54)

B.4 What is causation? (pp. 54–55)

B.5 Define burden of proof and explain its shifting character in a negligence action. (p. 58)

B.6 What is contributory negligence and how does it affect and award of damages? (pp. 58–59)

B.7 What standard of care do we owe in hazardous situations? (p. 60)

B.8 Explain the significance of the *Donoghue* v. *Stevenson* case. (p. 62)

Objective C: Describe occupier's liability.

C.1 Name the three categories of visitors. (pp. 65–66)

C.2 Describe the obligations owed to each category of visitor that you listed in C.1 above. (pp. 65–66)

Objective D: Examine several torts other than negligence.

D.1 What is a private nuisance? (p. 66)

D.2 Define trespass. (p. 67)

D.3 Distinguish an assault from a battery. (p. 68)

D.4 Define false imprisonment and explain the type of restraint necessary to establish it. (p. 68)

D.5 Distinguish libel from slander. (p. 68)

D.6 List and describe the three defences to a defamation suit. (pp. 68–69)

D.7 List and describe the two main categories of economic torts. (pp. 69–70)

Answers to Questions on Learning Objectives

A.1 The primary purpose of tort law is to compensate the victim, not to punish wrongdoers.

A.2 Liability in tort can either be strict or based on fault. Strict liability means that liability is imposed on a person who has committed a wrong regardless of whether it was the person's fault. Where fault is the basis of liability, the law considers whether the conduct that caused the damage was blameworthy or culpable, that is, whether it was the fault of the wrongdoer. Liability only exists when there is fault.

A.3 The defects of a compensation system based on fault are that victims unable to establish the fault of the other party may go uncompensated and that such a system involves enormous costs and numerous delays, thereby deterring potential claims.

A.4 Vicarious liability is the imputation of liability to an employer for acts his employee committed while in the course of employment.

B.1 In any tort action, the plaintiff must prove that the defendant owed her a duty of care, that the defendant breached the duty by acting as he did and that the defendant's breach caused the plaintiff damage.

B.2 You owe a duty of care to those persons whom it is reasonably foreseeable will be affected by your actions.

B.3 The standard of care which you owe is to take reasonable care not to injure others. Whether or not you act reasonably is a question of foreseeability of harm.

B.4 Causation deals with the question of whether the actions of a wrongdoer can be considered the operative cause of the harm. While you can often link a wrongful action to the damage suffered, the wrongdoing is not necessarily the direct cause of the damages. Generally speaking, the closer in time a person's conduct is to the injury suffered, the more likely it is to be found to be the cause of the injury.

B.5 The burden of proof in a civil action is the burden of proving an issue on a balance of probabilities. In most cases the plaintiff bears the burden of proof. Where the evidence presented by both parties is equal, the party bearing the burden of proof will lose.

In a tort action the plaintiff bears the burden of proving that the defendant caused the injury. The burden then shifts to the defendant to satisfy the court on the balance of probabilities that he was not in breach of his duty to the plaintiff.

B.6 Contributory negligence is the term that acknowledges that a plaintiff may have contributed to the damage he suffered. By statute, if contributory negligence occurs, there is an apportionment of loss between the two parties based on their relative contribution to the damage.

B.7 If you engage in hazardous activities you owe a standard of care higher than is normal. (See question and Answer B.3 above).

B.8 *Donoghue* v. *Stevenson* is significant as it acknowledges that manufacturers owe a duty of care to the ultimate consumers of their products.

C.1 An occupier owes a duty of care to invitees, licensees and trespassers.

C.2 An occupier owes the highest obligation to a person he invites onto the premises (invitee). That duty of care is to prevent injuries from hazards of which the occupier is aware and also those of which a reasonable person would be aware.

A licensee is a visitor who enters premises with the permission, express or implicit, of the occupier. The duty of an occupier to a licensee is to remove concealed dangers of which he has knowledge.

A trespasser is one who enters upon the premises unlawfully. An occupier owes a minimal duty to a trespasser. All that the occupier is bound to do is to eliminate any known dangers and not deliberately attempt to harm the trespasser.

D.1 Private nuisance is anything that interferes with the reasonable enjoyment and use of a person's land.

D.2 Trespass is the act of entering on the lands of another without consent or lawful right.

D.3 Assault is the threat of violence against a person. Battery is an attack against the person.

D.4 False imprisonment is the intentional restraint of another without lawful justification. Physical restraint, the threat of physical restraint, or a belief on the part of the victim that disobedience will lead to public humiliation are all seen as sufficient restraints to establish false imprisonment.

D.5 Libel is written defamation; slander is spoken defamation. Both require that a statement be made about anther that lowers that person's reputation in the eyes of right thinking members of the community.

D.6 Three defences to a charge of defamation are truth, absolute privilege and qualified privilege. Truth is, as its name suggests, proving that the defamatory comments made are actually true. Absolute privilege is a complete immunity accorded to certain people from defamation. This immunity is given in parliament, parliamentary debate, legal proceedings in inquests and royal commissions. Qualified privilege is a defence to defamation where the defamatory statement is made in good faith with an honest belief in its accuracy and in a statement where a person has been asked for the information.

D.7 One category refers to those torts that relate to the carrying on of business. A second category of torts relates to false advertising in relation to another's products.

Multiple-Choice Questions

1. Alexa awoke on a Monday morning and, realising that she was very late, quickly got dressed and jumped into her car. She checked her rear-view mirror and, thinking all was clear, she backed out of her driveway. Suddenly she heard a scream and realised that she had hit Jenny, the four-year-old from next door who was riding her tricycle. Jenny's mother Elsa also heard Jenny's scream and came running out only to see Jenny's tricycle crushed under the rear wheel of Alexa's car. Upon seeing the crushed tricycle Elsa fainted. After she came to, Elsa realised that the only injury that Jenny suffered was a broken leg. Can Elsa sue Alexa for negligence arising from the shock associated with seeing Jenny injured?

a) Yes, because under tort law, Alexa owes a duty of care to parents who witness their children being injured.
b) No, because it is only Jenny who was injured.
c) Yes, because under a statute, Alexa owes a duty of care to parents who witness their children being injured.
d) No, because there is no duty of care owed to Elsa.
e) No, because Elsa did not see the accident.

2. Alexa awoke on a Monday morning and, realising that she was very late, quickly got dressed and jumped into her car. She checked her rear-view mirror and, thinking all was clear, she backed out of her driveway. Suddenly she heard a scream and realised that she had hit Jenny, the six-year-old from next door who was riding her tricycle. Jenny's tricycle was crushed under the rear wheel of Alexa's car. However, the only injury that Jenny suffered was a broken leg. Can Jenny sue Alexa for negligence arising from the broken leg?

a) No, because Alexa did not owe a duty of care to Jenny.
b) Yes, because Alexa owed a duty of care to Jenny and did not fulfil the standard of care required.
c) No, because Alexa owed a duty of care to Jenny and fulfilled the standard of care required.
d) Yes, because Alexa caused Jenny's injuries.
e) Yes, because it was reasonable for Alexa to back up her car without doing more than look in the rear-view mirror.

3. Robert and James spent the afternoon drinking beer at their apartment. About 8 p.m., they went to a downtown bar to meet friends and to continue to drink beer. The two had taken Robert's car to the bar. At closing time, Robert and James left the bar and drove out of the parking lot with Robert behind the wheel and James attempting to direct him into traffic. As Robert accelerated into traffic, he was unable to control the car and crossed the centre line into the path of an on-coming car. The driver of the other car was killed, James was paralysed and Robert had a small bump on the head. Blood tests taken shortly after the accident showed that Robert's blood-alcohol level was three times the legal limit. Can the spouse of the other driver sue Robert for negligence?

a) No, because Robert did not owe a duty of care to other vehicles on the road.
b) Yes, because with a blood-alcohol level above the legal limit, Robert had to be the only cause of the accident.
c) No, because Robert owed a duty of care to other vehicles on the road, but the required standard of care was met.
d) Yes, because Robert owed a duty of care to others on the road, the standard of care was not met since the blood-alcohol level was above the legal limit, and Robert was the cause of the accident.
e) No, because Robert owed a duty of care to other vehicles on the road, the standard of care was not met since the blood-alcohol level was above the legal limit, but Robert was not the cause of the accident.

4. Robert and James spent the afternoon drinking beer at their apartment. About 8 p.m., they went to a downtown bar to meet friends and to continue to drink beer. The two had taken Robert's car to the bar. At closing time, even though the bartenders knew that Robert and James were very drunk, they let Robert and James leave the bar tossing the car keys between them. Robert drove out of the parking lot with James attempting to direct him into traffic. As Robert accelerated into traffic, he was unable to control the car and crossed the centre line and into the path of an on-coming car. The driver of the other car was killed, James was

paralysed and Robert had a small bump on the head. Blood tests taken shortly after the accident showed that Robert's blood-alcohol level was three times the legal limit. Can the spouse of the other driver sue the bar for negligence?

a) Yes, because a bar is responsible for the actions of every patron who walks through the door, whether or not they drink any alcohol.
b) No, because the bar owed no duty of care to the other driver.
c) Yes, because the bar had a duty of care not to serve alcohol to a drunk person and to ensure that a drunk did not leave the bar and get behind the wheel of a car.
d) No, because the bar did not the cause of the accident.
e) No, because the bar owed a duty of care to the other driver, but the required standard of care was met.

5. Eva carelessly threw a lit cigarette into a trashcan. An explosion follows because of a bottle of gasoline that an unknown person had put into the trash can earlier. The explosion caused serious injury to bystanders and damage to nearby property. In particular, the explosion knocked Jamie, a pedestrian, to the ground causing an undetected crack in his spine to completely break, resulting in paralysis. Can Jamie sue Eva for negligence?

a) Yes, because Eva owed a duty of care to Jamie and Eva met the required standard of care.
b) No, because Eva did not owe a duty of care to Jamie.
c) Yes, because the injury was directly connected to Eva's action.
d) No, because it was not foreseeable that a knock to the ground would result in paralysis.
e) Yes, because it was reasonably foreseeable that an explosion would injure pedestrians.

6. The Acme Moving Company is moving a family into the fourth storey of a condominium. The furniture includes a grand piano that does not fit through the front door of the building. In order to get the piano into the condominium, the movers remove a large window and erect a hoist to lift the piano up the side of the building and into the condominium through the window. Part-way up, something happens to the hoist and the piano falls back to the ground landing on a car parked outside the building on the road. On what basis could the owner of the car sue the movers?

a) On the basis of contributory negligence.
b) On the basis of negligence and *res ispa loquitur.*
c) On the basis of conversion to the car.
d) On the basis of trespass on the car.
e) On the basis of public nuisance.

7. George is walking down a busy sidewalk and reading a newspaper at the same time. Since he is not looking where he is going, George does not see the hole in the sidewalk and steps into it, breaking his leg. The hole did have barriers around it because some workers were repairing the sidewalk, but the barriers left a small gap that George managed to walk though. If George were to sue the workmen for his injury, would the workmen have any full or partial defence to the lawsuit?

a) Yes, because the workers had provided a barrier that completely sealed off the hole.
b) No, because the workers had done everything possible to prevent an accident.
c) Yes, because George was partially responsible for his own injury.
d) No, because the injury was too remote to be recoverable.
e) Yes, because George suffered no economic loss due to his injury.

8. Amy and Sarah were in a terrible oral argument. Sarah was holding a book throughout the argument that she was shaking at Amy to emphasise her points. Amy was worried that Sarah was going to hit her with the book. After about ten minutes, Sarah lost all control and hit Amy with the book, breaking her glasses and her nose. Can Amy sue Sarah?

a) Yes, for negligence.
b) Yes, for assault and battery.
c) Yes, for deceit.
d) Yes, for defamation.
e) Yes, for nuisance.

9. A truck driving down a road on the edge of town overturned, dumping ten tonnes of metal pipes all over the road and knocking down two power poles. The pipes blocked the road for two days, the time it took to clear up the mess. The power, however, was out for a week since the knocked-down power poles triggered a chain reaction that knocked out the whole local grid. The mayor of the town wants money to pay for the clean-up operation. On what basis can the town sue the trucking company?

a) Battery.
b) Deceit.
c) Defamation.
d) Public nuisance.
e) Private nuisance.

10. A truck driving down a road on the edge of town overturned, dumping ten tonnes of metal pipes all over the road and knocking down two power poles. The pipes blocked the road for two days, the time it took to clear up the mess. The power, however, was out for a week since the knocked-down power poles triggered a chain reaction that knocked out the whole local grid. It turns out that the road blockage and power outage was a particular problem for a cabinet-making business which had its driveway blocked by the pipes. As a result, the company suffered $20 000 in damages because it could not complete three

contracts. On what basis can the cabinet-making business sue the trucking company?

a) Battery.
b) Deceit.
c) Defamation.
d) Public nuisance.
e) Private nuisance.

11. Baxter, a nosy junior reporter, has been following a local politician for two weeks because of a tip he got that the politician had been seen frequently with a man other than her husband. Finally, he sees the two of them together in a compromising situation in a hotel room. Baxter writes a story that is printed in the newspaper. When the politician reads the article, she is furious and threatens to sue Baxter and the paper. On what basis could the politician sue Baxter and the paper, and would Baxter and the paper have a defence?

a) Battery and no defence.
b) Deceit and no defence.
c) Defamation and a defence of the truth.
d) Public nuisance and a defence of the public's right to know.
e) Negligence and a defence of contributory negligence.

12. What is the aim of remedies in torts and what are the usual remedies?

a) To put the parties in the position they would have been in if the tort had not been committed. Special damages, specific performance and injunction.
b) To compensate for the injuries that occurred. Damages, restitution and injunction.
c) To put the parties in the position they would have been in if the tort had not been committed. Damages and specific performance.
d) To compensate for the injuries that occurred. Damages and specific performance.
e) To put the parties in the position they would have been in if the tort had not been committed. Damages, restitution and injunction.

13. Adam is a good neighbour who always keeps his yard neat and the house in proper repair. He is reasonable about the noise if he throws a party in the backyard. On the other hand, Adam's neighbour Harold is not a good neighbour. Harold does no yard work and likes to play loud music most summer evenings until 3 a.m. The noise keeps Adam awake and is affecting Adam's talking parrot who has stopped talking. Can Adam successfully sue Harold to stop the noise?

a) Yes, based on assault.
b) Yes, based on private nuisance.
c) Yes, based on negligence.
d) Yes, based on public nuisance.
e) No, Harold has every right to play loud music on his property if he wants to.

14. George is walking down a busy sidewalk. To avoid walking into a hot dog vendor, George steps to his right and manages to step into a hole in the sidewalk, breaking his leg. The hole did have barriers around it because of the workers repairing the sidewalk, but the barriers left a small gap that George managed to walk though. Assuming the hot dog vendor had a right to be at that location (e.g., a permit for the spot), who may George sue for his injury?

a) The workers, and the hot dog vendor who was blocking the sidewalk.
b) The employer of the workers, and the hot dog vendor who was blocking the sidewalk.
c) The hot dog vendor who was blocking the sidewalk.
d) The workers and their employer.
e) None of the above.

15. What are the three bases of liability in torts?

a) Fault, absolute liability and vicarious liability.
b) Fault, strict liability and vicarious liability.
c) Workers' compensation, strict liability and vicarious liability.
d) Fault, strict liability and absolute liability.
e) Workers' compensation, absolute liability and vicarious liability.

16. Tom approached Ethel and threatened her by waving his fist at her face. Tom is guilty of:

a) Defamation.
b) Nuisance.
c) Negligence.
d) Assault.
e) Battery.

17. Rebecca invited Rachel over to her home for dinner. Rebecca owes Rachel all of the following duties EXCEPT:

a) A duty to prevent injury from hazards of which she is aware.
b) A duty to prevent injury from hazards of which a reasonable person out to be aware.
c) A duty to prevent Rachel from suffering any injury.
d) A duty to remove concealed dangers.
e) A duty to deliberately harm Rachel.

18. Which of the following is/are elements of a tort action?
I. The defendant owes the plaintiff a duty of care.
II. The defendant breaches that duty.
III. The defendant's breach causes injury to the plaintiff.

a) I only
b) II only

c) III only
d) I and II only
e) I, II, and III

Answers to Multiple-Choice Questions

1. a)
See pages 52–53 for more information.

2. b)
See pages 52–54 for more information.

3. d)
See pages 52–55 for more information.

4. c)
See pages 52–59 for more information.

5. e)
See pages 52–57 for more information

6. b)
See page 58 for more information.

7. c)
See pages 58–59 for more information.

8. b)
See page 68 for more information.

9. d)
See page 66 for more information.

10. d)
See page 66 for more information.

11. c)
See pages 68–69 for more information.

12. e)
See page 70 for more information.

13. b)
See page 66 for more information.

14. d)
See page 51 for more information.

15. b)
See pages 49–51 for more information.

16. d)
See pages 66–69 for more information.

17. c)
See pages 52–55 for more information.

18. e)
See pages 52 for more information.

True/False Questions

1. The primary purpose of tort law is to compensate the victim of a tort, not to punish wrongdoers.

2. The defects of a compensation system based on fault are that victims unable to establish the fault of the other party may go uncompensated and that such a system involves enormous costs and numerous delays, thereby deterring potential claims.

3. In any tort action, the defendant must prove that the plaintiff owed a duty of care, that the plaintiff breached the duty by acting as he did and that the plaintiff's breach caused the defendant damage.

4. The standard of care which we owe is to take the highest standard of care not to injure others. Whether or not you act reasonably is a question of foreseeability of harm.

5. A defendant in a negligence action will be liable for those types of damages that are reasonably foreseeable, regardless of whether the extent of damage could have been foreseen.

6. An occupier owes no duty of care to invitees, licensees, and trespassers.

Answers to True/False Questions

1. True.

2. True.

3. False. In any tort action, the plaintiff must prove that the defendant owed her a duty of care, that the defendant breached the duty by acting as he did and that the defendant's breach caused the plaintiff damage.

4. False. The standard of care which we owe is to take reasonable care not to injure others. Whether or not we act reasonably is a question of foreseeability of harm.

5. True.

6. False. An occupier owes a duty of care to invitees, licensees and trespassers.

4

Professional Liability

Purpose and Significance

Dealing with specialists has become part of our lives. Doctors, lawyers, teachers, engineers and architects at one time or another advise us on difficult questions and problems.

What, then, can we expect of professionals? Are they infallible? Of course not! This chapter examines the role of professionals and attempts to outline the scope of the duty that they owe and the liability they have for the advice they give and work they do.

This chapter is primarily concerned with the application of tort law to professionals. We have to determine: the special duties owed by professionals to their clients and to others; how the duties differ when they derive from contract, fiduciary, relationship or tort; the appropriate standard of care expected of professionals; how causation is determined when a loss is suffered; and the role of professional organisations in setting standards for professional conduct.

Chapter 4

Learning Objectives

A. Define professional liability.

B. Explore the scope of professional duty of care.

C. Discuss the liability for inaccurate statements.

D. Examine the standards set for professionals.

E. Describe the role of professional organisations.

Content Outline

I. Professional liability

II. Professional duty of care
    A. Contractual duty
    B. Fiduciary duty
    C. Duty in tort
    D. Choice of action

III. Liability for inaccurate statements
    A. Misrepresentation
    B. *Hedley Byrne* principle
    C. Limits to the *Hedley Byrne* principle
    D. Omissions

IV. The standard of care for professionals

V. Causation

VI. The role of professional organisations
    A. Origins
    B. Responsibilities and powers
    C. Codes of conduct
    D. Discipline
    E. Conflict of duty towards clients and the courts

Questions on Learning Objectives

Objective A: Define professional liability.

A.1 "The professional is not a guarantor of success." Discuss this statement as the basis for this chapter. (pp. 74–75)

A.2 What objectives must the law meet in setting professional liability? (pp.74–75)

Objective B: Explore the scope of professional duty of care.

B.1 Describe the fiduciary duty owed by a professional to a client. (pp. 76–77)

B.2 Why is it important to know whether a professional owes a duty in tort as well as in contract? (pp. 78–79)

Objective C: Discuss the liability for inaccurate statements.

C.1 What is negligent misrepresentation and what kind of damages will be awarded for negligent misrepresentation? (p. 80)

C.2 What is the legal significance of the *Hedley Byrne* v. *Heller* case? (pp. 80–81)

C.3 What limits are there to the *Hedley Byrne* principle and why are they necessary? (pp. 81–83)

C.4 What is informed consent? (p. 83)

Objective D: Examine the standards set for professionals.

D.1 Describe the approaches to setting standards for professional service. (pp. 84–86)

D.2 How are standards set for professionals? (pp. 84–86)

Objective E: Describe the role of professional organisations.

E.1 Describe the creation and role of a self-governing profession. (pp. 87–92)

Answers to Questions on Learning Objectives

A.1 Clients view professionals as having specialised knowledge. For that reason, they pay for the skills and knowledge that professionals possess. However, professionals cannot guarantee that everyone who relies on them will fully realise his or her goals. For example, in every lawsuit one party loses but clients are still expected to pay for their lawyers' work. This chapter explores the situations in which professionals are held liable to compensate their clients when advice given is inadequate or wrong, something very different than failing to achieve success.

A.2 The two objectives are the desire to assist innocent victims and the need to avoid discouraging legitimate professional activity.

B.1 A fiduciary duty arises from the relationship of trust in professional-client relations. This duty is the requirement of complete fidelity and loyalty by the professional to her client. It is a higher duty than that owed under a contract.

B.2 The measure of compensation given varies depending upon whether the professional breaches a contract or the duty of care owed in tort. Moreover, the class of people to whom a professional owes a duty of care is much broader in tort than it is in contract.

C.1 Negligent misrepresentation is a statement of fact made in breach of one's duty of care. Purely economic loss is recoverable as well as loss due to injury to persons or property.

C.2 *Hedley Byrne* establishes that a professional may be liable to persons other than his client. The professional owes a duty to those persons or groups of persons whom the maker of the statement should reasonably expect would rely upon his advice.

C.3 A professional cannot be held liable for statements made to anyone in the world so, while a wider group than those with whom the professional has a direct relationship can recover, the courts have limited liability to those who could be reasonably and foreseeably harmed, and who would reasonably rely on the statement. Normally there has to be some kind of a special relationship between the persons who rely on the statements and the maker.

C.4 Informed consent means that a patient cannot consent to any operation or treatment unless she has been fully apprised of the risks involved and the treatment to be undertaken. The doctor must disclose every risk she knew or ought to have known would be significant or material to the patient's decision.

D.1 Standards can be set by a hindsight approach. This approach means that you wait and see whether a client incurs any loss from relying on a professional's advice; if so, the professional is made to pay. A second approach is the forward looking approach. Under this approach, standards are set by assessing the quality of work prevailing at the time the work is done. Professionals must comply with that standard.

D.2 Standards can be set by the courts, members of the profession, through a published set of standards or through professional organisations.

E.1 Self-governing professional organisations are usually created by statute. Their role is to determine who is allowed to hold themselves out as professionals, to set standards for entrance, education and performance and to discipline members who fail to meet the standards. Although a self-governing profession must look after the welfare of its members, its primary obligation is protection of the public.

Multiple-Choice Questions

1. Mavis, a university student in need of money, volunteered for a medical experiment. She agreed to sleep in a lab with electrodes attached to various places on her body, including her head. The doctor told Mavis that there would be no side effects from the experiment. After the first night, Mavis felt uncomfortable, but there did not seem to be anything wrong. After the second night, places where the electrodes had been attached were red and sore. After the third night, the skin where the electrodes were attached was covered in blisters. Mavis went to see her family doctor and was told that the electrodes had caused second degree burns. Can Mavis successfully sue the doctor who is conducting the experiments?

a) No, because she agreed to the experiments.
b) Yes, because she was not adequately informed of the consequences of the electrodes being attached.
c) No, because she was paid for participating in the experiment.
d) Yes, because a doctor is strictly liable for any injury to his patients.
e) No, because the doctor had no way of knowing that the electrodes would cause burns.

2. In preparing the annual financial statements for a corporation, an accountant notices a minor discrepancy in the books. He asks the President of the corporation about it and is told that the discrepancy was an accounting mistake that had been corrected. Shortly after the financial statements are released to the shareholders and creditors, the corporation declares bankruptcy due to a lack of cash. An investigation reveals that the President had been stealing money for almost a year and that he had absconded to the Cayman Islands. Can either the shareholders or the creditors sue the accountant for the lost money?

a) Both can sue because the accountant did not take the money.
b) Only the shareholders can sue because the accountant owed them a duty of care and the required standard of care was not met when the accountant took the word of the President.
c) Only the creditors can sue because the accountant owed them a duty of care and the required standard of care was not met when the accountant took the word of the President.
d) Both can sue because the accountant owed both a duty of care and the required standard of care was not met when the accountant took the word of the President.
e) Neither can sue because the accountant did not owe the creditors a duty of care and, although he did owe a duty of care to the shareholders, the required standard of care was met.

3. Joe is a good used-car salesman. His monthly sales records for the last six months have been the highest in the dealership. Joe shows a car to Marge and tells her that it was driven by a little old lady who only used it on Sundays to go to church. Joe actually has no idea where the previous owner drove the car and does not care. Marge buys the car and within a month the engine seizes. Her mechanic tells her that the engine is worn out from prolonged use. Marge had been using the car to deliver goods from her business at home. Without the car, Marge has no way to make the deliveries. Is there anything that Marge can do?

a) Picket the car dealership to drive away customers.
b) Sue Joe and the dealership for negligent misrepresentation.
c) Sue Joe and the dealership for vicarious liability.
d) Sue Joe and the dealership for defamation.
e) Do nothing as Marge should have had a mechanic check out the car before she bought it.

4. Jerry, a stockbroker, prepared a monthly newsletter for his clients. The newsletter contained information on the general economy, what had happened to the stock market in the last month, and some stock tips. The newsletter was given only to his clients and was not made available to members of the general public (i.e., non-clients). One of his clients left the newsletter on the subway. Patrick found the newsletter on the seat and after reading it, decided to take one of the stock tips. He invested $10 000 in the stock later that day but two days later the stock ceased trading because of financial problems that the industry had been aware of for the past month. Does Patrick have any recourse against Jerry?

a) No, because Jerry could not have foreseen that a member of the public riding on the subway would read his newsletter so there is no duty of care.
b) Yes, because Jerry should have foreseen that any member of the public could rely on his stock tip so there is a duty of care.
c) No, because Jerry had met any required standard of care in issuing the stock tip.
d) Yes, because Jerry owed a duty of care to anybody who could possibly see his newsletter.
e) No, because the stock market is a risky venture and no stockbroker can be held liable if a client or a third party acts on the broker's advice.

5. Fine's Flowers sustained a serious loss from the freezing of flowers and plants in its greenhouse when the boilers shut down due to a lack of water. The interruption in the water supply was caused by a failure of a water pump. Fine's had arranged its insurance with the same agent for many years. They relied on the agent to recommend appropriate coverage and paid the necessary premiums without question. An inspector for the insurance company had advised the agent that the insurance policy with Fine's did not cover such matters as the failure of the water pump, but the agent had not said anything to Fine's. As a result, Fine's had no opportunity to arrange the required additional coverage. Does Fine's have any claim against the agent?

a) Yes, because the agent committed a negligent omission in not telling Fine's what the inspector said.
b) No, because the agent did not owe Fine's a duty of care to make sure every aspect of the business was covered by insurance.
c) Yes, because it was solely the agent's fault that the coverage was not sufficient.
d) No, because no one could have foreseen the pump breaking down long enough for the greenhouses to get cold enough for the flowers and plants to freeze.
e) No, because although the agent owed Fine's a duty of care, the required standard of care was met.

6. Janice goes to her family doctor about a pain in her hip. The doctor tells her that the pain is from a hip joint that should be replaced. The doctor performs the surgery following receipt of Janice's informed consent to the operation, but the pain is still present. On the advice of a friend, Janice goes to see a specialist in hip replacements and is told that there had been nothing wrong with her hip other than a bad case of arthritis. However, because the artificial hip was not positioned correctly, a second surgery was needed to correct the problem. Can Janice sue her family doctor?

a) Yes, she can sue for assault and battery since the doctor did such a bad job.
b) No, she cannot sue because the family doctor did everything that was expected.
c) Yes, she can sue in negligence for the family doctor not performing up to the standard of care expected of doctors.
d) No, she cannot sue because there is no connection with the pain in her hip to the actions of the family doctor.
e) Yes, she can sue in deceit because the family doctor did not tell her everything about the surgery.

7. An investing company became interested in an apparently prosperous family business. The investing company commissioned a report on the prospective acquisition from a well-known firm of investment analysts. The report estimated that the family business was worth over $4 million and considered it to be a sound investment. Without reading the report, the directors of the investing company decided that they should move quickly because there were rumours that there was another prospective purchaser. They purchased all the shares in the family business for $3.5 million. Subsequently, they learned that the major asset of the family business was almost worthless and that they had paid several times what the shares were worth. Can the investment company sue the analysts?

a) Yes, because the analysts owed a duty of care to the investment company.
b) No, because the analysts had met the required standard of care.
c) Yes, because the analysts had not met the required standard of care.
d) No, because the analysts were not the cause of the loss, as the investment company did not rely on the report.
e) Yes, because the analysts were the cause of the loss.

8. Jake is found guilty of misconduct by a disciplinary committee of a professional organisation. Following standard procedure, the committee publishes the results of the disciplinary proceeding in a newsletter circulated to members. The notice identifies the disciplined member, the nature of the offence, and the penalty imposed. Can Jake sue the organisation for the effect on his reputation?

a) Yes, a battery suit is possible for the damage to Jake's reputation.
b) No, a deceit suit is not possible because the organisation only published the truth.
c) Yes, a deceit suit is possible for spreading statements about Jake.
d) No, a defamation suit is not possible because the newsletter is not a communication to third parties.
e) Yes, a defamation suit is possible for damaging Jake's reputation.

9. Josie, a lawyer with a small law firm, learns that her client is planning to commit a murder because the client asks for information about the best way to avoid getting caught. When the client is caught by the police shortly after the murder is committed, the police come to speak to Josie about the client. Can Josie be required to answer the police's questions?

a) No, solicitor-client privilege would prevent Josie speaking to the police about any confidential knowledge.
b) Yes, Josie could speak to the police because solicitor-client privilege does not apply to information obtained related to future criminal activities.
c) No, solicitor-client privilege would prevent Josie speaking to the police except for confidential knowledge.
d) Yes, Josie could speak to the police because she counselled the client how to commit murder.
e) No, solicitor-client privilege would prevent Josie speaking to the police except for knowledge about the murder her client committed.

10. What are the responsibilities and powers of a professional organisation?

a) To set educational and entrance standards; to promote unethical conduct; to hear complaints and administer discipline to clients; and to defend the profession against unfair attacks.
b) To set educational and entrance standards; to set and adjust standards of ethical conduct; to hear complaints and administer discipline to members; and to defend the profession against attacks that it considers unfair.
c) To licence anyone who applies for entrance; to set and adjust standards of ethical conduct; to hear complaints and administer discipline to clients; and to defend the profession against unfair attacks.
d) To set educational and entrance standards; to promote unethical conduct; to hear complaints and administer discipline to members; and to defend the profession against any criticism, whether fair or not.
e) To licence anyone who applies for entrance; to set and adjust standards of ethical conduct; to hear complaints and administer discipline to clients; and to defend the profession against unfair attacks.

11. What is the distinction between hindsight and foresight?

a) In hindsight, if a client suffers any loss, then the advice must have been unsatisfactory. In foresight, the quality of advice given is compared with the standards prevailing at the time.
b) In hindsight, if a client suffers no loss, then the advice must have been satisfactory. In foresight, the quality of advice given is compared with the standards of the least educated member of the profession.
c) In hindsight, the quality of advice given is compared with the standards of the least educated member of the profession. In foresight, the quality of advice given is compared with the standards prevailing at the time.
d) In hindsight, if a client suffers no loss, then the advice must have been satisfactory. In foresight, if a client suffers any loss, then the advice must have been unsatisfactory.
e) In hindsight, if a client suffers a loss, the advice must have been unsatisfactory. In foresight, if a client suffers no loss, the advice must have been satisfactory.

12. What is the principle from *Hedley Byrne*?

a) Anyone who makes a misstatement may be held liable only for losses suffered by those with whom one has a direct contractual or fiduciary duty.
b) Anyone who makes a misstatement may be held liable only for losses suffered by those with whom one has a direct contractual duty.
c) Anyone who makes a misstatement may be held liable only for losses suffered by those with whom one has a direct fiduciary duty.
d) Anyone who makes a misstatement may be held liable for losses suffered by a wider group than those with whom one has a direct contractual or fiduciary duty.
e) Anyone who makes a misstatement may be held liable for losses suffered by the person with whom one has had direct communication.

13. What is a fiduciary duty?

a) A duty imposed on a person who has no relationship to another.
b) A duty imposed on a person based solely on a contractual relationship.
c) A duty imposed on a person who stands in a special relationship of trust to another.
d) A duty imposed on a person who stands in a special relationship of distrust to another.
e) A duty imposed on a person who stands in an ethical relationship to another.

14. What is the basis for the distinction among innocent, negligent and fraudulent misrepresentation?

a) The distinction is based on the court that would hear the case.
b) The distinction is based on the knowledge and intent of the person making the statement.
c) The distinction is based on the type of professional making the statement.
d) The distinction is based on the type of person receiving the statement.
e) The distinction is based on the existence of a fiduciary duty.

15. Is a person who does not have the appropriate professional designation allowed to practice that profession?

a) Yes, provided the person does not accept money.
b) No, because the person is not accredited and is probably committing an offence under the statute related to the profession.
c) Yes, provided the client knows about the lack of professional designation.
d) No, because the professional organisation would have no power to discipline the person.
e) Yes, provided the person understands the obligations.

16. Which of the following sets standards for professionals?
I. Professional organisations
II. The courts
III. Members of the professions themselves

a) I only
b) II only
c) III only
d) I and II only
e) I, II and III

17. All of the following statements are correct EXCEPT:

a) An agreement to provide professional services gives a client a right in contract law to demand an acceptable standard of work.
b) A professional owes a fiduciary duty to clients who repose a special trust in her.
c) A professional owes a duty of care to all persons who rely on his advice or services.

d) A professional owes a duty of care to those persons whom it is reasonably foreseeable will rely on his advice or services.
e) A professional may be liable for negligent omissions.

18. Which of the following statements is correct?

a) Victims of professional incompetence are always compensated for their losses.
b) The law attempts to compensate victims of professional incompetence without placing undue restrictions on legitimate professional activity.
c) The law relies on professionals to set their own standards.
d) Liability for professionals is decreasing.
e) Professionals are liable only to their clients.

Answers to Multiple-Choice Questions

1.b)
See pages 75–77 for more information.

2.d)
See pages 75–77 for more information.

3.b)
See pages 79–80 for more information.

4.a)
See pages 75–79 for more information.

5.a)
See pages 83–84 for more information

6.c)
See pages 84–86 for more information.

7.d)
See pages 84–86 for more information.

8.e)
See pages 84–86 for more information.

9.a)
See pages 84–86 for more information.

10.b)
See pages 88–91 for more information.

11.a)
See pages 79–83 for more information.

12.d)
See pages 79–83 for more information.

13.c)
See pages 83–85 for more information.

14.b)
See pages 79–81 for more information.

15.b)
See pages 87–88 for more information.

16.e)
See pages 87–88 for more information.

17.c)
See pages 84–87 for more information.

18.b)
See pages 84–87 for more information.

True/False Questions

1. The professional is a guarantor of success.

2. A professional owes a duty in tort but not in contract.

3. Negligent misrepresentation is a statement of fact made in breach of one's duty of care.

4. A professional cannot be held liable for statements made to anyone in the world so the courts have limited liability to those who could be reasonably and foreseeably harmed and who would reasonably rely on the statement.

5. Informed consent means that a patient cannot consent to any operation or treatment unless she has been fully apprised of the risks involved and the treatment to be undertaken.

6. The role of self-governing professional organisations is to determine who are allowed to identify themselves as professionals, to set standards for entrance, education and performance, and to discipline members who fail to meet the standards.

Answers to True/False Questions

1. False. Clients view professionals as having specialised knowledge. For that reason, they pay for the skills and knowledge that professionals possess. However, professionals cannot guarantee that everyone who relies on them will fully realise his or her goals. For example, in every lawsuit one party loses but clients are still expected to pay for their lawyers' work. This chapter explores the situations in which professionals are held liable to compensate their clients when advice given is inadequate or wrong, something very different than failing to achieve success.

2. False. The measure of compensation given varies depending upon whether the professional breaches a contract or the duty of care owed in tort. Moreover, the class of people to whom a professional owes a duty of care is much broader in tort than it is in contract.

3. True.

4. True.

5. True.

6. True.

5

Formation of a Contract: Offer and Acceptance

Purpose and Significance

We frequently are involved in contractual relationships. Every time we buy an item of clothing, go out to dinner, or put gas in a car, we have entered into a contract.

Before we can appreciate the legal significance of entering into a contract, it is important that we understand how a valid contract is made. The basis of a contract lies in two persons or more reaching an agreement. But, in order for that agreement to amount to a contract, it must meet certain requirements.

This chapter explores the first two requirements: offer and acceptance. The other necessary elements of consideration, intention to create legal relations, capacity, legality and (sometimes) writing will be discussed in Chapters 6, 7, 8 and 11.

Learning Objectives

A.   Outline the essential elements of an offer.

B.   Discuss standard form contracts.

C.   Describe the ways in which an offer may be terminated.

D.   Define the methods by which an offer may be accepted.

Content Outline

I. Role of contract law

II. Nature of a contract

III. Nature of an offer

IV. Communication of an offer

V. An offer made by tendering a written document to the offeree
    A. Standard form contracts: their risks and benefits
    B. Required notice of terms
    C. Unusual or unexpected terms

VI. Lapse and revocation of an offer

VII. Rejection and counter-offer by the offeree

VIII. Elements of acceptance
    A. Its positive nature
    B. Its communication to the offeror
    C. The moment of acceptance
    D. Business negotiations: tenders
    E. Whose offer has been accepted

IX. Transactions between parties at a distance from each other
    A. Modes of acceptance
    B. Modes of revocation
    C. Determining the jurisdiction where a contract is made

X. Unilateral and bilateral contracts
    A. The offer of a promise for an act
    B. The offer of a promise for a promise

XI. Uncertainty in the wording of an offer

XII. The effect of an incomplete agreement

Questions on Learning Objectives

Objective A: Outline the essential elements of an offer.

A.1 What is an offer? (pp. 99–100)

A.2 What requirements must be met to make a valid offer? (pp. 99–105)

A.3 Does an advertisement to sell goods at a stated price constitute an offer? (pp. 99–103)

A.4 In a self-service store, who is the offeror and who is the offeree? Explain.
(pp. 99–103)

Objective B: Discuss standard form contracts.

B.1 What is a standard form contract? (pp. 101–103)

B.2 What is the general rule regarding acceptance of an offer contained in a standard form? (pp. 101–103)

B.3 Describe the exception to the rule in question B.2 above. (p. 101–103)

Objective C: Describe the ways in which an offer may be terminated.

C.1 Describe the three ways in which an offer can lapse. (pp. 103–105)

C.2 Can an offeree accept an offer that has lapsed? (pp. 103–105)

C.3 Distinguish revocation from rejection of an offer. (pp. 104–106)

C.4 When is revocation of an offer effective? (pp. 104–105)

C.5 What is a counter-offer? (pp. 105–106)

C.6 What is the effect of making a counter-offer? (pp. 105–107)

Objective D: Describe the methods by which an offer may be accepted.

D.1 What requirements must be met to make a valid acceptance of an offer? (pp. 106–109)

D.2 What is the effect of accepting an offer? (pp. 106–109)

D.3 When acceptance of an offer is made through the mail, how is the time of acceptance determined? Discuss. (pp. 106–109)

D.4 How does one accept a unilateral offer? (pp. 112–113)

D.5 How does one accept a bilateral offer? (pp. 112–113)

Answers to Questions on Learning Objectives

A.1 An offer is a promise made by one party (the offeror) subject to a condition or containing a request to the other party (the offeree). The promise creates in the offeree a power of acceptance.

A.2 An offer can be made by act, words, writing or any combination of the three. The offer, however, must be precise. If it is vaguely worded or ambiguous then it does not amount to a valid offer and it cannot be accepted. Moreover, an offer must be complete. That is, it must contain all the major terms of the agreement. Finally, an offer must be communicated to the offeree before it is valid. To be communicated, the offeree must be made aware of the offer.

A.3 As a general rule, the courts have held that an advertisement of goods for sale at a stated price is not an offer to sell the goods at that price but merely an invitation to negotiate for their sale. However, if an advertisement contains a positive promise and a positive statement of what the advertiser demands in return, the courts may hold that the advertisement is an offer.

A.4 In a self-service store, the customer is the offeror and the cashier (acting for the store) is the offeree. You might think that the store is making the offer and thus is the offeror. But, the display of goods is simply an invitation to do business. It is the customer who makes the offer by taking the goods to the cashier.

B.1 A standard form contract is a written document whose terms are uniform for everyone. A common example for a standard form contract is an airline ticket.

B.2 In general, by accepting a standard form contract you are deemed to have accepted every term of it. That is, you are presumed to have knowledge of all of its terms and be bound by them.

B.3 If the offeree has no actual knowledge of a term in a standard form contract, she may be excused from liability. Liability depends upon whether the offeror took whatever steps were reasonably necessary to bring the term in question to the attention of the offeree. If the offeror has taken such steps than the offeree will be bound despite an absence of actual knowledge. In the absence of such steps, as for example where the term is in small print or is inconspicuous, the offeree may be excused from liability.

C.1 An offer lapses if:
(i) the offeree fails to accept within the time period specified by the offer,

(ii) there is no specific time period for acceptance and the offeree fails to accept within a reasonable time, or

(iii) either party dies or becomes insane prior to acceptance.

C.2 When an offer has lapsed the offeree can no longer accept it. A purported acceptance will not lead to the formation of a contract as one cannot accept something that no longer exists.

C.3 Revocation is the withdrawal of an offer, prior to acceptance, by the offeror. Rejection is the refusal of an offer by the offeree. Rejection may be done expressly, that is, by stating that the offeree will not accept the offer. Or, it may be indicated by acts, words or conduct, which would justify the offeror in believing that the offeree did not intend to, accept his offer.

C.4 Revocation of an offer is effective when notice of the revocation is actually received by the offeree. Anything less than actual notice may be held to be insufficient by the courts.

C.5 A modification of an offer usually amounts to a counter-offer. An inquiry by the offeree regarding the terms of the offer does not amount to a counter-offer or rejection: it does not terminate the original offer.

C.6 If the offeree responds to the offer by making a counter-offer he has rejected the original offer and it is terminated.

D.1 Acceptance, to be valid, must be:
(i) in a positive form, whether oral or by act,
(ii) unequivocal, and
(iii) communicated to the offeror.

D.2 The moment that an offer is accepted a contract is formed and each party is bound to comply with its terms.

D.3 Acceptance by mail is deemed to be effective when a properly addressed and stamped letter of acceptance is dropped in the mail unless the offer indicates that acceptance should be by means other than post. In that case, acceptance is not effective until the offeror receives the letter.

D.4 A unilateral offer is one that can be accepted by performance of an act. One example of a unilateral contract is the offer of a reward for the return of a lost dog.

D.5 A bilateral offer may be accepted by giving a promise. For example, the sale of goods on credit is a bilateral contract.

Multiple-Choice Questions

1. Jack owned three small islands on a popular vacation lake. Jack said to his friend Sarah, "I will sell you one of the islands for $5000." Sarah replied, "I accept." Is there a binding contract?

a) Yes, because there was an offer and an acceptance.
b) No, because the contract does not specify which of the three islands is involved.
c) Yes, because Jack communicated his offer to Sarah and it was not revoked prior to her acceptance.
d) No, because they are friends and friends cannot enter into contracts with each other.
e) No, because land contracts must be in writing.

2. Jimmy is trying to sell a bunch of tickets for a hockey game. Jimmy goes to see Emily and offers her six tickets for their stated value of $60 each. Emily accepts immediately and pays Jimmy cash. After seeing Emily, Jimmy goes to see Sarah who he hears is interested in three tickets. Sarah is not home, so he leaves a note stating that he has three tickets for her at $60 each. Emily then decides that she has too many tickets for her friends so offers the three extra tickets to Sarah for $60 per ticket. Sarah accepts Emily's offer and pays for the tickets. Can Jimmy sue Emily for selling the tickets to Sarah?

a) Yes, because Jimmy left an offer for Sarah before Emily made her offer to Sarah.
b) No, because Jimmy's note was just a counter-offer, not an offer.
c) Yes, because Jimmy's note was accepting Sarah's offer to buy the tickets.
d) No, because Emily did nothing wrong as Jimmy's note was just an invitation to treat.
e) Yes, because Emily interfered in Jimmy's business transaction with Sarah.

3. Gillian sent a letter to Michael offering to buy his house in a small town for $50 000. Two days later, Michael sent a letter back stating he would sell the house for $55 000. Michael's letter was received by Gillian on Friday the 1st. On Tuesday the 5th, Gillian mailed a letter to Michael accepting the offer, with the letter being received on Thursday the 7th. On Saturday the 2nd, Michael agreed to sell the house to Brian for $60 000. On the same day he mailed a letter to Gillian revoking his offer. The letter of revocation is received by Gillian on Wednesday the 6th. With whom does Michael have a contract?

a) With Brian because that contract was concluded first.
b) With Gillian because her letter of acceptance was mailed before the letter of revocation was received.
c) With Brian because Michael's letter of revocation was mailed before Gillian's letter of acceptance was mailed.
d) With Gillian because Michael had no right to negotiate with Brian while he was still in negotiations with Gillian.
e) With Brian because Michael's letter of revocation was received before Gillian's letter of acceptance was received.

4. On April 1, Gillian sent a letter to Michael offering to buy his house in a small town for $50 000. On April 3, Michael sent a letter back stating he would sell the house for $55 000. Michael's letter was received by Gillian on April 7. On April 11 Gillian mailed a letter to Michael accepting the offer, and the letter was received on April 13. In the meantime, on April 10, Michael had agreed to sell the house to Brian for $60 000 and, on the same day, he had delivered a letter to Gillian's house revoking his offer. With whom does Michael have a contract?

a) With Brian because Michael's offer to Gillian was revoked before Gillian accepted it.
b) With Gillian because Michael was not entitled to revoke his offer.
c) With Brian because neither Michael nor Gillian had made an offer capable of being accepted, only invitations to treat.
d) With Gillian because leaving a letter of revocation at someone's house is not sufficient notice of the revocation.
e) With Brian because Gillian's offer had lapsed when Michael accepted Brian's offer.

5. On January 3, George offered to sell Grace his cottage for $30 000. In the offer, George indicated that he was short of cash and needed to sell the cottage within two weeks or he would be forced into bankruptcy. On January 26, Grace sent George a letter by courier saying she accepted his offer, had arranged financing, and was ready to close the deal in two days. George sent a message back that he had sold the cottage on January 10 to Percy. Can Grace sue George for breach of contract?

a) Yes, because they had a contract that George broke by selling the cottage to Percy.
b) No, because George revoked the offer to Grace when he agreed to sell the cottage to Percy.
c) Yes, because George never revoked the offer to Grace.
d) No, because George's offer to Grace had lapsed.
e) No, because George's statement was just an invitation to treat so it could not be accepted.

6. Shane wrote to Clare offering to sell his car for $4000. Clare replied, "I will give you $2000 for the car." Shane replied, "What about $3500?" Upon receipt of the letter, Clare immediately wrote, "For $3000 you have a deal." Two days later, after having reconsidered the issue, Clare wrote again and said, "I have reconsidered and accept your offer of $3500 after all." Do Shane and Clare have a contract?

a) Yes, because there was offer and acceptance.
b) No, because they still have not settled on a price.
c) Yes, because the $3000 statement was just an invitation to treat, not a counter-offer.
d) No, because Clare's counter-offer of $3000 nullified Shane's offer of $3500.
e) No, because Shane has not accepted any offer.

7. On October 12, Frank wrote to Jane asking at what price she would be willing to sell her house. Jane wrote back on the 14th, stating the asking price was $75 000. On the 16th, Frank wrote back and asked, "Would you take $50 000?" On the 20th, Jane replied, "I won't go lower than $70 000." On the 25th, the letter from Frank stated, "You've got a deal at $68 000." On the 26th, Jane called Frank and agreed to $68 000. How would each communication be described?

a) 12th - invitation to treat; 14th - offer; 16th - counter-offer; 20th - counter-offer; 25th - counter-offer; 26th - acceptance.
b) 12th - offer; 14th - invitation to treat; 16th - offer; 20th - counter-offer; 25th - revocation; 26th - acceptance.
c) 12th - invitation to treat; 14th - offer; 16th - revocation; 20th - offer; 25th - counter-offer; 26th - acceptance.
d) 12th - offer; 14th - invitation to treat; 16th - offer; 20th - counter-offer; 25th - counter-offer; 26th - acceptance.
e) 12th - invitation to treat; 14th - offer; 16th - counter-offer; 20th - revocation; 25th - offer; 26th - counter-offer.

8. Chris wants to go home for the weekend so buys a VIA Rail ticket to the closest station to home. Since it is near the end of the university year, Chris checks two boxes of stuff to be stored at her parents for the summer. During the journey the train hits a cow and derails. Everything in the baggage car is destroyed when a stray spark ignites two cans of gasoline in the car. Chris is very upset because the boxes contained some expensive items, including an antique box worth $2000 and some jewellery. Chris sues VIA Rail for the loss, but is told by VIA Rail that the most she can claim is $40 per box as stated on her ticket. Is this correct?

a) No, because Chris was not given an opportunity to bargain with VIA Rail about the terms of the ticket/contract.
b) Yes, because Chris's only choice was to accept the terms of the ticket/contract or not take the train.
c) No, because Chris had not read the exemption terms in the ticket/contract.
d) Yes, because an exemption clause in a contract always applies, regardless of whether either of the parties reads the contract or has notice of the exemption terms in the contract.
e) No, because the limits in the ticket/contract are unfair.

9. Townhouse Limited is planning to build a set of townhouses downtown on a partially vacant lot. Townhouse needs all of the owners of the occupied lots to sell their land to it. What is the best way for Townhouse to ensure that it gets all the lots and not have one owner hold out for an absurd amount of money?

a) Ask each owner to make Townhouse an offer and then accept none of them until every owner has made an offer.
b) Enter into contracts with each owner who agrees and hope that no one holds out.

c) Enter into contracts with each owner who agrees and ask each owner not to tell their neighbours about the deal.

d) Make an offer to each owner and do not acknowledge any acceptance until acceptances are received from every owner.

e) Enter into an option with each owner that is not exercised until every owner has agreed to the option.

10. On July 2, Grace said to Percy that she would pay him $2000 if he would paint the outside of her house white. On July 3, Percy starts painting the house. When he finishes on July 10, Percy asks Grace for the $2000. Grace refuses to pay Percy and thanks him for the gift of the paint job. Can Percy force Grace to pay him?

a) No, because Percy never communicated his acceptance of the offer to Grace.

b) Yes, because Percy's conduct in painting amounted to communication of acceptance.

c) No, because Grace's statement was merely an invitation to treat.

d) Yes, because an owner of a house has to pay anybody who does work on the house.

e) No, because Grace's offer had lapsed so could not be accepted.

11. The local city government called for tenders to build a new city hall. Six local construction companies filed bids in accordance with the call for tenders. The city government selected one of the construction companies to do the job. How would the three stages be described in terms of contract law?

a) The call for tenders is an offer. The bids are invitations to treat. The selection is acceptance.

b) The call for tenders is an offer. The bids are counter-offers. The selection is a counter-offer.

c) The call for tenders is an invitation to treat. The bids are offers. The selection is acceptance.

d) The call for tenders is an invitation to treat. The bids are invitations to treat. The selection is an offer.

e) The call for tenders is an offer. The bids are an inquiry. The selection is acceptance.

12. Is there a distinction between the mailbox rule for acceptances and revocations?

a) Yes, acceptance occurs when the letter is mailed, provided that it is properly addressed and stamped, and revocation occurs when the letter is received.

b) No, acceptance and revocation occur when the letter is mailed, provided that it is properly addressed and stamped.

c) Yes, acceptance occurs when the letter is received and revocation occurs when the letter is mailed, provided that it is properly addressed and stamped.

d) No, acceptance and revocation occur when the letter is received.

e) Yes, acceptance occurs when the letter is mailed, provided that it is properly addressed and stamped, and revocation occurs two days after the letter is mailed, provided that it is properly addressed and stamped.

13. Jamie offers to sell Paul his shares in two weeks. Paul accepts the offer, but the price is left to be determined as the stock market price on the day of the sale. Do Jamie and Paul have a contract?

a) Yes, because there is offer, acceptance and no method to fix the price in the contract.
b) No, because the price is unknown and there is no method to fix the price in the contract.
c) Yes, because there is offer, acceptance and a method to fix the price in the contract.
d) No, because an essential term of the contract is missing.
e) No, because shares can only be sold through a stock market.

14. Howard of Ottawa has been negotiating with Bruce of New York to buy 40 000 pounds of bananas which are located in Colombia. On December 12, Howard faxes Bruce an offer for the bananas. On December 16, Bruce faxes an acceptance of the offer to Howard. Which country's law governs the contract and would it make a difference if the method of communication was mail?

a) Canada and no difference if by mail.
b) U.S. and no difference if by mail.
c) Colombia and no difference if by mail.
d) Canada and yes a difference if by mail.
e) U.S. and yes a difference if by mail.

15. What are the three ways in which an offer may lapse?

a) When the offeree fails to accept before another offeree accepts the offer; when the offeree fails to accept within two weeks if the offer has not specified any time limit; and when either of the parties dies or becomes insane prior to acceptance.
b) When the offeree fails to accept before another offeree accepts the offer; when the offeree fails to accept within a reasonable time if the offer has specified an unreasonable time limit; and when either of the parties dies or becomes insane or bankrupt
c) When the offeree fails to accept within a time specified in the offer; when the offeree fails to accept within two weeks if the offer has not specified any time limit; and when either of the parties dies or becomes insane prior to acceptance.
d) When the offeree fails to accept within a time specified in the offer; when the offeree fails to accept within a reasonable time if the offer has specified an unreasonable time limit; and when either party dies or becomes bankrupt prior to acceptance.
e) When the offeree fails to accept within a time specified in the offer; when the offeree fails to accept within a reasonable time if the offer has not specified any time limit; and when either of the parties dies or becomes insane prior to acceptance.

16. Which of the following is/are valid offer(s)?
I. A newspaper advertisement of goods
II. Raising a finger at an auction

III. Taking goods in a self-service store to a cashier

a) I only
b) II only
c) III only
d) II and III
e) I and III

17. Sarah offers to sell Vanessa her stereo system for $1,000. Vanessa decides to think about it for a few days. The next morning Sarah phones and tells Vanessa that she has changed her mind and the asking price is $1,200. Sarah has:

a) Rejected the original offer.
b) Revoked the original offer.
c) Made the original offer lapse.
d) Made a counter-offer.
e) Made a unilateral offer.

18. Walter arrived home from college one day to find a set of encyclopaedias on his doorstep. They were sent on a 30-day trial basis. All of the following are statements correctly describe Walter's legal position EXCEPT:

a) Walter may accept the offer by keeping and using the books.
b) Response A (above) is an example of a unilateral contract.
c) If Walter does nothing he will be bound.
d) Walter may accept the offer by letter, telegram or telephone.
e) If Walter accepts by letter, a contract will be formed when he puts a properly addressed and stamped letter in the mail.

Answers to Multiple-Choice Questions

1.b)
See pages 111-113 for more information.

2.d)
See pages 99-102 for more information.

3.b)
See pages 109-111 for more information.

4.a)
See pages 104-105 for more information.

5.d)
See pages 103-104 for more information

6.d)
See pages 105-106 for more information.

7.d)
See pages 99-105 for more information.

8.b)
See pages 101-103 for more information.

9.e)
See pages 106-109 for more information.

10.a)
See pages 106-110 for more information.

11.c)
See pages 108-109 for more information.

12.a)
See pages 109-111 for more information.

13.c)
See pages 99-106 for more information.

14.d)
See pages 109-110 for more information.

15.e)
See pages 103-107 for more information.

16.d)
See pages 121-122 for more information.

17.b)
See pages 120-121 for more information.

18.c)
See pages 121-122 for more information.

True/False Questions

1. An offer is a promise made by one party (the offeror) subject to a condition or containing a request to the other party (the offeree).

2. In a self-service store, the customer is the offeree and the cashier (acting for the store) is the offeror.

3. In general, by accepting a standard form contract we are deemed to have accepted every term of it.

4. When an offer has lapsed, the offeree can still accept it.

5. A modification of an offer usually amounts to a counter-offer.

6. The moment that an offer is communicated, a contract is formed and each party is bound to comply with its terms.

Answers to True/False Questions

1. True.

2. False. In a self-service store, the customer is the offeror and the cashier (acting for the store) is the offeree. We might think that the store is making the offer and thus is the offeror. But, the display of goods is simply an invitation to do business. It is the customer who makes the offer by taking the goods to the cashier.

3. True.

4. False. When an offer has lapsed the offeree can no longer accept it. A purported acceptance will not lead to the formation of a contract as one cannot accept something that no longer exists.

5. True.

6. False. The moment that an offer is accepted, a contract is formed and each party is bound to comply with its terms.

6

Formation of a Contract: Consideration, and Intention to Create Legal Relations

Purpose and Significance

In Chapter 5 we learned that the courts do not enforce all promises that have been made by one person and accepted by another. They also require that consideration be given. The first part of this chapter examines the concept of consideration and its role in contract law. Consideration can be defined as the price paid for the promise given. One of the most common forms of consideration is a promise made in return for another promise. For instance, if someone promises to renovate a shed for $500.00 and a promise is made to pay the money upon completion of the work, the consideration that has flowed between the parties is the exchange of promises.

Even when an apparently valid offer has been accepted and consideration is present, there will be no legally binding contract unless both sides intend to create a legally enforceable agreement. The second part of this chapter focuses on the intention to create legal relations.

Learning Objectives

A. Understand the term consideration.

B. Discuss the intention to create legal relations.

Content Outline

I. Meaning of consideration

II. Gratuitous promises

III. Adequacy of consideration

IV. Motive contrasted with consideration: past consideration

V. Relation between existing legal duty and consideration

VI. Gratuitous reduction of a debt

VII. Injurious reliance (equitable estoppel)
    A. Evolution of the principle
    B. Estoppel based on fact
    C. Estoppel based on reasonable reliance

VIII. Effect of a request for goods or services

IX. Use of a seal

X. Intention to create legal relations

Questions on Learning Objectives

Objective A: Understand the term consideration.

A.1 What is consideration? (pp. 119–120)

A.2 Distinguish consideration from gratuitous promises and from motive. (pp. 120–123)

A.3 Does the magnitude of consideration matter? (pp. 121–122)

A.4 Is a promise to pay something extra for an existing legal obligation binding? Explain. (pp. 121–126)

A.5 Debts may be settled by payment of something less than the full amount. When will such settlements be binding? Explain. (pp. 125–126)

A.6 What is the relationship between equitable estoppel and consideration? Between a seal and consideration? (pp. 126–130)

Objective B: **Discuss the intention to create legal relations.**

B.1 Describe the intention to create legal relations. Give two examples of situations where it is likely that such an intention exists. (pp. 132–133)

B.2 What is the legal test used to determine whether an intention to create legal relations exists? (pp. 132–133)

B.3 What is the legal effect of an absence of an intention to be legally bound? (pp. 132–133)

Answers to Questions on Learning Objectives

A.1 Consideration is the price for which the promise or act of another is bought. Consideration makes a contract binding in law and thus enforceable.

A.2 A gratuitous promise is one made for no consideration. For example, if you promise to give someone a birthday present, you have made a gratuitous promise. Such a promise is not enforceable because the party never gave any consideration for the promise.

Motive means a person's reason for making a promise. Consideration is the price paid for another's promise. The courts do not look at motive whereas they do look for consideration.

A.3 The magnitude of consideration does not matter in the absence of factors such as fraud or undue influence. The consideration must have some value in the eyes of the law but the courts will not assess its adequacy. The courts also will not assess a promise. A promise to pay can be adequate consideration as can the act of refraining from suing on a legal claim.

A.4 No. Where one party is bound by an existing contractual duty, a later promise to pay her something extra to perform is not binding. For example, if a moving company quotes a price to perform a job and later realises that the quote is low, it may not then demand an additional sum.

A.5 A debtor is legally bound to pay her debts. An agreement to pay only part of the debt is not supported by consideration and, therefore, is generally not binding on the creditor. However, such an agreement will be enforceable where payment is made before the due date of the debt, goods are given in addition to the part payment, or the agreement is between the debtor and a third party.

A.6 The law will enforce promises not supported by consideration in two situations. In equitable estoppel, one person asserts certain facts are true and another relies on the statement to his detriment. The maker of the statement will be estopped (prevented) from denying the truth of the original statement despite the fact that consideration has not flowed. The law recognises and enforces agreements made under seal as the seal is accepted in lieu of consideration.

B.1 Both parties to an agreement must intend to create a legally enforceable agreement in order for a valid contract to be formed. Where agreements are made between family members or close friends such an intention may not exist. For example, failure to attend a dinner invitation would rarely entitle the host to sue in damages. Promises between spouses also are not generally legally binding.

B.2 The law presumes that people entering into agreements intend their promises to be legally binding. Where it is questionable whether a party intended to be legally bound, the courts use the objective bystander test. That is, the courts ask whether an objective onlooker would have viewed the conduct of the party as evincing an intention to enter into a binding agreement.

B.3 Lack of an intention to create legal relations makes the agreement legally unenforceable.

Multiple-Choice Questions

1. Arlene, a wealthy widow, was approached by a women's group for a donation that the group intended to use to construct a women's centre in the community. Arlene offered to donate an amount that would cover twenty-five percent of the cost of the proposed building. If Arlene were to later refuse to fulfil the pledge, could the group force her to pay?

a) Yes, because all the essential elements of a contract are present — offer, acceptance, and consideration.
b) No, because Arlene's pledge is merely a gratuitous promise.
c) Yes, because Arlene has a moral obligation to fulfil the pledge.
d) No, because the community does not need another women's shelter.
e) Yes, if the women's group can show that they commenced construction of the centre in reliance on Arlene's pledge.

2. Scott offered to deliver a package to an office for Trisha, as he would pass by the office on his way to school. Trisha agreed and gave Scott the package that he delivered the same day. The next day, Trisha told Scott she would give him $20 for delivering the package. Scott accepted Trisha's offer, but later Trisha refused to pay the $20. Can Scott force Trisha to pay?

a) Yes, because all the essential elements of a contract are present — offer, acceptance, and consideration.
b) No, because Trisha's promise is merely a gratuitous promise since the consideration is in the past.
c) Yes, because Trisha has a moral obligation to fulfil the promise.
d) No, because $20 is too much for delivering a package.
e) Yes, because Scott changed his course of action and delivered the package based on Trisha's promise of $20.

3. Michael agreed to mow his grandmother's lawn for the summer, and in exchange his grandmother would give him lunch and his grandfather's old watch which did not work. For two months, Michael faithfully mowed his grandmother's lawn, but found that the job was very time consuming and reduced the amount of money he could make mowing lawns for other people. Michael's usual charge for mowing a lawn was $15, and he feels he is working for nothing. Can Michael force his grandmother to pay his usual charge of $15 per mowing?

a) Yes, because it is unfair that Michael gets paid less by his grandmother than by everyone else.
b) No, because there is a binding contract and the courts are not concerned with the adequacy of the consideration.
c) Yes, because $15 is what the labour is worth.
d) No, because special favours are always done for grandmothers.
e) Yes, because a few lunches and a broken watch are not adequate consideration for the labour.

4. Adams, a creditor of Brown, threatened to sue Brown for the amount of an overdue account. Cox, a friend of Brown, promised to pay Adams the amount due if Adams would refrain from suing, and Adams agreed. If Cox failed to pay Adams as agreed and Adams sued him for breach of contract, would Adams succeed?

a) Yes, because the consideration was the promise not to sue Brown.
b) No, because Cox's promise was a gratuitous promise.
c) Yes, because Cox had a moral obligation to pay Adams.
d) No, because Cox is not a party to the debt contract between Adams and Brown.
e) No, because Cox has not breached his contract with Adams.

5. Adams saved Bodnar from drowning. Afterwards, Bodnar promised to pay Adams $2000 out of gratitude. If Bodnar refuses to pay, can Adams force Bodnar to pay?

a) Yes, because all the essential terms of a contract are present - offer, acceptance, and consideration.
b) No, because the consideration is out of proportion to the labour or act required.
c) Yes, because the consideration is not out of proportion to the labour or act required.
d) No, because the labour or act was done before the promise to pay was made.
e) No, because not all the essential terms of a contract are present — namely no acceptance.

6. David owes Sean $1000, due on the first of March. On February 28, David is a little short so he asks Sean to accept $900 in satisfaction of the debt. Sean accepts the $900 and two days later commences a lawsuit against David for the missing $100. Can Sean succeed in the lawsuit?

a) Yes, because David has not fulfilled his obligations since the full amount was not paid.
b) No, because accepting the money one day early is consideration for the reduction.
c) Yes, because terms of a contract cannot be varied once the agreement is signed.
d) No, because David relied on Sean's agreement to accept $900.
e) Yes, because $900 is not adequate consideration for a $1000 debt.

7. A supplier's invoice for goods has the following common term printed on it: "Terms - Net price thirty days; two percent discount if paid within ten days." If the buyer pays the price less two percent within ten days, can the supplier later successfully sue for the sum deducted?

a) Yes, because the buyer has not fulfilled his obligations since the full amount was not paid.
b) No, because the buyer was just following the terms of the agreement.
c) Yes, because payment by a third party is consideration for the reduction.
d) No, because accepting the money early is consideration for the reduction.
e) Yes, because a two-percent discount is not adequate

8. Olive decided to operate an ice cream stand as a summer job. She had an old shed that could be fixed up as a storehouse for supplies. Her friend Martin offered to do the renovations for a total price of $150. Olive gladly accepted. A week after Martin started work on the shed, he realised that the price he had quoted was too low and demanded an extra $100 to finish the work. Olive grudgingly agreed, but later refused to pay anything more than $150. What will the court declare if Martin sues for the $100?

a) No agreement exists because there was no intent to create legal relations.
b) No agreement exists because Olive gave no consideration for Martin's promise to perform.
c) Olive was not given any consideration for her promise to pay the extra $100.
d) Martin must prove the price for the renovation was reasonable.
e) Olive must pay a reasonable price for the renovations.

9. Bruce asked a lawyer, Shane, for legal advice. After the advice was provided, Bruce asked Shane his fee and Shane suggested a reasonable sum. Bruce refused to pay the figure. Can Shane successfully sue Bruce for the sum mentioned?

a) Yes, because the essential elements of a contract are present - offer, acceptance, and consideration.
b) No, because Shane's provision of legal advice was a gratuitous service.
c) Yes, because a reasonable payment is required when there has been a request for services.
d) No, because past consideration is no consideration.
e) No, because Bruce and Shane had no intention to create legal relations.

10. A seal replaces which of the following essential elements of a contract?

a) Offer
b) Acceptance
c) Consideration
d) Intention to create legal relations
e) All of the above

11. What is the distinction between consideration in a unilateral contract and consideration in a bilateral contract?

a) The consideration in a unilateral contract is the promise of the other party. The consideration in a bilateral contract is the act done by the acceptor.
b) The consideration in a unilateral contract is the promise of the other party to pay money. The consideration in a bilateral contract is the act done by the acceptor to pay money.
c) The consideration in a unilateral contract is the act done by the acceptor. The consideration in a bilateral contract is the payment of money.

d) The consideration in a unilateral contract is the act done by the acceptor. The consideration in a bilateral contract is the promise of the other party.
e) The consideration in a unilateral contract is payment of money. The consideration in a bilateral contract is the promise of the other party.

12. John, who has just ordered a new 90-HP outboard motor, tells his friend Iris that he will give her his old 35-HP motor as soon as the new one arrives. To make use of the 35-HP motor, Iris will have to make expensive modifications to her small boat. Instead, at John's suggestion, Iris buys a new boat for $3000. Subsequently, John's brother reminds him that he had promised the old motor to him, and rather than promote a family quarrel, John tells Iris she cannot have the 35-HP motor. Can Iris successfully sue John for the motor?

a) Yes, because the contract between John and Iris had all the essential elements - offer, acceptance, and consideration.
b) No, because John's promise of the engine was a gratuitous promise.
c) Yes, because Iris reasonably relied on John's promise to her detriment.
d) No, because past consideration is no consideration.
e) No, because the promise to John's brother was made first.

13. As part of the preparations for a high school dance, the organising committee hires an off-duty police officer for security. When the officer asks for his payment at the end of the dance, the committee refuses to pay because the officer was just acting within his usual police officer duties. Can the officer successfully sue the committee for payment?

a) Yes, because it is not part of an officer's usual duty to provide security at a high school dance.
b) No, because providing security is part of an officer's usual duty.
c) Yes, because the essential elements of a contract are present and the person being a police officer is irrelevant.
d) No, because acting as a security officer conflicts with an officer's usual duty.
e) Yes, because the committee, relying on the officer's promise, did not arrange other forms of security.

14. How are the common law rules about the need for consideration unsatisfactory for business purposes?

a) A business may find it advantageous to settle a debt for a lesser sum.
b) A business may find it advantageous to fulfil a gratuitous promise to a long-term business client.
c) A business may find it advantageous to pay an extra amount for an existing contractual duty.
d) All of the above.
e) None of the above.

15. A student asserts that consideration is present in most promises to donate money to charitable organisations because the promisor has an economic benefit from his promise in the form of a deduction from his taxable income. Is this good reasoning?

a) No, because no one is required to claim a charitable donation on their income taxes.
b) Yes, because any consideration is sufficient.
c) No, because not all charitable organisations issue tax receipts.
d) Yes, because the law may provide the consideration necessary for a contract.
e) No, because the consideration must flow from the charitable organisation for a binding contract.

16. All of the following statements concerning the intention to create legal relations are correct EXCEPT:

a) The law presumes that people who enter into agreements intend to be legally bound.
b) The test for determining whether the parties intend to be bound is objective; that is, would a reasonable bystander assume from the outward conduct of the parties that they intended to create a contract?
c) It is less likely that intent to create legal relations exists between friends or family members than between strangers.
d) Promises contained in advertisements are enforceable because buyers intend them to be legally binding.
e) A term in a contract to the effect that neither party may sue the other is binding.

17. Which of the following correctly describes consideration?
I. Consideration is the price paid by one for the promise or act of another.
II. Consideration must be of a certain magnitude to make the contract binding.
III. An agreement will never be binding in the absence of consideration.

a) I only
b) II only
c) III only
d) I and III only
e) I, II, and III

Answers to Multiple-Choice Questions

1. e)
See pages 120–121 for more information.

2. b)
See pages 120–121 for more information.

3. b)
See pages 121–122 for more information.

4. a)
See pages 122–125 for more information.

5. d)
See pages 125–126 for more information

6. b)
See pages 125–126 for more information.

7. d)
See pages 125–126 for more information.

8. c)
See pages 125–128 for more information.

9. c)
See page 131 for more information.

10. c)
See pages 119–120 for more information.

11. d)
See pages 119–120 for more information.

12. c)
See pages 126–130 for more information.

13. a)
See pages 126–130 for more information.

14. d)
See pages 125–126 for more information.

15. e)
See pages 125–126 for more information.

16. d)
See pages 120–121 for more information.

17.a)
See pages 121–122 for more information.

True/False Questions

1. Consideration is not needed to make a contract binding and enforceable.

2. A gratuitous promise is one made for a small consideration.

3. Consideration must have some value in the eyes of the law but the courts will not assess its adequacy.

4. Both parties to an agreement must intend to create a legally enforceable agreement in order for a valid contract to be formed.

5. The law does not presume that people entering into agreements intend their promises to be legally binding.

6. Lack of an intention to create legal relations makes the agreement unenforceable by law.

Answers to True/False Questions

1. False. Consideration is the price for which the promise or act of another is bought. Consideration makes a contract binding in law and thus enforceable.

2. False. A gratuitous promise is one made for no consideration. For example, if a person promises to give you a birthday present, that person made a gratuitous promise. Such a promise is not enforceable because you never gave any consideration for the promise. Motive means a person's reason for making a promise. Consideration is the price paid for another's promise. The courts do not look at motive whereas they do look for consideration.

3. True.

4. True.

5. False. The law presumes that people entering into agreements intend their promises to be legally binding. Where it is questionable whether a party intended to be legally bound, the courts use the "objective bystander" test. That is, the courts ask whether an objective onlooker would have viewed the conduct of the party as evincing an intention to enter into a binding agreement.

6. True.

7

Formation of a Contract: Capacity to Contract and Legality of Object

Purpose and Significance

Our legal system precludes people in certain circumstances from entering into contracts. Others are allowed to contract but only in restricted circumstances. Who can contract? In what circumstances? Who cannot contract? Why not? These questions of capacity and are dealt with in this chapter.

A requisite element for a valid contract is legality of object. Simply put, the subject matter of a contract must be legal for the contract to be enforceable. For example, someone asks an individual to burn down a restaurant so that the owner can collect the insurance proceeds. The owner promises to pay $10,000 in return. If the person succeeds in burning the restaurant but the owner refuses to pay the money, can the individual successfully sue the owner? Of course not. A court would not assist the individual in the claim because to do so would be contrary to the public interest.

Legality of object encompasses more than agreements whose purposes are patently wrong. This chapter explores some of the less obvious forms of illegality such as those created by statute and agreements in restraint of trade.

Learning Objectives

A. Outline a minor's capacity to contract.

B. Describe those, other than minors, who are limited in their capacity to contract.

C. Examine contracts that are illegal or contrary to public policy.

Content Outline

I. Capacity to contract

II. Minors
    A. Contracts creating liability for a minor
    B. Contracts creating no liability for a minor
    C. Contracts indirectly affecting a minor
    D. Contractual liability of minors upon attaining majority

III. Other persons of diminished contractual capacity

IV. Corporations

V. Labour unions

VI. Enemy aliens

VII. Aboriginal peoples

VIII. Role of legality in the formation of a contract

IX. Difference between a void and an illegal contract

X. Contracts affected by a statute
    A. Significance of the wording of a statute
    B. Contracts void by statute
    C. Contracts exempt from the betting prohibition
    D. Agreements illegal by statute

XI. Contracts illegal by the common law and public policy
    A. Common law
    B. Public Policy

XII. Agreements in restraint of trade
    A. Agreements between vendor and purchaser of a business
    B. Agreements between employee and employer

Questions on Learning Objectives

Objective A: Outline a minor's capacity to contract.

A.1 When does a minor reach the age of majority? (p. 139)

A.2 What is the general rule describing a minor's capacity to contract? (pp. 139–142)

A.3 Describe two exceptions to the rule in Question A.2. (pp. 139–142)

A.4 Describe a minor's legal rights and obligations for non-necessaries. (pp. 139–140)

A.5 In what situations will a contract become enforceable against a minor unless the minor repudiates the contract upon reaching the age of majority? (pp. 139–142)

A.6 In what situations must a minor expressly ratify a contract upon reaching the age of majority to make it enforceable against her? (p. 142)

Objective B: Describe those, other than minors, who are limited in their capacity to contract.

B.1 Describe the legal view of the capacity of insane persons and those incapacitated by drugs or alcohol to contract. (p. 143)

B.2 What do the two groups of persons listed in B.1 have to prove to escape contractual liability? (p. 143)

B.3 Does a corporation have capacity to contract? (p. 143)

B.4 Describe a labour union's capacity to contract. (p. 144)

B.5 Describe a native person's capacity to contract. Does it matter where she lives? (pp. 144–145)

Objective C: **Examine contracts that are illegal or contrary to public policy.**

C.1 Distinguish between a void contract and one that is illegal. (p. 145)

C.2 Why might a statute make a contract illegal and not merely void? (pp. 146–149)

C.3 List the three categories of agreements that the common law treats as illegal. Give one example of each. (pp. 150–152)

C.4 What is the most common type of agreement that is contrary to public policy? Why are such agreements prohibited? (pp. 151–152)

Answers to Questions on Learning Objectives

A.1 Under common law, a minor reached the age of majority at age 21. The provinces have lowered, by statute, this age limit. For example, the age of majority in Ontario is 18 and is 19 in British Columbia.

A.2 A minor does not have the capacity to enter into binding contracts. As a general rule, the contract of a minor is unenforceable against him but enforceable by him against the other side.

A.3 A minor will be liable to pay a reasonable amount (not always the contract price) for all necessaries that she purchases. For something to be a necessary, it must be necessary in relation to the minor's station in life and the minor cannot already have an adequate supply of the same. Contracts of employment deemed to be for the minor's benefit are also enforced.

A.4 A minor may repudiate contracts for non-necessaries. That is, the minor can ignore the bargain. However, if he obtained goods under the contract, he will be required to return the goods to the other party.

A.5 Where contracts concern interests of a permanent or continuous nature, minors will be bound by the contracts unless repudiated promptly after coming of age. Examples of this type of contract are those dealing with land, shares, or partnerships.

A.6 In order to be binding, contracts that are not continuous or permanent in nature must be expressly ratified upon attaining the age of majority.

B.1 Like a minor, these categories of persons are seen to have capacity only to make contracts for necessaries. All other contracts can be avoided.

B.2 In order to avoid a contract on the basis of insanity or incapacity due to drink or drugs, the party alleging the incapacity must prove not only that she was incapable of rational decision at the time of the making of the agreement, but also that the other party was aware of her incapacity. While it is easy to prove that one is under age, it is difficult to prove intoxication or insanity. It is even more difficult to prove the requisite awareness in the other party.

B.3 In general, corporations have full capacity to contract. Some public corporations, such as municipalities, may contract only for limited things.

B.4 It is unclear what capacity, if any, a trade union has and the rules in this area change from province to province. Despite the lack of clarity with respect to legal status, they may bring and defend actions through a variety of legal techniques.

B.5 A native on a reserve has capacity to contract except in relation to property on the reserve. One who leaves the reserve has the same capacity as any other sane adult.

C.1 The words "void contract" are really misleading. A void contract is one that, in the eyes of the law, has never been. If either party to a void contract has partly performed, the court will attempt to restore the parties to their original positions. That may take the form of ordering the money that was paid be returned or that property transferred be returned.

As well, since the contract doesn't exist, both parties are released from further performance. If only a term of a contract is void, that term will be severed if it leaves the meaning of the rest of the contract intact and the balance of the contract will be upheld.

Where the contract is illegal, a court will refuse to aid either party who knowingly agreed to the illegal purpose. Any moneys or goods that have been transferred will not be recoverable.

C.2 Some statutes make contracts illegal, not merely void, in order to express positive disapproval of the actions contemplated in the statute.

C.3 The three categories of illegal agreements of common law are:
(i) where the agreement contemplates the commission of a tort;
(ii) where the agreement contains an undertaking by one party to indemnify the other against any damages arising from a wrong to be committed in the course of performance; and
(iii) where the subject matter of the agreement is held to be prejudicial to the public interest.

C.4 Contracts in restraint of trade are the most common type of agreement to be litigated on the grounds they are contrary to the public interest. That is because competition is considered to be necessary to Canadian life and restraint of trade is felt to inhibit competition.

Multiple-Choice Questions

1. When Jones was 17 years old, she took her CD player into the Mariposa Service Centre for an extensive repair job, which cost $175. If she does not pay, can the Mariposa successfully sue her?

a) No, because the contract was not for a necessity of life.
b) Yes, because the contract was for a necessity of life.
c) No, because the contract was not of a continuous nature.
d) Yes, because the contract was of a continuous nature.
e) No, because there was no consideration for the contract.

2. When Jones was 17 years old, she took her CD player into the Mariposa Service Centre for an extensive repair job, which cost $175. After Jones becomes of age, she picks up the repaired stereo and does nothing to acknowledge her liability to Mariposa. If she does not pay, can the Mariposa successfully sue her?

a) Yes, because only contracts with minors are unenforceable.
b) No, because the contract was entered into with a minor.

c) Yes, because, on attaining age of majority, all contracts are binding unless expressly repudiated.

d) No, because, on attaining age of majority, a contract for a non-necessity which is not of a continuous nature must be ratified.

e) Yes, because, on attaining age of majority, all contracts are not binding unless expressly ratified.

3. At 17 years of age, Watson entered into a contract of employment with an oil company to join its one-year training and familiarisation program, including travel to various company properties, for promising young employees. Shortly after Watson went to work for the company, it proposed to send her, with an adequate living allowance, to its oil fields in the Northwest Territories for a few months as part of the training program. If Watson refuses to go, can the company successfully sue her?

a) Yes, because it is part of a contract for necessities of life.
b) No, because it is part of a contract for non-necessities of life.
c) Yes, because it is a contract of an on-going or continuous nature.
d) Yes, because it is part of a beneficial contract of service.
e) No, because it is part of an exploitive contract of service.

4. Shirley, a 17 year old, is desperate for clothes. She borrows $500 from an adult family friend to buy some clothes. If Shirley fails to repay the debt, can the family friend successfully sue Shirley for the debt?

a) No, because the loaning of money is not a necessity.
b) Yes, because the loaning of money is a necessity.
c) No, because not all the essential elements of a contract are present — offer, acceptance and consideration.
d) Yes, because the money was used to purchase non-necessary items.
e) Yes, because the money was used to purchase necessary items.

5. Susan decides to make some extra money by selling cigarettes on the street. Since her friend Joan is going to the United States for the weekend, they agree that Joan will buy Susan $500 worth of cigarettes. When Joan returns from the States, Canada Customs finds the cigarettes and confiscates them. When Susan asks Joan to return the $500, Joan refuses. Will Susan succeed in suing Joan for the $500?

a) Yes, because all the essential elements of a contract are present — offer, acceptance and consideration.
b) No, because Joan's promise to buy the cigarettes is a gratuitous promise.
c) Yes, because Joan failed to perform her part of the contract.
d) No, because the object of the contract violated the law.
e) No, because the contract is void due to Customs' confiscation of the cigarettes.

6. Sean will graduate from trade school one month after attaining the age of majority. In anticipation, two months before graduation, Sean buys a house in the country where he intends to start a fix-it business. What, if anything, must Sean do on his birthday to make the contract enforceable?

a) Do nothing.
b) Ratify the contract since it is a contract for a necessity.
c) Repudiate the contract since it is a contract for a non-necessity.
d) Ratify the contract since it is a contract of a permanent continuous nature.
e) Repudiate the contract since it is a contract of a permanent continuous nature.

7. Sean will graduate from trade school one month after attaining the age of majority. In anticipation, two months before graduation Sean buys a house in the country where he intends to start a fix-it business. Since the house is on a lake, Sean enters a second contract to buy a sailboat. The contract for the sailboat is to be completed on his graduation day. What, if anything, must Sean do on his birthday to make the contract enforceable?

a) Do nothing.
b) Ratify the contract since it is a contract for a non-necessity.
c) Repudiate the contract since it is a contract for a non-necessity.
d) Ratify the contract since it is a contract of a permanent continuous nature.
e) Repudiate the contract since it is a contract of a permanent continuous nature.

8. Sean, age 17, purchased a bicycle on credit for the purpose of transportation to and from his place of employment. He made no payments on the bicycle. Can the seller successfully sue Sean for the debt?

a) Yes, because the bike is considered a non-necessity since it is needed to get to his place of employment.
b) No, because the bike is considered a non-necessity since it is needed to get to his place of employment.
c) Yes, because the bike is considered a necessity since it is needed to get to his place of employment.
d) No, because the bike is considered a necessity since it is needed to get to his place of employment.
e) Yes, because Sean has used the bike for free for a number of months.

9. Jamie is a nine-year-old hockey player. Because his father insisted that he play competitive hockey, Jamie liked good equipment and one afternoon bought a $100 aluminum hockey stick. His father was furious at the cost. Can the father do anything to avoid paying for the stick?

a) No, because a $100 hockey stick is a necessity for a competitive hockey player.
b) Yes, because a $100 hockey stick is not a necessity for a nine-year-old hockey player.

c) No, because $100 is a reasonable price for an aluminum hockey stick.
d) Yes, because no contract is binding against someone under the age of 12.
e) Yes, because $100 is an unreasonable price for an aluminum hockey stick.

10. Jason, a university student, participated in a pub-crawl for new students and then spent the rest of the evening drinking in the university pub. By 2 a.m. he is incapable of driving and is barely able to walk, let alone walk in a straight line. Jason hails a cab to drive him home even though he lives only one mile from campus. He has trouble remembering his address since he only moved in that day. After driving around for 30 minutes, the cab finally arrives at the correct house, but Jason discovers he has no money. The cab driver is fed up with this customer so agrees to come back the next day for payment. The next day, after he has sobered up, Jason refuses to pay the $50 fare. Can the cab driver successfully sue Jason for the fare?

a) Yes, because, unlike minors, adults are responsible for any contracts that they enter.
b) No, because Jason was too drunk at the time to have entered into a binding contract for a non-necessity.
c) Yes, because the contract was for a necessity and the driver was aware Jason was drunk.
d) No, because the contract was for a non-necessity and the driver was aware Jason was drunk.
e) Yes, because the fare was a reasonable price for the drive.

11. What is the distinction between a void and an illegal contract?

a) If the contract is void, the court will attempt to restore the parties to their original positions. If the contract is illegal, the court will not assist the parties.
b) If the contract is void, the court will not assist the parties. If the contract is illegal, the court will attempt to restore the parties to their original positions.
c) If the contract is void, the court will force the parties to complete the contract. If the contract is illegal, the court will attempt to restore the parties to their original positions.
d) If the contract is void, the court will attempt to restore the parties to their original positions. If the contract is illegal, the court will force the parties to complete the contract.
e) If the contract is void, the court will force the parties to complete the contract. If the contract is illegal, the court will not assist the parties.

12. What is the distinction between a wager and insurance?

a) One is illegal and one is not.
b) One has an insurable interest and one does not.
c) One is legal with government sanction and one is legal by itself.
d) One hopes that an event will occur and one hopes that an event will not occur.
e) All of the above.

13. How is the public interest affected in an agreement in restraint of trade?

a) It is in the public interest to strictly control business in order to promote the economy.
b) It is in the public interest to have open competition in order to promote the economy.
c) It is in the public interest to have trade restrained in order to protect consumers.
d) It is in the public interest to have open competition in order to protect consumers.
e) It is in the public interest to have reasonable contracts promoted by the courts.

14. Which of the following may have diminished contractual capacity?

a) Corporations
b) Labour unions
c) Enemy aliens
d) Bankrupt debtors
e) All of the above

15. Great Sea Corp. was incorporated under the laws of Canada. Although its head office is in Canada, most of its manufacturing facilities are in Panama where labour and raw materials are cheap. Great Sea Corp. entered into a large contract with a chain of food stores in Canada who agreed to carry its product. The contract called for monthly deliveries with payment in U.S. dollars. Since then, the Canadian government has declared war on Panama. As a result, the food stores refuse to make any payments to Great Sea Corp. and refuse to accept any more deliveries. Can Great Sea Corp. successfully sue the food stores for breach of contract?

a) Yes, because all the necessary elements of a contract are present — offer, acceptance and consideration.
b) No, because it is illegal to import food products from a country with which Canada is at war.
c) Yes, because there is nothing wrong with importing food products from a country with which Canada is at war.
d) No, because as an enemy alien, Great Sea Corp. does not have contractual capacity.
e) Yes, because Great Sea Corp. is not an enemy alien.

16. Which of the following has/have a limited capacity to contract?
I. Natives
II. Married women
III. Labour Unions

a) I only
b) II only
c) III only
d) I and III only
e) I, II, and III

17. All of the following correctly describe a minor's capacity to contract EXCEPT:

a) A minor must repudiate partnership agreements upon attaining the age of majority; otherwise, they become binding upon her.
b) A minor is bound to pay the contract price for necessaries.
c) A minor is bound by employment contracts for his benefit.
d) A minor may escape contractual liability but still be liable in tort law.
e) A minor must ratify a contract for non-necessary, non-permanent goods when he attains the age of majority in order for the contract to bind him.

18. The legal test for a necessary good for a minor is:

a) The good must be reasonably necessary to maintain the minor's standard of living.
b) The good must be reasonably necessary to maintain the minor's standard of living and be of benefit to her.
c) The good must be necessary in relation to the minor's station in life and he cannot have an adequate supply of it already.
d) The good cannot be a luxury.
e) The good must be necessary to maintain the minor's standard of living and she cannot have an adequate supply of it already.

19. The following statements are all correct EXCEPT:

a) A restrictive covenant between employer and employee will be upheld if it is reasonable as between the parties and not contrary to the public interest.
b) A restrictive covenant between employer and employee will be upheld if it is reasonable as between the vendor and purchaser of a business.
c) A restrictive covenant between an employer and an employee is more difficult to uphold than one between the vendor and a purchaser of a business.
d) The courts will sever an unreasonable restriction so long as the meaning of the remaining portion is unchanged.
e) The courts will redraft an unduly restrictive covenant to make it reasonable.

20. Which of the following is/are illegal?

a) An agreement to exclude an employee from the benefits of Workers' Compensation.
b) An agreement not to testify at a trial.
c) A bet on who will win the Grey Cup.
d) All of the above.
e) None of the above.

Answers to Multiple-Choice Questions

1. a)
See pages 139–140 for more information.

2. d)
See pages 139–141 for more information.

3. d)
See pages 139–141 for more information.

4. e)
See pages 139–141 for more information.

5. e)
See pages 148–150 for more information

6. a)
See page 142 for more information.

7. b)
See page 142 for more information.

8. c)
See pages 139–141 for more information.

9. b)
See pages 139–141 for more information.

10. d)
See page 143 for more information.

11. a)
See page 145 for more information.

12. e)
See pages 147–148 for more information.

13. b)
See pages 153–156 for more information.

14. e)
See pages 143–145 for more information.

15. d)
See page 144 for more information.

16. d)
See pages 144–145 for more information.

17. b)
See pages 139–141 for more information.

18. c)
See pages 139–141 for more information.

19. e)
See pages 153–156 for more information.

20. b)
See page 145 for more information.

True/False Questions

1. The provinces have lowered the common law age limit of 21 by statute.

2. A minor may repudiate contracts for non-necessaries.

3. Contracts, which are not continuous or permanent in nature, do not need to be expressly ratified upon attaining the age of majority in order to be binding upon the minor.

4. In order to avoid a contract on the basis of insanity or incapacity due to drink or drugs, the party alleging the incapacity must prove that they were incapable of rational decision at the time of the making of the agreement.

5. A native on a reserve has capacity to contract except in relation to property on the reserve.

6. Because the courts will not assist either party to an illegal contract (where both are aware of the illegality), a plaintiff is unable to recover any money or goods it has given to the defendant as part performance of the contract.

Answers to True/False Questions

1. True.

2. True.

3. False. Contracts that are not continuous or permanent in nature must be expressly ratified upon attaining the age of majority in order to be binding upon the minor.

4. False. In order to avoid a contract on the basis of insanity or incapacity due to drink or drugs, the party alleging the incapacity must prove not only that she was incapable of rational decision at the time of the making of the agreement but also that the other party was aware of her incapacity. While it is easy to prove that one is under age it is difficult to prove intoxication or insanity. It is even more difficult to prove the requisite awareness in the other party.

5. True.

6. True.

8

Grounds Upon Which a Contract May Be Impeached: Mistake

Purpose and Significance

Thus far we have concentrated on how to make a contract. In the next two chapters, we will explore four grounds upon which a contract may be set aside.

The subject matter of this chapter is mistake. What are mistakes in the legal sense? When will a court allow you to avoid a contract on the basis of a mistake? What tests are used to decide these issues? In this chapter we will explore these questions and the answers to them.

Learning Objectives

A. Discuss the legal consequences of a mistake about the terms of a contract.

B. Outline the legal consequences of a mistake in an assumption that underlies a contract.

C. Define void and voidable contracts.

D. Examine how the law of mistake affects third parties.

E. Describe the defence of *non est factum*.

Content Outline

I. Restricted meaning of mistake

II. Mistakes about the terms
    A. Words used inadvertently
    B. Errors in recording an agreement
    C. Misunderstandings about the meanings of words

III. Mistakes in assumptions
    A. About the existence of the subject matter of a contract
    B. About the value of the subject matter: allocation of risk
    C. The challenge of achieving a fair result
    D. Unforeseen future events

IV. Mistake and innocent third parties
    A. How the problem arises
    B. Void and voidable contracts
        1. Consequences of a void contract
        2. Consequences of a voidable contract
    C. Mistake about the identity of a party to a contract
    D. Mistake about the nature of a signed document: *non est factum*

V. Mistakes in performance

Questions on Learning Objectives

Objective A: **Discuss the legal consequences of a mistake about the terms of a contract.**

A.1 What is the legal meaning of mistake? (pp. 162–163)

A.2 Words are sometimes inadvertently used in stating the terms of a contract. How do the courts deal with this problem? (pp. 163–165)

A.3 What is rectification and when will it be granted? (p. 165)

A.4 How do the courts resolve a misunderstanding about the meaning of words actually used in a contract? (pp. 163–167)

Objective B: **Outline the legal consequences of a mistake in an assumption that underlies a contract.**

B.1 What happens if the subject matter of a contract does not exist at the time the contract is made? (pp. 167–169)

B.2 What happens if the subject matter of the contract turns out to be very different from that contemplated by the parties? (pp. 167–169)

Objective C: **Define void and voidable contracts.**

C.1 What is a void contract? (pp. 171–172)

C.2 What is a voidable contract? (pp. 171–172)

C.3 What is the significance of finding that a contract is void? (pp. 171–172)

Objective D: **Examine how the law of mistake affects third parties.**

D.1 Explain the legal significance of the case *Cundy* v. *Lindsay*. (pp. 173–174)

D.2 Can you reconcile *Cundy* v. *Lindsay* with the *King's Norton Metal* case? Explain. (pp. 173–174)

D.3 With *Phillips v. Brooks*? (p. 174)

Objective E: **Describe the defence of *non est factum*.**

E.1 What is *non est factum*? (p. 175)

E.2 What effect does a successful plea of *non est factum* have? (p. 175)

E.3 What role does carelessness by the signor play in a plea of *non est factum*? (pp. 175–176)

Answers to Questions on Learning Objectives

A.1 A legal mistake is a mistake that the law will recognise as excusing its maker from obligations under a contract. A legal mistake must be distinguished from the lay use of the word "mistake" meaning an error in judgement.

A.2 If words are used inadvertently, the courts may do one of two things. First, if it was reasonable for the second party to rely on those words and enter into the contract, then the contract will be held to be binding on the first party. However, if it would be clear to a reasonable bystander that the first party had made a mistake in expressing the terms of the contract, then the contract is voidable at the option of the first party.

A.3 Rectification is a court order to alter a contract to make it reflect the true agreement between parties.

A.4 If there is a misunderstanding about the meaning of words actually used in a contract, courts will decide which meaning is more reasonable in all the circumstances and attribute that meaning to the terms of the document. If the court is unable to decide which of two meanings is more reasonable, the court will refuse to decide between them with the result that the defendant's position becomes stronger than the plaintiff's does.

B.1 Where the subject matter of a contract does not exist at the time that the parties enter into the contract, the contract will be held void.

B.2 If the subject matter of the contract is very different from that which was contemplated by the parties, the courts will first decide upon whose shoulders the risk of loss or damage should fall. If the party adversely affected was the one who should bear the risk then the court will not grant relief. Conversely, if the party adversely affected should not bear the risk, relief will be granted.

C.1 A void contract is one that has never been forced at all.

C.2 A voidable contract is one that can, in certain circumstances, be set aside or rescinded at the option of the injured party.

C.3 The biggest significance of finding that a contract is void is that property that has been exchanged under the alleged contract will be returned to the original owner. Under a voidable contract, if a third party's rights will be affected, the injured party loses his right to avoid the contract.

D.1 In *Cundy* v. *Lindsay* there were two innocent parties, both victims of a fraud. Normally, the more careless of the two persons bears the loss. However, in that case, the more innocent of the two bore the loss because the original contract was declared void.

D.2 *King's Norton Metal* case cannot be reconciled with *Cundy* v. *Lindsay* because in the former case the contract was held voidable for fraud. As an innocent third party's rights had been affected, the injured party lost his rights to rescission.

D.3 In *Phillips* v. *Brooks*, the contract was again held to be voidable and not void and, as a result, a subsequent innocent purchaser was protected.

E.1 *Non est factum* literally means "it is not my doing." It is a plea that the signor of a document makes if he was unaware of the effect of the document he signed.

E.2 A successful plea of *non est factum* will lead the court to hold that the contract is void. Innocent third parties will suffer.

E.3 Until recently in Canada, a careless signor could escape liability by pleading *non est factum*. In 1982, the Supreme Court of Canada held that a careless signor could not escape liability. However, the rule is not absolute. It depends on the facts of each case including the magnitude and extent of the carelessness.

Multiple-Choice Questions

1. Sheila just purchased some expensive second-hand dining-room furniture for cash from Jock. Unknown to Sheila, Jock had himself just bought it on credit from the original owner by representing himself to be another person with good credit standing. The negotiations with the original owner took place face-to-face. If the original owner does not get paid, can Sheila keep the furniture?

a) Yes, because there was nothing illegal about the contract involving Sheila.
b) No, because there was something illegal about the contract involving Sheila.
c) Yes, because the contract between Jock and the original owner was only voidable.
d) No, because the contract between Jock and the original owner was void.
e) Yes, because Sheila is not connected in any way to the contract between Jock and the original owner.

2. Sheila just purchased some expensive second-hand dining-room furniture for cash from Jock. Unknown to Sheila, Jock had himself just bought it on credit from the original owner by representing himself to be another person with good credit standing. The negotiations with the original owner took place over the phone. If the original owner does not get paid, can Sheila keep the furniture?

a) Yes, because there was nothing illegal about the contract involving Sheila.
b) No, because there was something illegal about the contract involving Sheila.
c) Yes, because the contract between Jock and the original owner was only voidable.
d) No, because the contract between Jock and the original owner was void.
e) Yes, because Sheila is not connected in any way to the contract between Jock and the original owner.

3. Zack leaves a note for Alan stating, "I will sell you my car for $2400 cash." Alan delivers $2400 to Zack, and obtains possession and a transfer of the registration on the car. Zack immediately realises that he had made an error in his note as he intended to write $2700 rather than $2400. However, Alan was unaware of the error. He simply thought the price was an attractive one. Has there been a mistake according to the law?

a) Yes, because Zack mistakenly wrote the wrong number.
b) No, because the error was entirely Zack's doing and Alan reasonably relied on the statement.

c) Yes, because Zack made an error in judgement in selling his car for $2400.

d) No, because Alan should have known that the price was an error.

e) Yes, because a reasonable bystander would know that the price in the note was wrong.

4. Zack and Alan have been negotiating for Alan to buy Zack's car. Through a series of notes, the price for the car ranged between $7200 and $7800. Zack then leaves a note for Alan stating, "I will sell you my car for $760 cash." Alan delivers $760 to Zack and asks for the registration papers. Zack immediately realises that he had made an error in his last note as he intended to write $7600 rather than $760. Can Alan force Zack to sell his car for $760?

a) Yes, because there has been an offer, acceptance and consideration.

b) No, because there has been no intention to create legal relations.

c) Yes, because that was the price that Zack stated in his note.

d) Yes, because it would be clear to a reasonable bystander that the price was reasonable.

e) No, because it would be clear to a reasonable bystander that the price was absurdly low.

5. Following protracted negotiations, Clare Limited finally reach an oral agreement with McKenzie Co. to sell them 100 cords of wood for $431 per cord. In order to make sure that the terms of the contract were clear, Clare drew up a written version of the contract and both parties signed it. Shortly after delivery, Clare received a cheque for $13 400 as full payment. In reviewing the written contract, Clare was horrified to discover that the figures had been reversed so that the price read $134 instead of $431 per cord. Neither party had noticed the reversal at the time of signing. Can Clare successfully sue McKenzie for the missing amount?

a) Yes, because a court can rectify a typographical error.

b) No, because the mistake was Clare's fault so it cannot commence the lawsuit.

c) Yes, because a court will always attempt to achieve a fair result.

d) No, because there is no way for a court to know if the parties had not agreed to the change of price.

e) Yes, because the contract is voidable due to the mistake.

6. James, in England, is negotiating with Marc, in France, to buy 40 000 pounds of bananas grown in Brazil and currently on a ship in the mid-Atlantic. Unbeknownst to either James or Marc, the ship has encountered a hurricane and been sunk. After the ship was sunk, James and Marc conclude their contract with a price of 20¢ per pound. James pays the required amount to Marc and then learns that the ship has sunk. Can James successfully sue Marc to get his money back?

a) Yes, because Marc is in breach of contract for failing to deliver the required bananas.

b) No, because it is not Marc's fault that the ship sank.

c) Yes, because the contract was void since the goods had been destroyed before the contract was concluded.

d) No, because the contract was merely voidable since the goods had been destroyed after the contract was concluded.

e) Yes, because the risk of loss had not passed to James prior to the conclusion the contract.

7. James is negotiating with Marc to buy 10 000 shares of a company that trades bananas grown in South America. The shares are traded on the Toronto and New York stock exchanges. Unbeknownst to either James or Marc, there has been a terrible storm in South American that has wiped out the entire banana crop and caused the company to suffer a large drop in share price. After the storm, James and Marc conclude their contract for a price of $20 per share. James pays the required amount to Marc and then learns that the storm destroyed the crop. Can James successfully sue Marc to get his money back?

a) Yes, because Marc is in breach of contract for not telling James about the drop in stock price.

b) No, because it is not Marc's fault that the storm destroyed the crop and affected the stock price.

c) Yes, because the contract was void since the stock price had changed.

d) No, because the contract was merely voidable since the stock price had changed.

e) No, because a contract for shares should contemplate that there is a risk of quick changes in value.

8. Barney has arranged to borrow $100 000 from the bank in order to start up a high-tech business. The bank has agreed to loan the money but only if Barney's father Antonio signs a mortgage on his farm as security for the loan. Antonio is an immigrant farmer who has never learned English, but owns a farm worth $250,000. Antonio goes into the bank with his son and it is explained to him that the paper he is signing is only a guarantee to Barney's loan. He is told that the guarantee could never affect his farm. The papers are actually a mortgage on the farm. After six months, Barney defaults on the loan and the bank moves to sell the farm. Does Antonio have any defence to prevent the bank from selling the farm?

a) Yes, he could argue that he lacked privity of contract to the loan agreement.

b) No, he signed the mortgage documents.

c) Yes, he could argue *non est factum*.

d) No, it was his mistake not to read the papers.

e) Yes, he could argue that the bank was in a conflict of interest situation.

9. Lucy signs a five-year lease to rent a shop on a busy main street. She has misread a street map and believes that a city bus route uses the street, and that a bus stop is close to the shop. In fact the bus route runs along a parallel route two blocks to the south. The landlord is completely unaware of Lucy's erroneous belief. When Lucy discovers her mistake, can she get out of the contract based on the error?

a) No, because the contract is merely voidable based on Lucy's mistaken assumption.

b) Yes, because the contract is void based on Lucy's mistaken assumption.

c) No, because although there has been a legal mistake, the landlord did not know about Lucy's assumption.

d) No, because there has been no legal mistake since the landlord did not know about Lucy's assumption.

e) Yes, because the contract never existed since Lucy thought she was renting a shop on a city bus route.

10. What is the distinction between a void and a voidable contract?

a) A void contract exists until such time as one party chooses to rescind it whereas a voidable contract never existed.

b) A void contract never existed whereas a voidable contract exists until such time as one party chooses to rescind it.

c) A void contract allows a court to award damages whereas a voidable contract does not allow a court to award damages.

d) A void contract does not allow a court to award damages whereas a voidable contract allows a court to award damages.

e) A void contract allows a court to award damages whereas a voidable contract never existed.

11. In what circumstances may neither party have a remedy for mistake about the terms of a contract?

a) When a court finds that the mistake involved only one party.

b) When a court finds that both parties are being unreasonable in their demands.

c) When a court finds that the disagreement is better settled by arbitration than by a court.

d) When a court finds that the remedies requested are excessive for the circumstances.

e) When a court finds that it is impossible to decide which of the parties' interpretations is more reasonable.

12. What are the conditions that have to be satisfied for a court to order rectification of a contract?

a) There is an incomplete agreement between the parties; the parties did not engage in further negotiations to amend the contract; and the error can be easily explained as no more than an error in recording.

b) There is a complete agreement between the parties; the parties engaged in further negotiations to amend the contract; and the error can be easily explained as an error in recording.

c) There is an incomplete agreement between the parties; the parties did not engage in further negotiations to amend the contract; and the error can be easily explained as no more than an error in recording.

d) There is a complete agreement between the parties; the parties did not engage in further negotiations to amend the contract; and the error can be easily explained as an error in recording.

e) There is an incomplete agreement between the parties; the parties engaged in further negotiations to amend the contract; and the error can be easily explained as an error in recording.

13. Helen asked Joyce, "What will you give me for 75 shares of Eastern Cafeterias of Canada?" Joyce said she would make inquiries and then make an offer. Later in the day, Joyce replied, "I will give you $10 a share for your Eastern Cafeterias." Helen replied, "I accept your offer." Helen delivered the shares for Eastern Cafeterias of Canada Limited and received a cheque in full payment. Joyce then realised that Eastern Cafeterias Limited and Eastern Cafeterias of Canada Limited were two different companies and that she had the former company in mind when she made her offer to buy the shares. Joyce stopped payment on the cheque. Can Helen successfully sue Joyce for breach of contract?

a) Yes, because there is no ambiguity about the company of which Helen was trying to sell the shares.

b) No, because it was ambiguous which company Joyce meant when she made her offer.

c) Yes, because was a mistake about the subject matter of the contract.

d) No, because there was a mistake about the subject matter of the contract.

e) No, because a court will not be able to determine whose interpretation of the contract is right.

14. What is the legal definition of mistake?

a) When a contract is entered which is quite different from the one intended.

b) When an error in judgement has been made.

c) When there has been an unintentional act, omission or error by one party.

d) When the parties agree that they made a mistake.

e) None of the above.

15. Margaret bought a stereo system from a local pawn shop for $1000. Margaret bought the stereo system knowing that she could sell it to Beth, the local school disc jockey, for $1500. Shortly after the sale to Beth was completed, the police arrived to seize the stereo alleging that the stereo was stolen property. Can Beth keep the stereo system?

a) No, because the police are allowed to seize anything they believe is stolen.

b) Yes, because Beth lawfully acquired the stereo from Margaret.

c) No, because the contract between Margaret and the pawn shop was illegal and, therefore, void.

d) Yes, because the contract between Margaret and the pawn shop was merely voidable.

e) Yes, because the police will return it to her after their investigation is complete.

16. Rectification of a contract will be ordered when:

a) One party to a contract was induced to sign the document.
b) The words of a contract do not have the meaning that one of the parties to the contract believed they did.
c) The value of the subject matter of a contract is very different from that contemplated by the parties.
d) There is a complete, unambiguous, absolute agreement between parties which has not been changed and which was recorded incorrectly.
e) The subject matter of the contract was not in existence at the time the contract was made.

17. Which of the following is/are correct?
I. A void contract is one that was never formed.
II. A voidable contract is one that was never formed.
III. A third party is protected if a contract is void but not if it is voidable.

a) I only
b) II only
c) III only
d) I and II only
e) I and III only

18. All of the following statements are correct EXCEPT:

a) It is difficult to have a contract set aside for a mistake.
b) The rules of interpretation as well as the law of mistake solve mistakes about the meanings of words used in contracts.
c) If the subject matter of a contract does not exist when the contract is made, the contract will be declared void.
d) If the subject matter of a contract exists but its qualities are radically different from those contemplated by the parties, the contract will be void.
e) Innocent third party rights bar the right to have a contract declared voidable.

Answers to Multiple-Choice Questions

1. c)
See pages 171–172 for more information.

2. d)
See pages 171–172 for more information.

3. b)
See pages 163–172 for more information.

4. e)
See pages 163–172 for more information.

5. a)
See pages 163–172 for more information

6. c)
See pages 171–172 for more information.

7. e)
See pages 171–172 for more information.

8. c)
See pages 175–176 for more information.

9. d)
See pages 163–172 for more information.

10. b)
See pages 171–172 for more information.

11. e)
See pages 163–170 for more information.

12. d)
See pages 163–170 for more information.

13. a)
See pages 163–170 for more information.

14. e)
See pages 163–170 for more information.

15. c)
See pages 163–170 for more information.

16. d)
See page 165 for more information.

17. a)
See pages 171–172 for more information.

18. d)
See pages 163–170 for more information.

True/False Questions

1. A legal mistake is a mistake that the law will recognise as excusing its maker from obligations under a contract.

2. Where the subject matter of a contract does not exist at the time that the parties enter into the contract, the contract will be held void.

3. A void contract is one that has been forced but then declared illegal.

4. In *Cundy* v. *Lindsay* the more careless of the two parties bore the loss because the original contract was declared void.

5. *Non est factum* literally means "it's my doing."

6. In 1982, the Supreme Court of Canada held that a careless signor could not escape liability by pleading *non est factum*.

Answers to True/False Questions

1. True.

2. True.

3. False. A void contract is one that has never been forced at all.

4. False. In *Cundy* v. *Lindsay*, the more innocent of the two bore the loss because the original contract was declared void.

5. False. *Non est factum* literally means "it is not my doing." It is a plea that the signor of a document makes if he was unaware of the effect of the document he signed.

6. True.

9

Grounds Upon Which a Contract May Be Impeached: Misrepresentation, Undue Influence, and Duress

Purpose and Significance

We have encountered the concept of misrepresentation in the previous chapters. In this chapter, we will explore misrepresentation from a contractual point of view. When is misrepresentation a contractual wrong? Are the remedies of an injured party different if the misrepresentation is contractual than if it is tortious? What is a misrepresentation? These questions and their answers will be explored.

The related wrongs of undue influence and duress will be discussed. Both undue influence and duress prevent a person from making an independent decision to enter into a contract. Contracts formed as a result of either are voidable at the option of the victim. These similarities as well as the differences between undue influence and duress will be explored.

Learning Objectives

A. Examine the differences between misrepresentation as a tort and as a contractual wrong.

B. Discuss undue influence and duress.

Content Outline

I. Misrepresentation and torts

II. Misrepresentation and contracts

III. Consequences of misrepresentation in contracts

IV. Opinion versus fact

V. Signed documents and misrepresentation by omission

VI. Contracts requiring disclosure
    A. When one party has special knowledge
    B. Contracts of insurance
    C. Sale of corporation securities
    D. Sale of goods compared with sale of lands

VII. Undue Influence
    A. Special relationships
    B. Dire circumstances
    C. Burden of proof
    D. Arrangements between husband and wife
    E. Importance of independent legal advice
    F. Loan transactions
    G. Threat of prosecution
    H. Inequality of bargaining power

VIII. Duress

Questions on Learning Objectives

Objective A: **Examine the differences between misrepresentation as a tort and as a contractual wrong.**

A.1 Name and describe the three types of misrepresentation. (p. 181)

A.2 What type of misrepresentation is dealt with by the law of contract? (pp. 181–183)

A.3 What remedies can an injured party obtain for innocent misrepresentation? (pp. 181–182)

A.4 What kind of assertions amount to a misrepresentation? (pp. 181–182)

A.5 In A.4 above, we describe the first element of misrepresentation. What are the others? (p. 181–183)

A.6 Can silence ever amount to misrepresentation? (pp. 181–183)

Objective B: **Discuss undue influence and duress.**

B.1 What is undue influence? (p. 186)

B.2 What remedies does a victim have if a contract is formed as a result of undue influence? (pp. 186–188)

B.3 How does a victim lose her right to avoid contracts made as a result of undue influence? (p. 186–190)

B.4 Describe three factors that will be considered by the courts to see whether undue influence exists. (pp. 186–190)

B.5 What is the most effective way to prevent an allegation of undue influence? (pp. 186–190)

B.6 Define duress. (pp. 190–191)

B.7 What legal rights does a victim of duress have? (pp. 190–191)

Answers to Questions on Learning Objectives

A.1 Misrepresentation can be fraudulent, negligent or innocent. Fraudulent misrepresentation is a misstatement that was made recklessly or with the knowledge that it was false, without regard for its truth or falseness. An innocent misrepresentation becomes fraudulent if the party who made the misstatement learns of its falsity and fails to inform the other party of the true situation. Innocent misrepresentation is a misstatement made neither fraudulently nor negligently but which nevertheless is false.

A.2 It is innocent misrepresentation that the law of contract governs. Fraudulent and negligent misrepresentation are governed by the law of tort, not contract.

A.3 The remedy that an injured party obtains for innocent misrepresentation depends upon the stage in the bargaining at which the innocent misrepresentation is made. If the innocent misrepresentation precedes the making of the contract (induces the innocent party to enter into it) then the injured party may rescind (repudiate) the contract and, in addition, be compensated for any losses that have arisen directly out of performance of the contract. If, however, the innocent misrepresentation is a term of the contract, the injured party is able to have the normal remedies based on breach of contract. At this stage, however, you should note that the injured party may repudiate the contract and receive damages or may simply get damages. Damages are usually substantially more than compensation for losses suffered.

A.4 In order for an assertion to amount to misrepresentation, the assertion must be of fact and not merely opinion.

A.5 The injured party must rely on the false statement of fact and must suffer damages as a result of such reliance.

A.6 The concept of misrepresentation has been enlarged to include silence where the silence is a failure to disclose relevant information in circumstances requiring the utmost good faith. The most common example of a contract of utmost good faith is a contract of insurance. For example, if you have heart disease and you fail to tell your life insurance company, your silence amounts to misrepresentation of the state of your health.

B.1 Undue influence is the domination of one party over the will of the other party to such a degree that the latter is deprived of the ability to make an independent decision in relation to the contract.

B.2 A victim of undue influence has the right to avoid the contract.

B.3 A victim of undue influence loses her right to avoid the contract if she fails to act properly after being freed from the domination. Any acquiescence or delay will lead to a refusal of the court's assistance.

B.4 In determining whether undue influence exists, the courts look at the degree of domination of the stronger party, the extent of the advantage received and whether or not a special relationship exists between the two parties.

B.5 In order to prevent an allegation of undue influence, each party should take the precaution of having the other obtain independent legal advice about his rights and duties before entering into the contract.

B.6 Duress is actual or threatened violence or imprisonment against the party entering into the contract or someone close to her.

B.7 A victim of duress has the same rights as a victim of undue influence. That is, the victim has the right to avoid the contract so long as she acts promptly.

Multiple-Choice Questions

1. Susan owns a 1970 MG sports car. The body is fine, but mechanically the car needs a large amount of work. In need of money, Susan contacts Fred who has always wanted to buy the car. Susan offers to sell the car to Fred for $5000 and intentionally says that the car is in excellent condition. Fred accepts the offer. Later, Susan discovers she wants the car back and claims that there is no contract because of her fraudulent misrepresentation. Can Susan successfully sue Fred for the return of the car?

a) Yes, because any misrepresentation is a reason for rescission.
b) No, because a party cannot rely on their own misconduct to have a contract rescinded.
c) Yes, because there was a fraudulent misrepresentation that induced Fred to enter into the contract.

d) No, because there was no misrepresentation since the body of the car was in excellent condition.

e) No, because there is no remedy for innocent misrepresentations.

2. Susan owns a 1970 MG sports car. The body is fine, but mechanically the car needs a large amount of work. In need of money, Susan contacts Fred who has always wanted to buy the car. Susan offers to sell the car to Fred for $5000 and intentionally says that the car is in excellent condition. Fred accepts the offer. After Fred gets the car he discovers how bad the engine really is. Can Fred successfully sue Susan for the return of his money?

a) No, because there is no remedy for innocent misrepresentations.

b) Yes, because any false statement entitles the aggrieved party to rescind the contract.

c) No, because Fred had an obligation to check out the car for himself.

d) Yes, because there was a fraudulent misrepresentation that induced Fred into entering the contract.

e) No, because there was no misrepresentation since the body of the car was in excellent condition.

3. Joe, a used-car salesman, had the best sales record in the dealership. Janice was looking for an affordable, reliable car that she could use to get to university and to her part-time job. Joe showed her a little yellow compact that had a list price of $4000. Joe told her that the dealership had just picked up the car for $3800 so that is what he could sell it for. Also, Joe claimed that it was the best car on the lot. In reality, the car had cost the dealership only $500 because of its bad condition. Relying on Joe's recommendation, Janice bought the car. Within six weeks the engine gave out and Janice was told that it could not be fixed. Can she successfully sue Joe and the dealership to get her money back?

a) Yes, because Joe intentionally misrepresented the dealership's price of obtaining the car that is a statement of fact.

b) No, because Joe's statements about the car's price and its being the best car on the lot were just statements of opinion.

c) Yes, because Joe's statements about the car's price and it's being the best car on the lot were statements of fact.

d) No, because neither of Joe's statements could be considered material to Janice's decision to buy the car.

e) Yes, because Joe intentionally misrepresented that the car was the best on the lot and this is a statement of fact.

4. Jacob, a 16 year old, has just bought a used car and needs to get insurance. The insurance premium for a car owned by a 16 year old is very high. As a result, Jacob's father agreed to register the car in his name and take out the insurance. This way the premium is much lower. Jacob has a car accident and the insurance company refuses to pay for the damages when they learn that Jacob really owns the car and is the primary driver. Can Jacob force the insurance company to pay the claim?

a) Yes, because there is a binding contract and the accident is within the coverage provided.

b) No, because Jacob and his father have not provided the insurance company with all the pertinent aspects of the risk.

c) Yes, because the insurance company must pay all claims that are made by the insured.

d) No, because the insurance contract only covered Jacob's father.

e) No, because the insurance contract is based on an innocent misrepresentation.

5. Joe, a used-car salesman, had the best sales record in the dealership. Janice was looking for an affordable, reliable car that she could use to get to university and to her part-time job. Joe showed her a little yellow compact that had a list price of $4000. Joe made no representations about the car, including not telling Janice that the engine required extensive work to be usable. Janice decided to buy the car. Within six weeks the engine gave out and she was told that it could not be fixed. Can Janice successfully sue Joe and the dealership to get her money back?

a) No, because six weeks exceeded the warranty period.

b) Yes, because Joe and the dealership were selling shoddy merchandise.

c) No, because there was a binding contract.

d) Yes, because Joe failed to tell her about the state of the engine.

e) No, because it is Janice's responsibility to check out the car and its engine.

6. A whaling ship three years at sea sailed into a thick fog near the Bering Strait and ran onto the rocks. The coast was barren and the ocean navigable only two months of the year. Although winter was due within two or three weeks, another ship came along, rescued the crew and bought the cargo of whale oil at a bargain price. The captain of the wrecked ship readily agreed to the price. The owners of the contract want to repudiate the contract because of the low price. Can they succeed?

a) Yes, because the captain of the wrecked ship lacked independent legal advice before agreeing to the price.

b) Yes, because there was duress on the captain of the wrecked ship due to the dire circumstances.

c) No, because the captain of the wrecked ship voluntarily agreed to the price.

d) Yes, because there was undue influence on the captain of the wrecked ship due to the dire circumstances.

e) No, because the captain of the wrecked ship knew what he was doing when he agreed to the price.

7. Brian is a businessman who has been having difficulties lately in meeting his liabilities as they become due. Brian approached a bank for a loan to pay off all his creditors and start up a new business. The bank agrees to the loan only if Brian's wife, Jennifer, agrees to sign a security agreement on her personal assets. Jennifer inherited two pieces of land from her mother which are worth $750 000. After having the transaction explained by the bank and her husband, Jennifer signs the agreement. A few months later, Brian defaults on the loan and absconds from

115

the jurisdiction. The bank comes after Jennifer to pay back the loan and is threatening to sell her land for the money. Is there anything Jennifer can do to get out of the security agreement?

a) Yes, claim undue influence since she lacked independent legal advice.
b) No, she signed a binding agreement with the bank.
c) Yes, locate her husband and force him to pay the bank.
d) No, a claim of undue influence between a husband and wife never works.
e) Yes, claim duress since she lacked independent legal advice.

8. Jimmy really wanted to buy a piece of coastal land owned by Cheryl because it was a perfect location to import drugs. Cheryl refused to sell because the land had been in her family for generations and it was the only asset she had. Jimmy's offering price was four times what the land was worth. After two weeks of Cheryl's refusals, Jimmy arranged to meet Cheryl one last time at his house. The meeting took place in a third-storey room. When Cheryl once again refused, Jimmy said she was not leaving the house until she signed the agreement and then Jimmy left the room. The door was not locked, but when Cheryl looked out a man with a bulge (that looked like a gun) in his pocket was just outside the door. The two windows in the room were also not locked, but outside was a straight drop to the concrete patio below. After three hours, Cheryl signed the agreement, was given a cheque for the full amount of the purchase and was driven home. The next day Cheryl wanted out of the contract. Is there anything Cheryl can do to get out of the agreement?

a) Yes, she can claim undue influence.
b) No, she signed a contract with all the essential elements — offer, acceptance and consideration.
c) Yes, she can claim duress.
d) No, Jimmy made no misrepresentations about the agreement.
e) Yes, she can claim a lack of independent legal advice.

9. Grace arranged to store her vintage sports car at a garage for a month at a price of $110. Payment was made when the car was put in the garage. During the month that the car was there, the owner sold the garage and forgot to tell the new owner that Grace had prepaid for the month. When Grace went to pick up her car, the new owner demanded a further payment of $110. After paying the $110 under protest, Grace obtained her car. Can Grace successfully sue the new owner for the $110?

a) Yes, if she claims dire circumstances.
b) Yes, if she claims there was no contract between herself and the new owner.
c) Yes, if she claims undue influence.
d) No, she must sue the old owner for the $110.
e) Yes, if she claims fraudulent misrepresentation.

10. Caroline is in dire financial straits and is forced to borrow $10 000 from Mark at an annual interest rate of 70 percent. Caroline defaults on her first payment of interest and Mark sues. How will the court respond?

a) The court will allow Mark to recover both the principal of the loan and the interest at the given rate.
b) The court will allow Mark to recover the principal of the loan but not the interest.
c) The court will allow Mark to recover the interest at the given rate on the loan but not the principal.
d) The court will allow Mark to recover both the principal of the loan and the interest, but will set the interest rate at the Bank of Canada prime rate.
e) The court will allow Mark to recover neither the principal of the loan nor the interest at any rate.

11. What are the exceptions to the rule that a court will not consider the adequacy of consideration, just whether or not consideration is present?

a) Where someone claims to be the victim of undue influence.
b) Where there is a concern about the capacity of one of the parties to the contract.
c) Where it is determined that the consideration was grossly inadequate.
d) Where someone claims to be the victim of duress.
e) All of the above.

12. Under what circumstances does a victim of misrepresentation lose the right to rescind?

a) If the party who relied on the misrepresentation does not renounce the contract promptly.
b) If the party who relied on the misrepresentation allows an unreasonable length of time to elapse without repudiating the contract.
c) If the party who relied on the misrepresentation takes further benefits under the contract.
d) If the party who relied on the misrepresentation does not come to the court with clean hands.
e) All of the above.

13. If a court presumes that the signer has notice of all the terms in the contract he or she is signing, can the presumption be rebutted?

a) No, the presumption is not rebuttable.
b) Yes, if the signer can show that he cannot read and the terms were not explained to him.
c) Yes, if the signer can allege *non est factum*.
d) Yes, if the signer is expected to sign a document hurriedly and without an opportunity to read it.
e) Yes, if the signer believes on reasonable grounds that the terms are truly the express intention of the other party.

117

14. What is the distinction between undue influence and duress?

a) Undue influence involves two independent people while duress involves two people in a special relationship.
b) Undue influence is a lack of utmost good faith while duress is a lack of independent legal advice.
c) Undue influence is a lack of independent legal advice while duress is a lack of utmost good faith.
d) Undue influence is physical pressure while duress is mental pressure.
e) Undue influence is mental pressure while duress is physical pressure.

15. Wilma decides to bring a lawsuit for fraudulent misrepresentation against Jerry. For remedies, Wilma claims damages in the amount of $1 million. At the trial the court finds that there was misrepresentation, but it was innocent, not fraudulent. What could the court award after making its finding in this case?

a) The court will award rescission of the contract.
b) The court will award damages.
c) The court will award rescission of the contract and damages.
d) The court will award nothing.
e) The court will award an injunction to prevent Jerry from doing the misrepresentation again.

16. All of the following statements are correct EXCEPT:

a) One requirement for misrepresentation is that a false assertion of fact be made.
b) Silence can never amount to misrepresentation.
c) Failure to disclose pertinent information in contracts requiring utmost good faith may amount to misrepresentation.
d) Misrepresentation can occur before a contract is made or it can form part of the contract itself.

17. Which of the following remedies may be available to victims of innocent misrepresentation?
I. Damages for deceit
II. Rescission
III. Damages for breach of contract

a) I only
b) II only
c) III only
d) II and III only
e) I, II, and III

18. Which of the following statements correctly describes the factors a court will consider in a case of undue influence?

a) Whether there has been actual violence as a means of coercion.

b) Whether there has been threatened violence as a means of coercion.

c) Whether there was domination by one party over the mind of another.

d) Whether a special relationship existed between the parties to a contract, the degree of domination of the stronger party and the extent of the advantage she received from the bargain.

e) Whether a victim has been deprived of the will to make an independent decision.

Answers to Multiple-Choice Questions

1.b)
See pages 181–183 for more information.

2.d)
See pages 181–183 for more information.

3.a)
See pages 181–184 for more information.

4.b)
See pages 184–185 for more information.

5.e)
See pages 181–184 for more information

6.d)
See pages 186–190 for more information.

7.a)
See pages 186–190 for more information.

8.c)
See pages 190–191 for more information.

9.b)
See pages 181–191 for more information.

10.b)
See pages 188–189 for more information.

11.e)
See pages 186–190 for more information.

12.e)
See pages 181–191 for more information.

13.d)
See pages 181–191 for more information.

14.e)
See pages 186–190 for more information.

15.d)
See pages 181–191 for more information.

16.b)
See pages 181–186 for more information.

17.d)
See pages 181–186 for more information.

18.d)
See pages 186–191 for more information.

True/False Questions

1. Misrepresentation can only be innocent.

2. The remedies that an injured party obtains for innocent misrepresentation depends upon the knowledge of the information obtained during the discussions to complete the contract.

3. The injured party must rely on the false statement of fact and must suffer damages as a result of such reliance.

4. The concept of misrepresentation has been restricted not to include silence where the silence is a failure to disclose relevant information in circumstances requiring the utmost good faith.

5. A victim of undue influence has the right to avoid the contract.

6. In determining whether undue influence exists, the courts look at the degree of influence of the weaker party, the extent of the advantage received and whether or not a special relationship exists between the two parties.

Answers to True/False Questions

1. False. Misrepresentation can be fraudulent, negligent or innocent. Fraudulent misrepresentation is a misstatement that was made knowing that it was false. A negligent misrepresentation is made recklessly, without regard for its truth or falseness. An innocent misrepresentation becomes fraudulent if the party who made the misstatement learns of its falsity and fails to inform the other party of the true situation. Innocent misrepresentation is a misstatement made neither fraudulently nor negligently but which nevertheless is false.

2. False. The remedy that an injured party obtains for innocent misrepresentation depends upon the stage in the bargaining at which the innocent misrepresentation is made. If the innocent misrepresentation precedes the making of the contract (induces the innocent party to enter into it) then the injured party may rescind (repudiate) the contract and, in addition, be compensated for any losses that have arisen directly out of performance of the contract. If, however, the innocent misrepresentation is a term of the contract, the injured party is able to have the normal remedies based on breach of contract. At this stage, however, we should note that the injured party may repudiate the contract and receive damages or may simply get damages. Damages are usually substantially more than compensation for losses suffered.

3. True.

4. False. The concept of misrepresentation has been enlarged to include silence where the silence is a failure to disclose relevant information in circumstances requiring the utmost good faith. The most common example of a contract of utmost good faith is a contract of insurance. For example, if an individual has a heart disease and we fail to tell the life insurance company, the silence amounts to misrepresentation of the state of health of the individual.

5. True.

6. False. In determining whether undue influence exists, the courts look at the degree of domination of the stronger party, the extent of the advantage received and whether or not a special relationship exists between the two parties.

10

The Requirement of Writing

Purpose and Significance

Up to this point we have been concerned with the substance of a contract. That is, offer, acceptance, consideration, intention, capacity, legality, and vitiating elements. This chapter focuses instead on the form that a contract takes. Is it oral? Written? Some combination of the two? Does it matter? The answer to the last question is a resounding "yes." The *Statute of Frauds* decrees that certain contracts, to be enforceable, must be in writing.

In this chapter we will learn what types of contracts must be in writing to be legally enforceable and what essential elements of a contract must be reduced to writing. We will examine how the writing requirements have been relaxed through the doctrine of part performance.

Learning Objectives

A. Discuss the types of contracts that must be in writing to be enforceable.

B. Describe the requirements that a written document must meet to satisfy the *Statute of Frauds*.

C. Explain the doctrine of part performance.

D. Outline the Sale of Goods Act.

Content Outline

I. Distinction between substance and form
    A. Benefits of a written record
    B. *Statute of Frauds*
    C. Consequences of the *Statute of Frauds*

II. Types of contract affected by the *Statute of Frauds*
    A. A promise to answer for the debt or default or miscarriage of another
    B. An agreement made in consideration of marriage
    C. A contract concerning an interest in land
    D. An agreement not to be performed by either party within one year
    E. Ratification of infants' contracts

III. Requirements for a written memorandum
    A. All essential terms must be included
    B. Signed by the defendant

IV. Effect of the statute on contracts within its scope
    A. Recovery of money paid under a contract
    B. Recovery for goods and services
    C. Effect of a subsequent written memorandum
    D. Defendant must expressly plead the statute
    E. Effect on a prior written contract
    F. Only the party who has signed can be sued

V. Doctrine of part performance

VI. Requirements of the *Sale of Goods Act*
    A. What constitutes a sale of goods under the act?
    B. Evidence that satisfies the act
    C. When both acts apply
    D. Criticism of the *Sale of Goods Act*

VII. Consumer protection legislation

Questions on Learning Objectives

Objective A: Discuss the types of contracts that must be in writing to be enforceable.

A.1 What is the difference between the substance and form of a contract? (pp. 195–197)

A.2 Distinguish a guarantee from an indemnity and state which of the two must be in writing. (pp. 197–198)

A.3 Many contracts concern land. Which must be in writing? Why? (p. 199)

A.4 Discuss the enforceability of an oral contract that may be performed within one year. (pp. 199–200)

Objective B: Describe the requirements that a written document must meet to satisfy the *Statute of Frauds*.

B.1 To comply with the *Statute of Frauds*, what items must be contained in a note or written memorandum? (pp. 201–202)

B.2 Who must sign the memorandum? (pp. 201–203)

B.3 What form can the memorandum take? (pp. 201–203)

B.4 When must the note or memorandum be made? (pp. 201–203)

B.5 Explain the consequences of holding that a contract fails to comply with the writing requirements of the *Statute of Frauds*. (pp. 202–204)

B.6 Which party to an action must raise the issue of the requirements of the *Statute of Frauds*? (pp. 202–204)

Objective C: **Explain the doctrine of part performance.**

C.1 Which system of courts developed the doctrine of part performance? (pp. 204–205)

C.2 What three requirements must be met in order for the doctrine of part performance to apply? (pp. 204–205)

C.3 What is the legal effect of holding that the doctrine applies? (p. 205)

Objective D: **Outline the Sale of Goods Act.**

D.1 Describe the general effect of the *Sale of Goods Act*. (pp. 207–208)

D.2 Compare the writing requirements under the *Statute of Frauds* with those of the *Sale of Goods Act*. (pp. 207–209)

Answers to Questions on Learning Objectives

A.1 The terms of a contract are its substance. The form of the contract is the physical form it takes. Usually, the contract's form is oral or written or some combination of the two.

A.2 A guarantee is a promise to pay if a debtor defaults. The debtor retains primary obligation to repay the debt and it is only if the debtor defaults that the guarantor must pay. In contrast, a person who makes a promise to indemnify makes himself primarily liable to pay the debt. That is, the creditor may claim directly from the person giving the indemnity regardless of whether he has first sought repayment from the debtor himself. Guarantees must be in writing to be enforceable.

A.3 As a general rule, all contracts concerning land must be in writing. However, the courts have held that some agreements are so remotely connected with land that they need not be in writing to be enforceable.

A.4 The duration of a contract may be a year or less, longer than a year of uncertain. If performance is to be within a one-year period then the writing requirement does not apply. If performance is for an indefinite period, the *Act* similarly does not apply. However, if performance by both parties is to be for a period longer than a year, then the contract must be in writing to be enforceable.

B.1 A memorandum must contain all essential terms of the contract including the identity of the parties, a description of the subject matter of the contract and all material terms such as price.

B.2 The Statute requires that a memorandum be signed by the party to be charged. That means that the memorandum must be signed by the party who is being sued; the other party need not have signed.

B.3 The memorandum may be one document or several taken together. It may be a formal contract or something less formal such as a letter or note.

B.4 The note or memorandum must be in existence before a lawsuit is started. It is not necessary that it exist at the date the contract is made.

B.5 If a contract is required to be in writing and the parties make it orally, then it is unenforceable. It is important that you distinguish an unenforceable contract from a void one. A void contract is one that was never made. If goods or moneys have changed hands, the courts will try to restore the parties to their original positions. If a contract is unenforceable, the courts do not get involved at all: neither party will be able to force the other to perform. Thus, if one party has made a down payment to the other, he cannot recover it.

B.6 It is the defendant (the party being sued) who must plead the statute as a defence to an action. If she fails to plead the statute, the court will decide the case without reference to it.

C.1 The courts of equity developed this doctrine.

C.2 The doctrine of part performance requires:
(i) that the contract concern land;
(ii) that the acts unequivocally refer to the alleged contract; and
(iii) that the plaintiff and not the defendant performed the acts in question and has suffered a loss by his performance.

C.3 If the doctrine of part performance applies, the contract will be enforced despite the fact that the contract is not in writing.

D.1 Contracts for the sale of goods priced over a certain amount must be evidenced in writing or by one of three types of conduct.

D.2 The *Sale of Goods Act* permits consideration to be other than by way of fixed price. Apart from that, the writing requirements are the same as those of the *Statute of Frauds* (see Questions B.1–B.4 above). A second difference, however, lies in the fact that the *Sale of Goods Act* permits the enforcement of the contract where there is acceptance and receipt of the goods by the buyer, part payment has been made or something "of earnest" has been given from the buyer to the seller.

Multiple-Choice Questions

1. Which of the following contracts is within the *Statute of Frauds*?

a) Purchase of a piece of land.
b) Contract for the building of a house on a piece of land.
c) An agreement to rescind an earlier written contract.
d) A contract of indemnity.
e) All of the above.

2. Ajax Limited entered into an oral contract with Dean where Dean will act as supervisor for setting up an electronic data-processing system. The contract did not include a schedule of work or payments. Although the contract by its terms is to extend beyond one year, it is not certain to do so. Dean decides he wants to get out of the contract and claims it is not enforceable because it is not in writing. Is Dean correct?

a) Yes, because an employment contract must be in writing according to the *Statute of Frauds*.
b) No, because the main objective of the contract is a data-processing system which is not within the *Statute of Frauds*.
c) Yes, because the main objective of the contract is a data-processing system that is within the *Statute of Frauds*.
d) Yes, because it is a contract that by its terms is to extend beyond one year.
e) No, because there is no guarantee that the contract will last more than one year.

3. Donut Limited hires Timothy for its marketing division. The oral contract is for an indefinite time period. If Timothy wants to get out of the contract, can he argue that the contract should have been in writing?

a) Yes, because an employment contract must be in writing according to the *Statute of Frauds*.
b) No, because the main objective of the contract is marketing which is not within the *Statute of Frauds*.
c) Yes, because the main objective of the contract is a marketing that is within the *Statute of Frauds*.
d) Yes, because it is an indefinite contract that will be performed by both parties for a period longer than one year.
e) No, because there is no guarantee that the contract will last more than one year.

4. Sutton & Co. were stockbrokers and members of the Vancouver Stock Exchange with access to its facilities. Grey was not a member, but he had contacts with prospective investors. The parties made an oral agreement by which Grey

was to receive half the commission from transactions for his clients completed through Sutton and was to pay half of any bad debts that might develop out of the transactions. When a loss resulted from one of the transactions, Grey refused to pay half the loss. Can Sutton successfully sue Grey?

a) Yes because Grey agreed to cover half of any loss.
b) No because the main objective of the contract was for a guarantee and, therefore, must be in writing under the *Statute of Frauds*.
c) Yes because the main objective of the contract was for an indemnity and, therefore, did not have to be in writing.
d) No because the main objective of the contract was for stock transactions and the indemnity was only a minor element.
e) Yes because the main objective of the contract was for stock transactions and the guarantee was only a minor element.

5. Jim owns a cottage on a lake in a popular vacation area. At the start of the summer, Jim enters into two contracts. The first is a contract with Ralph to replace the roof of the cottage that suffered winter storm damage. The second is with Mercy who will rent the cottage for the month of July. Both contracts were concluded over the phone. Unfortunately for Jim, both contracts ran into problems and the disputes have landed in court. Both Ralph and Mercy are pleading the *Statute of Frauds*. Can Jim succeed in either lawsuit?

a) Jim can succeed in both lawsuits since neither contract had to be in writing.
b) Jim can succeed in the lawsuit against Ralph since only the contract with Mercy had to be in writing.
c) Jim can succeed in the lawsuit against Mercy since only the contract with Ralph had to be in writing.
d) Jim cannot succeed in either lawsuit since both contracts needed to be in writing.
e) The *Statute of Frauds* is not relevant to the question.

6. Paula orally agrees to buy Blackacre from Victoria. Paula then refuses to complete the sale. Victoria sends Paula a letter outlining the contract and demanding that she carry out her obligations. Paula replies by letter saying that she has decided not to go through with the contract referred to in Victoria's letter and that she is not bound since the contract is not in writing. Is Paula correct?

a) Yes because all contracts concerning land must be in writing.
b) No because the contract's main objective was not the transfer of land.
c) Yes because the two letters are not sufficient written evidence of the contract for the *Statute of Frauds*.
d) No because the two letters are sufficient written evidence of the contract for the *Statute of Frauds*.
e) Yes because the written evidence occurred after the contract was entered which is insufficient for the *Statute of Frauds*.

7. Elmer, a farmer, has decided to retire and wants to sell his farm to a young couple who wants to start a farm. Elmer meets and orally agrees to sell the farm to Rob and Jane Smith. The deal is set to close on June 30 because Jane gets access to a trust fund in June that will provide the money for the purchase. However, in order to make any money this year the fields need to be planted in April and May. Elmer agrees to vacate the farmhouse and let the Smiths take over the farm in March although he will not be paid until the end of June. On June 30, Elmer changes his mind, refuses to sign the deed and demands that the Smiths vacate the farm. Can the Smiths force Elmer to finish the transaction?

a) No because agreements concerning land must be in writing under the *Statute of Frauds*.
b) Yes because of the doctrine of part performance.
c) No because of the doctrine of frustration.
d) Yes because the agreement's main objective is not the transfer of land and, therefore, does not have to be in writing under the *Statute of Frauds*.
e) No because of the parol evidence rule.

8. Susan orally offers to sell her typewriter to David for $150. David orally accepts and then hands Susan a deposit of $10, which Susan accepts. Susan then receives an offer to buy her typewriter for $250 that she accepts. Can Susan successfully argue that the contract with David is void because it was not in writing?

a) No because the sale of chattels is not within the *Statute of Frauds*.
b) Yes because the contract needs to be in writing under the *Sale of Goods Act*.
c) No because the *Sale of Goods Act* will accept part payment as evidence of the existence of the contract.
d) Yes because none of the essential information is in writing.
e) No because the *Sale of Goods Act* only applies to sales over $250.

9. Susan orally offers to sell a number of items to David. No item is worth more than $20, but the total price for the items is $340. David orally accepts the offer. Susan then receives an offer to buy all the items for $450 that she accepts. Can Susan successfully argue that the contract with David is unenforceable for not being in writing?

a) No because the sale of chattels is not within the *Statute of Frauds*.
b) Yes because the total price in the contract is more than the limit in the *Sale of Goods Act*.
c) No because the individual price of each item is less than the limit in the *Sale of Goods Act*.
d) Yes because none of the essential information is in writing.
e) No because the *Sale of Goods Act* only applies to sales over $500.

10. What does it mean when one says that a contract comes within the *Statute of Frauds*?

a) The Statute requires the contract to be oral.
b) The Statute requires the contract to be partially written and partially oral.
c) The Statute requires the contract to be in writing.
d) The Statute requires the contract to be under seal.
e) None of the above.

11. What is the distinction between an unenforceable contract and a void contract?

a) An unenforceable contract never existed. A void contract exists but cannot be the subject of a lawsuit.
b) An unenforceable contract exists but cannot be the subject of a lawsuit. A void contract never existed.
c) An unenforceable contract is illegal. A void contract never existed.
d) An unenforceable contract never existed. A void contract is illegal.
e) An unenforceable contract exists but cannot be the subject of a lawsuit. A void contract is illegal.

12. Hansel orally agreed with Gretel to sell her his land and house on the coast. The agreement set the price at $100 000 and was to close on October 31. To make sure everything was clear, Hansel wrote a letter to Gretel that specified the terms agreed to (i.e., the parties, the price, the land covered and the closing date). Gretel received the letter and called Hansel to acknowledge receipt. On October 31, Gretel refused to complete the sale. Can Hansel force Gretel to purchase the land and house?

a) No because a contract concerning land must be in writing under the *Statute of Frauds*.
b) Yes because all the essential elements of a contract are present — offer, acceptance and consideration.
c) No because only Hansel, not Gretel, has signed the written memorandum required by the *Statute of Frauds*.
d) Yes because the letter from Hansel is sufficient for the requirement of writing under the *Statute of Frauds*.
e) No because not all the essential terms of the contract are listed in the letter.

13. What type of conduct can replace the need for a written memorandum?

a) Receipt of the goods by the buyer.
b) Part payment tendered by the buyer and accepted by the seller.
c) Something by way of earnest given by the buyer to the seller.
d) An act of performance that clearly suggests the existence of a contract.
e) All of the above.

14. What is the connecting factor of consumer protection legislation?

a) Protection of the seller in a consumer transaction.
b) Protection of the buyer in a consumer transaction.
c) Protection of both the seller and the buyer in a consumer transaction.
d) There is no connecting factor.
e) None of the above.

15. May the *Statute of Frauds* and the *Sale of Goods Act* apply to the same contract and, if so, do the requirements of both acts have to be met?

a) Yes both acts can apply, and the requirements of both have to be met.
b) No both acts cannot apply.
c) Yes both acts can apply, but if they do, only the requirements of the *Statute of Frauds* have to be met.
d) Yes both acts can apply, but if they do, only the requirements of the *Sale of Goods Act* have to be met.
e) Yes both acts can apply, but if they do, only the requirements of one of the acts have to be met, at the seller's choice.

16. Which of the following contracts are subject to the writing requirements of the *Statute of Frauds*?
I. A month-to-month lease
II. An agreement to build a house
III. A personal guarantee

a) I only
b) II only
c) III only
d) I, II and III
e) I and III only

17. All of the following statements about the doctrine of part performance are correct EXCEPT:

a) It limits the effect of the *Statute of Frauds*.
b) It applies to only contracts concerning land.
c) Its application makes an otherwise unenforceable contract enforceable.
d) The acts relied upon by the courts must be unequivocally related to the alleged contract.
e) The doctrine applies so long as one of the parties to the contract has performed a portion of the contract.

18. Which of the following statements correctly describes the elements that a memorandum must contain to comply with the *Statute of Frauds*?

a) It is a document that contains all the essential terms of a contract.
b) It is a document or series of documents that contains all the essential terms of a contract.

c) It is a document or series of documents that contains all the essential terms of a contract and is signed by the party to be charged.

d) It is a document or series of documents that contains all the essential terms of a contract and is signed by the party to be charged or the party's authorised agent.

e) It is a document or series of documents that contains a description of the agreement reached and is signed by the parties to it.

Answers to Multiple-Choice Questions

1. a)
See page 199 for more information.

2. d)
See pages 199–200 for more information.

3. e)
See pages 199–200 for more information.

4. e)
See pages 197–198 for more information.

5. b)
See pages 201–202 for more information

6. d)
See page 201–202 for more information.

7. b)
See pages 204–205 for more information.

8. c)
See page 208 for more information.

9. b)
See page 207 for more information.

10. c)
See page 201 for more information.

11. b)
See page 202 for more information.

12. c)
See pages 203–204 for more information.

13. e)
See pages 203–204 for more information.

14. b)
See pages 209–210 for more information.

15. a)
See pages 197–209 for more information.

16. e)
See pages 197–200 for more information.

17. e)
See pages 204–206 for more information.

18. d)
See pages 201–202 for more information.

True/False Questions

1. A contract's form is the physical form it takes, either oral or written or a combination of the two.

2. As a general rule, all contracts concerning land must be in writing.

3. A memorandum does not need to contain all essential terms of the contract except for the identity of the parties and a description of the subject matter of the contract.

4. The note or memorandum must be in existence after a lawsuit is started. It is necessary that it exist after the date the contract is made.

5. It is the defendant (the party being sued) who must plead the Statute as a defence to an action.

6. The doctrine of part performance requires:
(i) that the contract concern land, and
(ii) that the acts unequivocally refer to the alleged contract, and
(iii) that the plaintiff and not the defendant performed the acts in question and has suffered a loss by his performance.

Answers to True/False Questions

1. True.

2. True.

3. False. A memorandum must contain all essential terms of the contract including the identity of the parties, a description of the subject matter of the contract and all material terms such as price.

4. False. The note or memorandum must be in existence before a lawsuit is started. It is not necessary that it exist at the date the contract is made.

5. True.

6. True.

11

The Interpretation of Contracts

Purpose and Significance

Think of misunderstandings individuals have with others. Often, the cause is that we have a different interpretation of the words than does the other person. The same thing can happen with contracts. Let's take the renovation of a shed. What if a contractor decides to put a window into a shed? The client might reply that that was "not part of the deal." The client might feel that when the word "restoration" was used, the client meant that the shed was to be made usable whatever that took.

If we ask for part payment in advance, we might get the same response: "That's not part of the deal!" But, we could reply, "We always get a deposit before we start work on a project!"

This example illustrates that there are two kinds of problems in interpreting a contract. First, what do the words used actually mean? Secondly, when will new terms be added or implied? Are the rules of interpretation different for terms that are stipulated than for silent ones? This assignment explores how courts interpret contracts and, in so doing, answers those questions.

Learning Objectives

A. Describe the rules for interpretation of express terms of a contract.

B. Discuss the parol evidence rule.

C. Explain when and how terms may be implied in a contract.

Content Outline

I. The Relationship Between Formation and Interpretation of Contracts

II. The Interpretation of Express Terms
    A. Two approaches to interpretation
    B. How the courts apply the approaches
    C. How the courts choose between conflicting testimony
    D. Special usage of words
    E. Predicting the likely decision of a court
    F. The goal of the courts: To give validity contracts

III. The Parol Evidence Rule
    A. The meaning of the rule
    B. The consequences of the rule
    C. The scope of the rule
        1. Does the document contain the whole contract?
        2. Interpretation of the contract
        3. Subsequent oral agreement
        4. Collateral agreement
        5. Condition precedent

IV. The Limits of *The Moorcock Doctrine*

Questions on Learning Objectives

Objective A: Describe the rules for interpretation of express terms of a contract.

A.1 Explain the plain-meaning approach to interpretation of contracts. (p. 215)

A.2 Describe the liberal approach to interpretation of contracts. (p. 215)

A.3 Describe two other means courts use to interpret contracts. (pp. 216–218)

Objective B: Discuss the parol evidence rule.

B.1 What is the parol evidence rule? (p. 219)

B.2 Describe the circumstances in which parol evidence is admissible. (p. 219)

B.3 What is the relationship between a condition precedent and the parol evidence rule? (pp. 221–222)

Objective C: Explain when and how terms may be implied in a contract.

C.1 What is an implied term? (p. 222)

C.2 In what two situations will a court often imply a term of contract? (pp. 223–224)

C.3 Describe the importance of the *Moorcock* case. (pp. 224–225)

Answers to Questions on Learning Objectives

A.1 When a court interprets a contract, its goal is to explain the meaning of the agreement in a way that would most fairly give effect to the expectations of the contracting parties. The literal or plain-meaning approach to interpretation relies on the dictionary meaning of words to determine what meaning a term of a contract should bear.

A.2 The liberal approach refers to the process where the purposes the parties had in drafting a contract (or term) are first determined. Then the words actually used are construed in light of that purpose.

A.3 First, the oral evidence of the parties is considered and weight given to that which is corroborated or most credible. Second, account is taken of evidence of special usage of words in trades, business and geographical regions.

B.1 Parol evidence is oral evidence. According to the parol evidence rule, oral evidence from outside a contract may not be used to add to, alter, or vary the terms of a written agreement.

B.2 The rule in B.1 above has exceptions. Parol evidence is admissible to prove that a contract is illegal or invalid due to incapacity, misrepresentation, fraud, duress, or undue influence. Parol evidence may also be used to prove a subsequent contract or to explain an ambiguous or incomplete contract. Finally, parol evidence is admissible to assist in interpretation of the express terms of the contract.

B.3 Parol evidence is also admissible to show that an agreement would not be effective unless specified, uncertain future event happened. That specified, uncertain future event is known as a condition precedent.

C.1 An implied term is not expressed in the contract. Rather, it is one that the court believes would have been included if the parties, as reasonable people, had thought about it.

C.2 Often, terms are implied where there is a long-established custom in a particular trade or type of transaction, or where they are necessary for the contract to take effect.

C.3 The *Moorcock* case is important because it sets out the criteria for when terms will be implied to enable the contract to be effective.

Multiple-Choice Questions

1. Acme Limited is negotiating to sell its manufacturing division to New Age Co. The process takes three months to reach a final agreement, with the negotiations involving meetings, faxes, telephone calls and letters. To clarify the terms of the agreement, Acme draws up a formal written agreement that both parties sign to signify its acceptance. As the arrangements are made to transfer ownership of the factories involved, New Age notices that a term of critical importance to them is missing from the written contract. Can New Age do anything about the missing term?

a) Yes because the term was part of the negotiated agreement.
b) No because the parol evidence rule would not allow evidence of a term to be added to the agreement.
c) Yes because the parol evidence rule does not apply since the final signed agreement does not encompass the entire agreement.

d) No because rectification only applies to typographical errors.

e) Yes because rectification can be used to correct any error in recording.

2. New Media Inc. leases a computing system to Corporate Limited, a small but prosperous manufacturing company. An attractive part of the deal for Corporate is the promise by New Media to provide, without further charge, a new software program for inventory and accounts receivable records. New Media explains that the written contract contains no reference to this new software program because it is in its final stage of development and has yet to be publicly announced. The manager of Corporate signs the contract without a term referring to the software program. The equipment is delivered several weeks later along with the promised program, but the program does not function properly and proves to be a failure. Can Corporate successfully sue New Media for breach of the oral promise?

a) Yes because the oral promise was part of the contract.

b) No because the oral promise is merely a gratuitous promise.

c) Yes because the parol evidence rule does not apply since the final signed agreement does not encompass the entire agreement.

d) No because the parol evidence rule would not allow evidence of a term to be added to the agreement.

e) Yes because the oral promise was a separate contract with separate consideration.

3. Trucking Co. orally agrees with Paving Limited, a paving company, to transport 9000 cubic meters of gravel within three months and to provide any related documents that Paving may require for financing the project. To finance the paving operations, Paving applies for a bank loan and the bank requests evidence that the paving work can be started immediately. Paving, therefore, asks Trucking to sign a statement saying that 3000 cubic meters of gravel can be delivered within the next month. Soon after Trucking starts to make the deliveries, it finds that it quoted a price that was too low. Can Trucking terminate the agreement after delivering the 3000 cubic meters?

a) No because the contract does not have to be in writing under the *Sale of Goods Act*.

b) Yes because only delivery of 3000 cubic meters has been reduced to writing and the parol evidence rule would exclude evidence of any other agreement.

c) No because the document concerning 3000 cubic meters was not intended to be the entire contract.

d) Yes because the contract must be in writing under the *Statute of Frauds*.

e) Yes because Trucking can rely on *non est factum* to say it did not understand the nature of the document it was required to sign for the bank.

4. Sam offers to sell Frank his car for $15 000. Frank orally agrees to buy the car provided the bank agrees to loan him $10 000. Sam orally agrees to this stipulation and then draws up a written contract for the sale of the car for $15 000 which both parties sign. The written agreement makes no mention of the need for

a bank loan. When the bank refuses to loan Frank the money, Frank informs Sam and expresses regret at not being able to buy the car. Can Sam successfully sue Frank to force him to buy the car?

a) Yes because the parol evidence rule would exclude evidence about the bank loan requirement.
b) No because the written contract contains the entire agreement.
c) Yes because a contract for the sale of a car must be completely in writing.
d) No because the bank loan requirement would amount to a condition precedent which is an exception to the parol evidence rule.
e) No because the bank loan requirement would amount to a collateral agreement which is an exception to the parol evidence rule.

5. What is the parol evidence rule?

a) It is a rule that allows a party to a contract to add a term previously agreed upon by the parties but not included in the final written form of the contract.
b) It is a rule that prevents a party to a contract from adding a term previously agreed upon by the parties but not included in the final written form of the contract.
c) It is a rule that prevents oral evidence from being used to interpret the terms of a contract.
d) It is a rule that regulates the evidence that can be used to interpret the terms of a contract when the contract is partially in writing and partially oral.
e) It is a rule that regulates the written evidence that can be used to establish the oral terms of a contract.

6. Bell agrees to sell his house to Dan for $250 000. While inspecting the house and land before accepting Bell's offer, Dan notices a sailboat that needs a bit of work but seems to have a sound hull. Dan asks Bell to include the sailboat in the sale of the house. Bell is hesitant, but eventually orally agrees to sell the sailboat for an extra $1000. The written agreement sets out the parties, the land and fixtures covered and the purchase price, but makes no mention of the sailboat. When Dan receives possession of the house, he finds that the sailboat is gone. Can Dan force Bell to return the sailboat?

a) Yes because it was part of the agreement for the sale of the house.
b) No because the parol evidence rule would exclude evidence of an additional term of the contract.
c) Yes because the sale of the sailboat would amount to a collateral agreement that is an exception to the parol evidence rule.
d) No because the sailboat is not a fixture of the house.
e) Yes because the sale of the sailboat would amount to a condition precedent that is an exception to the parol evidence rule.

7. What is the principle of the *Moorcock* decision?

a) The courts will not imply terms to a written contract due to the parol evidence rule.
b) The courts will imply terms to a written contract as an exception to the parol evidence rule.
c) The courts will not imply terms to a contract unless the parties agree to the terms.
d) The courts will imply terms to a contract when the court cannot decide between the interpretations suggested by the parties.
e) The courts will imply terms necessary to give effect to a contract when otherwise the fair expectations of a party would be defeated.

8. Mavis hired W. Drilling Limited to drill a well on her property for $9 per metre plus the cost of the pipe. Mavis and W. Drilling sign a written agreement setting out the terms of the contract. W. Drilling drills to a depth of 300 meters, but stops when Mavis refuses to pay for the work done since no water has been located. Can W. Drilling successfully sue Mavis for the cost of the work done and the materials supplied?

a) No because the contract contained an implied term that water would be located.
b) Yes because all the essential elements of a contract are present — offer, acceptance and consideration.
c) No because W. Drilling guaranteed that water would be located within 100 meters of the surface.
d) Yes because the parol evidence rule would exclude evidence of a term that guaranteed water would be located.
e) No because the location of water would amount to a condition precedent which is an exception to the parol evidence rule.

9. In a written contract Sean promises to pay Bruce $1000 if Bruce will bring a truckload of boxes from Vancouver to Sean's residence in Thunder Bay. Bruce makes the delivery based on the agreement. Sean fails to pay Bruce the $1000 and Bruce sues. In defence Sean offers evidence that Bruce knew that the cases contained liquor and that their importation into Ontario was a violation of the Liquor Control Act (Ontario). Will Sean's defence be successful in preventing the court from ordering him to pay $1000 to Bruce?

a) No because the parol evidence rule would exclude evidence that would have the effect of adding to, deleting from or varying the terms of the written agreement.
b) Yes because the parol evidence rule would not exclude evidence related to the interpretation of the contract.
c) No because the fact that the boxes contain liquor is not a condition precedent nor a collateral agreement, the two exceptions to the parol evidence rule.
d) Yes because the parol evidence rule would not exclude evidence related to the formation and legality of the contract.

e) Yes because the parol evidence rule would exclude evidence as to duress, undue influence and fraud related to the contract.

10. What is the distinction between the plain-meaning and the liberal approach to the interpretation of contracts?

a) The plain-meaning approach confines court to the dictionary meaning of words whereas the liberal approach allows the court to look at the purpose of the parties.
b) The plain-meaning approach allows the court to look at the purpose of the parties whereas the liberal approach confines court to the dictionary meaning of words.
c) The plain-meaning approach confines court to the trade usage of words whereas the liberal approach confines the court to the dictionary meaning of words.
d) The plain-meaning approach allows court to look at any source that it wants to find the meaning of words whereas the liberal approach allows the court to look at the purpose of the parties.
e) The plain-meaning approach allows the court to look at the purpose of the parties whereas the liberal approach confines the court to the trade usage of words.

11. Jill and Jack enter into a contract whereby Jill agrees to deliver 100 pounds of wood to Jack in exchange for $200. Jill delivers the wood but Jack refuses to pay arguing that the wood was supposed to be cut for use in a wood stove. Jill argues that there was nothing in the contract about the wood having to be cut up and she did deliver 100 pounds of logs as specified in the contract. Which of the following kinds of evidence can be considered by a court in deciding how to interpret the contract?

a) Dictionaries.
b) Trade usage.
c) Knowledge of the parties.
d) Circumstances of the negotiations.
e) All of the above.

12. What is the distinction between an express term and an implied term?

a) An express term is not in a contract but is a term that reasonable people would have included if they had thought about it whereas an implied term is actually in a contract.
b) An express term is actually in a contract whereas an implied term is not in a contract but is a term that reasonable people would have included if they had thought about it.
c) An express term is a written term in a contract whereas an implied term is an oral term in a contract.
d) An express term is an oral term in a contract whereas an implied term is a written term in a contract.
e) An express term is actually in the contract whereas an implied term is an oral term of a contract.

13. Rudolph agrees to sell his house to Teresa for $50 000. The negotiations for the agreement of purchase and sale have taken place through a series of emails and include a number of complicated terms concerning repairs that need to be done before the sale is completed. Rudolph writes a letter to Teresa stating that he wants to clarify the terms of the agreement concerning repairs. Teresa writes back confirming that the letter is accurate. Will the parol evidence rule apply to this situation?

a) Yes because the agreement has been reduced to a formal written agreement.

b) No because the agreement is for more than just the sale of the house.

c) Yes because the agreement concerns land.

d) No because the letter was not intended to encompass the entire agreement of purchase and sale.

e) Yes because the courts apply to all contracts where a written format is involved.

14. How is the parol evidence rule reconciled with the doctrine of implied term?

a) The parol evidence rule excludes evidence of terms to be added to the contract. The doctrine of implied term includes evidence of terms to be added to the contract.

b) The parol evidence rule includes evidence of terms to be added to the contract. The doctrine of implied term excludes evidence of terms to be added to the contract.

c) The parol evidence rule applies to terms that were discussed but excluded from the written contract. The doctrine of implied term applies to terms that were never discussed.

d) The parol evidence rule applies to terms that were never discussed. The doctrine of implied term applies to terms that were discussed but excluded from the written contract.

e) The parol evidence rule applies to the interpretation of contracts. The doctrine of implied term applies to the performance of contracts.

15. For what matters does the parol evidence rule not exclude evidence?

Note: answer choices in this exercise are randomised.

a) Interpretation of the contract; to prove the existence of prior oral terms; to prove the existence of collateral agreements; and to prove the existence of a condition subsequent.

b) Interpretation of the contract; to prove the existence of a subsequent oral agreement; to prove the existence of collateral agreements; and to prove the existence of a condition precedent.

c) To prove the existence of prior oral terms; to prove the existence of amendments to the contract; and to prove the existence of a condition precedent.

d) To prove the existence of a subsequent oral agreement; to prove the existence of collateral agreements; and to prove the existence of a condition subsequent.

e) Interpretation of the contract; to prove the existence of prior oral terms; to prove the existence of amendments to the contract; and to prove the existence of a condition precedent.

16. All of the following statements are correct EXCEPT:

a) Implied terms are those that reasonable people would have inserted in the contract had they thought of it.
b) Implied terms are often the result of long established custom.
c) The courts will imply terms reasonable necessary to give effect to a contract.
d) Implied terms are based on the presumed intention of the parties.
e) Implied terms are necessary because of the operation of the parol evidence rule.

17. The rule that words in a contract will be interpreted according to trade usage means that:

a) A local trade council will resolve any contract dispute.
b) The words of the contract will usually be read according to the meaning they normally have in that trade.
c) The contract language will be read as a person inexperienced in that trade would read it.
d) The party who is most experienced in the trade will be responsible for explaining any vague language in the contract.
e) The words of the contract will be interpreted according to their standard dictionary meaning.

18. Which of the following will be allowed in to assist in interpretation of a contract?
I. Evidence showing that the contract was induced by fraud.
II. Evidence that explains ambiguous terms of the contract.
III. Evidence to prove the contents of the contract.

a) I only
b) II only
c) III only
d) I and II only
e) I, II and III

Answers to Multiple-Choice Questions

1. b
See page 219 for more information.

2. d
See pages 219–220 for more information.

3. c
See page 220 for more information.

4. d
See page 221 for more information.

5. b
See page 219 for more information

6. c
See page 221 for more information.

7. e
See page 223 for more information.

8. b
See page 224 for more information.

9 . d
See page 219 for more information.

10. a
See pages 215–216 for more information.

11. e
See pages 215–217 for more information.

12. b
See page 222 for more information.

13. d
See page 221 for more information.

14. c
See pages 219 and 222 for more information.

15. b
See pages 220–221 for more information.

16. e
See page 223 for more information.

17. b
See page 217 for more information.

18. d
See page 220 for more information.

True/False Questions

1. When a court interprets a contract, its goal is to describe the meaning of the agreement in a way that would most fairly give effect to the expectations of the contracting parties.

2. Oral evidence of the parties is considered and weight given to that which is corroborated or most credible.

3. According to the parol evidence rule, oral evidence from outside a contract may not be used to add to, alter, or vary the terms of a written agreement.

4. Parol evidence is not admissible to show that an agreement would not be effective unless a specified, certain future event happened.

5. An implied term is expressed in the contract.

6. The *Moorcock* case is important because it sets out the criteria for implying terms that enable the contract to be effective.

Answers to True/False Questions

1. False. When a court interprets a contract, its goal is to explain the meaning of the agreement in a way that would most fairly give effect to the expectations of the contracting parties.

2. True.

3. True.

4. False. Parol evidence is also admissible to show that an agreement would not be effective unless a specified, uncertain future event happened. That specified, uncertain future event is known as a condition precedent.

5. False. An implied term is not expressed in the contract. Rather, it is one that the court believes would have been included if the parties, as reasonable people, had thought about it.

6. True.

12

Privity of Contract and the Assignment of Contractual Rights

Purpose and Significance

So far we have focused our attention on the original parties to the contract. Sometimes, however, the contract affects people outside it. Those people are termed third persons or third parties to the contract. In this chapter we examine the rule that prohibits a third party from suing on a contract. That rule is known as the privity of contract rule.

We go on to learn how you can circumvent the privity of contract rules through novation and trusts. We then examine exceptions to the privity of contract rule.

Contracts also affect third parties when one party to the contract gives away (assigns) his rights to the third party. Assignment is an everyday occurrence in the world of business so we examine what assignment is, the requirements for a valid assignment, and when it is allowed.

Learning Objectives

A. Discover the meaning of the privity of contract rule.

B. Discover how to circumvent the privity of contract rule.

C. Examine the exceptions to the privity of contract rule.

D. Discuss the concept of, requirements for and types of assignment of contractual rights.

Content Outline

I. Privity of Contract
      A. Limits on the scope of contractual rights and duties
      B. Comparison with rights and duties in tort
            1. Liability of sellers of goods
            2. Liability of manufacturers

II. Novation

III. Vicarious Performance
      A. How it occurs
      B. When is vicarious performance allowed
      C. Tort liability
      D. Exemption clauses

IV. Trusts
      A. How a trust is created
      B. The relation of the trust concept to third parties: constructive trusts
      C. The requirement that a trust cannot be revoked

V. Exceptions to the Privity of Contract Rule
      A. Insurance
      B. The undisclosed principal
      C. Contracts concerning land
      D. Special concessions to commercial practice
            1. Collateral contracts
            2. Exemption clauses and the allocation of risk

VI. The Nature of Rights
      A. The nature of the assignment
      B. The importance of the assignments
      C. The role of equity

Questions on Learning Objectives

Objective A: Discover the meaning of the privity of contract rule.

A.1 Explain the privity of contract rule. (p. 232)

A.2 Describe the arguments for and against the privity of contract rule. (pp. 232–233)

Objective B: Discover how to circumvent the privity of contract rule.

B.1 How can you replace another person as a party to a contract? (pp. 233–234)

B.2 What requirement is necessary to achieve a replacement as described in B.1 above? (p. 233–234)

B.3 What is vicarious performance? (p. 234)

B.4 Is vicarious performance an exception to the privity of contract rule? (p. 234)

B.5 What is a trust? (p. 236)

B.6 Is a trust an exception to the privity of contract rule? (pp. 236–237)

Objective C: Examine the exceptions to the privity of contract rule.

C.1 Explain why an insurance contract is an exception to the privity of contract rule. (p. 237)

C.2 Explain how a landlord/tenant relationship can avoid the privity of contract rule. (p. 238)

C.3 Explain the significance of the *Shanklin Pier* case. (p. 238)

Objective D: Discuss the concept of, requirements for and types of assignment of contractual rights.

D.1 Define the words assignment, assignor and assignee. (p. 240)

D.2 In equity, who are the parties to a lawsuit dealing with an assignment? Why? (p. 241)

D.3 Explain the requirements for a statutory assignment. (pp. 243)

D.4 What risk do you run if you ignore notice of an assignment? (p. 244)

D.5 If a debtor has notice from two or more assignees, whom should he pay? (pp. 244)

D.6 Explain the statement that an assignee "takes subject to the equities." (p. 245)

D.7 When you die someone must assert your rights and fulfill your obligations. How is that done? (p. 247)

D.8 What is negotiation? (p. 248)

D.9 Describe three differences between negotiation and assignment. (pp. 248–249)

Answers to Questions on Learning Objectives

A.1 The privity of contract rule prohibits a person who is not party to a contract from suing on it.

A.2 The privity of contract rule was designed because it was felt that only the people who created the contract should have a say in its disposition. It also prevents undue amounts of litigation on a single contract. Moreover, third parties to the contract have not given consideration and it is arguable that without consideration they should not be recognized.

The arguments against retaining the privity of contract rule include the fact that the rule can be circumvented and there are a series of exceptions to it. Moreover, in tort there is no requirement for privity and, finally, the main purpose of the contract may be to confer benefits on a third party. It seems unduly harsh that the party who is to benefit is unable to enforce the contract.

B.1 Novation refers to the procedure whereby a third party replaces an existing party to the contract. The existing party is then relieved of rights and obligations under the contract and the new party assumes them. Novation can also amount to the substitution of a new contract for an old one.

B.2 Novation must be voluntary to be achieved.

B.3 Vicarious performance refers to the situation where a party to the contract obtains someone else to carry out his duties for him. Under vicarious performance, the original promisor remains accountable for proper performance. The employee who actually does the work can only look to the promisor (not the promisee) for payment.

B.4 Vicarious performance is not an exception to the privity of contract rule. The original parties remain liable to one another and must perform according to the contract. Vicarious performance simply means that one party to the contract has delegated his duties to an employee to be performed.

B.5 A trust is an arrangement where property is transferred from person A to person B with the intent that person B look after the property and administer it for person C's benefit. B has title to the property but must hold all benefits for C.

B.6 A trust is not a true exception to the privity of contract rule. The beneficiary of a trust is like the third party to a contract as the beneficiary neither created the trust nor is the person appointed to administer it. The difference is that the privity of contract rule is a common law concept and the trust is recognized by equity. Equity refused to accept the strict privity of contract rule because it felt that the beneficiary had a legitimate right that should be enforced.

C.1 An insurance contract is an exception to the privity of contract rule because the person who insures his life through an insurance contract is not the person who is entitled to the proceeds under the contract and who has the right to force the insurance contract to pay.

C.2 In a landlord/tenant relationship, rent must be paid regardless of whether the landlord and tenant are the original parties to the lease or not. In that way, the privity of contract rule does not apply.

C.3 In the *Shanklin Pier* case, the court allowed persons who were closely associated with a business transaction but were not parties to a specific contract to be subject to the terms of the contract. This case has been followed in Canada.

D.1 An assignment is the transfer of contractual rights from one of the original parties to the contract to a third party. The person who does the assigning is called the assignor and the person to whom the rights are assigned is called the assignee.

D.2 Equity requires that all three parties "the assignor, the assignee and the promisor" be parties to the action. This is so because the equity courts will not decide a dispute unless all persons affected by its decision are parties to the action and have had an opportunity to argue on their own behalf.

D.3 By statute, an assignment may be made so long as the assignment is absolute (unconditional and complete), is in writing and notice has been given to the promisor of the assignment.

D.4 If a debtor ignores notice of an assignment and pays the original party, he can be sued by the assignee and required to pay the debt a second time.

D.5 Where notice is received from two or more assignees, the debtor must pay the assignee who first gave her notice.

D.6 That statement refers to the fact that an assignee can never be in a better position to sue the promisor then the assignor was. So, if the promisor had defences to an action by the assignor, the promisor would have the same defences to an action by the assignee.

D.7 When someone dies, the law automatically assigns her rights and obligations to a personal representative. Through that assignment, the personal representative is able to stand in the deceased's shoes and assert her rights and fulfill her obligations.

D.8 Negotiation is the process of assigning a negotiable instrument. You will recall that the most common negotiable instruments are checks and promissory notes.

D.9 If a negotiable instrument is negotiated, notice does not have to be given to the promisor. Second, an assignee of a negotiable instrument may stand in a better position then the assignor. The promisor in a negotiable instrument may not raise the defences it has against the assignor. Finally, an assignee of a negotiable instrument can sue in his own name without joining the assignor as a party to the action.

Multiple-Choice Questions

1. Larry, a contractor, enters into a contract with Darryl to construct a house for him. Larry engages Carol, a plumber, to install the plumbing in the house. If Carol installs the plumbing negligently, can Darryl successfully sue Larry or Carol?

a) Sue Larry because that is the person with whom Darryl has a contract.
b) Sue Carol because she did the work negligently.
c) Sue Larry because the contract required personal performance.

d) Sue Larry and Carol because they were both involved in the contract.
e) Sue neither Larry nor Carol because there was no breach of contract.

2. Dennis, a carpenter, owes $1000 to Percy. Dennis offers to renovate Kate's kitchen if Kate will promise to pay Dennis's debt to Percy. Kate accepts the offer. Although Dennis completes the renovation, Kate fails to pay the debt to Percy. On failing to receive payment, who should Percy sue?

a. Sue Kate because she agreed to pay the debt.
b. Sue Dennis because that is the person with whom Percy has the contract.
c. Sue Kate because she took an assignment of the debt.
d. Sue Dennis because Percy never received notice of the assignment.
e. Sue neither Dennis nor Kate because neither is responsible for paying the debt.

3. Holly is excited about the new purple car that she has just ordered from the dealer. A week after the order is placed, the dealer calls Holly and tells her that the car has to be ordered directly from the factory and that will take three months. Holly and the dealer agree to substitute a white car for the purple one. What has just happened to the contract?

a) Nothing.
b) Vicarious performance.
c) Privity of contract.
d) Novation.
e) Assignment.

4. Jennifer agrees to select and supply logs to Stacey for carving into wooden sculptures. Jennifer then hires Mark to choose and cut the trees for Stacey's logs. If Stacey does not like the logs chosen, can she successfully sue Jennifer or Mark for breach of contract?

a) Sue Mark because he selected the logs.
b) Sue Jennifer because the contract required personal performance.
c) Sue Mark because the contract required personal performance.
d) Sue Jennifer and Mark because Mark selected the logs.
e) Sue neither Jennifer nor Mark because there is no breach of contract.

5. Jason, a plumbing contractor, agreed to install a new bathroom in Margo's house. The standard form contract that they signed included a clause exempting Jason from liability for problems that are caused to the rest of the plumbing system in the house if the work in the new bathroom is done negligently. Jason arranged for his newest plumber, Justine, to do the installation. In the course of installing the new bathroom, Justine attached a pipe backwards. This caused the main water pipe in the basement to break, flooding the entire basement. Jason claims that he is not liable for the damage caused by the flooding nor is he liable for repairing the main water pipe. Who can Margo sue?

a) Sue Jason because he is liable for any negligence despite the exemption clause.
b) Sue Justine because she caused the problem and cannot be covered by an exemption clause.
c) Sue Jason because exemption clauses do not apply in vicarious performance situations.
d) Sue Jason and Justine because it is only fair that one of them is liable for the damages.
e) Sue neither Jason nor Justine because they are both covered by the exemption clause.

6. Carol enters into a contract with Norm whereby Norm will pay $100 a month to Sheila for three years out of a fund that Carol gives to Norm for this purpose. If Norm stops making payments to Sheila, can Sheila successfully sue Norm?

a) Yes because Sheila has privity to the contract as the named beneficiary.
b) No because Sheila has no privity to the contact.
c) Yes because Sheila is the beneficial owner of the money in the fund.
d) No because the money is owned by Norm who can do with it whatever he wants.
e) Yes because Carol has assigned her part of the contract to Sheila.

7. Gerry leased his cottage to Shane for two years at a rent of $200 per month. Part of the lease agreement was that Shane was to keep the cottage in good repair and pay the annual taxes. About a year into the lease, Gerry sells his ownership in the cottage to Linda, promising that Shane will be given proper notice of the change in ownership. After receiving notice, Shane stops doing repairs and stops paying the taxes. Can Linda successfully sue Shane for breach of the lease?

a) No because Linda has no privity to the contract.
b) Yes because Linda has privity in the contract due to being the new owner of the land.
c) No because Gerry has assigned his part of the contract to Linda.
d) Yes because Linda is the beneficial owner of the land.
e) No because Shane has not breached the lease.

8. What are the necessary elements of a statutory assignment?

a) The assignment must be conditional and oral, and the notice to the other party must be in writing.
b) The assignment must be oral, unconditional and complete, and the notice to the other party must be oral.
c) The assignment must be conditional and in writing, and the notice to the other party must be oral.
d) The assignment must be absolute and in writing, and the notice to the other party must be in writing.
e) The assignment must absolute and in writing, and the notice to the other party must be oral.

9. In what circumstances does an assignment occur by operation of the law?

a) Upon the death of a party and upon bankruptcy.
b) Upon the death of a party and upon a person attaining an age of majority.
c) Upon a person attaining an age of majority and upon a person becoming insane.
d) Upon the death of a party and upon a person becoming insane.
e) Upon the death of a party, upon a person attaining an age of majority, upon a person becoming insane and upon bankruptcy.

10. Zeta Limited, a building contractor, has erected a building for Stanley. Under the terms of their contract, Stanley still owes Zeta Limited $10 000, to be paid one month after completion of the building. Zeta Limited has purchased $12 000 worth of materials from Supply Co. In settlement of its debt to Supply Co., Zeta Limited pays $2000 in cash and assigns in writing its rights to the $10 000 still owing by Stanley. Supply Co. then notifies Stanley that he should pay the money to it rather than to Zeta Limited when the debt falls due. What is wrong with this scenario?

a) The notice given to Stanley was not proper.
b) Money owing on building contracts cannot be assigned.
c) Stanley has no privity of contract with Supply Co. so cannot be forced to pay Supply Co.
d) Zeta Limited still owes Supply Co. $10 000.
e) Nothing.

11. A debtor owed his creditor $200. The creditor assigned her right to collect this debt to another person, Z. The assignee, Z, delayed in sending notice to the debtor that he was now the party entitled to payment. The debtor, before receiving any notice of the assignment, paid his original creditor $125 on account. Who can Z successfully sue for the $125?

a) Sue the debtor because that is who owed the money.
b) Sue the original creditor because the debtor has not received notice of the assignment.
c) Sue the debtor because in certain circumstances a debtor can be forced to pay twice.
d) Sue the original creditor and the debtor because it is only fair that one of them should have to pay.
e) Sue neither the original creditor nor the debtor because it is Z's own fault that notice was not sent.

12. James lent $800 to Tim on April 1 with repayment due on April 30. James, in writing, assigned the whole debt to Brent on April 7. On April 8, James, in writing, assigned the whole debt to George. On April 9 Tim received notice of the assignment of the debt to George. On April 10 Tim received notice of the assignment of the debt to Brent. On April 30, who should Tim pay and who may be sued if payment is not received?

a) Tim should pay Brent, and George should sue James if payment is not received.
b) Tim should pay James, and Brent should sue George if payment is not received.
c) Tim should pay George, and Brent should sue James if payment is not received.
d) Tim should pay James, and George should sue Brent if payment is not received.
e) Tim should pay George, and James should sue Brent if payment is not received.

13. What limits are placed on the defences available to the non-changing party if an assignee sues for non-payment or breach of contract?

a) Only equitable defences are available.
b) Only statutory defences are available.
c) Only common law defences are available.
d) There are no limits on the defences available.
e) There are no defences available.

14. Mike loans $1000 to Donald. Mike then assigns, in writing, his right to collect the debt to Geoff. When Geoff notifies Donald of the assignment by letter, Donald informs Geoff that he intends to set off a claim of $500, which he is owed by Mike, against the $1000 debt. Who can Geoff sue and for how much?

a) Sue Mike for $1000 because that is the person with whom he had a contract.
b) Sue Donald for $1000 because that is the full amount of the loan.
c) Sue Mike for $500 because that is the difference relying on the set off and just absorb the $500 loss.
d) Sue Donald for $500 because that is the difference relying on the set off and just absorb the $500 loss.
e) Sue Mike for $500 and Donald for $500 because of the set off.

15. What is the distinction between an assignment and a negotiable instrument?

Note: answer choices in this exercise are randomized.

a) The holder of a negotiable instrument can only sue in the name of the original party, notice to the non-changing party is required within 24 hours and a holder has fewer rights to enforce payment than the previous holder of the negotiable instrument.

b) The holder of a negotiable instrument can sue in his own name, notice to the non-changing party is required within 24 hours and a holder has less rights to enforce payment than the previous holder of the negotiable instrument.
c) The holder of a negotiable instrument can sue in his own name, notice to the non-changing party is not required and a holder may have better rights to enforce payment than the previous holder of the negotiable instrument.
d) The holder of a negotiable instrument can only sue in the name of the original party and a holder may have better rights to enforce payment than the previous holder of the negotiable instrument.

e) The holder of a negotiable instrument can sue in his own name and a holder has fewer rights to enforce payment than the previous holder of the negotiable instrument.

16. Which of the following are necessary for a valid statutory assignment?
I. The assignment must be unconditional and complete.
II. The assignment must be in writing.
III. Notice in writing of the assignment must be given to the promisor.

a) I only
b) II only
c) III only
d) I and III only
e) I, II and III

17. All of the following are exceptions to the privity of contract rule EXCEPT:

a) An insurance contract.
b) A trust.
c) A lease agreement.
d) An implied collateral contract.
e) An assignment of contractual rights.

18. Which of the following statements correctly describes the privity of contract rule?

a) Privity of contract precludes third parties from suing on a contract.
b) Privity of contract prevents third parties from obtaining benefits from a contract.
c) Privity of contract precludes third parties from suing in tort.
d) Privity of contract prevents the replacement of one party to a contract with another.
e) Privity of contract prevents parties to a contract from having someone else carry out their obligations under the contract.

Answers to Multiple-Choice Questions

1. c)
See page 234 for more information.

2. b)
See page 232 for more information.

3. d)
See pages 233–234 for more information.

4. b)
See page 234 for more information.

5. e)
See page 235 for more information

6. c)
See page 236 for more information.

7. b)
See page 238 for more information.

8. d)
See page 243 for more information.

9. a)
See page 247 for more information.

10. e)
See page 240 for more information.

11. b)
See page 244 for more information.

12. c)
See page 244 for more information.

13. d)
See page 245 for more information.

14. e)
See pages 245–246 for more information.

15. c)
See page 248 for more information.

16. e)
See page 243 for more information.

17. b)
See pages 237–240 for more information.

18. a)
See page 232 for more information.

True/False Questions

1. The privity of contract rule prohibits a person who is not party to a contract from suing on it.

2. Novation must be voluntary to be achieved.

3. A trust is an arrangement in which property is sold from person A to person B with the intent that person B look after the property and administer it for person C's benefit.

4. In a landlord/tenant relationship, rent must be paid regardless of whether the landlord and tenant are the original parties to the lease or not.

5. Equity requires that two parties — the assignor and the assignee — be parties to the action.

6. Where notice is received from two or more assignees, the creditor must pay the assignee who first gave her notice.

Answers to True/False Questions

1. True.

2. True.

3. False. A trust is an arrangement in which property is transferred from person A to person B with the intent that person B look after the property and administer it for person C's benefit.

4. True.

5. False. Equity requires that all three parties — the assignor, the assignee and the promisor — be parties to the action. This is so because the equity courts will not decide a dispute unless all persons affected by its decision are parties to the action and have had an opportunity to argue on their own behalf.

6. False. Where notice is received from two or more assignees, the debtor must pay the assignee who first gave her notice.

13

The Discharge of Contracts

Purpose and Significance

When and how does a contract end? Parties are obligated to perform according to the terms of a contract as soon as it is entered into and they are obligated to perform as promised under its terms. Once a contract is fully and completely performed, it ends.

However, contracts do not always end through performance. They may end in three other ways. First, the parties to the contract may agree to end it before completion. Second, it may become impossible for one party or the other to perform its obligations under the contract. Finally, in some instances the law will excuse a party from further performance under the contract. This assignment examines performance and the other three "endings" to a contract.

Learning Objectives

A. Discuss discharge of a contract through performance.

B. Discuss the meaning of waiver, substitution, accord and satisfaction, and novation.

C. Explain the meaning and effects of a condition precedent and a condition subsequent.

D. Examine the doctrine of frustration.

E. Discuss limitation acts.

Content Outline

I. The Easy Ways in Which a Contract May be Discharged

II. Discharge by Performance
    A. The nature of discharge by performance
    B. Tender of performance

III. Discharge by Agreement
    A. Waiver
    B. Substituted agreement
        1. Material alteration of the terms
        2. Accord and satisfaction
        3. Novation
    C. A contract provides for its own dissolution
        1. Condition precedent
        2. Condition subsequent
        3. Option to terminate

IV. Discharge by Frustration
    A. Effect of absolute promises
    B. Doctrine of frustration
    C. Self-induced frustration
    D. The effect of frustration
        1. Harshness of the Common Law
        2. The court's attempt to ameliorate the harshness
        3. Statutory reform
    E. The Sale of Goods
        1. Where the Sale of Goods Act applies
        2. In provinces where the Frustrated Contracts Act applies

3. Where the Common Law applies
4. When the source of goods is destroyed

V. Discharge by Operation of Law

Questions on Learning Objectives

Objective A: Discuss discharge of a contract through performance.

A.1 What does it mean to say a contract has been discharged? (p. 254)

A.2 Describe discharge by way of performance. (p. 255)

A.3 Explain the meaning and consequences of "a tender of performance." (p. 255)

Objective B: Discuss the meaning of waiver, substitution, accord and satisfaction, and novation.

B.1 What is a waiver? (p. 256)

B.2 How can a material alteration be made to the terms of a contract? What is the effect of the alteration if properly made? (pp. 256–257)

B.3 Distinguish accord and satisfaction from novation. (pp. 257)

Objective C: Explain the meaning and effects of a condition precedent and a condition subsequent.

C.1 How can a condition alter the general rule requiring parties to a contract to perform? (p. 258)

C.2 How is a condition created? (p. 258)

C.3 What is the difference between a condition precedent and a condition subsequent? (pp. 258–259)

Objective D: **Examine the doctrine of frustration.**

D.1 Is it wise to make an absolute promise? (pp. 260–261)

D.2 What is the doctrine of frustration? (p. 261)

D.3 Describe three situations in which the doctrine of frustration might apply. (p. 262–263)

D.4 What is self-induced frustration? (p. 263)

D.5 Discuss the effects of the doctrine of frustration at common law. (pp. 265–267)

D.6 Discuss the decision in the *Fibrosa* case. (p. 266)

D.7 Explain how the *Frustrated Contracts Act* has modified the common law. (pp. 268)

Objective E: **Discuss limitations acts.**

E.1 What does it mean to say a contractual obligation has become statute barred? (p. 271)

E.2 Describe the effects of a *Limitations Act*. (pp. 271)

Answers to Questions on Learning Objectives

A.1 To discharge a contract means to end it thereby ending any obligations created thereunder.

A.2 Discharge through performance occurs when both parties satisfactorily perform their respective obligations. Performance by one is insufficient.

A.3 An attempt to perform one's obligations under a contract is called a tender of performance. Failure by one party to accept the other's tender of performance entitles the latter to immediately sue for breach of contract.

B.1 A waiver is an agreement not to proceed with performance of a contract when one or both of the parties has not performed its part of the bargain. If neither party has fully performed, by agreeing to forego the performance of the other they have given consideration to one another for the waiver. If one party has fully performed then it receives no consideration for its waiver of the other's performance; to be enforceable, the waiver must be under seal.

B.2 Both sides to the contract must agree upon a material alteration to a contract. If the alteration is material then, in effect, the parties have discharged the original contract and replaced it with a new one.

B.3 There are two aspects to the meaning of accord and satisfaction. First, the parties to the contract agree that they want to discharge the contract (i.e. they reach accord). Second, they agree to release one another for a sum of money or its equivalent, that is, they give satisfaction. they do so in order to be released from their contractual obligations.

Novation, on the other hand, is the discharge of the original agreement and substitution of a new one. Unlike a material alteration, in which the discharge of the old contract is incidental, the primary objective of the parties in novation is to discharge the original contract and put a new one in place.

C.1 In a condition, the parties agree that contractual liability will only be triggered if some event occurs. You will recall that performance is not required until contractual liability exists.

C.2 A condition is created by agreement amongst all the parties to the contract.

C.3 A condition precedent is a contractual term that a future event must happen (or not happen) before the promisor's liability is established. A condition subsequent is an uncertain future event that, if it occurs, brings the promisor's liability to an end. That is, liability based on the contract exists but one of the parties has an "out" in certain prescribed circumstances.

D.1 The danger of making an absolute promise is that if circumstances change and you are unable to perform, you will not be relieved from your contractual liability. Thus, it is not wise to make promises in absolute terms.

D.2 The doctrine of frustration excuses parties to a contract from failure to perform in circumstances where they are not at fault.

D.3 First, the doctrine applies where performance becomes impossible. Second, the doctrine applies where performance could be undertaken but would have a very different meaning from that envisioned in the original contract. Finally, a contract may be discharged for frustration where performance becomes purposeless, after the agreement was made, for reasons beyond the control of the parties.

D.4 Self-induced frustration refers to the situation where one party to a contract willfully disables itself from performing. Self-induced frustration will not excuse non-performance.

D.5 At common law, if the doctrine of frustration applies, the contract is discharged and both parties are freed from further performance under its terms. Any performance already due under the contract is still enforceable, however.

D.6 The *Fibrosa* case changed the then-existing caselaw that losses were held to lie where they had fallen at the time the frustrating event occurred. In the *Fibrosa* case, the House of Lords permitted a purchaser of goods or services who had prepaid to recover the money, provided he had received no benefits from the other party when the frustrating even took place. It did not permit recovery of expenses incurred in reliance upon the contract. However, if even the slightest benefit had been conferred in exchange for the prepayment, the seller could retain the whole deposit. There was not attempt at apportionment of the loss between the parties.

D.7 The *Frustrated Contracts Act* attempts to remedy the common law by undertaking some apportionment of loss. First, a party who has undertaken performance may retain money already paid by the other to the extent that she (the first party) has incurred expenses to the time of frustration. Second, the performing party may recover such expenses even if the money has not been paid but is due and owing at the time of frustration. Third, the performing party may obtain a just amount as remuneration for a valuable benefit received by the other regardless of whether a deposit has been paid.

E.1 A contractual obligation becomes statute barred when a person who is entitled to have a contract performed neglects to take legal action to enforce the obligation for such a long time that he loses the right to bring the action.

E.2 The *Limitations Act* bars a right of action for failure to pursue a remedy. In effect, it means that you have to sue on a contract within a stipulated period of time or forego your rights.

Multiple-Choice Questions

1. Gilbert owed Sullivan $100. Sullivan pressed Gilbert for payment and in a moment of irritation Gilbert tendered the entire sum in quarters. Is Sullivan required to accept this payment?

a) No because a payment to a creditor is always required to be a negotiable instrument.
b) Yes because a creditor must accept any payment in legal tender and silver coins are legal tender.
c) No because a creditor can refuse to accept payment in silver coins.
d) Yes because a creditor must accept any form of payment that fulfills the requirements of the loan.
e) No because a creditor always has a choice in the form of payment he or she will accept.

2. Gilbert owed Sullivan $100. Suppose that Sullivan claimed that the amount was $125 instead of $100 (e.g., interest). When Gilbert tried to pay Sullivan $100 with a $100 bill, Sullivan refused the payment because he wanted $125. What should Gilbert do first?

a) Gilbert should sue Sullivan for breach of contract for refusing to accept the payment.
b) Gilbert should send Sullivan a letter asking for an acknowledgement that Gilbert tendered performance and Sullivan refused.
c) Gilbert should send the bill to Sullivan by registered mail.
d) Gilbert should pay the money into court.
e) Gilbert should do nothing.

3. Gilbert owed Sullivan $100. Suppose that Sullivan claimed that the amount was $125 instead of $100 (e.g., interest) as offered by Gilbert. Gilbert deposited $100 with the proper court official, and Sullivan sued him for $125. If the court awarded Sullivan only $100, who should have to pay the court costs? What if the court awarded $115?

a) For a court award of $100, Sullivan would have to pay the court costs. For a court award of $115, the costs would be apportioned between Gilbert and Sullivan.
b) For a court award of $100, Gilbert would have to pay the court costs. For a court award of $115, Sullivan would have to pay the court costs.
c) For a court award of $100, Sullivan would have to pay the court costs. For a court award of $115, Gilbert would have to pay the court costs.
d) For a court award of $100, Gilbert would have to pay the court costs. For a court award of $115, the costs would be apportioned between Gilbert and Sullivan.

e) For a court award of $100, Sullivan would have to pay the court costs. For a court award of $115, Sullivan would have to pay the court costs.

4. Jane agrees to pay Tim $20 if Tim will shovel her driveway, sidewalk and front walk. Jane pays Tim the money and then decides to do the work herself. Because Jane knows that Tim is saving for university, Jane gives Tim a waiver stating he doesn't have to do the work or return the money. Can Jane demand her money back in three days time if she changes her mind again?

a) No because a waiver is a method of discharging a contract.
b) Yes because there was no consideration for the waiver.
c) No because the $20 payment amounted to consideration for the waiver.
d) Yes because the $20 was just a gratuitous promise, not part of a contract.
e) No because Jane shovelling the driveway, etc. amounted to consideration for the waiver.

5. Conrad agreed to mow Matthew's lawn while Matthew was on vacation for four weeks. Matthew agreed to pay Conrad $20 for each time the lawn was mowed. During the four weeks, Conrad mowed the lawn three times. Upon returning from vacation, Matthew paid Conrad $60 plus a $10 tip. Can either party successfully sue the other for breach of contract?

a) Conrad can sue Matthew under contract law for overpaying him.
b) Matthew can sue Conrad under contract law for the return of the $10.
c) Neither party can sue the other because the contract has been discharged by agreement.
d) Each party can sue the other because neither party has fulfilled its obligations under the contract.
e) Neither party can sue the other because the contract has been discharged by performance.

6. Elk Farm Equipment agrees to sell Cynthia a new state-of-the-art tractor. After signing the agreement, Cynthia instructs Elk to change the tire size and to install a special steering area that includes a stereo system and a TV set. Elk refuses, treats the contract as breached and sells the tractor to another purchaser for a higher price. Can Cynthia successfully sue Elk for breach of contract?

a) Yes because Elk's refusal to deliver the tractor as ordered amounts to breach of contract.
b) No because Cynthia's changes to the tractor after the agreement was signed amounted to a material alteration of the terms.
c) Yes because Elk is not ordering Cynthia another tractor that would meet her specifications.
d) No because Elk can just order a new tractor for Cynthia.
e) Yes because Elk sold Cynthia's tractor to another person.

7. In what ways may a contract be discharged?

a) By non-performance, by novation, by a term of the contract and by fundamental breach.
b) By performance, by separate agreement or as a term of the contract, by frustration and by operation of law.
c) By novation, by frustration and by operation of law.
d) By non-performance, by separate agreement or as a term of the contract and by frustration.
e) By performance, by novation, by fundamental breach and by operation of law.

8. On December 1, Jamie entered into an agreement with a local construction company to renovate his basement for $10,000 starting January 2nd if he could obtain a loan for $5,000 from his parents before that date. On December 26th, Jamie asked his parents for a loan and was turned down. Jamie reported to the construction company that he was unable to obtain financing and would not require the company to do the renovations. Can the construction company successfully sue Jamie for breach of contract?

a) Yes because Jamie is not fulfilling his obligations under the contract.
b) No because Jamie withdrew from the contract before the construction company had done any work.
c) Yes because the construction company suffered a loss in preparing for the repairs.
d) No because the contract included a condition precedent that was not fulfilled.
e) No because the contract included a condition subsequent that was fulfilled.

9. As a special present, Harold bought two tickets to a local baseball game so he could take his daughter. On the day of the game, it rained all morning but by game time the sky had cleared. However, in the third inning the rain started again. After an hour's rain delay, the umpire called the game on the account of rain. On the back of the tickets, there was a clause that stated "If a game is called for rain before the fifth inning, this ticket may be turned in for a ticket to another game." If the box office refuses to give Harold two tickets to a later game, can Harold successfully sue the box office for the tickets?

a) No because the statement on the back of the ticket is a gratuitous promise.
b) Yes because the statement on the back of the ticket is part of the contract of sale and is considered a condition subsequent.
c) No because the statement on the back of the ticket is only met if the game is cancelled after the fifth inning.
d) Yes because the statement on the back of the ticket is part of the contract of sale and is considered a condition precedent.
e) Yes because the statement on the back of the ticket does not apply since the contract was discharged by frustration.

10. Joyce, a wine producer in the Niagara Peninsula, has agreed to sell 100 cases of ice wine to a European consortium. The contract is for the wine to be delivered following its production from the current crop of grapes. To make ice wine, the grapes must freeze on the vines before they are harvested and pressed. Due to an ice storm in January, all the grapes were destroyed on the vines so no wine could be produced for that year. Can the European consortium successfully sue Joyce for breach of contract?

a) No because the contract was conditional on the grapes freezing on the vines.
b) Yes because there has been a fundamental breach of the contract.
c) No because the contract has been frustrated by the ice storm.
d) Yes because Joyce has failed to fulfil her obligations under the contract.
e) Yes because Joyce can buy grapes from another source and fulfil her obligations.

11. Frank, being a wine connoisseur, agrees to buy 100 bottles of wine from a small wine producer in southern Ontario. Unknown to either Frank or the winery, a prohibitionist has broken into the winery's cellar and broken every bottle of wine in the cellar. The winery then tells Frank that they will not be delivering the bottles. Can Frank successfully sue the winery for breach of contract?

a) Yes because the winery will not fulfil its obligations under the contract.
b) No because the contract cannot be legal if a prohibitionist breaks the bottles.
c) Yes because the winery can fulfil its obligations with wine from another winery.
d) No because the contract has been frustrated by the action of the prohibitionist.
e) Yes because there has been a fundamental breach of the contract.

12. Frank, being a wine connoisseur, agrees to buy 100 bottles of wine from a small wine producer in southern Ontario. The winery thinks that the price in the contract is too low so it decides to break every bottle of wine in the cellar. The winery then tells Frank that they will not be delivering the bottles. Can Frank successfully sue the winery for breach of contract?

a) Yes because the winery will fulfil its obligations under the contract.
b) No because the contract cannot be legal if the price is so low that the winery felt the need to break every bottle in the cellar.
c) Yes because the winery can fulfil its obligations with wine from another winery.
d) No because the contract has been frustrated by the actions of the winery.
e) Yes because the winery willfully disabled itself from performing.

13. Phillip agreed to rent an apartment from Caroline for one year commencing April 1 with rent set at $350 per month. Phillip paid $900 as a deposit on the signing of the lease. In preparation for the lease beginning, Caroline spent $300 to have the apartment painted. On March 23, the apartment building burnt down in a fire started by lightning. Caroline intends to rebuild the building, but it will take

15 months to complete construction. If the building is located in Halifax, can Phillip get back the money he has already paid?

a) He can get all the money back because the contract was discharged by frustration before either party had performed their obligations.
b) He can get none of the money back because Caroline had started performance by having the apartment painted.
c) He can get all but $300 of the money back because of the Frustrated Contracts Act.
d) He can get all the money back because incurring expenses without the other side receiving any benefit is not sufficient reason to retain a deposit.
e) He can get $300 of the money back because the contract is valid.

14. Phillip agreed to rent an apartment from Caroline for one year commencing April 1 with rent set at $350 per month. Phillip paid $900 as a deposit on the signing of the lease. In preparation for the lease beginning, Caroline spent $300 to have the apartment painted. On March 23, the apartment building burnt down in a fire started by lightning. Caroline intends to rebuild the building, but it will take 15 months to complete construction. If the building is located in Ottawa, can Phillip get back the money he has already paid?

a) He can get all the money back because the contract was discharged by frustration before either party had performed their obligations.
b) He can get none of the money back because Caroline had started performance by having the apartment painted.
c) He can get all but $300 of the money back because of the *Frustrated Contracts Act*.
d) He can get all the money back because incurring expenses without the other side receiving any benefit is not sufficient reason to retain a deposit.
e) He can get $300 of the money back because of the *Fibrosa* case.

15. How can a contract be discharged by law?

Note: answer choices in this exercise are randomized.

a) Under the *Bankruptcy and Insolvency Act* and the *Limitations Act*.
b) Under the *Frustrated Contracts Act* and the *Limitations Act*.
c) Under the *Bankruptcy and Insolvency Act* and the *Frustrated Contracts Act*.
d) Under the *Frustrated Contracts Act*.
e) Under the *Limitations Act*.

16. To which of the following would the doctrine of frustration apply?
I. Martha and the Muffins, a rock band, agree to play in Toronto for three nights and then in Montreal for the following four. The band is exhausted by the end of the Toronto concerts and asks to be released from its obligations to play in Montreal.

II. Martha and the Muffins agree to play in Toronto for three nights and in Montreal for the following four. On their last night in Toronto the drummer has a heart attack and is unable to play. The band asks to be released from its obligation to play in Montreal.

III. Olga agrees to buy goods from an American company and to pay for the goods in U.S. dollars. By the time she receives the goods, the value of the Canadian dollar has dropped substantially. If she pays for them, she will be unable to make a profit on resale. She asks to be released from her obligation to buy the goods.

a) I only
b) II only
c) III only
d) II and III only
e) I, II and III

17. All of the following statements correctly describe the discharge of a contract by agreement EXCEPT:

a) Novation is the discharge of one contract by substitution of another.
b) If parties to a contract agree to a material alteration of its terms, they have in effect agreed to discharge the contract and replace it with a new one.
c) Waiver is the discharge of one agreement by substitution of another.
d) One party to a contract may accept a money payment instead of performance and thus discharge an existing contract.
e) The parties to an agreement may include an express term that excuses one or both from performance.

18. Which of the following statements correctly describes the applicability of the doctrine of frustration?

a) The doctrine of frustration excuses performance of a contract where performance becomes impossible, has a very different meaning from that which was originally conceived, or becomes impossible or purposeless after the agreement was made for reasons beyond the control of the parties.
b) Where a party to a contract is unable to perform without hardship, the doctrine of frustration will excuse performance.
c) The doctrine of frustration discharges a contract and frees one party from further performance of it.
d) The doctrine of frustration only applies to absolute promises.
e) The doctrine of frustration excuses contractual performance based on fault.

Answers to Multiple-Choice Questions

1. c)
See page 255 for more information.

2. d)
See pages 255–256 for more information.

3. a)
See pages 255–256 for more information.

4. b)
See page 256 for more information.

5. e)
See page 255 for more information

6. b)
See pages 256–257 for more information.

7. b)
See pages 254, 255, 256, 260 and 271 for more information.

8. d)
See page 258 for more information.

9. b)
See pages 259–260 for more information.

10. c)
See pages 260–261 for more information.

11. d)
See pages 260–261 for more information.

12. e)
See page 263 for more information.

13. d)
See pages 266–267 for more information.

14. c)
See pages 266–267 for more information.

15. a)
See page 271 for more information.

16. b)
See page 256 for more information.

17. c)
See page 256 for more information.

18. a)
See pages 261–263 for more information.

True/False Questions

1. To discharge a contract means to end it, thereby ending any obligations created thereunder.

2. A waiver is an agreement to proceed with performance of a contract.

3. There are two aspects to the meaning of accord and satisfaction. First, the parties to the contract agree that they want to discharge the contract (i.e. they reach accord). Second, they agree to release one another for of their obligations

4. A condition is created by agreement amongst all the parties to the contract.

5. The doctrine of frustration excuses parties to a contract from failure to perform in circumstances where they are not at fault.

6. A contractual obligation becomes statute barred when a person who is entitled to have a contract performed neglects to take legal action to enforce the obligation for such a long time that he loses the right to bring the action.

7. Novation is the discharge of the original agreement and substitution of a new one.

Answers to True/False Questions

1. True.

2. False. A waiver is an agreement not to proceed with performance of a contract when one or both of the parties has not performed its part of the bargain. If neither party has fully performed, by agreeing to forego the performance of the other they have given consideration to one another for the waiver. If one party has fully performed then it receives no consideration for its waiver of the other's performance. To be enforceable, the waiver must be under seal.

3. False. There are two aspects to the meaning of accord and satisfaction. First, the parties to the contract agree that they want to discharge the contract (i.e. they reach accord). Second, they agree to release one another for a sum of money or its equivalent, that is, they give satisfaction. They do so in order to be released from their contractual obligations.

4. True.

5. True.

6. True.

7. True.

14

The Effect of Breach

Purpose and Significance

In Chapter 13, we have learned of four ways that a contract might end. In this chapter we will examine a fifth — breach of contract. Breach is dealt with separately for two reasons. First, not all breaches are serious enough to warrant termination. Second, even those breaches that are sufficiently serious do not lead to automatic termination. They give the injured party the right to elect to end the contract.

We begin this chapter by examining the types of breach that lead to the right to discharge a contract. We also look at how breaches may occur. Finally, as exemption clauses are used to protect parties from liability for breaches of contract, we will examine the meaning and functions of such clauses.

Learning Objectives

A. Discover the effects of a breach of contract.

B. Examine breach of contract by express repudiation.

C. Examine breach of contract through failure to perform.

D. Discover the meaning and functions of exemption clauses.

Content Outline

I. Implications of Breach

II. How Breach May Occur

III. Express Repudiation

IV. One Party Renders Performance Impossible

V. Failure of Performance
  A. Types of failure
  B. The doctrine of substantiated performance
  C. When the right to treat the contract as discharged is lost
  D. Exemption Clauses
    1. Their purpose
    2. Attitude of the courts: requirement of adequate notice
    3. Strict interpretations of exemption clauses
    4. Fundamental breach

VI. Possible Criminal Consequences of Breach

VII. The Business Significance of Breach

Questions on Learning Objectives

Objective A: Discover the effects of a breach of contract.

A.1 When can a party elect to treat the contract as discharged for breach? (p. 277)

A.2 If one party to a contract breaches a minor term, what is the injured party entitled to? (p. 277)

A.3 How can you lose the right to treat a contract as discharged for breach? (pp. 282)

Objective B: Examine breach of contract by express repudiation.

B.1 What is express repudiation? (p. 279)

B.2 If one party expressly repudiates a contract, what rights does the other have? (p. 279)

B.3 What is anticipatory breach? (pp. 279–280)

Objective C: Examine breach of contract through a failure to perform.

C.1 Distinguish the situation of frustration from one where a party renders performance of the contract impossible. What is the significance of making this distinction? (p. 280)

C.2 What remedy exists for performance that is slightly inadequate? (p. 281)

C.3 Explain the doctrine of substantial performance. (p. 282)

Objective D: Discover the meaning and functions of exemption clauses.

D.1 What purpose do exemption clauses serve? (p. 283)

D.2 How do the courts limit the use of an exemption clause? (p. 284)

D.3 What is fundamental breach? (pp. 285)

D.4 What is the relationship between fundamental breach and an exemption clause? (p. 285–286)

D.5 Describe the significance of the *Suisse Atlantique* case. (p. 285–286)

Answers to Questions on Learning Objectives

A.1 Where there has been a breach of either the whole contract or an essential term of a contract, the injured party can elect to treat the contract as discharged.

A.2 If the breach of contract is of a minor term, the injured party is not entitled to repudiate the contract but instead can only sue for whatever damages it sustains.

A.3 If an injured party elects to proceed with the contract and take benefits under it in the face of a breach, the injured party may not later treat the contract as discharged. Second, if the injured party does not learn of the breach until performance was complete and it has received the benefit of the contract, it may not treat the contract as discharged.

B.1 Express repudiation is a declaration by one contracting party to the other that it will not perform under the contract as promised.

B.2 In the face of an express repudiation, the injured party may treat the contract as at an end, find another party to perform and sue for damages of breach.

Alternatively, the injured party may continue to insist on performance. If it does and performance is not undertaken, the injured party is still entitled to damages for breach of contract. The injured party does take a risk, however, as intervening events may provide the other party with an excuse for non-performance.

B.3 Whenever breach occurs in advance of the time agreed upon for performance in the contract, an anticipatory breach has occurred.

C.1 In frustration, performance is rendered impossible through no fault of the parties to the contract. An act that constitutes a breach of contract is a willful act of a party. Rendering performance impossible is an example of a willful act. The remedies available to an aggrieved party differ when the cause is frustration rather than breach.

C.2 Where performance is only slightly inadequate, the injured party may not repudiate the contract but may sue for damages.

C.3 The doctrine of substantial performance is the recognition by the courts that where a contract is substantially performed but defective or incomplete in some minor respect, the other party must perform its part of the bargain.

Naturally, the injured party is entitled to damages for the amount of the defective performance. The doctrine of substantial performance prevents a party from seizing upon a trivial failure of performance to avoid its own obligations under the contract.

D.1 Exemption clauses serve to limit the liability of one party to the contract. The clauses may excuse liability completely for certain things or they may limit liability to a fixed dollar amount.

D.2 Exemption clauses may prevent a person from recovering for damage or loss to his person or property. The courts are thus wary of exemption clauses and attempt to circumscribe their application. They do so in two ways. First, if there was inadequate notice of the term given to the party, then the court would find it unreasonable to have the injured party bound by such a term. Second, exemption clauses will be very strictly construed against the party that draws them.

D.3 Fundamental breach is a breach of contract that is so serious that it defeats the whole purpose of the contract.

D.4 An exemption clause will not be held to excuse a fundamental breach of contract unless the clause directly excuses such a breach.

D.5 In the *Suisse Atlantique* case, the House of Lords held that exemption clauses could excuse fundamental breaches when the clause was intended by the parties to the contract to have such an effect.

Multiple-Choice Questions

1. Bill and Ted entered into a contract where Ted would pay Bill for maintaining his yard for an entire year. This meant that Bill was responsible for clearing the driveway and front walk all winter, planting the flower beds in the spring, mowing the lawn and weeding the flower beds in the summer, and raking the leaves and preparing the flower beds in the fall. Ted was to pay Bill monthly installments for the work. After Bill planted the flowerbeds, he took a four-week vacation to the United States in June and did not arrange for someone to replace him. As a result, the lawn grew very long and the flowerbeds became overgrown with weeds. Can Ted successfully sue Bill?

a) Yes, sue Bill for breach of contract asking for damages.
b) Yes, sue Bill for breach of contract asking for the contract to be rescinded.

c) No, Ted should treat the contract as being finished and arrange for someone else to do the work.

d) Yes, sue Bill for breach of contract asking for specific performance.

e) No, Ted should do nothing and let Bill finish out the contract.

2. Alpha Corp. contracts to buy manufactured materials from Beta Limited with delivery in six months. A week later, Beta Limited discovers that it has agreed to a price that is much too low and informs Alpha that it will not deliver the materials as promised. What would be Alpha's best course of action?

a) Continue to wait for Beta's delivery.

b) Locate someone else to make the goods and just write off the contract with Beta.

c) Immediately sue Beta for breach of contract and do nothing about locating another supplier.

d) Ask a court to rescind the contract between Alpha and Beta.

e) Immediately sue Beta for breach of contract and locate another supplier.

3. Albert agrees to sell his Ferrari sports car to Brian for $30 000 and to deliver the car and registration in three weeks. A few days later, John, unaware of the agreement between Albert and Brian, offers Albert $35 000 for the car. Albert accepts the offer and immediately delivers the car to John. What is Brian's best course of action?

a) Sue John for return of the car.

b) Sue Albert for breach of contract by rendering the contract impossible to perform.

c) Sue Albert and John for breach of contract and for return of the car.

d) Just walk away from the transaction and be happy that no money had been lost.

e) Wait and see if Albert gets the car back before the closing of the deal in three weeks and, if not, sue for breach of contract.

4. Coal Co. contracts to deliver 6000 tonnes of coal in 12 monthly installments of 500 tonnes each. The contract requires the buyer to provide the trucks to transport the coal. In the first month, the buyer sends sufficient trucks to transport only 400 tonnes. What is Coal Co.'s best course of action?

a) Treat the contract as discharged and sue the buyer for breach of contract.

b) Continue to perform the contract, but sue the buyer for breach of contract associated with the first delivery.

c) Immediately sue the buyer for breach of the entire contract and ask for damages.

d) Continue to perform the contract and see if the extra 100 tonnes are picked up next month.

e) Immediately sue the buyer for breach of the entire contract and ask for specific performance.

5. Coal Co. contracts to deliver 6000 tonnes of coal in 12 monthly installments of 500 tonnes each. In the first month, Coal Co. only delivers 50 tonnes. What is the buyer's best course of action?

a) Treat the contract as discharged and sue Coal Co. for breach of contract.
b) Continue to expect performance of the contract, but sue Coal Co. for breach of contract associated with the first delivery.
c) Immediately sue Coal Co. for breach of the entire contract and ask for an injunction.
d) Continue to perform the contract and see if the extra 450 tonnes are delivered next month.
e) Immediately sue Coal Co. for breach of the entire contract and ask for specific performance.

6. Harold has been talked into trying downhill skiing by his university friends. On a bright, sunny Saturday, they all head off to a local ski hill. Being a novice, Harold rents all his equipment at the rental hut and, on the way out, is asked to sign a piece of paper, which is the rental contract. The contract contains an exemption clause. On his very first time down the hill Harold collides with a tree breaking both his legs. After being released from the hospital, Harold contacts a lawyer about suing the ski hill for renting him the equipment. What is the likely outcome to the lawsuit?

a) That Harold has to cover his own losses because skiing is a risky hobby.
b) That the ski hill is liable because the exemption clause was not explained to Harold.
c) That Harold has to cover his own losses because of the exemption clause in the contract.
d) That the ski hill is liable because the crash was a fundamental breach of the rental contract so the exemption clause did not apply.
e) That the ski hill is liable because exemption clauses do not apply to dangerous situations.

7. Fred bought 1000 kilograms of white corn seeds from a local farm supplier. Fred explicitly wanted white corn because it had a much higher selling price than the regular yellow corn. The sale contract included a clause that exempted the supplier from any liability for any problems that arose from growing the seeds, including any problem that resulted from the supplier giving the buyer the wrong seeds. When the ears of corn finally appeared, Fred discovered that the corn was yellow, not white as he intended. Fred was furious and wanted to sue the supplier. What would be Fred's best course of action?

a) Do nothing because he can still get cash for his crop.
b) Sue the supplier because there has been a fundamental breach and exemption clauses do not apply in such situations.
c) Sue the supplier for misrepresenting the seeds as white corn seeds.
d) Do nothing because he could have only rejected the seeds prior to planting.

e) Do nothing because the exemption clause explicitly covers situations of fundamental breach.

8. Barney and John entered into a contract where Barney will build a cottage for John in exchange for $50 000 that John will pay on completion. All summer Barney works on the cottage and in August tells John that it is finished and that he wants his money. John inspects the cottage and finds that a few things have not been done. There are no cover plates on any electrical switches and no doors on any interior doorframe. John refuses to pay Barney anything and threatens to sue if Barney does not finish the job. Barney refuses to do anything else arguing that the job is done and that he has another job that takes all his time. What is the likely outcome of a lawsuit?

a) John will be forced to pay Barney as the job has been substantially completed.
b) John will not be forced to pay Barney anything and John should hire someone to do the few remaining items.
c) John will be forced to pay Barney after Barney has done every last little thing.
d) John will not be forced to pay Barney anything and Barney will be forced to do every last little thing.
e) John will be forced to pay Barney for the work minus the few remaining things after Barney has done every last little thing.

9. Fred bought 1000 kilograms of superior cabbage seeds from a local farm supplier. Payment for the seeds would be made after the crop was sold in the fall. Fred explicitly wanted superior cabbage seeds because they had a much higher selling price than the regular cabbage seeds. After the plants appeared, Fred discovered that the seeds were the regular variety. Fred was furious and wanted to sue the supplier. What would be Fred's best course of action?

a) Treat the contract as discharged as the type of seed was a major term of the contract and pay the supplier nothing.
b) Sue the supplier for breach of a minor term of the contract and ask for damages.
c) Accept the difference in the seeds and try again next year, but pay the supplier nothing.
d) Sue the supplier for breach of a major term of the contract, but accept that discharge of the contract is not possible.
e) Sue the supplier for a minor breach of a major term of the contract and ask for damages.

10. How does express repudiation of a warranty differ in effect from the express repudiation of a condition?

a) If there is repudiation of a condition, the contract can be treated as discharged. If there is repudiation of a warranty, the injured party can only sue for damages.
b) If there is repudiation of a condition, the injured party can only sue for damages. If there is repudiation of a warranty, the contract can be treated as discharged.

c) If there is repudiation of a condition, the injured party has access to the equitable remedies, such as specific performance. If there is repudiation of a warranty, the injured party can only seek common law damages.

d) If there is repudiation of a condition, the contract can be treated as discharged. If there is repudiation of a warranty, the injured party has no recourse.

e) If there is repudiation of a condition, the injured party has no recourse. If there is repudiation of a warranty, the injured party can only sue for damages.

11. Under what circumstances is the victim of a breach of condition limited to money damages as a remedy?

a) When the aggrieved party has elected to proceed with the contract and to accept benefits under it despite the breach; and the aggrieved party received the benefit of the contract and did not learn of the breach until performance was complete.

b) When the aggrieved party has elected to treat the contract as discharged and sues for damages; and the aggrieved party continues with the contract anyway and sues for damages.

c) When the aggrieved party has elected to proceed with the contract and to accept benefits under it despite the breach.

d) When the aggrieved party received the benefit of the contract and did not learn of the breach until performance was complete.

e) When the aggrieved party did not know about the breach; and the aggrieved party continues with the contract anyway and sues for damages.

12. If the goods delivered are different in quantity from those ordered, when can the buyer treat the contract as discharged?

a) If either the expected deficiency or the actual deficiency to date is important relative to the whole performance promised.

b) If the buyer thinks that this is the normal practice of the seller and if the quantity delivered is substantially less than the quantity required.

c) If the buyer thinks that there is good reason to think that future performance will be equally deficient and if either the expected deficiency or the actual deficiency to date is important relative to the whole performance promised.

d) If the buyer thinks that there is good reason to think that future performance will be equally deficient.

e) If the buyer thinks that this is the normal practice of the seller and if the quantity delivered is substantially greater than the quantity required.

13. On May 16, Alpha Limited contracts to deliver goods to Beta Inc. by May 31, with payment due on June 30. On May 23, Beta closes up his business and moves to another district without giving any notice to "Alpha." Has any breach of contract occurred before May 31?

a) No because the goods can still be delivered on May 31, just at another address.

b) Yes because Alpha has not delivered the goods before Beta moved.

c) Yes because Beta has made himself unable to receive delivery of the goods so has rendered performance impossible.
d) No because Beta has made no express repudiation of the contract.
e) Yes because moving breached the identification of the parties section of the contract.

14. What is the distinction between substantial performance and part performance?

a) Substantial performance is when performance does not comply in any way with the requirements of the contract. Part performance is when a contract has been partially performed.
b) Substantial performance is when performance does not comply in some minor particular with the requirements of the contract. Part performance is when a contract has been partially performed.
c) Substantial performance is when performance does not substantially comply with the requirements of the contract. Part performance is when one party to the contract has completely performed while the other party has not.
d) Substantial performance is when performance does not comply in some minor particular with the requirements of the contract. Part performance is when an act of performance is used to establish the existence of a contract.
e) Substantial performance is when performance does not comply in any way with the requirements of the contract. Part performance is when an act of performance is used to establish the existence of a contract.

15. Is it possible for a breach of contract to have criminal consequences?

Note: answer choices in this exercise are randomized.

a) Yes if the contract involved a criminal act.
b) No because breach of contract is a civil issue, not a criminal issue.
c) Yes if the party breaching the contract does so with the knowledge that the action will endanger human life or cause bodily harm.
d) No because the remedies for breach of a contract do not include imprisonment.
e) Yes if the contract was illegal.

16. All of the following statements about exemption clauses are correct EXCEPT:

a) The use of exemption clauses enhances the ability of a supplier to keep its price low.
b) Where the bargaining power of two parties is roughly equal, exemption clauses work reasonably well.
c) An alternative to using an exemption clause is to purchase insurance.
d) An exemption clause cannot excuse non-performance of the contract.
e) Exemption clauses are strictly construed against the party that draws them.

17. Which of the following statements is correct?

a) A fundamental breach is a breach of contract that is slightly inadequate.
b) A fundamental breach cannot be excused by an exemption clause that expressly covers the breach.
c) A fundamental breach may never be excused.
d) A fundamental breach renders exemption clauses ineffective to excuse the breach.
e) A fundamental breach is a serious breach of contract that defeats the purpose of the contract.

18. For which of the following is an injured party entitled to repudiate the contract?
I. For an anticipatory breach.
II. For breach of a fundamental term.
III. For breach of a minor term.

a) I only.
b) II only.
c) III only.
d) I and II only.
e) I, II, and III.

Answers to Multiple-Choice Questions

1. a)
See page 281 for more information.

2. e)
See page 279 for more information.

3. b)
See pages 280–281 for more information.

4. d)
See page 281 for more information.

5. a)
See page 281 for more information

6. c)
See pages 283–284 for more information.

7. e)
See pages 285–286 for more information.

8. a)
See page 282 for more information.

9. d)
See pages 282–283 for more information.

10. a)
See pages 278–279 for more information.

11. a)
See page 282 for more information.

12. c)
See page 281 for more information.

13 . c)
See page 280 for more information.

14. d)
See pages 204 and 282 for more information.

15. c)
See page 286 for more information.

16. d)
See pages 283–284 for more information.

17. e)
See page 285 for more information.

18. d)
See pages 279–280 for more information.

True/False Questions

1. Where there has been a breach of either the whole contract or an essential term of a contract, the injured party can elect to treat the contract as discharged.

2. If an injured party elects to proceed with the contract and take benefits under it in the face of a breach, the injured party may treat the contract as discharged.

3. In the face of an express repudiation, the injured party may not treat the contract as at an end, find another party to perform and sue for damages of breach.

4. In frustration, performance is rendered possible through the fault of the parties to the contract. An act that constitutes a breach of contract is a tort in law.

5. Exemption clauses do prevent a person from recovering for damage or loss to his person or property. The courts are thus wary of exemption clauses and attempt to circumscribe their application.

6. In the *Suisse Atlantique* case, the House of Lords held that exemption clauses does not permit fundamental breaches when the clause was intended by the parties to the contract to have such an effect.

Answers to True/False Questions

1. True.

2. False. If an injured party elects to proceed with the contract and take benefits under it in the face of a breach, the injured party may not later treat the contract as discharged.

3. False. In the face of an express repudiation, the injured party may treat the contract as at an end, find another party to perform and sue for damages of breach.

4. False. In frustration, performance is rendered impossible through no fault of the parties to the contract. An act that constitutes a breach of contract is a willful act of a party. Rendering performance impossible is an example of a willful act. The remedies available to an aggrieved party differ when the cause is frustration rather than breach.

5. False. Exemption clauses may prevent a person from recovering for damage or loss to his person or property. The courts are thus wary of exemption clauses and attempt to circumscribe their application. They do so in two ways. First, if there was inadequate notice of the term given to the party, then the court would find it unreasonable to have the injured party bound by such a term. Second, exemption clauses will be very strictly construed against the party that draws them.

6. False. In the *Suisse Atlantique* case, the House of Lords held that exemption clauses could excuse fundamental breaches when the clause was intended by the parties to the contract to have such an effect.

15

Remedies for Breach

Purpose and Significance

In the previous chapter, we discussed breach of contract and the injured party's right to repudiation for certain types of breach. In this chapter we look at other remedies for breach, namely, damages, specific performance, injunction, rescission and *quantum meruit*.

Damages are the most common remedy; thus we will explore the various types of damage awards that may be obtained and when damages are recoverable. As three of the remedies (specific performance, injunction and rescission) are equitable in nature, we will consider the special circumstances in which they can be obtained. The final remedy of *quantum meruit* will be discussed thereafter.

Learning Objectives

A. Examine the nature of, and principles underlying, an award of damages.

B. Examine the types of damages available and when each can be obtained.

C. Discuss the equitable remedies of specific performance, injunction and rescission.

D. Examine the bars to obtaining equitable remedies.

E. Discuss the remedy of *quantum meruit*.

Content Outline

I. Types of Remedies

II. Damages
    A. The purpose of award of damages
    B. Mitigation of damages
    C. Prerequisites for an award of damages

III. The Measurement of Damages
    A. Expectation damages
        1. Differences between tort and contract
        2. Opportunity cost
        3. Contracts of sale
    B. Consequential damages
    C. General damages
    D. Reliance damages
    E. Liquidated damages
    F. Nominal damages

IV. Problems in Measuring Damages
    A. Mental anguish
        1. Wrongful dismissal
        2. Lost holidays
        3. Attitude of the courts
    B. Cost of performance versus economic loss

V. Equitable Remedies
    A. Reasons for the intervention of equity
    B. Reasons for denying a remedy
    C. Specific performance
    D. Injunction
        1. Interlocutory injunction
        2. Injunction against an employee

E. Rescission
    1. The choice between damages and rescission
    2. Opportunity cost
    3. *Quantum meruit*

VI. Methods of Enforcing Judgement

Questions on Learning Objectives

Objective A: Examine the nature of, and principles underlying an award of damages.

A.1 What is the basic purpose that underlies an award of damages? (p. 292)

A.2 Explain the duty to mitigate damages. (p. 293)

A.3 Are all damages arising from a breach of contract recoverable? Explain. (p. 293–294)

A.4 Give the legal test for recoverability of damages. (p. 294)

Objective B: Examine the types of damages available and when each can be obtained.

B.1 What are expectation damages and when are they recoverable? (pp. 294–295)

B.2 What are consequential damages and when are they recoverable? (p. 296)

B.3 Distinguish general damages from reliance damages. (p. 297)

B.4 What are liquidated damages? Do you understand the relationship between liquidated damages and a penalty clause? (pp. 297–298)

B.5 What form of non-economic harm is compensable by damages and when? (pp. 298–299)

Objective C: Discuss the equitable remedies of specified performance, injunction and rescission.

C.1 What is specific performance? (p. 302)

C.2 When will specific performance be granted? When will it not be granted? (pp. 302–303)

C.3 What is an injunction? (p. 303)

C.4 When will an injunction be granted? (pp. 303–304)

C.5 Describe the remedy of rescission. (p. 304)

C.6 When is rescission not available as a remedy? (p. 304)

C.7 When might you want to make a claim for rescission? (pp. 304–305)

Objective D: Examine the bars to obtaining equitable remedies.

D.1 What does it mean to say that equitable remedies are discretionary? (p. 301)

D.2 Describe five bars to obtaining an equitable remedy. (p. 301)

Objective E: **Discuss the remedy of *quantum meruit*.**

E.1 What is *quantum meruit*? (p. 307)

E.2 When is *quantum meruit* available for breach of contract? (p. 307)

Answers to Questions on Learning Objectives

A.1 An award of damages attempts to place the injured party in the same position as if the contract had been completed. The purpose is not to punish the party that breached the contract but rather to compensate the injured party for the loss caused by the breach.

A.2 If you sustain a loss as a result of breach of contract, you are required to do as much as is reasonable to limit the extent of the loss you suffer. This obligation is called the duty to mitigate damages.

A.3 Not all damages arising from a breach of contract are recoverable. To qualify for recovery, the damage must "flow naturally from the breach." That is, the loss must be a foreseeable consequence of the breach.

A.4 The test set for recoverability of damages is whether from past dealings between the parties and the knowledge of both at the time of the contract, the parties could reasonably foresee such a loss to result from breach. If so, damages will be awarded.

B.1 Expectation damages are damages to compensate an injured party for lost profits. They are the amount that the injured party "expected" to earn from the contract if it had been properly fulfilled.

B.2 Consequential damages are those damages other than lost profits that are suffered and which flow from the breach and were reasonably foreseeable at the time the contract was made.

B.3 General damages are the amount that a court awards for harm that cannot be quantified with precision but which the court believes are necessary to fairly compensate the injured party. They are often awarded to compensate for pain and suffering. Reliance damages, on the other hand, are damages that compensate the injured party for time, effort and expenditures made in preparation for performance of the contract. That is, it is compensation for the expenditures made "in reliance" on the contract.

B.4 Liquidated damages are the amount that the parties to a contract agree in advance will be paid for breach of contract. The dollar amount agreed upon must be a genuine attempt to estimate the loss and cannot be a penalty clause, an exorbitant amount out of all relation to the probable consequences of the breach.

B.5 The courts are slowly coming to recognize mental anguish as a form of non-economic harm that is compensable by damages. These awards are found in wrongful dismissal cases and breach of contract for holiday travel and accommodation. Outside of those areas, very few awards of damages for mental anguish for breach of contract have been awarded.

C.1 Specific performance requires one party to the contract to perform that which she has agreed to do in the contract.

C.2 Specific performance will be granted where damages are inadequate compensation. It is commonly granted in contracts dealing with land for unique chattels. It will not be granted where the courts must supervise the parties or where the goods are not unique.

C.3 An injunction is a court order restraining a party from acting in a particular manner.

C.4 An injunction will be granted where there is a negative covenant, that is, a requirement in the contract that a party not do something. It is an order to stop from acting in a certain fashion.

C.5 Rescission is a remedy that attempts to return the parties to the positions they were in before the contract was made.

C.6 Rescission is not available if the subject matter of the contract cannot be returned or the goods have been damaged or have deteriorated.

C.7 We may want to claim for rescission if the contract was a bad bargain.

D.1 To say that equitable remedies are discretionary is to emphasize that the court is free to look at all the circumstances to determine whether or not it should give the equitable remedy. It means that a plaintiff cannot claim such a right automatically on showing a breach.

D.2 Five bars to obtaining an equitable remedy are: lack of clean hands in the plaintiff, unreasonable delay by the plaintiff in bringing the action, adverse effect on an innocent third party, lack of valuable consideration and where the plaintiff could not have had the remedy awarded against him had he been the defendant.

E.1 *Quantum meruit* is awarded where no amount has been specified in the contract so the court awards what is reasonable in the circumstances.

E.2 *Quantum meruit* is available as a remedy for a breach of contract where there is no express agreement on how much is to be paid or where the work that has been done is less than that which had been contracted for and there is no express agreement covering progress payments.

Multiple-Choice Questions

1. George contracted to sell 10 000 kilograms of fresh fish to Ethel. The contract provided that the fish would be delivered in two equal installments on May 1 and June 1. When the first installment was delivered, Ethel refused the fish saying it was not good enough quality. The fish was returned to George's warehouse. If George sues Ethel for breach of contract, what should he do or ask for?

a) Keep the fish so he remains willing and able to deliver it.
b) Ask for rescission since neither side has performed.
c) Ask for expectation damages.
d) Sell the fish to another buyer to mitigate the losses.
e) Ask for general damages.

2. Grace contracted to sell 100 000 garden hoes to Mark for $2 each. The profit on such a contract would be $20 000. Shortly afterwards, Grace received an offer from Brian to buy 200 000 garden hoes at a profit of $60 000, but she does not have enough hoes to accept the offer if she fulfilled the contract with Mark. Grace learned that a competing manufacturer can supply garden hoes of equal quality to Mark at $2.25 each, or $25 000 more than at Grace's price. Using a strictly economic analysis, what would be Grace's best course of action?

a) Fulfil the contract with Mark and do not enter into a contract with Brian.
b) Break the contract with Mark and do not enter into a contract with Brian.
c) Fulfil the contract with Mark and enter into a contract with Brian.
d) Break the contract with Mark and enter into a contract with Brian.
e) None of the above.

3. Grace contracted to sell 100 000 garden hoes to Mark for $2 each. The profit on such a contract would be $20 000. Shortly afterwards, Grace received a letter from Mark saying he would not accept receipt of any garden hoes because he has found a cheaper supplier. Grace commences an action for breach of contract and wins. What would be the objective of the remedies order?

a) Put the aggrieved party in the position he or she would have been in if the contract had been completed.
b) To rescind the contract as neither party had performed.
c) Put the aggrieved party in the position he or she would have been in if the contract had never been entered.
d) To order specific performance to force Mark to accept the garden hoes.
e) Put the parties in the position they were in when Grace received notice of the breach.

4. While examining the items for sale at an antiques auction, Jennifer overhears a local antiques expert comment on a small wooden table saying that it was very valuable being a rare example of a Linquest and that he expects that it is worth $10 000. As a result, Jennifer bids on the table and buys it for $700. Jennifer then takes the table to an appraiser and is told that the table is a 30-year-old reproduction worth $50. Jennifer sues the auctioneer and asks for expectation damages. What amount could she sue for?

a) $9950.
b) $9300.
c) $700.
d) $650.
e) $0.

5. Big Parts Manufacturing entered into a contract to buy steel from the local steel supplier. The contract called for periodic deliveries for two years. As a result of the constant supply of steel, Big Parts entered into a contract with a local car manufacturer to supply panels for use in the production of cars. In turn, the car manufacturer entered into contracts with car retailers to sell the cars that it manufactured. The car retailers sold those cars to rental companies with expected delivery dates based on when shipments were due from the car manufacturer. The rental companies then arranged contracts with taxi companies who rented fleets of cars each year. The taxi companies rented the cars to their drivers for a certain percentage of the daily take. The steel supplier breaches its contract with Big Parts because of a difficulty in locating the coal necessary to run its steel producing plant. Which of the many contracts would the steel manufacturer be responsible for as part of consequential damages?

a) The contract with Big Parts; between Big Parts and the car manufacturer; between the car manufacturer and the retailers; between the retailers and the taxi companies; and between the taxi companies and their drivers.
b) The contract with Big Parts; between Big Parts and the car manufacturer; between the car manufacturer and the retailers; and between the retailers and the taxi companies.
c) The contract with Big Parts; between Big Parts and the car manufacturer; and between the car manufacturer and the retailers.
d) The contract with Big Parts; and between Big Parts and the car manufacturer.
e) The contract with Big Parts.

6. As part of a major deal worth $50 million in profit, Gold Inc. and Resources Limited entered into a contract with a damages clause which read: "In the event that either party breaches their part of the agreement, damages will be limited to $1 million." As it turns out, Gold Inc. did breach its part of the bargain. However, the breach occurred early on so Resources Limited had only spent $500 000 in performance of its part of the agreement. Gold Inc. had spent $100 000 on its part of the contract before breaching the contract. What could be the amount of the damages award?

a) $50 million.
b) $25 million.
c) $1 million.
d) $500 000.
e) $400 000.

7. Fred and his brother Joe were business associates where Fred ran a vegetable supply company that supplied the vegetables for Joe's restaurant. Fred and Joe argued constantly about the price and quality of the vegetables that Fred supplied to Joe. Finally, Joe had enough and refused any more deliveries despite the written contract between Fred and Joe. While Fred was able to easily sell the vegetables elsewhere, Fred wanted to prove to Joe that the price and quality of his vegetables was top notch. So Fred started a breach of contract action against Joe. If Fred wins, what sort of damage award is likely?

a) Liquidated damages for having to sell his vegetables elsewhere.
b) Nominal damages, as there was no real loss.
c) Expectation damages for the expected profit that had been lost.
d) General damages for Fred's hurt pride.
e) Consequential damages for the profits lost at Joe's restaurant.

8. John entered into a contract to buy an antique Victorian lapel pin from Bonnie. The lapel pin was valued at $5 000 and was irreplaceable since there was not another one like it in the world. Two days before delivery, Bonnie changed her mind and refused to sell the lapel pin to John. In a breach of contract suit, what type of remedy would John be seeking?

a) Damages.
b) Rescission.
c) Interlocutory injunction.
d) Injunction.
e) Specific performance.

9. Linda agreed to paint the outside of Michael's house for $2000 with the full amount paid at completion. After painting two of the walls, Michael tells Linda to quit painting the house because he has changed his mind about having the job done. Michael refuses to pay Linda anything for the work already completed since no payment was due until completion. Can Linda successfully sue Michael and, if so, for what amount?

a) Yes, for the full $2000.
b) No because nothing was due prior to completion.
c) Yes, for the value or market price of the work done.
d) No because Michael had a right to withdraw his offer of payment at any time prior to completion.
e) Yes, for the cost of the paint only, but nothing for Linda's labour.

10. What is the difference between the objective of damages in contracts and in torts?

a) Contracts aim to put the parties in the position they would have been in prior to the breach and torts aim to put the parties in the position they would have been in if the tort had been completed.
b) Contracts aim to put the parties in the position they would have been in if the contract had been completed and torts aim to put the parties in the position they were in prior to the tort.
c) Contracts aim to cover expectation damages and torts do not aim to cover expectation damages.
d) Torts aim at compensating for injuries and contracts aim at compensating for breaches.
e) Torts aim to cover medical bills and contracts aim to cover opportunity costs.

11. What is the distinction between a liquidated damages clause and a penalty clause?

a) A penalty clause is usually not enforced by a court.
b) A court generally enforces a liquidated damages clause.
c) A liquidated damages clause is a genuine attempt to estimate the amount of the damages.
d) A penalty clause is an amount to force the parties to perform the contract.
e) All of the above.

12. When might a court order an injunction, but not specific performance?

a) When the court would have to supervise an order of specific performance, but would not be required to supervise an injunction.
b) When the conduct of the defendant is reprehensible, the court would order an injunction, but not specific performance.
c) When the court would have to supervise an injunction, but would not be required to supervise an order of specific performance.
d) When the aim is to prevent the defendant from doing particular activities.
e) When the aim is to prevent the defendant from doing particular activities and force the defendant to do other activities.

13. For what reasons may a court refuse to order an equitable remedy?

a) The plaintiff does not have clean hands.
b) The plaintiff unreasonably delays in commencing the court action.
c) Where an innocent purchaser or third party is involved.
d) The plaintiff would not be a party against whom the remedy would be awarded if the plaintiff were the defendant.
e) All of the above.

14. What methods can be used to enforce a judgement?

a) Imprisonment, levy execution, execution order or garnishee order.
b) Levy execution, execution order or garnishee order.
c) Imprisonment, execution order or garnishee order.
d) Execution order or garnishee order.
e) Imprisonment or garnishee order.

15. Mavis agreed to let the Mini Mining Company remove minerals that are in the ground in the back half of her farm. The contract required the Company to restore the land to its original appearance, which was estimated to cost $50 000. After strip mining for two years, the Company figured they had all the minerals they could easily reach, so quit mining. They have decided not to restore the land because the actual cost of restoration is $40 000 cost and the difference in value of the land without the restoration is $1000. Mavis is mad and commences an action for breach of contract. What would be the amount of the damages if the *Peevyhouse* decision were applied?

a) $50 000 as estimated.
b) $40 000 the actual cost.
c) $1000 the difference in land value.
d) $49 000 the estimated cost minus the difference in land value.
e) $39 000 the actual cost minus the difference in land value.

16. Carlos agreed to buy an antique dining room set from Pedro for $7,500.00. He made a down payment of $750.00 and agreed to return and pick up the furniture at a later date. When her returned, Pedro refused to give him the furniture saying that he had found a buyer who would pay a higher price. Carols may be entitled to which of the following equitable remedies:
I. Specific performance
II. An injunction
III. Rescission

a) I only
b) II only
c) III only
d) I and III only
e) I, II and III

17. (This carries on from Question 16). Carlos intended to resell the furniture at a profit. Pedro's refusal to carry out the agreement entitles Carlos to which of the following?

a) Expectation damages.
b) General damages.
c) Reliance damages.
d) Liquidated damages.
e) Damages for mental anguish.

18. All of the following may bar Carlos from obtaining an equitable remedy
EXCEPT:

a) Unreasonable delays by Carlos in taking Pedro to court.
b) No attempt by Carlos to mitigate damages.
c) Carlos himself did something wrong.
d) If Carlos is a minor he may be unable to sue.
e) If Pedro sold the antique furniture to a third party who had no knowledge of the
agreed Pedro and Carlos.

Answers to Multiple-Choice Questions

1. d)
See page 293 for more information.

2. d)
See page 292 for more information.

3. a)
See page 292 for more information.

4. d)
See page 295 for more information.

5. d)
See pages 296–297 for more information

6. c)
See pages 297–298 for more information.

7. b)
See page 298 for more information.

8. e)
See page 302 for more information.

9. c)
See page 307 for more information.

10. b)
See page 294 for more information.

11. e)
See page 298 for more information.

12. a)
See page 303 for more information.

13. e)
See pages 301–302 for more information.

14. d)
See pages 307–308 for more information.

15. c)
See pages 300–301 for more information.

16. d)
See pages 302–305 for more information.

17. a)
See page 294 for more information.

18. b)
See pages 301–302 for more information.

True/False Questions

1. An award of damages attempts to place the injured party in the same position as if the contract had been completed. The purpose is not to punish the party that breached the contract but rather to compensate the injured party for the loss caused by the breach.

2. Expectation damages are damages to compensate an injured party for torts.

3. Liquidated damages are the amount that the parties to a contract agree will be paid for breach of contract when a condition occurs.

4. Specific performance will be granted where damages are inadequate compensation. It is commonly granted in contracts dealing with land or unique chattels. It will not be granted where the courts must supervise the parties or where the goods are not unique.

5. Rescission is a remedy that attempts to return the parties to the positions they were in after they completed their contractual obligations.

6. *Quantum meruit* is awarded where an amount has been specified in the contract.

Answers to True/False Questions

1. True.

2. False. Expectation damages are damages to compensate an injured party for lost profits. They are the amount that the injured party "expected" to earn from the contract if it had been properly fulfilled.

3. False. Liquidated damages are the amount that the parties to a contract agree in advance will be paid for breach of contract. The dollar amount agreed upon must be a genuine attempt to estimate the loss and cannot be a penalty clause, an exorbitant amount out of all relation to the probable consequences of the breach.

4. True.

5. False. Rescission is a remedy that attempts to return the parties to the positions they were in before the contract was made.

6. False. *Quantum meruit* is awarded where no amount has been specified in the contract so the court awards what is reasonable in the circumstances.

16

Sale of Goods

Purpose and Significance

In chapters 5 to 15, we have learned how the common law deals with contracts in general. In this chapter, we examine one particular kind of contract, namely, a contract for sale of goods. We will discuss specific terms that the *Sale of Goods Act* may imply and those terms of a contract not changed by the Act. Additionally, we will examine bills of lading. In Chapter 15, we discussed the contractual remedies that exist for an injured party to a contract. Where the contract is for the sale of goods, there are special remedies available to the seller. We will examine those additional remedies. Then, after a brief review of the seller's liability and the buyer's remedies, we will examine consumer protection legislation.

Contracts for the sale of goods are very common. We could not live without them. How else would you obtain food, clothing, shelter and transportation? Because such contracts are common, the legislatures enacted the *Sale of Goods Act*. All Canadian provinces (except Quebec) have adopted a standardized form of this act. Its purpose is to make the law more certain in transactions between persons who deal in goods of the kind involved in the transaction or who hold themselves out as having special knowledge or skill with respect to the goods.

Learning Objectives

A. Discuss the application of the *Sale of Goods Act*.

B. Discuss what terms of a contract the *Sale of Goods Act* affects.

C. Discuss common terms of a contract that are not governed by the *Sale of Goods Act*.

D. Describe the types and functions of bills of lading.

E. Describe the remedies that a seller of goods has.

F. State the types of liability that a seller of goods might have.

Content Outline

I. The *Sale of Goods Act*
    A. History
    B. Ownership and possession
    C. Definition of goods
    D. Types of contract of sale

II. Terms in a Contract of Sale
    A. The *caveat emptor* principle
    B. Statutory protection for the buyer: implied terms
        1. Conditions and warranties
        2. Seller's title
        3. Suitability and quality
        4. Sale by sample
        5. Exemption clauses

III. Title to Goods
    A. Specific goods
        1. Rule 1
        2. Rule 2
        3. Rule 3
        4. Rule 4
    B. Unascertained goods
        1. Rule 5
    C. The effect of agency
    D. Bills of lading

IV. Remedies of the Seller
    A. Lien
    B. Stoppage in transit

C. Repossession
D. Resale
E. Damages for non-acceptance
F. Action for the price
G. Retention of deposit

V. The Seller's Liability
A. Misrepresentation
B. Breach of a term
C. Wrongful withholding or disposition by the seller

VI. Remedies of the Buyer

Questions on Learning Objectives

Objective A: **Discuss the application of the *Sale of Goods Act*.**

A.1 Explain the difference between title and possession. (p. 317)

A.2 Describe the types of contracts to which the *Sale of Goods Act* applies. (p. 317)

A.3 Describe the difference between a contract of sale and an agreement to sell. (p. 318)

A.4 Describe the difference between a contract of sale and a consignment. To which does the *Sale of Goods Act* apply? (pp. 318–319)

Objective B: **Discuss what terms of a contract the *Sale of Goods Act* affects.**

B.1 Distinguish a condition from a warranty, as the terms are used in the *Sale of Goods Act*. (p. 320)

B.2 Why is it important to make the distinction drawn in B.1 above? (p. 320)

B.3 What terms concerning a seller's ownership of goods are implied by the *Sale of Goods Act*? (pp. 321–322)

B.4 Describe the impact of the *Sale of Goods Act* on the suitability and quality of goods. (pp. 319, 321–323)

B.5 State, in your own words, the rules of the *Sale of Goods Act* to determine when title to specific goods passes. (pp. 328–330)

Objective C: Discuss common terms of a contract that are not governed by the *Sale of Goods Act*.

C.1 Explain the meaning and impact of s.53 of *Sale of Goods Act*. (p. 325)

C.2 Describe the limitations on a seller's ability to exempt herself from liability under the *Sale of Goods Act*. (pp. 325–326)

C.3 When must a party pay for goods that she has purchased? (p. 326)

C.4 Describe three terms relating to delivery that should be included in a contract of sale. (p. 327)

C.5 If no time for delivery is specified in the contract, what term will the courts imply? (p. 327)

C.6 When does the risk of loss pass from the seller to the buyer in a contract? Why do you care? (p. 327–328)

Objective D: Describe the types and functions of bills of lading.

D.1 What three purposes do bills of lading serve? (p. 331–332)

D.2 Describe a straight bill of lading. (p. 332)

D.3 Describe an order bill of lading. (p. 332)

D.4 What is the relationship between an order bill of lading and ownership? (p. 332)

Objective E: Describe the remedies that a seller of goods has.

E.1 What is a lien? (p. 332)

E.2 When is it available to a seller of goods? (p. 332)

E.3 Describe the right of "stoppage *in transit*" and when it is available to an unpaid seller. (p. 333)

E.4 Describe a seller's right of resale. (p. 334)

E.5 When does a seller sue for damages for non-acceptance? For the contract price of the goods? (pp. 334–335)

E.6 Why is it important to distinguish a deposit from a down payment? (pp. 335–336)

Objective F: State the types of liability that a seller of goods might have.

F.1 How does the *Sale of Goods Act* affect a seller's liability for breach of contract? (pp. 336–338)

F.2 What is the difference between wrongful detention and conversation of goods? (p. 338)

F.3 What remedies does a buyer have if a sale of goods goes wrong? (p. 338)

Answers to Questions on Learning Objectives

A.1 An owner of goods has title to them. An owner has the right to complete enjoyment, disposal and use of the goods. Possession can be in the hands of someone other than the owner. A person who has dominion and control over the goods but is not the owner is said to have possession of them.

A.2 The *Sale of Goods Act* applies to contracts whose subject matter is goods, not services. It applies to both contracts of sale and agreements to sell.

A.3 In a sale, ownership of (title to) goods passes from the seller to the buyer at the moment the contract is made. In an agreement to sell, the transfer of title to the buyer is deferred until a future date. That date may be specified or indefinite.

A.4 A consignment does not amount to a transfer of title. It deals with a change in possession. It is an agreement to ship goods from one business to another. In a sale, title to (ownership of) goods passes from seller to buyer when the contract is made. The *Sale of Goods Act* applies to sales, not consignments.

B.1 The Act uses the word "condition" to mean an essential term of contract. A "warranty" is used to refer to a minor, non-essential term.

B.2 The importance of the distinction is that breach of a condition allows the injured party to repudiate the contract and relieves him from any further duty to perform under the contract. Breach of a warranty may allow the injured party to recover damages but it does not relieve him from performing his side of the bargain.

B.3 The *Sale of Goods Act* implies that the seller has the right to sell the goods, that the buyer will have and enjoy quiet possession of the goods and that the goods will be free from charges and encumbrances in favour of any third party, not declared or known to the buyer before or at the time the contract was made.

B.4 The common law provision as to suitability and quality of goods is *caveat emptor,* buyer beware. Under the *Sale of Goods Act*, however, where the buyer makes known to the seller the particular purpose for which the goods are required and relies on the seller's skill or judgement, there is an implied condition that the goods will be reasonably fit for such a purpose. As well, where the goods are bought by description from a seller who deals in that kind of goods, there is an implied condition that the goods will be of merchantable quality. If the buyer examines the goods, the condition does not extend to defects, which the examination ought to have revealed.

B.5 In an unconditional contract for the sale of specific goods, title to the goods passes to the buyer when the contract is made. Where the contract is for the sale of specific goods to put them into a deliverable state, property passes when the thing is done and the buyer has notice that it is done. Where there is a contract for the sale of goods but the seller is bound to do some act or thing with reference to the goods for the purpose of ascertaining their price, property passes when that act or thing is done and the buyer has notice. When goods are delivered on approval, property passes when the buyer signifies his approval or acceptance or he retains the goods without giving notice of rejection.

C.1 Section 53 enables a seller to exclude or modify the terms implied by *the Sale of Goods Act* by express agreement or by course dealing between the parties.

C.2 Exemption clauses are very strictly construed against the seller in order to limit her ability to exempt herself from the Act. Moreover, the clause may not so completely exempt the seller from liability that she may default with impunity.

C.3 Where the contract stipulates a time for payment, the buyer must pay at that time. If a time for payment is implied, the buyer must pay then. Where the contract is silent about when and how the buyer is to pay, the courts assume that delivery and payment are to be made at the same time.

C.4 When drafting a contract relating to delivery, you should specify the quantity to be delivered, the time of delivery and the place of delivery.

C.5 If no time for delivery is specified, the courts will imply that the goods were to be delivered within a reasonable time. What amounts to a reasonable time varies according to the place of delivery.

C.6 Risk of loss passes at the time stipulated in the contact. Where a contract is silent about the risk of loss, normally the owner bears any loss that is sustained to the goods.

Under both an f.o.b. and a c.i.f. contract, the risk of loss usually remains with the seller until he has delivered the goods to the *carrier*. In contrast, under a c.o.d. contract, the risk of loss remains with the seller until he has delivered them to the *buyer*.

D.1 First, they act as a receipt from the carrier. Second, they provide evidence of the terms of the contract between the shipper and carrier. Finally, the bill of lading may itself be evidence of title to (ownership of) the goods.

D.2 A straight bill of lading specifies the name and address of the party that is to receive an arrival notice once the goods reach their destination. Anyone holding the arrival notice and representing the consignee named in the bill of lading is entitled to receive the merchandise.

D.3 An order bill of lading is made to the order of a specified party. The bill of lading acts to transfer title to the named party.

D.4 Because an order bill of lading transfers title to the specified party, it can be used like a negotiable instrument. That is, it can be used to transfer title to third parties independent of a transfer of possession.

E.1 The right of a seller to withhold goods from a buyer until he is paid is called a lien.

E.2 In order for a seller to have a right of lien, she must have possession of the goods. Once she loses possession, she loses the right to the lien. However, even with possession of the goods, she may not have a lien. The right to a lien exists only if:
i) the contract makes no stipulation that the buyer is to have credit so payment is required upon delivery, or
ii) the goods have been sold on credit, the term of credit has expired without payment being made and the seller still possesses the goods, or
iii) the buyer becomes insolvent before the seller has delivered the goods. Insolvency must be proven. It is insufficient to prove that the buyer is merely financially precarious.

E.3 If a seller gives goods to a carrier for the purpose of delivering them to a buyer but during the course of the delivery notifies the carrier that he wishes the goods to be returned to him and not delivered to the buyer, he has stopped the goods *in transit*.

This remedy is not available to the seller once the goods are in the possession of the buyer.

E.4 After exercising the right of lien of stoppage *in transit* a seller may resell the goods. He must first give notice of the intended resale to the buyer.

An unpaid seller also obtains the right to resell goods whenever a buyer refuses to accept goods delivered according to the terms of the contract.

E.5 A seller has the right to receive the full contract price when title in the goods has passed to the buyer. In such a situation a seller would sue for the contract price.

Where title has not passed to the buyer, a seller would sue for damages of non-acceptance. The amount of the damages depends on whether the seller could resell the goods. If she could, damages are the value of lost profits. If she could not, damages are the excess of the contract price over resale price.

E.6 A deposit is a sum of money paid by the buyer to the seller to compel performance of the contract. The purpose of a down payment is not to compel the seller to perform but to constitute a part payment of the contract price.

If the contract falls through, the party with a deposit (the seller) is entitled to keep it. If it is a down payment, he usually has to return the money less any claims he may have for damages.

F.1 At common law, a breach of a very important term of contract entitles the injured party to repudiate the contract and her obligations under it. The *Sale of Goods Act* prevents repudiation when complete delivery is made and the buyer has indicated an intent to keep the goods.

F.2 When title to goods has passed to a buyer and the seller refuses to deliver, the seller is guilty of wrongful detention. If the seller not only fails to deliver but also transfers the goods to someone else, he is liable for conversion.

F.3 A buyer may get damages, rescission or specific performances for breach of the contract of sale. Damages are a sum of money that compensates the buyer for the seller's breach. Rescission restores the parties to their original position. This releases the parties from further obligations under the contract and returns whatever goods or money one has given to the other. Specific performance requires the seller to deliver the specified goods to the buyer.

Multiple-Choice Questions

1. What is the definition of goods?

a) All personal property.
b) All personal chattels other than choses in action and money.
c) All personal chattels and personal property.
d) All personal property and real property.
e) All personal chattels other than those in possession.

2. What is a sale of goods?

a) A transfer of possession to goods in exchange for other goods.
b) A transfer of ownership to goods in exchange for other goods.
c) A transfer of possession to goods in exchange for money.
d) A transfer of ownership to goods in exchange for money.
e) A transfer of ownership or possession to goods in exchange for money or other goods.

3. Jack wants to buy a new television set. He goes to a local store and views the various sets on display. The store is having a display sale so all the sets actually on the floor of the store are 25% off. After watching the various pictures for a few

minutes, Jack selects the set that he wants and points it out to the sales person. The sales person says, "That is a good set and should give you years of good viewing." Jack pays for the television and takes it home immediately. Three weeks later, Jack turns on the television and the set sparks and does not light up. Jack takes the set to a repair shop and is informed that the electrical cord is frayed and caused the television to short-circuit. As a result, all the television components need to be replaced. Can Jack force the local store to replace the television set?

a) Yes because the set was not suitable for the purposes for which it was purchased.
b) No because it is not the store's activities that destroyed the set.
c) Yes because the sales person guaranteed that the set would work for years.
d) No because Jack bought specific goods that he had an opportunity to inspect.
e) Yes because there was no way for Jack to inspect the interior of the television set.

4. Maple Leaf Appliances Limited is having its annual January sale. Late on Saturday afternoon, Dennis buys a new television set displayed on the floor and pays for it by cheque postdated for five days later. The set is to be delivered on Monday. The parties never discussed which of them is to take the risk of loss before the set is delivered. On Sunday, burglars break into the seller's premises and steal the television set. Dennis stops payment on the cheque. Can Maple Leaf Appliances successfully sue Dennis for the price of the television set?

a) Yes because the television was owned by Dennis once the sales contract was agreed to.
b) No because delivery was not to take place until Monday, after the burglary took place.
c) Yes because the actual television set had been unconditionally appropriated to Dennis.
d) No because payment was not to take place until Thursday, after the burglary took place.
e) No because title to the television set had not passed to Dennis.

5. Maple Leaf Appliances Limited is having its annual January sale. Late on Saturday afternoon, Dennis buys a new television set from the samples displayed on the floor and pays for it by cheque postdated for five days later. From the stock in the warehouse, a set is to be delivered on Monday. The parties never discussed which of them is to take the risk of loss before the set is delivered. On Sunday, burglars break into the seller's premises and steal the television set. Dennis stops payment on the cheque. Can Maple Leaf Appliances successfully sue Dennis for the price of the television set?

a) Yes because the television was owned by Dennis once the sales contract was agreed to.

b) No because delivery was not to take place until Monday, after the burglary took place.

c) Yes because title to the television set had not passed to Dennis.

d) No because payment was not to take place until Thursday, after the burglary took place.

e) No because the actual television set had not been unconditionally appropriated to Dennis.

6. What is the distinction between a condition and a warranty under the *Sale of Goods Act*?

a) A condition that is breached allows the injured party to treat the contract as discharged whereas a warranty that is breached allows the injured party to do nothing.

b) A condition that is breached allows the injured party to complete performance and then sue for damages whereas a warranty that is breached allows the injured party to treat the contract as discharged.

c) A condition is a major or essential term of the contract whereas a warranty is a minor or non-essential term of the contract.

d) A condition is a minor or non-essential term of the contract whereas a warranty is a major or essential term of the contract.

e) A condition is a term of the contract concerning the seller's title whereas a warranty is a term of the contract concerning the buyer's title.

7. Albert purchases a second-hand refrigerator from Blake. Five days after Albert receives the refrigerator, Cowan arrives and demands the refrigerator, claiming he is the proper owner. It turns out that Cowan, not Blake, was the owner all along. What can Albert do in the circumstances?

a) Keep the refrigerator and tell Cowan to sue Blake for the money.

b) Give the refrigerator to Cowan and accept that he should check on ownership more closely before buying second-hand goods.

c) Keep the refrigerator and charge Cowan with trespass if he tries to take the refrigerator.

d) Give the refrigerator to Cowan and sue Blake for breach of implied term as to title.

e) Give the refrigerator to a court and sue both Cowan and Blake to determine ownership.

8. Bill has decided it is time to replace his ten-year-old computer. Not being particularly knowledgeable about computers, Bill goes into Total Computer World and asks a sales person, Susan, about the different machines. Bill explains to Susan that he is a university student so wants a computer that can do word processing, allow access to the Internet and will not be out of date for at least three or four years. Susan recommends a particular model and gives Bill an hour to examine it and try it out on the Internet. At the end of the trial, Bill agrees to buy the computer. After Bill gets it home, his friend who is an expert on

computers, comes over to see the new machine. The friend informs Bill that his new machine is a two-year old model that will not work with the latest Internet software or with the latest version of Bill's preferred word processing package. When Bill tries to return the computer, the store refuses. Can Bill force the store to take the machine back?

a) No because of caveat emptor.

b) Yes because Bill relied on Susan's expertise.

c) No because Bill was given an opportunity to try out the computer.

d) Yes because the store has breached the implied term as to title.

e) No because the difficulties with the computer are not those ordinarily encountered with proper use of a computer.

9. Allan agrees to purchase a car from Lambeth Motors Limited. In the contract the car is described as "a new 190-H.P., 6-cylinder sedan." There is also a clause, inserted by the seller, that "All conditions, warranties and liabilities implied by statute, common law, or otherwise are hereby excluded." After taking delivery, Allan discovers that the car is not new and has only four cylinders. Can Allan successfully sue Lambeth Motors for breach of contract?

a) No because the exemption clause in the contract excludes any liability.

b) Yes because the car does not meet the suitability requirements of Allan.

c) No because the exemption clause in the contract only excludes liability for any express terms.

d) Yes because the exemption clause in the contract only excludes liability for any implied terms.

e) No because the car still meets the suitability requirements of Allan.

10. Weiss purchases from Powell, a seed dealer, some seeds described in the catalogue as Red Wave Petunias. When the seeds grow, they turn out to be yellow geraniums. Can Weiss successfully sue Powell for breach of contract?

a) Yes because the seeds do not meet the description in the catalogue.

b) No because Weiss did not reject the seeds once he had a chance to examine them.

c) Yes because the yellow geraniums clash with the rest of Weiss's garden.

d) No because the seeds were of good quality.

e) Yes because the flowers grown from the seeds were not of merchantable quality.

11. Olive went into an antiques store and saw an old pocket watch which she wanted to buy. After negotiating over the price for a few minutes, a deal was struck. Olive paid cash and the store agreed to polish the case of the watch and deliver it in three days. That night a fire started in the back room of the store and everything was destroyed. Can Olive successfully sue the store to return her money?

a) Yes because title would not pass until the case had been polished.

b) No because title passed when the contract was agreed to.

c) Yes because title would not pass until the store delivered the watch.
d) No because title passed when Susan paid for the watch.
e) Yes because title would not pass until Olive had an opportunity to inspect the watch.

12. McVale, a wheat farmer, agrees to sell his entire crop of wheat to a local bread factory for $1 per kilogram. Before agreeing to the purchase, experts from the bread factory inspected the wheat and determined that it was of a very high quality. The wheat had already been harvested, the bread factory simply had to come and get it. The day before the bread factory truck arrived, the barn was struck by lightning and burned to the ground. Can McVale still sue the bread factory for the price of the wheat?

a) Yes because title passed when the contract was agreed to.
b) No because title would not pass until the factory picked up the wheat.
c) No because title would not pass until the wheat had been weighed to determine the price.
d) No because title would not pass until the bread factory paid for the wheat.
e) Yes because title passed when the bread factory inspected the wheat.

13. What are the remedies available to the buyer in a contract for the sale of goods?

a) Damages, lien, and action for the price.
b) Damages, rescission, and specific performance.
c) Rescission, injunction, and lien.
d) Rescission, injunction, and specific performance.
e) Damages, rescission, injunction, specific performance, lien, and action for the price.

14. The Wool Sweater Store of St. John's, Newfoundland, agrees to sell 100 sweaters to West Coast Sweater Emporium of Vancouver, British Columbia. The Sweater Emporium has been a customer of the Wool Sweater Store for ten years so the Store ships the sweaters before actually receiving payment from the Emporium. While the sweaters are still travelling to Vancouver, the Wool Sweater Store learns that the Emporium is insolvent and will not be paying any of its bills for the next two months. What remedy should the Wool Sweater Store use to solve its problem?

a) Damages.
b) Lien on the sweaters.
c) Stoppage in transit.
d) Retention of deposit.
e) None of the above.

15. What are the remedies available to a seller for breach of a contract in the sale of goods?

Note: answer choices in this exercise are randomized.

a) Lien, stoppage *in transit*, repossession, resale, damages, action for the price, and retention of deposit.
b) Lien, resale, rescission, and injunction.
c) Stoppage *in transit*, action for the price, specific performance.
d) Lien, repossession, resale, injunction, and specific performance.
e) Repossession, damages, injunction and retention of deposit.

16. Which of the following statements correctly describes how a seller of goods can control the impact of the *Sale of Goods Act*?
a. She can never control the legislation.
b. She can tell the buyer that the Act does not apply.
c. She could give written notice to the buyer that the terms of the Act do not apply.
d. She could insert an express term in the contract to the effect that the Act does not apply.
e. She can ignore the legislation.

17. The *Sale of Goods Act* applies to which of the following contracts?
I. A contract to have your apartment painted.
II. Buying the paint.
III. An agreement to buy the paint when it arrives in stock.

a) I only
b) II only
c) III only
d) II and III only
e) I, II and III

18. All of the following statements are correct EXCEPT:

a) When made to the order of a particular person, a bill of lading can be used to transfer title.
b) A bill of lading may be used as a receipt.
c) A bill of lading may be evidence of title of goods.
d) A bill of lading may be endorsed and used like a negotiable instrument.
e) A bill of lading is a form of contract.

19. You agree to buy a car from a used car business. After signing the contract you realize you cannot afford the car and you refuse to accept it. All of the following statements concerning the seller's remedies are correct EXCEPT:

a) The seller may retain the deposit you made on the car.
b) The seller may sue you for breach of contract.
c) The seller may sue you for damages.
d) The seller may resell the car and sue you for the full sale price.
e) The seller may resell the car.

20. Which of the following contracts may be affected by consumer protection legislation?
I. Purchase of a regularly priced item of clothing from a department store.
II. Goods sent to you in the mail on a 30-day trial basis.
III. Purchase of a car over time.

a) I only
b) II only
c) III only
d) II and III only
e) I, II and III

21. Which of the following statements correctly describes a lien?

a) A lien is the right to withhold goods in one's possession until a debt is paid.
b) A lien is the right to order a shipper to withhold goods from a buyer.
c) A lien is the right to prevent a buyer from passing a valid title to goods.
d) A lien is the right to resell goods that a buyer has refused to accept.
e) A lien is the right to hold goods as a deposit to ensure further performance of a contract.

Answers to Multiple-Choice Questions

1. b)
See page 317 for more information.

2. d)
See page 318 for more information.

3. d)
See page 321 for more information.

4. a)
See page 328 for more information.

5. e)
See pages 327–328 for more information

6. c)
See page 320 for more information.

7. d)
See page 320 for more information.

8. b)
See page 321 for more information.

9. d)
See page 325 for more information.

10. a)
See page 320 for more information.

11. a)
See page 329 for more information.

12. c)
See page 329 for more information.

13. b)
See page 338 for more information.

14. c)
See page 333 for more information.

15. a)
See pages 332–336 for more information.

16. d)
See page 325 for more information.

17. d)
See page 318 for more information.

18. e)
See pages 331–332 for more information.

19. d)
See page 334 for more information.

20. d)
See page 335 for more information.

21. a)
See page 332 for more information.

True/False Questions

1. An owner of goods has title to them. An owner has the right to complete enjoyment, disposal and use of the goods. Possession cannot be in the hands of someone other than the owner.

2. The Act uses the word "condition" to mean an essential term of contract. A "warranty" is used to refer to a guarantee.

3. Section 53 enables a seller to include the terms implied by the *Sale of Goods Act* by express agreement or by course dealing between the parties.

4. The bill of lading may never be evidence of title to (ownership of) the goods.

5. Because an order bill of lading transfers title to the specified party, it can be used like a negotiable instrument. That is, it can be used to transfer title to third parties independent of a transfer of possession.

6. In order for a seller to have a right of lien, she must have possession of the goods. Once she loses possession, she loses the right to the lien. However, even with possession of the goods, she may not have a lien. The right to a lien exists only if:
i) the contract makes no stipulation that the buyer is to have credit so payment is required upon delivery, or
ii) the goods have been sold on credit, the term of credit has expired without payment being made and the seller still possesses the goods, or
iii) the buyer becomes insolvent before the seller has delivered the goods. Insolvency must be proven. It is insufficient to prove that the buyer is merely financially precarious.

Answers to True/False Questions

1. False. An owner of goods has title to them. An owner has the right to complete enjoyment, disposal and use of the goods. Possession can be in the hands of someone other than the owner. A person who has dominion and control over the goods but is not the owner is said to have possession of them.

2. False. The Act uses the word "condition" to mean an essential term of contract. A "warranty" is used to refer to a minor, non-essential term.

3. False. Section 53 enables a seller to exclude or modify the terms implied by the *Sale of Goods Act* by express agreement or by course dealing between the parties.

4. False. First, a bill of lading acts as a receipt from the carrier. Second, it will provide evidence of the terms of the contract between the shipper and carrier. Finally, the bill of lading may itself be evidence of title to (ownership of) the goods.

5. True.

6. True.

17

Leasing and Bailment

Purpose and Significance

In a contract of sale, one person buys a product from another and immediately takes titles and becomes the owner. Ownership and possession always reside in a single person. In leases and bailments, possession and ownership of property reside in two different parties. (We should remember that the word "property" has various meanings and can refer to a specific object such as an automobile or the legal rights connected with an object.)

A lease occurs where a party (the lessee) takes possession of and uses another person's property (the lessor) in return for rent. The lessor retains ownership during the lease term but it may be transferred to the lessee at the term's end for an additional sum.

Bailment occurs when the owner of personal property (the bailor) delivers possession of it to another (the bailee), who takes control of the item but is obligated to return it to the bailor when the bailment ends.

Leasing has become a popular alternative to sale in recent years. A lease may enable a person to purchase items that would otherwise be prohibitively expensive. Leases are often structured so that ownership is transferred at the end of the term; in a bailment, on the other hand, ownership normally remains with the original party. We may be surprised to learn that we have entered into bailments on countless occasions already. Every time we borrow a library book, drive our parents' car or rent a VCR, we are entering into a bailment.

In this assignment, you will learn about the nature of leases and bailments. Leasing is defined and various types of leases are discussed. Common lease terms are explained, as are rights of the lessor and the lessee. We then go on to examine the bailment relationship. Various rights, duties and liabilities that may arise for the bailor and the bailee during the bailment are explored. Finally, we will examine two of the more common, important bailment situations — carriers and hotelkeepers.

Learning Objectives

A. Discuss the nature of a lease.

B. Explore lessor and lessee rights.

C. Discuss the nature of a bailment.

D. Examine the legal position of a bailee.

E. Examine the legal position of carriers and hotelkeepers as bailees.

Content Outline

I. Leasing

II. Types of Chattel Leases
      A. Operating leases
      B. Purchase leases
      C. Security and finance leases
      D. Sale-and-leaseback

III. Reasons for Chattel Leasing

IV. Common Terms in Chattel Leases
      A. Duration
      B. Rent
      C. Insurance and other costs payable by the lessee
      D. Purchase option
      E. Early termination-minimum payment
      F. Implied terms

V. Rights of the Parties
      A. The lessor
      B. The lessee

VI. Bailment
      A. Definition
      B. Non-contractual bailments
      C. Bailment compared with sale
      D. Bailment compared with trust
      E. Bailment compared with debt
      F. Bailment compared with licence
      G. The benefit of bailment

VII. Rights and Duties of a Bailee
    A. Liability under contract and tort
    B. Sub-bailment
    C. The standard of care
    D. Remedies of a bailee for the value of services rendered
    E. Lien
    F. The right of sale

VIII. Special Types of Bailment
    A. Storage and safekeeping
    B. Repairs and work on a chattel
    C. Transportation
        1. Types of carriers
        2. Liability of a common carrier
        3. Remedies
    D. Hotelkeepers and innkeepers
        1. Definition of an innkeeper
        2. Liability
        3. The Innkeepers (or hotelkeepers) Act
        4. Remedies
    E. Pledge or Pawn

Questions on Learning Objectives

Objective A: Discuss the nature of a lease.

A.1 Distinguish an operating lease from a purchase lease. (pp. 343–344)

A.2 Discuss the importance of the distinction between operating and purchase leases. (p. 344)

A.3 The owner of a leased chattel is not always the lessor. How and why might this occur? (p. 344)

Objective B: Explore lessor and lessee legal rights derived from a lease.

B.1 A lease will likely confer a tax advantage upon the lessor. When in the lease arrangement is the greatest tax relief experienced by the lessor? (pp. 345–346)

B.2 Describe the remedy available to a lessee who suffers from a breach of the warranty of fitness. (p. 347)

Objective C: Discuss the nature of a bailment.

C.1 Define the word "bailment" and give three examples of bailment. (p. 349)

C.2 Describe the two general classes of bailments and the significance of distinguishing between them. (p. 349)

Objective D: Examine the legal position of a bailee.

D.1 Describe the different standards of care that a bailee may owe to the bailor. (p. 353)

D.2 When bailed goods are damaged or lost, who has the burden of proof of explaining how the damage or loss occurred? (p. 351)

D.3 A bailee may be compensated for his services by being paid the contract price, damages or *quantum meruit*. Describe the differences among these three remedies. (p. 353)

D.4 What is a lien? Is a bailee entitled to one? (p. 354)

D.5 How can a bailee realize on her lien? (p. 354)

Objective E: Examine the legal position of carriers and hotelkeepers as bailees.

E.1 Distinguish a private carrier from a common carrier. (pp. 356–357)

E.2 Why is it important to make the distinction drawn in D.1 above? (p. 357)

E.3 How might a carrier limit his liability? (p. 357)

E.4 Does a hotelkeeper owe a higher duty of care than a boarding house? Why or why not? (pp. 358–359)

E.5 Describe the impact of provincial legislation on a hotel's liability. (pp. 358–359)

E.6 When is a hotel unable to rely on such legislation? (pp. 358–359)

Answers to Questions on Learning Objectives

A.1 In both operating and purchase leases, the owner of a good (the lessor) permits the property to be possessed by another (the lessee). The lessor in return for rent authorizes possession and use of the property by the lessee. However, the lessor in an operating lease retains ownership but it is generally intended that the lessee will gain ownership through a purchase lease.

A.2 Ownership of property generally entitles the owner to certain benefits and may impose obligations. A capital purchase lease will have to be recorded, for accounting purposes, in the lessee's balance sheet. The item must be shown as an asset of the lessee and the outstanding payments as a liability. For tax purposes, the two types of leases are treated differently. If ownership in the property is to be transferred to the lessee, as in a purchase lease, payments will not be tax deductible. However, in an operating lease, the lessee will be able to make a tax deduction for the rental payments. Furthermore, the owner of capital property may claim a tax deduction for its depreciation. Finally, the type of lease will determine how security in the property must be obtained.

A.3 A finance lease is one in which the vendor sells the chattel to a second party who arranges to lease the item to a third party, the lessee. The lessor, or financing party, is an intermediary who facilitates possession and use of the item by the lessee. The lessor owns the property until the lessee satisfies the terms of the lease.

B.1 The lessor may claim capital cost allowance for leased items, which the lessor owns. The greatest deductions on an asset occur early in an asset's useful life. Since rental payments are often consistent over the lease period, the lessor normally experiences greater savings during the first few years of ownership.

B.2 Lessees will likely be able to avail themselves of the warranty of fitness. This warranty, like all warranties, entitles the offended party to damages. The implied term warrants that leased items are reasonably fit for the purpose for which it was leased. The lessee may be entitled to damages for losses resulting from the goods not being in compliance with the warranty.

C.1 A bailment is created when a bailor delivers some item of personal property to a bailee who accepts it and agrees to return it at a later date. Three examples are lending, pledging or renting an item of personal property.

C.2 Bailments may be gratuitous or for reward. Gratuitous bailments may be for the benefit of the bailor, the bailee or both. Bailments for reward are of benefit to both.

The liability of the bailee for loss or damage to the bailed property varies depending on whether the bailment is gratuitous or for reward.

D.1 The bailee must use a reasonable degree of care to protect the bailed property during the time he has possession of it. If such care is not exercised, the bailee may be liable to the bailor if the property is lost or damaged. The degree of care due depends partly on the classification of the particular bailment. If it is a mutual benefit bailment, the bailee is held to a duty of ordinary care, that which a reasonable person would use to protect his own property. If the bailment is for the benefit of the bailor, a lower degree of care is required on the part of the bailee. On the other hand, if the bailment is for the bailee's benefit, the bailee is held to a higher degree of care. Other factors relevant to the degree of care due include the nature and value of the property, how easily the property can be damaged or stolen, whether the bailment was for reward or for free, and the experience of the bailee.

D.2 As the bailee is the person with possession of the goods, she normally is better able to establish the facts and thus has the burden of proof for showing that she was not negligent.

D.3 If the bailment is contractual, the bailee will have the usual contractual remedies. For complete performance, he is entitled to the contract price. Where performance is incomplete, the bailee may be entitled to damages for payment for services rendered on a *quantum meruit* basis. Damages are normally less than the full contract price. *Quantum meruit* is based on what is reasonable, not what the contract price was.

D.4 A lien is the right to retain possession of goods owned by another. The right arises when services have been performed with respect to the good and payment is due by the owner.

Only some bailees are entitled to liens. Entitlement comes from the common law and from statutes. At common law, for example, bailees who make repairs or improvements to goods may have a right of lien. Thus, a garage which repairs your car may hold it until paid for its services.

D.5 Mere retention of a person's goods (i.e., a lien) may lead to a bailee being paid for her services. If it doesn't, the bailee may, by power of statute, sell the goods. Any surplus after payment of the bailee's charges and costs must be given to the bailor.

E.1 A private carrier transports goods for reward but reserves the right to select his customers and restrict the type of good he's willing to carry. A common carrier acts for reward and does not discriminate amongst customers. His services may be limited to a particular geographical region or type of goods.

E.2 The liability of a common carrier is extremely high. In effect, a common carrier is an insurer of the goods as liability is imposed regardless of fault. The only defences to liability that a common carrier may have are that damage or loss occurred through an act of God, inherent vice in the goods or the fault of the shipper. A private carrier, however, owes only the normal standard of care.

E.3 A carrier may limit his liability by inserting an exemption clause in the bailment contract. Such a clause stipulates that liability is limited to a set dollar amount.

E.4 A hotel (or inn) offers lodging to the public at large. A boarding house is free to decide whom it will accommodate. A hotel has a much higher standard of care than that of a boarding house that has a duty to take reasonable care of guest and their belongings.

E.5 Provincial legislation enables a hotel to limit liability for loss or theft of goods. (The amount varies from province to province).

E.6 If the loss or theft occurs through willful act of a hotel's employees or if the hotel refuses to accept a guest's goods for safekeeping, it is unable to rely on the legislation's limitations of liability.

Multiple-Choice Questions

1. Jones took her outboard motor to Martin's Marina and Repair Centre for its annual overhaul and storage. Since considerable repairs and parts were needed, Jones left a deposit of $500 with Martin. Shortly afterwards and before making any repairs, Martin went bankrupt. Can Jones get her motor and $500 back without being part of the bankruptcy proceedings?

a) No, the motor and money can only be retrieved as part of the bankruptcy proceedings.

b) Yes, title to the motor and money remained with Jones.

c) Yes Jones can get the motor back as she has title to it, but for the money she will have to be part of the bankruptcy proceedings.

d) No, the motor and money were lost as part of the declaration of bankruptcy.

e) Yes, but only if Martin still has the motor and money separate from the rest of his assets.

2. JJ agreed to help his friend Ruby move. When he arrives at Ruby's apartment, he finds a note saying she has gone out to find more boxes. Finding a pile of boxes with "books" crossed out on the side, he loads them into his minivan. The first boxes he picks up seem very light for books, but he figures Ruby knows what she is doing and places the boxes in the bottom of the van with heavier boxes on top. While driving over to Ruby's new place he takes a corner too fast. The boxes shift and he hears a sound like glass shattering. At the new place JJ opens the crushed boxes and finds broken dishes and glasses. It turns out the boxes contained Ruby's china and crystal glasses, not books. Ruby is very upset when she finds out what has happened. Can Ruby force JJ to replace everything that was broken?

a) No, the standard of care for a bailment for the benefit of the bailor allowed JJ to treat the boxes as the label indicated.

b) Yes, the standard of care for a bailment for the benefit of the bailor suggested that JJ should have treated the boxes, not as how they were labelled, but as their light weight indicated.

c) No, the standard of care for a bailment for the benefit of the bailee is very low.

d) Yes, the standard of care for a bailment for the benefit of the bailor is very high.

e) Yes, the standard of care for a bailment for the benefit of the bailor is low, but the contents require special considerations.

3. An army officer took his uniform to a firm of dry cleaners to be cleaned. The cleaners gave him a receipt in which they disclaim all liability for damage arising in the course of "necessary handling." The uniform was never returned. It turned out that the uniform had been sent to someone else for cleaning. Can the officer successfully sue the dry cleaners for the uniform's value?

a) No because it is assumed that dry cleaners will periodically lose clothes.

b) Yes because it is assumed that dry cleaners will never lose clothes.

c) No because of the exemption clause.

d) Yes because sending the uniform to another cleaners was not "necessary handling."

e) No because the situation deals with bailment law which is independent of both contract and tort law.

4. What are the possible remedies of the bailee?

a) Damages, right of sale, and injunction.

b) Quantum meruit, lien, injunction, and specific performance.

c) Damages, quantum meruit, lien, and right of sale.

d) Quantum meruit, right of sale, and specific performance.

e) Damages, quantum meruit, lien, and injunction.

5. Farmer Brown has stored 3000 kilograms of grain at the local grain elevator. The elevator put Brown's grain in the main elevator, mixed with grain from other farmers. After Brown arranges for the sale of the grain to a factory, Brown demands the grain elevator return his grain. On receiving the grain, Brown decides that the quality of the grain does not match the quality of the grain he gave the elevator for storage. Can Brown successfully sue the grain elevator for not returning the grain he put into storage?

a) Yes because the grain elevator did not return the exact goods stored.

b) No because the grain elevator returned the exact goods stored as required.

c) Yes because, although grain is a fungible good, the goods returned were not of the same quality as the goods stored.

d) No because, although grain is a fungible good, the goods returned were of the same quality as the goods stored.

e) Yes because the grain stored should never have been mixed with grain from other farmers.

6. Simon took his power lawn mower to a repair shop to have it fixed. At the shop he signed an "authorization to repair" sheet that directed the repair shop to "repair the engine." The shop did so, but apparently found it necessary to replace most of the internal parts of the engine. The repair bill was $250, almost the price of a new machine. Simon refused to pay the account when he realized the cost of the repairs, and the repair shop refused to release the repaired mower to him. Does the repair shop have any remedy to get its money?

a) Yes, place a lien on the lawn mower and just wait for Simon to pay.

b) No, Simon is within his right to refuse to pay for the repairs.

c) Yes, sue Simon for breach of contract asking for damages equal to the cost of repairs and the value of the repaired mower.

d) No, there is an exemption clause in the contract that precludes any liability for Simon.

e) Yes, place a lien on the lawn mower and sell the mower if provincial law gives the repairer a right to sell.

7. BK Moving Limited, a common carrier, contracted with Sean to move the contents of his house from Halifax to Calgary. When Sean opened the boxes in Calgary he discovered that everything that was breakable was broken due to a natural catastrophe. Can Sean successfully sue BK Moving for the replacement value of the things broken?

a) Yes because the carrier is liable for all losses that occurred during transit.

b) No because the carrier is not responsible for any breakage that occurs if the owner packs the boxes.

c) Yes because the carrier is liable for any losses due to its negligence in transporting the boxes.

d) No because the carrier is not responsible for any losses that occur as the owner is responsible for taking out insurance.

e) No because the carrier is not responsible for any losses due to a natural catastrophe.

8. Tim and Joanne go out to a restaurant for dinner and leave their coats on the coat rack near the front door. There is a sign that states that the restaurant is not responsible for any articles placed on the coat rack. After dinner, Joanne's coat is no longer on the coat rack. If the restaurant refuses to pay for a replacement coat, can Joanne successfully sue the restaurant?

a) No because there has been no transfer of ownership.

b) Yes because there has been a transfer of ownership.

c) No because there has been no transfer of possession.

d) Yes because there has been a transfer of possession.

e) Yes because there has been a transfer of both possession and ownership.

9. While wandering along the banks of the town river, Brian finds a box with no identifying marks, which had washed up on the shore. Looking inside the box, Brian finds a glass figurine. Brian places the box in the trunk of his car, and the next day places an ad in the local paper for the owner. A few days later, Brian receives a phone call and arranges to meet the owner. When he takes the box out of his trunk the figurine inside is broken. The owner is very upset because it turns out the figurine is worth $3000. Can the owner claim the value of the figurine from Brian?

a) No because a gratuitous bailment for the benefit of the bailee was created and Brian met the required standard of care.

b) Yes because a gratuitous bailment for the benefit of the bailee was created and Brian did not meet the required standard of care.

c) No because a gratuitous bailment for the benefit of the bailor was created and Brian met the required standard of care.

d) Yes because a gratuitous bailment for the benefit of the bailor was created and Brian did not meet the required standard of care.

e) Yes because a gratuitous bailment for the benefit of the bailor and the bailee was created and Brian met the required standard of care.

10. Jim is finding the cost of parking his car downtown everyday for work very expensive. In order to save a bit of money, Jim takes advantage of an early bird special at a particular lot. One of the catches with the special is that Jim must leave the keys to his car with the attendant. As Jim leaves the lot, he sees a large board with words on it near the entrance, but does not read what it says. The board

lists the parking lot's limits on liability. When Jim returns after work, his car is gone. Can Jim successfully sue the parking lot under bailment law?

a) No because no bailment was created since possession of the car had not changed.
b) Yes because a bailment was created since possession of the car changed.
c) No because a stolen car is always within the exemption clause in a contract with a parking lot.
d) Yes because a parking lot cannot exempt itself from liability with an exemption clause.
e) No because a bailment was created, but the parking lot cannot be held negligent for having a car stolen.

11. What are the principal differences between a lease-to-own contract and a conditional sale?

a) A lease-to-own contract is a lease with an option to purchase the chattel at the end of the lease. A conditional sale is a security device where the seller retains title while the purchaser makes periodic payments.
b) In a lease-to-own contract, the buyer agrees to purchase the chattel at the start of the lease. A conditional sale is a security device where the seller retains possession while the purchaser gets ownership while he or she makes periodic payments.
c) A lease-to-own contract is a lease with an option to purchase the chattel at the end of the lease. A conditional sale is a security device where the seller retains possession while the purchaser gets ownership while he or she makes periodic payments.
d) In a lease-to-own contract, the buyer agrees to purchase the chattel at the start of the lease. A conditional sale is a security device where the seller retains title while the purchaser makes periodic payments.
e) A lease-to-own contract is a lease with an option to purchase the chattel at the start or end of the lease. A conditional sale is a security device where the seller retains possession and the purchaser gets ownership while making periodic payments.

12. What is a finance lease?

a) An agreement where one party provides credit financing, sells the property to a finance institution and then the institution leases the property to a third party.
b) An agreement where a finance institution provides credit financing, takes possession of the property and then leases it back to the owner.
c) An agreement where a finance institution provides credit financing, becomes owner of the property and then leases it to the lessee.
d) An agreement where a finance institution finances the construction and then leases it for itself.

e) An agreement where a finance institution who provided financing for its construction becomes owner of the property and then leases it to a third party until the debt associated with the construction is paid off.

13. What is the distinction between an operating lease and a capital lease?

a) In an operating lease, an operating asset is acquired. In a capital lease, there is no intention to transfer ownership of the item leased.
b) In an operating lease, there is no intention to transfer ownership of the item leased. In a capital lease, a capital asset is acquired.
c) In an operating lease, an operating asset is acquired. In a capital lease, a capital asset is acquired.
d) In an operating lease, is no intention to transfer ownership of the item leased. In a capital lease, ownership and possession are transferred after the required payments have been made.
e) In an operating lease, an operating asset is acquired. In a capital lease, ownership and possession are transferred after the required payments have been made.

14. Roxburgh rented a portable steam engine from Reynolds to power a woodcutting saw. The engine exploded immediately after it was put into use because the safety gauge and valve did not work. Can Reynolds successfully sue Roxburgh for the value of the destroyed engine?

a) No because the lease was invalid for a lack of the essential terms.
b) Yes because the standard of care did not required the lessor to ensure that the engine worked perfectly before leasing it.
c) No because the standard of care required the lessor to ensure that the engine worked perfectly before leasing it.
d) Yes because the standard of care required the lessee to test the safety gauge and valve prior to use.
e) No because the standard of care did not require the lessee to test the safety gauge and valve prior to use.

15. What two implied terms from real property leases are also implied in chattel leases?

a) Restrictions on the use of the chattel and requirement to make repairs.
b) Quiet possession and warranty of fitness.
c) Restrictions on the use of the chattel and quiet possession.
d) Quiet possession and requirement to make repairs.
e) Restrictions on the use of the chattel and warranty of fitness.

16. Which of the following is/are most likely to be leases?
I. Items purchased on "layaway" whereby ownership is transferred after payment has been made in full.
II. Appliance rental.

III. Purchase of farming equipment after a period of use.

a) I only
b) II only
c) III only
d) I and II only
e) II and III only

17. All of the following statements are correct EXCEPT:

a) A bailee may get damages for breach of a contractual bailment.
b) A bailee is entitled to a reasonable amount for the value of the services he has performed.
c) A bailee may have a right to a lien on the bailed goods in his possession.
d) A bailee's standard of care is very high when he is a carrier of goods.
e) A bailee may have a right to sell bailed goods left in his possession.

18. You begin a moving business. Based on your knowledge of law you decide that there should be a contract in place that should be signed by any person whose goods you are moving. A term of the contract is that liability for damage or loss to goods will be limited to $50. You agree with Ms. Coghill to move her household goods. Somehow they are damaged in transport. Which of the following would be the result?

a) You will be liable to Ms. Coghill for the full amount of the damage.
b) You will be liable only if the damage occurred through your fault.
c) You will be liable unless the damage was caused by act of God, inherent vice in the goods themselves or default of Ms. Coghill.
d) Your liability depends upon whether you are a private or a common carrier and whether the exemption clause applies.
e) You will be liable to Ms. Coghill for $50.00.

Answers to Multiple-Choice Questions

1. b)
See page 349 for more information.

2. a)
See pages 351 and 353 for more information.

3. d)
See page 351 for more information.

4. c)
See pages 353–354 for more information.

5. c)

See page 355 for more information

6. e)

See page 356 for more information.

7. e)

See pages 357 for more information.

8. c)

See page 349 for more information.

9. d)

See page 353 for more information.

10. b)

See page 355 for more information.

11. a)

See pages 343,344 and 677 for more information.

12. c)

See page 344 for more information.

13. b)

See pages 343–344 for more information.

14. e)

See page 348 for more information.

15. b)

See page 347 for more information.

16. e)

See pages 343–344 for more information.

17. d)

See pages 356–357 for more information.

18. d)

See pages 357–358 for more information.

True/False Questions

1. In both operating and purchase leases, the owner of a good (the lessor) permits the property to be possessed by another (the lessee). The lessor in return for rent

authorizes possession and use of the property by the lessee. However, the lessor in an operating lease retains ownership but it is generally intended that the lessee will gain ownership through a purchase lease.

2. The lessor may claim capital cost allowance for leased items that the lessor owns. The greatest deductions on an asset occur early in an asset's useful life. Since rental payments are often consistent over the lease period, the lessor normally experiences greater savings during the first few years of ownership.

3. A bailment is created when a bailor buys some item of personal property to a bailee who accepts it and agrees to sell them at a later date.

4. The bailee is the person with possession of the goods.

5. Mere retention of a person's goods (i.e., a lien) may lead to a bailee being paid for her services. If it doesn't, the bailee may, by power of statute, sell the goods. Any surplus after payment of the bailee's charges and costs must be given to the bailor.

6. A carrier cannot limit his liability by inserting an exemption clause in the bailment contract.

Answers to True/False Questions

1. True.

2. True.

3. False. A bailment is created when a bailor delivers some item of personal property to a bailee who accepts it and agrees to return it at a later date. Three examples are lending, pledging or renting an item of personal property.

4. True.

5. True.

6. False. A carrier may limit his liability by inserting an exemption clause in the bailment contract. Such a clause stipulates that liability is limited to a set dollar amount.

18

Insurance and Guarantee

Purpose and Significance

Insurance touches every aspect of our lives. If we drive a car, we will have insurance to cover damage to the automobile and injury to others in case of an accident. If we live in an apartment, we probably have contents insurance. In a house, we have mortgage insurance, fire insurance, and contents insurance. It is important to realize that insurance has become a part of everyone's life.

This chapter begins by examining the nature of insurance and the laws that regulate it. It goes on to discuss the different types of insurance that we will come in contact with on a daily basis. Finally, it highlights special aspects of the insurance contract.

A separate topic covered in this chapter is the guarantee. Many of us will give or ask for a guarantee at some point. As it is an onerous undertaking, it is important that we appreciate what a guarantee is and what rights and obligations both parties have under a guarantee.

236

Learning Objectives

A. Discuss insurance contracts at common law and under statute.

B. Discuss various types of insurance.

C. Examine certain aspects of the insurance contract.

D. Discuss the role and function of a guarantee.

Content Outline

I. The Nature of Insurance

II. Insurance Terminology

III. Regulation of Insurance Business

IV. Insurance of Business Premises and Other Assets
    A. Fire, accident, and theft insurance
    B. Vehicle insurance
    C. Marine insurance

V. Insurance on the Operation of a Business
    A. Business interruption insurance
    B. Credit insurance
    C. Fidelity insurance
    D. Key-Person insurance
    E. Insurance for employees
    F. Public liability insurance

VI. Special Aspects of the Contract of Insurance
    A. Legality of object-wrongful act of the insured
    B. Insurable interest
    C. Formation of the contract
        1. Life insurance
        2. Property insurance
    D. Renewal
    E. Terms of contract
    F. Disclosure
    G. Assignment
    H. Subrogation
    I. Co-Insurance

VII. Guarantee
  A. The nature of a guarantee
  B. Continuing guarantee
  C. Consideration
  D. Discharge of guarantee
  E. Rights of the guarantor on default
    1. Defences
    2. Subrogation
  F. Requirement of writing

Questions on Learning Objectives

Objective A: Discuss insurance contracts at common law and under statute.

A.1 What purposes does insurance serve? (pp. 364–365)

A.2 Explain the meaning of: insurance policy, insured, insurer, premium, rider and endorsement. (pp. 365–366)

A.3 Distinguish an insurance agent from an insurance broker and an insurance adjuster. (p. 366)

A.4 Why were statutes passed to regulate insurance? (p. 367)

A.5 List five matters which statutes govern in insurance contracts. (pp. 367)

Objective B: Discuss various types of insurance.

B.1 Describe the protection that fire insurance gives. (p. 367)

B.2 Describe the losses that a fire insurance policy does *not* cover. (p. 367)

B.3 How can you obtain protection for risks not covered by fire insurance? (p. 367)

B.4 What three types of insurance should a business that uses automobiles obtain? (p. 368)

B.5 What is a deductible? (p. 369)

B.6 What is a factor? (p. 369)

B.7 How can you protect yourself against theft by an employee? (p. 369)

B.8 How can you insure against theft from outside parties? (p. 368)

B.9 List and briefly describe four types of insurance that a business owner should obtain. (pp. 367–370)

Objective C: Examine certain aspects of the insurance contract.

C.1 When is a life insurance policy effective? (p. 373)

C.2 When is a property insurance contract effective? (p. 373)

C.3 When is a renewal of an insurance policy effective? (pp. 373–374)

C.4 How does an insurance contract differ from a wager? (p. 372)

C.5 When do you have an insurable interest in a contract for property insurance?

For life insurance? Why is it important to know the answers to these questions? (pp. 372–373)

C.6 What is utmost good faith and what part does it play in insurance law? (pp. 374–375)

C.7 What role does notice play with respect to insurance contracts? (p. 375)

C.8 How do you assign a life insurance contract? A property insurance contract? (pp. 375–376)

C.9 What is co-insurance? (p. 376)

Objective D: Discuss the role and the function of a guarantee.

D.1 List three important characteristics of a guarantee. (p. 377)

D.2 Must a creditor sue the debtor before it sues the guarantor? (p. 378)

D.3 Distinguish a guarantee from an indemnity and note the significance of the distinction. (p. 378)

D.4 What consideration does a guarantor receive for giving a guarantee? (p. 379)

D.5 What acts of the creditor will discharge the guarantor's obligation? (pp. 380–381)

D.6 What rights does a guarantor have if the debtor defaults? (pp. 381–382)

D.7 Define the word subrogation and explain how the concept of subrogation works in insurance law. (pp. 381–382)

D.8 Must a guarantee be in writing to be enforceable? (p. 382)

Answers to Questions on Learning Objectives

A.1 Insurance serves to shift the risk of damage from the insured to the insurance company. It also spreads the risk among a number of parties so that no single individual must bear the full amount of the damage or loss.

A.2 An insurance policy is the written insurance contract. The insured is the party that obtains the insurance protection. The insurer is the insurance company. A premium is the price paid by the insured for coverage and which varies according to the amount of risk associated with the particular insured. A rider is a separate clause incorporated in the insurance contract to supplement the standard contract's terms. An endorsement changes the terms of the existing insurance contract.

A.3 An insurance agent is the person who arranges the insurance contract on behalf of an insurance company. An insurance broker acts for the insured not the insurer. An insurance broker will deal with a number of insurance companies and choose the insurance policy that best suits the insured. An insurance adjuster is the individual who appraises damage or loss, determines whether the loss is covered by the insurance contract and, if so, what the amount of the loss (compensation) should be.

A.4 Statutes act to protect the public by requiring insurance companies to abide by certain rules and regulations.

A.5 The statutes require that a Superintendent of Insurance be appointed to oversee the operation of licensed insurance companies. They also specify what requirements insurers; agents, brokers and adjusters must meet and describe what terms must be included in each and every insurance policy. In addition, the statutes outline the types of risks that are not covered unless expressly included in the insurance contract and they define the extent to which an insurer may limit its liability. Other areas that are regulated by statute are the effects of misrepresentation and suicide, conditions necessary for an insurable interest, recognition of rights of beneficiaries and assignees and nature of the proof that an insurer may demand before it pays on a claim.

B.1 Fire insurance covers loss to buildings and contents caused by fire.

B.2 Fire insurance does not cover loss of important papers, theft that occurs during the fire, loss of property belonging to people other than the insured that is kept on the premises, medical expenses, loss of profits caused by suspended business operations, increased hazards due to vacancy of the premises, losses due to explosives kept on the property, damage caused by a fire used for heating or industrial purposes which is under the control of the insured, damage caused by riots or intentionally caused by the insured.

B.3 In order to obtain protection for the risks not covered by fire insurance you must either buy extra insurance coverage or have special terms inserted in the policy by way of a rider or endorsement.

B.4 It should maintain insurance against damage to the vehicle and the health and property of third parties.

B.5 A deductible is the amount that an insured himself must pay in the event of a claim. For example, if you have a $50.00 deductible and you are in an accident, you must pay the first $50.00 worth of damage and the insurance company will pay the balance.

B.6 A factor buys another's accounts receivable and attempts to collect on them. A factor may be with or without recourse.

B.7 Fidelity insurance protects against the risk of theft by an employee of the insured.

B.8 Robbery, burglary and theft insurance protect against losses willfully caused by outside parties.

B.9 A business enterprise should obtain business interruption insurance, life insurance on the lives of key officers, public liability insurance and property damage insurance.

C.1 As with any contract, the date the contract becomes effective is when there is acceptance by the offeree. With a life insurance contract, the offer is not accepted until the insurance company actually delivers the policy to the insured.

C.2 Property insurance agreements are effective when the agent acting on behalf of the insurance company signs the agreement regardless of whether the insured has paid a premium or actually received the policy. The agent must prepare a memorandum as evidence of the request for insurance and his acceptance thereof.

C.3 A mere renewal notice does not effectively extend insurance contracts. There must be a new agreement between the insurance company and the insured before the renewal is effective. Such evidence can take the form of delivery of a renewal policy or memorandum of agreement of past actions. In any event, there must be communication of the insured's acceptance in order to make the renewal effective.

C.4 In an insurance contract, the insured must have an insurable interest whereas in a wager she need not.

C.5 In a property insurance contract, the insured must have an insurable interest at the time the contract was formed and at the time the claim arises. Where the contract is for life insurance, the person buying the insurance must either obtain written consent of the person whose life is being insured or have an insurable interest at the time the contract is formed. It is important to know whether an insured has an insurable interest because without it the insurance contract is void.

C.6 Utmost good faith requires the insured to reveal any relevant information to the insurance company. If utmost good faith is not displayed, an insurance claim may be defeated.

C.7 There is a statutory term requiring the insured to notify the insurer promptly of any change that is material to the risk and within the control and knowledge of the insured. Where prompt notice is not given by the insured, the insurer is absolved from liability under the policy.

C.8 To assign a life insurance contract, you need only properly pass the rights under the insurance to a third party. The insurer's consent is not required. Under a property insurance contract, you cannot assign without the consent of the insurer.

C.9 Co-insurance refers to the situation where an insured does not purchase coverage for the total value of the property. Thus the insured becomes a co-insurer with the insurance company and the insured will not recover the total loss for damages from a fire but must bear a certain proportion of the loss himself.

D.1 In a guarantee, a guarantor makes a promise to a creditor that if a debtor defaults, she will perform the debtor's obligation. Second, a claim under the guarantee arises only if the debtor himself defaults. Third, a guarantor's obligation to pay arises immediately upon default by the principal debtor.

D.2 A creditor need not sue the primary debtor before it sues the guarantor. However, the debtor must default before the creditor can sue the guarantor.

D.3 In an indemnity, the person giving the indemnity becomes primarily liable for the debt and the promise of indemnity is independent of any obligation of another. A guarantee must be in writing, an indemnity need not be.

D.4 Normally, the consideration is that the creditor forebears from suing the debtor or else grants credit to the debtor when he otherwise would not. Consideration is not automatic, however, and must be proven to exist.

D.5 If a creditor agrees to a material change in the scope of the debtor's liability without obtaining the consent of the guarantor, the guarantor is discharged from his obligation under the guarantee.

D.6 The guarantor may plead any rights of set-off that the debtor has.

D.7 Subrogation is a substitution of one person for another so that the rights and duties that attach to the original person become attached to the substituted one. In other words, one party is said to "stand in another's shoes." Where an insured is reimbursed for a claim by the insurance company, the insurer steps into the shoes of the insured and has the right to sue any third party.

D.8 By virtue of the *Statute of Frauds*, a guarantee must be in writing to be enforceable.

Multiple-Choice Questions

1. Black purchases a life insurance policy, naming his wife as beneficiary. Afterwards, Black is shot and killed while attempting to hold up a bank. Can Mrs. Black collect the insurance money?

a) No because Black did not practice utmost good faith with the insurance company.
b) Yes because Mrs. Black is the named beneficiary in a valid insurance contract.
c) Yes because Mrs. Black had an insurable interest in Mr. Black.
d) Yes because Black died and there was a valid insurance contract.
e) No because public policy would prevent payment.

2. Good Groceterias Limited recently lost one of its stores in a fire. It had insured the stores over the years with Pyro Fire Insurance Company, without changing the coverage against losses by fire. When it first insured the store in question, the property had an actual value of $50 000, but at the time the loss occurred, the replacement value had increased to $75 000. Good Groceterias' policy with Pyro included the following clause: "This company shall not be liable for a greater proportion of any loss or damage to the property described herein than the sum hereby insured bears to 80% of the actual cash replacement value of said property at the time such loss shall happen." What amount can Good Groceterias recover if the loss amounted to $36 000 and the insurance carried was $36 000?

a) $36 000.
b) $32 400.
c) $28 800.
d) $21 600.
e) $18 000.

3. Gary learns that he has a serious disease and applies for life insurance without disclosing this information. He is later killed in an automobile accident. Does the insurer have grounds for refusing to pay the claim?

a) Yes because public policy would prevent payment.
b) No because the cause of death was unrelated to the disease.
c) Yes because Gary did not practice utmost good faith with the insurer.
d) No because Gary had an insurable interest in himself.
e) No because Gary died and there was a valid insurance contract.

4. Acme Limited owns a building worth $155 000 and takes out two fire insurance policies for $120 000 each, one with Ajax Insurance Inc. and the other with Hercules Insurance Limited. In the event of a fire, could Acme collect $120 000 from each insurance company?

a) Yes because that is what each policy is worth.
b) No because that would allow Acme to recover more than the property's value. Ajax would pay $120 000 and Hercules would pay $35 000.
c) No because that would allow Acme to recover more than the property's value. Ajax would pay $35 000 and Hercules would pay $120 000.
d) No because that would allow Acme to recover more than the property's value. Ajax would pay $77 500 and Hercules would pay $77 500.
e) Yes because the value of the loss is unrelated to the amount each insurance company is required to pay.

5. Sarah and Stacey are partners in a profitable plumbing supply company. If either of them dies, the partnership has to pay the estate a half interest in the assets of the business. Therefore, Sarah and Stacey have each taken out life insurance on the other to provide the necessary funds. Stacey is involved in a bad car accident and dies. Does the insurer have grounds for refusing to pay the claim?

a) Yes because Sarah does not have an insurable interest in Stacey.
b) No because Sarah does have an insurable interest in Stacey.
c) Yes because the cause of Stacey's death is unrelated to the business.
d) No because Stacey was not the cause of her own death.
e) Yes because Sarah did not practice utmost good faith with the insurer.

6. Under a life insurance policy, a premium payment became due on July 26. The grace period expired and the company sent a "late payment offer," offering to receive late payment under certain conditions. Four months later, the company sent a letter to the insured saying that the policy was "technically out of force," and that immediate payment of the premium was required. In February of the following year, the company sent a further letter stating that the insurance had lapsed. The letters did not come to the insured's attention until the following April and in July he sent a cheque. By then his life had become uninsurable and he died a month later. Does the insurer have to pay the claim?

a) Yes because the insured had an insurable interest.
b) No because the policy expired due to the wrongful acts of the insured.
c) Yes because the insured did not tell the insurer about his ill health.
d) No because the policy had expired and the July payment was too late.

e) Yes because, although the policy had expired, the July payment renewed the policy back to the original letter.

7. New Age Inc. owned a factory and associated equipment as its principal asset. Diane, who owned all of the shares of New Age, took out a fire insurance policy on the factory and associated equipment. If lightning starts a fire that destroys the factory and the equipment, does the insurer have to pay the claim?

a) No because Diane did not have an insurable interest.
b) Yes because Diane did have an insurable interest.
c) No because the insured did not practice utmost good faith with the insurer.
d) No because lightning is an Act of God.
e) Yes because a fire started by lightning is one of the events covered by a fire insurance policy.

8. Roberta, a 16 year old, bought a used car for $3000. Because of the high cost of insurance, Roberta's father registered the car in his name and took out car insurance, which listed Roberta as a secondary driver. In fact, Roberta was the only one to drive the car. After a bad accident, which Roberta caused, the car needed $4000 worth of repairs. Does the insurer have to pay the claim?

a) Yes because Roberta's father had an insurable interest in the car.
b) No because Roberta and her father did not practice utmost good faith with the insurer.
c) No because the cost of the repairs exceeded the purchase price of the car.
d) No because the accident was caused by Roberta.
e) Yes because there was a valid contract of insurance.

9. While the Smiths were away on vacation for two weeks, their house was broken into and many things were stolen. On returning from vacation and finding the thefts, the Smiths did nothing for two months. At that time, the Smiths notified their insurer about the thefts and gave the insurer a list of things stolen and the value of each item. Does the insurer have to pay the claim?

a) Yes because the Smiths had an insurable interest in the items stolen.
b) No because the Smiths had practiced utmost good faith with the insurer.
c) Yes because there was a valid contract of insurance.
d) No because they waited too long to notify the insurer about the thefts.
e) No because the insurer had been notified about the Smiths' vacation.

10. Jane was in a car accident caused solely by the other driver. As a result of the accident, Jane spent three months in hospital and another six at home recuperating and going for physical therapy. Under her car insurance policy, her insurer paid all the extra bills and replaced her lost income for the nine months. Jane is also contemplating suing the driver who caused the accident. If Jane decides not to sue, is there anything the insurer can do?

a) Yes because the insurer can use the principle of insurable interest.

b) No because only the person who is injured has a right to sue.

c) Yes because the insurer can use the principle of subrogation.

d) No because the insurer is not in a position of co-insurance.

e) Yes because the insurer can use the principle of public liability insurance.

11. Can a property insurance contract be assigned?

a) Yes, without the consent of the insurer.

b) No, it can never be assigned.

c) Yes, it is automatically assigned if the property covered is sold.

d) No, novation is the only possibility.

e) Yes, if the new owner is a member of the old owner's family.

12. Jenny tries to rent a launch from Boat Rentals Limited but is refused because of her age. William, Jenny's father, a reputable businessman, informs the manager of Boat Rentals that if the company will rent the launch to his daughter, he will be responsible for any damage caused by her negligent acts if Jenny does not reimburse the company for any such damage. Boat Rentals rents the launch to Jenny and she promptly runs it aground on rocks, putting a large hole in the bottom. Can Boat Rentals successfully sue William for the damages?

a) No because the agreement is like an insurance contract and Jenny does not have an insurable interest in the launch.

b) Yes because the agreement is like an insurance contract and Jenny does have an insurable interest in the launch.

c) No because the agreement is like a guarantee and is oral.

d) Yes because the agreement is like a guarantee and is oral.

e) No because the statement was just a gratuitous promise by William.

13. Creely threatens to sue Dobbs for his past-due debt. Dobbs asks for 60 days more to raise the money, but Creely refuses to give the extra time unless Dobbs obtains a guarantee from his cousin Guara. Dobbs takes a form of guarantee to his cousin, explains the situation and requests her signature. Guara signs the guarantee and mails it to Creely. Creely delays suing Dobbs for 60 days. When Dobbs defaults again, can Creely successfully sue Guara for the amount of the debt?

a) Yes because the guarantee is in writing and there is consideration for it.

b) No because, although the guarantee is in writing, there is no consideration for it.

c) Yes because a collateral agreement is sufficient to accept a time delay in the repayment of the debt.

d) No because, in relation to the debt, there is no consideration since the only consideration is past consideration.

e) No because, by waiting 60 days to sue for repayment, Creely materially altered the guarantee, which relieves the guarantor.

14. What types of acts will discharge a guarantor from his or her obligations?

a) If the debtor breaches the contract of guarantee; if the debt contract is varied without the guarantor's consent; and if the debtor does something to impair the value of any security given by the creditor.
b) If the creditor breaches the contract of guarantee; if the debt contract is varied without the guarantor's consent; and if the creditor does something to impair the value of any security given by the debtor.
c) If the debtor breaches the contract of guarantee; if the debt contract is varied with the guarantor's consent; and if the debtor does something to impair the value of any security given by the creditor.
d) If the creditor breaches the contract of guarantee; if the debt contract is varied without the guarantor's consent; and if the debtor does something to impair the value of any security given by the creditor.
e) If the debtor breaches the contract of guarantee; if the debt contract is varied with the guarantor's consent; and if the creditor does something to impair the value of any security given by the debtor.

15. What are the rights of the guarantor upon default?

a) The guarantor is limited to defences available to the creditor.
b) The guarantor cannot turn around and sue the debtor once he has paid the creditor.
c) The guarantor may raise any defence that would have been available to the debtor.
d) The guarantor may step into the shoes of the debtor and sue the creditor.
e) The guarantor may simply refuse to pay the creditor.

16. You decide to go into business as a sole proprietor with no employees. You realize that you must arrange appropriate insurance. You would purchase all the following types of insurance EXCEPT:

a) Fire insurance
b) Public liability insurance
c) Property damage insurance
d) Hospital insurance for employees
e) Fidelity insurance

17. A guarantee is:

a) An indemnity
b) A promise to pay a creditor if the debtor defaults.
c) A promise to a debtor to assist in the event of default.
d) A promise to pay a creditor.
f) A contract to induce a perspective creditor to advance money or goods.

18. Which of the following is or are special aspects of the insurance contract?

I. The insured must have an insurable interest.

II. the insured must act with utmost good faith.

III. The insured must notify the insurer of any material change within his control and knowledge.

a) I only.

b) II only.

c) III only.

d) I and II only.

e) I, II, and III.

Answers to Multiple-Choice Questions

1. e)
See page 371 for more information.

2. d)
See pages 376–377 for more information.

3. c)
See pages 374–375 for more information.

4. d)
See pages 376–377 for more information.

5. b)
See page 370 for more information

6. d)
See page 373 for more information.

7. a)
See page 372 for more information.

8. b)
See pages 374–375 for more information.

9. d)
See page 375 for more information.

10. c)
See page 376 for more information.

11. d)
See page 376 for more information.

12. c)
See pages 378, 382 for more information.

13. a)
See page 379 for more information.

14. b)
See pages 380–381 for more information.

15. c)
See pages 381–382 for more information.

16. d)
See pages 369–370 for more information.

17. b)
See page 377 for more information.

18. e)
See pages for more information.

True/False Questions

1. Insurance serves to shift the risk of damage from the insured to the insurance company. It also spreads the risk among a number of parties so that no single individual must bear the full amount of the damage or loss.

2. Fire insurance covers only loss to buildings caused by fire.

3. A responsible person should maintain insurance against damage to their vehicle and health.

4. Fidelity insurance protects against the risk of theft by a client of the insured.

5. A mere renewal notice does effectively extend insurance contracts.

6. In an indemnity, the person giving the indemnity becomes primarily liable for the debt and the promise of indemnity is independent of any obligation of another.

7. A guarantee must be in writing, an indemnity need not be.

Answers to True/False Questions

1. True.

2. False. Fire insurance covers loss to buildings and contents caused by fire.

3. True.

4. False. Fidelity insurance protects against the risk of theft by an employee of the insured.

5. False. A mere renewal notice does not effectively extend insurance contracts. There must be a new agreement between the insurance company and the insured before the renewal is effective. Such evidence can take the form of delivery of a renewal policy or memorandum of agreement of past actions. In any event, there must be communication of the insured's acceptance in order to make the renewal effective.

6. True.

7. True.

19

Agency and Franchising

Purpose and Significance

As life gets more complicated, we rely on others to do more and more work for us. Agents are those persons who enter into contracts on our behalf. An agent is often, but not necessarily, an employee. Conversely, an employee need not necessarily be an agent.

Because agency relationships are so common, we begin this chapter by exploring the nature of an agency relationship and how it is formed. We go on to describe the duties that an agent owes to her principal and those that a principal owes to her agent. Finally, as agents enter into contracts with third parties, it is important to know when the agent will be liable to the third party, when the principal will be so liable and when both will be liable.

Franchising, another type of contract, facilitates the expansion of business. A franchise is characterized by the granting of a license by the franchisor to another party (the franchisee) to use the franchisor's product, name, and trademark in return for a payment of a franchise fee. Franchises help to reduce barriers to entry into a market. Despite franchises being independently owned by the franchisee, the franchise relationship often includes an element of support for persons lacking adequate skills or for those who are unable to afford the initial start-up cost of the franchise. Assistance may be provided by the franchisor by way of marketing expertise, training programs, and through provision of a loan. These, and other elements of a franchise, are explored below.

Learning Objectives

A. Discuss the agency relationship.

B. Describe the ways an agent obtains authority to act for her principal.

C. Explain the meaning of ratification.

D. Describe an agent's duties to her principal.

E. Describe a principal's duties to her agent.

F. Discuss the liability of an agent or her principal to a third party.

G. Discuss the nature of franchising.

Content Outline

I. The Nature of Agency

II. Creation of Agency Relationship
    A. The parties to the relationship
    B. Express agreement
    C. Ratification
    D. Estoppel
        1. Apparent authority
        2. Holding out
    E. Agency by necessity

III. The Duties of an Agency to the Principal
    A. Duty to comply with the contract
    B. Duty of care
    C. Personal performance
    D. Good faith
        1. Fiduciary relationship
        2. Acting for two principals
        3. Contracts between agent and principal

IV. The Duties of the Principal to the Agent
    A. Remuneration
    B. Expenses

V. Liability of Principal and Agent
    A. The principal alone is liable on the contract
    B. The agent alone is liable on the contract

C. Either the principal or the agent may be held liable on the contract
D. The undisclosed principal
E. Liability for misrepresentation
F. Breach of warranty of authority

VI. Terminating an agency relationship

VII. Franchising
    A. The growth of franchising
    B. The nature of franchising
    C. Typical contents of a franchising agreement
        1. Consideration provided by the franchisor
        2. Consideration provided by the franchisee
        3. Conduct of business
        4. Termination of the franchise
        5. Restrictive covenants
        6. Dispute resolution
    D. Legal relationships created by franchising

VIII. Franchise Legislation
    A. Disclosure
    B. Fair dealing
    C. Right to associate
    D. Industry self-management
    E. Enforcement and dispute resolution

Questions on Learning Objectives

Objective A: Discuss the agency relationship.

A.1 What is an agency relationship? (pp. 385–386)

A.2 Who has the capacity to enter into an agency relationship? (p. 386)

A.3 How can an agency relationship be terminated? (p. 399)

A.4 Give three examples of common agency relationships. (p. 386)

Objective B: **Describe the ways an agent obtains authority to act for her principal.**

B.1 What is the basis of an express agency relationship? (pp. 386–387)

B.2 How does agency by estoppel arise? (p. 389)

B.3 What does "holding out" mean? (pp. 390–391)

Objective C: **Explain the meaning of ratification.**

C.1 What is ratification? (p. 387)

C.2 What is the effect of ratification? (p. 387)

C.3 What conditions must be satisfied to have a valid ratification? (p. 387)

C.4 Name the four circumstances in which an agent's acts cannot be ratified. (pp. 387–388)

Objective D: **Describe an agent's duties to her principal.**

D.1 Explain an agent's duty to obey her principal. (p. 391)

D.2 Describe an agent's duty of care. (p. 391)

D.3 Can an agent have someone else perform her duties? (p. 392)

D.4 Discuss an agent's duty of good faith. (pp. 392–393)

Objective E: Describe a principal's duties to her agent.

E.1 What payment is an agent entitled to recover from her principal? (p. 394)

E.2 Describe the principal's obligation to pay her agent's expenses. (p. 394)

Objective F: Discuss the liability of an agent or her principal to a third party.

F.1 What liability does an agent who acts within the scope of her authority have to a third party? (p. 395)

F.2 What rights does a third party have against the agent of an unidentified principal? (p. 395)

F.3 When will an agent alone be liable on the contract? (p. 395)

F.4 When may a third party hold either the principal or agent liable for performance of a contract? (p. 396)

Objective G: Discuss the nature of franchising.

G.1 Describe the franchise relationship. (pp. 399–400)

G.2 Discuss likely incentives for entering into a franchise agreement as a franchisee. (pp. 400–401)

Answers to Questions on Learning Objectives

A.1 An agency relationship is one in which one party is authorized to bring another party for whom she acts (the principal) into contractual relations with third parties.

A.2 Any person who has the capacity to contract can engage a person to act as agent on her behalf. An agent has the same capacity to contract that her principal has. Thus, if the principal is a minor, contracts made by the agent for her are voidable at her option in the same fashion as if she had made them personally. While a principal must be competent to contract, an agent need not be capable of contracting in her own right: a principal may use an agent who is a minor to enter into binding contracts with third parties.

A.3 Generally, either party has the power to terminate an agency relationship. (We must remember that termination may amount to breach of contract). Where an agent is not also an employee, the agent's authority can be terminated by:
(i) expiry of the time period specified in the agency agreement,
(ii) completion of the particular project for which the agency was formed,
(iii) notice by one party to the other,
(iv) the death or insanity of either party,
(v) the bankruptcy of the principal, or
(vi) any event which makes performance of the agency agreement impossible.

A.4 Common examples of agency relationships are: partnerships, lawyers acting for their clients, stockbrokers, insurance agents, someone acting under a power of attorney and spouses.

B.1 An express agency relationship is one in which authority to act is explicitly conferred on the agent by the principal. It may be conferred either orally or in writing but the principal must tell the agent what acts the agent is to perform. If the agency agreement is to extend beyond one year, it must be in writing to be enforceable.

B.2 Agency by estoppel arises from the appearance of authority in the agent created by the principal or from trade custom and a third party has relied on that appearance. The test used to determine the extent of apparent authority is whether a third party should have been put on notice about the limits to the agent's authority or whether it could be reasonably assumed from the kind of business in which the agent is engaged that the agent had limits to her authority. It is *not* whether the third party dealing with the agent actually believed that the agent had authority.

B.3 Holding out refers to the situation where a principal represents that someone is her agent either by words or actions. If a person is held out to be an agent, the principal may not later deny the existence of the agency relationship.

C.1 A contract may be made by one person who knows she has no authority to act for another but purports to act as the other's agent anyway. If the principal later adopts the contract, there has been ratification.

Ratification can be done expressly or by implication as where a principal assumes the benefits of a contract made for her.

C.2 The legal effect of ratification is to make the principal liable on the contract and to release the agent from liability to the third party.

C.3 To be valid, ratification must be:
(i) complete,
(ii) made within a reasonable time after the "agent" acted, and
(iii) made by a person with the capacity to do the act personally.

C.4 First, where an agent purports to accept an offer "subject to the ratification of my principal," later ratification will not be retroactive. Second, a company cannot ratify contracts made for it before it was incorporated. Third, a principal cannot ratify a contract made for her if at the time she purports to ratify the act she could not have made that contract. Fourth, a principal cannot ratify when the rights of a third party would be affected.

D.1 An agent must obey all lawful instructions given by her principal. She must also keep her principal informed about all-important developments affecting her service. The principal should also pass along to the agent any new information that may affect the agent and that will assist her in carrying out her duties. Notice to an agent is equivalent to giving notice to a principal and vice versa.

D.2 An agent must act with the reasonable care, skill, and diligence that are required for that particular type of work. Such care must be taken whether or not the agent is paid and regardless of the actual degree of competence that the agent possesses. The parties involved are always free to make an agreement that would impose a greater or lesser degree of skill and care.

D.3 As a general rule, an agent must personally perform her duties and thus cannot delegate to another. This stems from the fact that the agent is usually selected for her own personal skills or experience.

There are certain circumstances in which an agent will have implied authority to delegate all or part of her duties. One is where delegation is necessary to effectively carry out the agency services. Another is where it is common trade usage to perform through a subagent.

D.4 An agency relationship is one in which special trust and confidence is reposed by the principal in the agent. Whenever such a relationship exists, the parties owe a high degree of good faith and loyalty to one another. Thus, any money that comes into an agent's possession through her role as agent belongs to the principal. The agent must account for money and property acquired in the course of business dealings. The agent is responsible for accounting for the funds and for keeping accurate records.

While it is not an actual duty to keep the principal's property separate from the agent's own property, it is highly recommendable because the property in her possession belonging to her principal cannot then be confused with assets of her own.

Good faith also requires that the agent place the interest of her principal above all else except the law. Normally, an agent is not acting in good faith when she serves two principals in respect of the same transaction or when she places her own interests in conflict with those of the principal.

E.1 Generally the agent will receive the amount specified in the agency agreement. If the amount of compensation is not specified, the agent will receive a reasonable rate of pay. That amount is determined by reference to the fees of an agent who performs comparable services.

E.2 An agent is entitled to reimbursement for reasonable outlays made on behalf of the principal. It is important that the agent acts only within the scope of her specified authority because the principal is under no obligation to reimburse the agent for unauthorized acts unless she later ratifies them.

F.1 An agent is not normally a party to the contract nor is she liable on it. To ensure that only the principal is liable, the agent must describe herself to the third party as an agent.

F.2 An agent may tell a third party that she is an agent for another but not disclose the name of that other. The other is called an unidentified principal. If the third party contracts on those terms, it has no recourse against the agent and limits its rights to the unidentified principal.

F.3 If an agent describes herself as a principal but is only an agent, she also is liable on the contract. The principal can neither sue nor be sued on the contract.

F.4 If the third party later discovers the existence and identity of the principal, it has the option of holding either the principal or agent liable for the performance of the contract. Once it elects to take action against one it cannot sue the other.

G.1 A franchise relationship is contractual. The franchisee obtains a license to sell the franchisor's product and to make use of the franchisor's name and trademarks. The franchisor and franchisee are separate and independent businesses that have agreed to perform or avoid certain activities. The obligations of each are set out in the franchise agreement.

G.2 A franchise offers the advantage to a franchisee of a recognized product. The franchisee generally has access to trademarks, product information, marketing support and broad business expertise accumulated by the franchisor. Furthermore, financial assistance may be provided by the franchisor to help with start-up costs. Franchisees are granted territories for which the franchisor may not grant subsequent licenses.

Multiple-Choice Questions

1. Alva arranges on behalf of Penny, but without Penny's authority, to buy six crates of dinnerware from Plates Inc. Penny runs a kitchen supply store and could use the dinnerware in her store. Can Plates Inc. successfully sue Penny if Penny does not pay?

a) No, there is no contract between Penny and Plates Inc.
b) Yes, if Penny ratifies the contract entered into by Alva.
c) No, Alva did not have the authority to bind Penny in a contract.
d) Yes, if Plates Inc. is estopped from denying that Alva is an agent of Penny.
e) No, because there is no way for Penny to retroactively accept the contract with Plates Inc.

2. What form can an express agreement creating an agency relationship take?

a) Written.
b) Oral.
c) Partially written and partially oral.
d) Under seal.
e) All of the above.

3. Katie entered into a contract with Franklin Co. for the purchase of a trailer. The contract was negotiated by an agent of Franklin, Sarah, whom the company held out as having authority to act on its behalf. But Sarah's authority was limited because any transaction required the approval of the head office. Katie knew of the limitation on Sarah's authority as Sarah had told her of it. After reaching an agreement, Sarah was unable to obtain the necessary approval from head office. After several attempts to change the head office's decision, Sarah told Katie that she had received approval by telephone and she signed the contract on behalf of Franklin Co. hoping that head office would ratify the contract. If Franklin Co. refused to honor the contract, can Katie successfully sue on the contract?

a) Katie can sue Franklin based on an agency by estoppel.
b) Katie can sue Franklin based on an express agency.
c) Katie can sue Franklin based on an agency by ratification.
d) Katie can sue Sarah based on her duty of good faith.
e) Katie can sue Sarah based on breach of warranty of authority.

4. Silverman was the captain of a ship transporting 40 000 pounds of bananas from Brazil to Vancouver. On the way, the ship stopped in Mexico to pick up a load of clothing. While in port, the port authorities went on strike and there was no way for the ship to leave the port. As the strike dragged on, Silverman realized that the bananas were about to fully ripen. Since he could not get hold of the owner of the bananas for instructions, Silverman sold the bananas to a businessperson from Mexico City. The price was the best Silverman could get, but

was significantly less than the bananas' value in Vancouver. Can the owner of the bananas successfully sue Silverman for the loss in the sale price of the bananas?

a) No, the captain was the owner's agent by express agreement.
b) Yes, the captain had no right to enter into the contract on behalf of the owner.
c) No, the captain was the owner's agent by necessity.
d) Yes, the captain should have waited until the bananas reached Vancouver before selling them.
e) No, the captain was the owner's agent by estoppel.

5. Bonnie lists her house for sale with Ida, a real estate agent. Ida submits an offer for the house from a friend, Sean. Ida successfully influences Bonnie to accept the offer that is $29 000 below the list price. When Sean withdraws from the sale before it is completed, Ida tells Bonnie of another purchaser for the house, for the same price. Bonnie agrees to the change of purchaser and completes the sale. Ida did not tell Bonnie that the new purchaser was a company controlled by Ida. Three weeks after the sale, the company resells house at a $30 000 profit. Can Bonnie sue Ida and the company for the profit?

a) Yes because Ida breached her duty of good faith.
b) No because Ida has not breached any of an agent's duties.
c) Yes because Ida beached her duty of care.
d) No because Bonnie agreed to the sale of the property to Ida's company.
e) Yes because Ida beached her duty of obedience.

6. A client gave a broker an order to buy tallow. The broker already held some tallow on his own account, and simply sent this tallow to the client. Can the client successfully sue the broker if the tallow is not the best quality?

a) Yes because the broker beached his duty of care.
b) No because the broker has not breached any of an agent's duties.
c) Yes because the broker breached his duty of good faith.
d) No because it is assumed that the broker got his client the best quality and at the best price available.
e) Yes because the broker breached his duty of obedience.

7. A client gave his stockbroker an order to buy 1000 shares of Acme Inc. Ten minutes earlier, the stockbroker had received an order from another client to sell 1000 shares of Acme Inc. If the stockbroker matches up to two orders, is there any problem?

a) No because the price is definitely the best that could be obtained on the open market.
b) Yes because the price is definitely not the best that could be obtained on the open market.
c) Yes because the broker is criminally liable for taking a kickback.

d) Yes, if the broker does not first make both orders available to other brokers.

e) No, it makes perfect sense.

8. The Browns were away on a winter vacation in Florida when a storm caused a tree in their yard to fall on the roof of their house, creating a large hole. Their neighbor, Green, realized that if the roof was not repaired quickly the contents of the house would also be badly damaged. Green had no way of contacting the Browns so, after obtaining three quotes, Green hired the cheapest to repair the roof. When the Browns return from vacation are they liable for the repair costs?

a) Yes because Green acted as an agent by necessity.

b) No because Green gave the cost of the repairs to the Browns as a gift.

c) No because Green did not act as an agent by necessity.

d) No because the Browns could not have ratified the contract.

e) Yes because Green acted as an agent by estoppel.

9. Julie, an agent of Blair, negotiated a contract on Blair's behalf with Seacoast Inc. During the negotiations Julie incurred expenses such as long-distance telephone and fax calls and two airplane tickets to meet with Seacoast in person. Also, it took Julie two months to conclude the contract. If Blair refuses to pay, can Julie force Blair to pay for the expenses and/or her time?

a) No, an agent is an independent contractor so must cover all expenses herself out of the agency contract price.

b) Yes, a principal has a duty to reimburse an agent for expenses and to pay remuneration.

c) Yes, a principal has a duty to reimburse an agent for expenses, but is not responsible for any form of salary.

d) Yes, provided the contract is in Blair's interest.

e) No, a principal owes no duties to the agent.

10. Julie, an agent of Blair, negotiated a contract on Blair's behalf with Seacoast Inc. Seacoast was aware that the principal parties to the contract would be Blair and itself. If Blair breaches the contract, who can Seacoast sue?

a) The principal, Blair.

b) The agent, Julie.

c) The principal, Blair, or the agent, Julie.

d) Neither the principal, Blair, nor the agent, Julie.

e) The agent, Julie, for breach of warranty of authority.

11. Andrew was employed as manager of a pub by Upstart Brewing Co. Upstart had expressly forbidden Andrew to purchase certain articles for the business, even though it was normal practice in the trade to give managers such authority. Andrew contracted to buy such articles from Patrick, without disclosing that he was Upstart's manager. On the license above the door of the pub, only Upstart's name appeared. If the contract is breached who can Patrick sue?

a) The principal, Upstart.
b) The agent, Andrew.
c) The principal, Upstart, or the agent, Andrew.
d) Neither the principal, Upstart, nor the agent, Andrew.
e) The agent, Andrew, for breach of warranty of authority.

12. Paula, who is not the agent of Bob, entered into a contract on Bob's behalf with Computer Inc. Paula thought that when Bob saw the good terms of the contract, he would ratify it. As it turned out, Bob did not ratify the contract and Computer Inc. was not paid for the goods it delivered to Bob's place of business. Who can Computer Inc. sue?

a) The principal, Bob.
b) Paula as the principal party to the contract.
c) The principal, Bob, or the agent, Paula.
d) Neither the principal, Bob, nor the agent, Paula.
e) The agent, Paula, for breach of warranty of authority.

13. Caroline has just accepted an offer from Jones to buy her principal's (i.e., Mark's) hardware store even though she knows that Mark died two days earlier. When Jones learns of the death, can Jones successfully sue Mark's estate to complete the sale?

a) No, the agency relationship terminated on the death of the principal.
b) Yes, Caroline was an agent of Mark and could bind him in contracts.
c) No, real estate cannot be sold through an agent.
d) Yes, an estate is always responsible for the contracts, liabilities and debts of the person who died.
e) Yes, although the agency relationship terminated by death, a second agency by estoppel was created until Jones learned about the death.

14. What is the relationship between a franchisor and the eventual customer?

a) The relationship is with the franchisor as licensee and the eventual customer as third party.
b) There is no relationship between the franchisor and the eventual customer.
c) The relationship is with the franchisor as agent and the eventual customer as third party.
d) The relationship is as immediate parties to a contract.
e) The relationship is through the franchisee as agent.

15. What is the essential characteristic of a franchise?

a) The right of the franchisee to bind the franchisor in contracts.
b) The right of the franchisor to receive a large percentage of the profits.
c) The right of the franchisee to ignore any directives concerning the business from the franchisor.

d) The right of the franchisee to market goods supplied by, or made to specifications provided by, the franchisor.

e) The right of the franchisor to control the entire business affairs of the franchisee.

16. Which of the following is/are examples of an agency relationship?

I. Employees acting for their employers

II. A pawnbroker

III. Stockbrokers acting for their clients

a) I only

b) II only

c) III only

d) II and III only

e) I, II and III

17. An agent owes her principal all the following duties EXCEPT:

a) To obey the principal's instructions except where they conflict with the law.

b) To use reasonable care, skill and diligence in carrying out her duties.

c) To delegate her duties when it is inconvenient or when she is unable to perform.

d) To place the interest of her principal above all else except the law.

e) To insure that she does not place her own interest in conflict with that of her principal.

18. Which of the following statements correctly describes the principal's liability to third parties for contracts negotiated by her agent?

a) The principal is liable if the agent did not disclose her existence.

b) The principal is liable if the third party knows that the representations made by the agent are unauthorized.

c) The principal is liable if the agent told the third party that she acted as an agent but did not disclose the name of the principal.

d) The principal is liable if the agent acted outside the scope of her authority.

e) The principal is liable if the agent acted within the scope of apparent authority.

Answers to Multiple-Choice Questions

1. b)
See page 387 for more information.

2. e)
See page 386 for more information.

3. e)
See page 398 for more information.

4. c)
See page 391 for more information.

5. a)
See pages 392–393 for more information

6. c)
See pages 392–393 for more information.

7. d)
See page 393 for more information.

8. c)
See page 391 for more information.

9. b)
See page 394 for more information.

10. a)
See page 395 for more information.

11. c)
See page 396 for more information.

12. e)
See page 398 for more information.

13. a)
See page 399 for more information.

14. b)
See pages 399–400 for more information.

15. d)
See pages 399–400 for more information.

16. c)
See page 386 for more information.

17. c)
See page 392 for more information.

18. c)
See page 389 for more information.

True/False Questions

1. An agency relationship is one in which one party is authorized to bring another party for whom she acts (the principal) into contractual relations with third parties.

2. Agency by estoppel arises from the legal obligations of authority in the agent created by the principal or from trade custom, and a third party has relied on that appearance.

3. The legal effect of ratification is to make the principal liable on the contract and to release the agent from liability to the third party.

4. As a general rule, an agent must personally perform her duties and thus but can delegate to another.

5. An agent is entitled to reimbursement for reasonable outlays made on behalf of the principal. It is important that the agent acts only within the scope of her specified authority because the principal is under no obligation to reimburse the agent for unauthorized acts unless she later ratifies them.

6. If an agent describes herself as a principal but is only an agent, she also is not liable on the contract.

Answers to True/False Questions

1. True.

2. False. Agency by estoppel arises from the appearance of authority in the agent created by the principal or from trade custom, and a third party has relied on that appearance. The test used to determine the extent of apparent authority is whether a third party should have been put on notice about the limits to the agent's authority or whether it could be reasonably assumed from the kind of business in which the agent is engaged that the agent had limits to her authority. It is not whether the third party dealing with the agent actually believed that the agent had authority.

3. True.

4. False. As a general rule, an agent must personally perform her duties and thus cannot delegate to another. This stems from the fact that the agent is usually selected for her own personal skills or experience.

There are certain circumstances in which an agent will have implied authority to delegate all or part of her duties. One is where delegation is necessary to effectively carry out the agency services. Another is where it is common trade usage to perform through a subagent.

5. True.

6. False. If an agent describes herself as a principal but is only an agent, she also is liable on the contract. The principal can neither sue nor be sued on the contract.

20

The Contract of Employment

Purpose and Significance

Everyone needs to know about the employment relationship. Either we will own a business and have employees or will be an employee. A basic understanding of the employment relationship is essential to each and every one of us.

In this chapter, we begin by learning what the employment relationship is. To do that, we will distinguish it from other types of legal relationships that are similar to the employment relationship. We then explore how and when employees may be discharged by the employer. Thereafter, we consider legislation that has been passed to improve the quality of employees' lives. Finally, the legal status and role of trade unions will be examined.

Learning Objectives

A. Discuss the master-servant (employment) relationship.

B. Describe the law relating to termination and discharge of employees.

C. Discuss employee welfare legislation.

D. Outline the legal role of trade unions.

Content Outline

I. Development of the Law Governing Employment

II. Relationship of Employer and Employee
    A. Compared With Agency
    B. Compared With an Independent Contractor
    C. The Relationship at Common Law

III. The Employer's Liability
    A. Liability in a contract
    B. Liability in tort

IV. Notice of Termination of Individual Employment Contracts

V. Grounds for Dismissal Without Notice
    A. The contractual basis
    B. Misconduct
    C. Disobedience
    D. Incompetence
    E. Illness
    F. Effect of dismissal
    G. Adverse economic conditions

VI. Wrongful Dismissal
    A. Damages
    B. Reinstatement

VII. Employee Welfare Legislation
    A. History
    B. Legislative jurisdiction
    C. Employee rights
        1. Human rights
        2. Pay equity
        3. Employment equity

Questions on Learning Objectives

Objective A: Discuss the master-servant (employment) relationship.

A.1 Is an employee also an agent? Explain. (pp. 411–412)

A.2 Give two reasons why it is important to determine whether an agent is also an employee. (pp. 411–412)

A.3 Distinguish an employee from an independent contractor. (p. 412)

A.4 What liability does an employer have for the actions of its employees? (p. 413)

A.5 When is an employer not liable for the torts of its employees? (p. 413)

Objective B: **Describe the law relating to termination and discharge of employees.**

B.1 At common law, when can an employer lawfully discharge an employee? (pp. 414–415)

B.2 When may an employer dismiss an employee without notice? (pp. 415–417)

B.3 What damages can an employee get for wrongful dismissal? (pp. 417–418)

B.4 What is reinstatement? When is it available as a remedy for wrongful dismissal? (pp. 419– 420)

Objective C: **Discuss employee welfare legislation.**

C.1 Why was legislation passed governing employees? (pp. 420–421)

C.2 Describe the purpose, in the employment context, of the following legislation: human rights, pay equity and employment equity. (pp. 421–423)

C.3 List five working conditions that are regulated by statute. (pp. 423–424)

C.4 When are unemployment insurance benefits payable? (p. 424)

C.5 Why were workers' compensation laws passed? (p. 425)

C.6 When can an employee collect workers' compensation benefits? (p. 426)

C.7 What employees are covered by workers' compensation? (p. 426)

Objective D: **Outline the legal role of trade unions.**

D.1 Explain the meaning of collective bargaining, certification and a collective agreement. (p. 427)

D.2 What terms does a collective agreement normally cover? (pp. 427–428)

D.3 List and briefly describe the types of disputes that affect a trade union. (p. 428)

D.4 How does legislation regulate an interest dispute? (p. 429)

D.5 How does legislation regulate a rights dispute? (p. 429)

D.6 What difference does it make to an individual employee if a collective agreement is in place? (pp. 430–431)

Answers to Questions on Learning Objectives

A.1 An agent is authorized to contract on behalf of his principal. An employee, on the other hand, gives his employer authority to direct and control the work that he is to perform. That work may or may not include the making of contracts with third parties.

A.2 It is important to determine whether an agent is also an employee because:
i) an agent may have no recourse against a principal who terminates the relationship without notice, and
ii) employers are generally liable for more acts of employees than principals are for agents.

A.3 An independent contractor is not subject to the supervision of the person who hires him. An employee is under the authority and control of an employer. An independent contractor has the obligation to produce a specified result; the means he employs to obtain that result are his own affair.

A.4 An employer is liable for any breach of contract caused by its employees. So, for example, if an employee of a moving company breaks or damages the furniture that he moves, the employer will have to pay damages.

An employer is also liable for any tort an employee commits in the course of employment.

A.5 An employer is not liable for the torts of employees caused when the employee is not engaged in the employer's work or if the employee delegates the work to someone else without the employer's consent.

B.1 If an employee is hired for a particular length of time and the time elapses, the employer may discharge the employee without notice. Where the employment relationship is for an indefinite period, an employer may discharge an employee only so long as he gives reasonable notice of the termination. What is reasonable depends on the circumstances.

B.2 An employer may dismiss an employee without notice when there is cause for dismissal. Cause is misconduct, disobedience, incompetence, permanent disability or constantly recurring illness.

B.3 An employee may get damages for breach of contract if he has been wrongfully dismissed. The amount of damages is that which will compensate the employee for failing to receive the required notice of termination. That requires a determination of what would have been reasonable notice in the circumstances. Compensation will also include losses other than salary such as pension benefits and travel expenses.

B.4 Reinstatement refers to the act of putting an employee back into the job from which he has been dismissed. It is not normally a remedy for wrongful dismissal. However, in large industrial enterprises, certain union jobs and universities, reinstatement does occur.

C.1 Before trade unions emerged, employers had all the advantage in bargaining power. Workers basically had to accept the terms that the employers offered or starve. Employee welfare legislation was passed to ensure that work conditions were safe and that the employees had some measure of power over certain terms of the employment relationship.

C.2 Human rights legislation was enacted to prohibit discrimination in employment on the basis of race, religion, age, sex and other prohibited grounds. Pay equity legislation is intended to redress gender discrimination in remuneration. Employment equity legislation was enacted to require certain employers to make their work force reflect more closely the representation of certain disadvantaged persons in society.

C.3 Employment conditions regulated by statute in each of the provinces are: minimum wages, maximum working hours per day and week, overtime rates, health and safety standards and minimum age for full-time employment.

C.4 Unemployment insurance benefits are payable to workers who have contributed in the past and are currently unemployed. Benefits are not payable where the loss of work is caused by strike.

C.5 Workers' compensation statutes were passed to ensure that workers would be compensated for job related injuries and to place the cost of industrial accidents on employers.

C.6 To collect workers' compensation benefits, an employee must show that she is disabled and the disease or injury is job related. An employee does not need to prove that her employer was negligent. Benefits are awarded regardless of fault.

C.7 Normally, workers' compensation laws cover workers in construction, mining, manufacturing, lumbering, fishing, transportation, communications and public utilities.

D.1 Collective bargaining is the process of establishing conditions of employment between a business and the bargaining agent for its employees.

A Labor Relations Board acknowledges certification that a union has enough members to justify its role as exclusive bargaining agent for employees.

A collective agreement is that agreement reached between an employee and union after they have finished the collective bargaining process.

D.2 A collective agreement normally includes terms that define what employees are covered, an outline of the steps for settling grievances, seniority provisions, wages, hours, vacations, length of time that the collective agreement operates for, the means by which it may be changed, discipline, efficiency, rights to grievances, strikes, lock-outs and dismissal procedures.

D.3 The four types of disputes are jurisdictional, recognition, interest and rights. A jurisdictional dispute is a disagreement between two unions about who has the right to represent one group of employees. A recognition dispute refers to a situation where an employer refuses to recognize a union as the employees' bargaining agent. An interest dispute is a disagreement between an employer and a union about the terms to be included in a collective agreement. A rights dispute is a disagreement between an employer and union on the interpretation of terms in an existing collective agreement.

D.4 Most provinces now have legislation that requires both employer and employee to genuinely attempt to bargain to reach agreement and, failing agreement, submit to conciliation procedures. Failing agreement at this stage, there is a mandatory cooling off period.

D.5 In order to settle rights disputes most provinces have imposed arbitration procedures.

D.6 Where a collective agreement is entered into by an employer with a union, an employer is not permitted to privately negotiate his contract of employment.

Multiple-Choice Questions

1. Why is it important to ascertain whether a person is an agent or an employee?

a) Both an agent and an employee may be subject to direction from senior officers.
b) An employee can sue for wrongful dismissal whereas an agent can be terminated without notice.
c) An employer's liability in torts for an employee may be greater than a principal's liability in torts for an agent.
d) Both an agent and an employee may be able to bind the employer/principal in contracts.
e) All of the above.

2. Parkinson Limited entered into a contract with Martin to have Martin erect an addition on Parkinson Limited's existing building. During the construction, a client of Parkinson Limited is injured when she trips over a stack of boards lying next to the walkway leading to the front door of the building. Who can the client sue for her injuries?

a) Parkinson Limited because the injury occurred on its land.
b) Martin because as an independent contractor, he is liable for any injuries that result from his work.
c) Parkinson Limited because Martin is an employee so cannot be sued for torts he commits during the course of employment.
d) Martin and Parkinson Limited because Parkinson Limited is responsible for the actions of both employees and independent contractors and Martin is responsible for any injuries that he causes.
e) Neither Martin nor Parkinson Limited because the client is responsible for her own clumsiness which caused the injury.

3. Patrick, a sales rep for a national company, has a business meeting in St. John's on a Monday. To save on airfare, Patrick arrives on Friday evening. With the weekend free, Patrick uses the car rented by the company to tour the Avalon Peninsula. Returning to St. John's after dark, Patrick swerves to avoid a moose

and has a head-on collision with another car. Can the other driver successfully sue the national company?

a) No because Patrick is on a frolic of his own.
b) Yes because an employer is responsible for all the actions of its employees.
c) No because Patrick did not have to be in St. John's until Monday.
d) Yes because Patrick was in St. John's for business and the company rented the car.
e) No because the sightseeing and the accident are unconnected to Patrick's job.

4. Part of Adrian's job is to explain the various advantages of the computers he delivers. While delivering a computer, Adrian becomes embroiled in an argument with a customer about the particular computer. Adrian pushes the customer, who falls and injures himself. Can the customer successfully sue Adrian's employer for assault?

a) Yes because the employer is responsible for all the actions of its employees.
b) No because the assault was carried out while Adrian and the customer were discussing a non-work-related topic.
c) Yes because the assault was carried out while Adrian was in the course of his employment.
d) No because the employer did not tell Adrian to argue with, or to push, the customers.
e) No because Adrian was on a frolic of his own.

5. How does an employer determine the period of notice for the termination of an employment contract?

a) Termination date in the employment contract; reasonable notice based on the industry, the length of employment and the frequency of pay; and no notice if there is just cause.
b) Frequency of pay; the start date if the employee has found another job; and no notice if there is just cause.
c) Termination date in the employment contract; one week for each year of employment; and the start date if the employee has found another job.
d) One week for each year of employment; the minimum required by statute; and no notice if there is just cause.
e) Termination date in the employment contract; the start date if the employee has found another job; and the minimum required by statute.

6. Mason, a bookkeeper for Phillips Inc., has been borrowing money without permission from the company to pay for his grandmother's nursing home expenses. In total, Mason borrowed $200 000. After Mason starts repaying the company, the discrepancies in the accounts are discovered and Mason confesses that he is responsible. Can the company dismiss Mason without notice?

a) Yes based on incompetence.
b) No because Mason was trying to repay the borrowed money.
c) Yes based on misconduct.
d) No because Mason had good reasons to borrow the money.
e) Yes based on disobedience.

7. Patrick, a sales rep for a large multinational, has been given the Middle East as his new sales area. While arranging to send a shipment to a Middle Eastern country, he is told to include a cash bribe of $4000 U.S. to be given to the customs officer of the foreign country. Patrick believes that bribes are wrong so does not include the cash. When the shipment is turned back, the company suffers a significant loss and immediately fires Patrick. Can the company justify the termination without notice?

a) Yes based on the economic loss that the company suffered due to Patrick's actions.
b) No because Patrick had done nothing wrong.
c) Yes based on disobedience since bribes are common in the industry.
d) No because an employee is allowed to disobey an unlawful order.
e) Yes based on misconduct since Patrick did not send the cash.

8. Following a lengthy court case, it is determined that the employer wrongfully dismissed Janice by not giving her notice of termination. Janice had worked for the company for ten years with a biweekly pay of $2000. The company provided extensive benefits valued at $100 per pay period. The company also gave most employees a Christmas bonus equal to an extra pay cheque. Because Janice was in sales, occasionally the company gave her an extra bonus of $500 when she located a new customer for the company. The previous year, Janice had signed up six new customers. Janice located new employment eight weeks after she was fired. The new salary was $1500 every two weeks. If the court decides that the appropriate notice period was 14 weeks, what should be the amount of damages?

a) $19 700.
b) $16 700.
c) $14 700.
d) $10 200.
e) $8 700

9. Patrick, a sales rep for a local tool manufacturer, has disobeyed lawful orders from his employer six times over the past two years. After suffering economic loss due to these actions, the manufacturer terminates Patrick without notice. Patrick does not think this is fair after ten years of employment so commences a wrongful dismissal action against the manufacturer. Can Patrick force the manufacturer to pay him a severance package?

a) Yes because even if Patrick disobeyed a lawful order of his employer, after ten years some form of severance package is required.

b) No because the manufacturer had just cause based on misconduct so no notice period or severance package is required.

c) Yes because Patrick's actions did not amount to enough for dismissal with just cause so a notice period or severance package is required.

d) No because the manufacturer had just cause based on disobedience so no notice period or severance package is required.

e) Yes because economic conditions are not a basis for dismissal without notice or a severance package.

10. James has just turned 65 years old and his employer has given him six months notice of dismissal. The dismissal is due to the company's mandatory retirement policy for persons over the age of 65. James does not think he is ready to retire just yet and objects to the dismissal notice. Is there anything James can do to challenge the mandatory retirement scheme as discriminatory?

a) Yes because all provincial human rights codes prohibit discrimination based on age without any limits on the age range.

b) Maybe, depending on whether the *Canadian Charter of Rights and Freedoms* or a provincial human rights code applies to the company and the wording of the provincial human rights code if it does apply.

c) Yes because section 15 of the *Canadian Charter of Rights and Freedoms* prohibits discrimination based on age and the *Canadian Charter of Rights and Freedoms* applies to all places of work.

d) No because the Supreme Court of Canada, relying on section 1, allows mandatory retirement schemes and the *Canadian Charter of Rights and Freedoms* applies to all places of work.

e) Maybe, depending on whether James' health is good enough to justify his continued employment.

11. Jeff was injured by a falling box full of nails at his place of work. The accident occurred because the employee who was stacking the boxes was being careless and not watching what he was doing. Also, Jeff was walking around the factory without the required safety clothing (e.g., a hard hat) so the injury was more severe than it might have been. Can Jeff force his employer to compensate him for his injuries?

a) No because Jeff contributed to his own injuries.

b) Yes because the employer is responsible in tort law for any injury incurred in the course of employment.

c) No because the accident was caused by a fellow employee.

d) Yes because the employer had obviously not provided all the necessary safety equipment or Jeff would not have been injured.

e) No because Jeff can be compensated under the provincial workers' compensation scheme.

12. Is specific performance available as a remedy for wrongful dismissal of an employee?

a) Yes, but it has never been ordered in any case.
b) No, it is not available because of the difficulty of a court having to supervise an employee.
c) Yes, but until recently it was usually ordered only under a collective agreement.
d) No, it is not available because courts do not view employment contracts as situations where personal performance is required.
e) Yes, but in any case where specific performance could have been ordered, the courts issued an injunction.

13. What are the types of labor disputes?

a) Certification disputes; recognition disputes; interest disputes; and rights disputes.
b) Recognition disputes; disinterest disputes; and disputes arising from wrongs committed by the employer.
c) Certification disputes; disinterest disputes; and rights disputes.
d) Jurisdictional disputes; recognition disputes; interest disputes; and rights disputes.
e) Jurisdictional disputes; certification disputes; disinterest disputes; and disputes arising from wrongs committed by the employer.

14. Acme Limited is in financial difficulties due to a downturn in the economy. As a result, it has decided to downsize 20 employees from each of its six factories. With their next pay cheque the affected employees receive a termination notice effective immediately. Can the affected employees successfully sue Acme for wrongful dismissal if no pay in lieu of notice is included in their pay cheques?

a) No because a decline in market conditions is just cause for termination without notice.
b) Yes because a decline in market conditions is not just cause for termination without notice.
c) No because downsizing is a normal part of doing business and does not required a notice period.
d) Yes because downsizing is an unusual part of doing business and, therefore, requires a notice period.
e) No because each of the employees selected for the downsizing committed some form of just cause justifying the company's termination without notice.

15. Hector is a student employed for the summer by Bob's Do-it-all Company. Union dues are deducted from Hector's first pay cheque. When he calls payroll to complain, payroll explains that union dues were deducted from every employee who is not management. Does the union represent Hector?

a) Yes because the union dues are taken from Hector's pay cheque.
b) No because Hector has chosen not to join the union.
c) No because as a summer student Hector is classified as management.
d) No because summer students can never be included in a bargaining unit.
e) Yes because the bargaining unit covers all employees, even those who do not choose to join the union.

16. An employer may dismiss an employee without notice for which of the following?
I. There is insufficient work for the employee to do.
II. The employee regularly misses work because his children are ill and he must stay home with them.
III. The employee is chronically absent from work because of illness.

a) I only
b) II only
c) III only
d) II and III only
e) I, II and III

17. All of the following statements correctly describe the employment relationship EXCEPT:

a) An employer is liable for contractual and tortious wrongs of its employees.
b) An employer is liable for the contractual wrongs of its employees.
c) An employer is liable for torts committed by an employee in the course of employment.
d) An employer has the authority to direct and control the work of its employees.
e) An employee may have no power to enter into contracts on behalf of his employer whereas an agent always will have such a power.

18. A collective agreement:

a) Is an acknowledgement that a particular union has sufficient support from some membership to act as its exclusive bargaining agent.
b) Is a type of contract that covers such job conditions as grievance procedures, seniority, wage rates, hours, vacation and procedure for dismissal.
c) Is a specified group of employees eligible to joint a union.
d) Is an agreement that empowers employees to strike.
e) Is the process of establishing the conditions of employment by negotiation.

Answers to Multiple-Choice Questions

1. e)
See pages 411–412 for more information.

2. b)
See page 412 for more information.

3. d)
See page 413 for more information.

4. c)
See pages 413–414 for more information.

5. a)
See pages 414–415 for more information

6. c)
See page 416 for more information.

7. d)
See page 416 for more information.

8. d)
See page 418 for more information.

9. d)
See pages 416–417 for more information.

10. b)
See pages 423–424 for more information.

11. e)
See page 425 for more information.

12. c)
See page 419 for more information.

13. d)
See page 428 for more information.

14. b)
See page 417 for more information.

15. e)
See page 427 for more information.

16. c)
See pages 415–417 for more information.

17. a)
See page 413 for more information.

18. b)
See page 427 for more information.

True/False Questions

1. An agent is authorized to contract on behalf of his principal. An employee, on the other hand, gives his employer authority to direct and control the work that he is to perform. That work may or may not include the making of contracts with third parties.

2. An independent contractor is subject to the supervision of the person who hires him.

3. If an employee is hired for a particular length of time and the time elapses, the employer cannot discharge the employee without notice.

4. Reinstatement refers to the act of putting an employee back into the job from which he has been dismissed.

5. Human rights legislation was enacted to prohibit discrimination in employment on the basis of race, religion, age, sex and other prohibited grounds. Pay equity legislation is intended to redress gender discrimination in remuneration. Employment equity legislation was enacted to require certain employers to make their work force reflect more closely the representation of certain disadvantaged persons in society.

6. To collect workers' compensation benefits, an employee must only need to show that she is disabled.

Answers to True/False Questions

1. True.

2. False. An independent contractor is not subject to the supervision of the person who hires him. An employee is under the authority and control of an employer. An independent contractor has the obligation to produce a specified result; the means he employs to obtain that result are his own affair.

3. False. If an employee is hired for a particular length of time and the time elapses, the employer may discharge the employee without notice. Where the employment relationship is for an indefinite period, an employer may discharge an employee only if he gives reasonable notice of the termination. What is reasonable depends on the circumstances.

4. True.

5. True.

6. False. To collect workers' compensation benefits, an employee must show that she is disabled and the disease or injury is job related. An employee does not need to prove that her employer was negligent. Benefits are awarded regardless of fault.

21

Negotiable Instruments

Purpose and Significance

The law seems to live on a sea of paper. Wills, contracts, statutes, deeds, and cases are all presented as written documents. Usually these documents are important because of what they represent (an agreement between contracting parties, for example) or for the information they contain (a deed of title or a statute).

Sometimes, however, a written document acquires legal value that goes beyond that which the document represents or the information it contains. One such document is the negotiable instrument. In this chapter we will explore negotiable instruments, their history, meaning and uses. We will also consider the liability that makers and users of negotiable instruments face and the defenses that may be raised against a claim by a holder of a negotiable instrument.

Learning Objectives

A. Discuss the development, types and uses of negotiable instruments.

B. Discuss the concept of negotiability and methods of negotiation.

C. Outline the liabilities that arise in the use, negotiation and endorsement of negotiable instruments.

D. Discuss the position of a holder in due course.

E. Consider the types of defenses available in the law of negotiable instruments.

Content Outline

I. History

II. Future Developments

III. Nature and Uses of Negotiable Instruments
   A. As personal property
   B. Types of instruments
   C. Bill of exchange (drafts)
   D. Promissory note
   E. Cheque
      1. Certification
      2. Postdated cheques
      3. "Stop payment"
      4. The predominant use of cheques

IV. Prerequisites for Liability

V. Negotiability
   A. Meaning of negotiability
   B. Consequences when a document is not negotiable

VI. Methods of Negotiation
   A. By endorsement and delivery
   B. By delivery only

VII. Endorsement
   A. Types of endorsement
      1. Endorsement in blank
      2. Special endorsement
      3. Restrictive endorsement

Questions on Learning Objectives

Objective A: Discuss the development, types and uses of negotiable instruments.

A.1 Who has the power to regulate negotiable instruments? (p. 439)

A.2 B sells A $1,000 worth of goods. In exchange A gives B a promissory note obliging A to pay $1,000 in 30 days. If A does not pay the $1,000 in 30 days, on what grounds can B sue A? (p. 439)

A.3 Does the *Bills of Exchange Act* in Canada govern all negotiable instruments? (p. 440)

A.4 What are the essential features of a bill of exchange or draft? (p. 440)

A.5 What is an acceptor? (p. 440)

A.6 What is the difference between a bill of exchange and a promissory note? (p. 442)

A.7 What is the difference between a bill of exchange and a cheque? (p. 443)

A.8 Can a cheque be used as legal tender? (p. 445)

Objective B: Discuss the concept of negotiability and methods of negotiation.

B.1 What features must an instrument possess in order to be negotiable? (p. 446)

B.2 Is endorsement necessary whenever a holder negotiates a negotiable instrument? (p. 447)

B.3 How can an instrument payable to a specified person become a bearer instrument? (p. 447)

B.4 What is a restrictive endorsement? (p. 448)

B.5 When someone endorses a negotiable instrument what liability is incurred by the endorser? (pp. 449–450)

Objective C: Outline the liabilities that arise in the use, negotiation and endorsement of negotiable instruments.

C.1 What is "dishonor"? (p. 450)

C.2 Is an endorser liable to a holder in due course if the negotiable instrument is a forgery? (p. 450)

C.3 Is an endorser entitled to notice of his liability? (pp. 450–451)

Objective D: Discuss the position of a "holder in due course."

D.1 What conditions must be met to be a "holder in due course"? (p. 453)

D.2 What is the practical effect of the legal recognition of negotiation and the rights of holders in due course? (p. 453)

D.3 What is the difference between immediate parties and remote parties? (p. 453)

Objective E: Consider the types of defenses available in the law of negotiable instrument.

E.1 What are the three principal categories of defenses? (pp. 455)

E.2 A gives B a promissory note obliging A to pay $1,000 to B in 60 days. B gives no consideration to A for the note. Will A be liable for the obligation contained in the note? (pp. 455–457)

E.3 A gives a promissory note to B obliging A to pay $1,000 to B in 60 days. B gives consideration to A, but later says to A, "You don't have to pay me anything." B then negotiates the promissory note to C. If C sues A, does A have a defense? (p. 457)

E.4 List several "real" defenses. (p. 458)

Answers to Questions on Learning Objectives

A.1 In Canada, negotiable instruments are within federal jurisdiction.

A.2 If B is still the holder of the note, he can sue either on the original contract (the sale of goods) or on his rights as holder of the promissory note. Though the note was consideration for the original sales contract, that contract revives if the note is dishonored.

The note contains an enforceable promise to pay. It amounts to a self-contained contract with necessary terms on its face. An "action on the instrument" can be a simpler legal undertaking than an action on other types of contract.

A.3 The *Bills of Exchange Act* governs the three basic types of negotiable instruments: bills of exchange (or drafts), promissory notes and cheques.

This does not mean that courts may not give other types of commercial instruments the special quality of negotiability. Disputes with respect to such instruments would be resolved by recourse to common law rather than statute law. For example, bearer bonds have been held to be negotiable instruments.

A.4 The essence of a bill of exchange is a written order by the drawer (often a purchaser or debtor), addressed to the drawee (often a bank or someone who owes money to the drawer), ordering the drawee to pay a specified sum of money to a named party, the payee (often a creditor of the drawer, or a seller).

A.5 The drawee of a bill of exchange becomes an acceptor when it indicates its willingness to comply with a demand for future payment of the bill by expressing that consent on the face of the bill with the word "accepted" and the date of acceptance.

A.6 A promissory note involves two essential parties, rather than the three essential parties of a bill of exchange. A promissory note contains an express promise to pay from the outset and never undergoes presentment for acceptance.

A.7 A cheque is a specialized form of a bill of exchange. It is drawn against a bank and contains an implied promise by the drawer that the drawer has funds on deposit at the bank sufficient to meet the amount of the cheque. A cheque is also payable on demand.

A.8 Cheques are widely used for cash transfers. They permit easy handling of large cash payments with relative safety through mail and in general commerce. However, a cheque, even one certified by a bank, is not legal tender. Only Bank of Canada notes and official coinage fit within the strict definition of legal tender.

B.1 (a) It must be in writing.
   (b) The obligation must be for money payment.
   (c) The money promised must be a "sum certain."
   (d) The promise or order must be unconditional.
   (e) The money must be payable at a fixed or determinable future time or on demand.
   (f) Negotiation must be of the whole instrument.
   (g) The drawer or an authorized agent must sign the negotiable instrument.

B.2 An order instrument must be endorsed as well as delivered in order to be adequately negotiated. A party who purchases an order instrument without requiring proper endorsement acquires limited rights, probably limited to rights against the immediate transferor.

Endorsement is not necessary for a bearer instrument.

B.3 An instrument payable to the order of a specified person becomes a bearer instrument if it is endorsed by that person without further words or instructions. It can, thereafter, be negotiated by delivery alone.

A cheque, payable to a specified person, who thereafter endorses it has turned the cheque into a bearer instrument.

B.4 The holder of an instrument may add limiting instructions to an endorsement, by writing "for deposit only" or "pay to Prometheus only." These would be restrictive endorsements.

The party entitled to payment on an order instrument renders it henceforth non-negotiable by specifying how payment shall be made as part of a restrictive endorsement.

B.5 If one becomes an endorser without words of qualified liability, the endorser becomes liable for payment to a holder in due course, if the party of primary liability (acceptor, maker or drawer) fails to make payment. This result follows though the endorser has never owned the instrument and is not in the act of negotiating it to someone else.

C.1 Dishonor is the failure by the party primarily liable (acceptor, maker or drawer) to pay the instrument according to its terms. If the instrument is a draft, dishonor may take the form of either the drawee's refusal to accept or, if he accepts, of his later refusal to pay as acceptor.

C.2 As long as the holder meets the proper criterion, the endorser becomes liable on the terms of the instrument even if the drawer's signature has been forged, or a prior endorsement is a forgery.

C.3 Both the endorser and drawer have a liability contingent on receiving prompt notice of dishonor. Notice of dishonor must be given to endorsers and drawers not later than the business day next following the dishonor. This notice must be express unless the right has been waived. It is not enough to show that the endorser heard about the dishonor from an independent source.

D.1 Four conditions attach to legal status as a holder in due course. These apply to the holder of an instrument:
    (a) who has taken the instrument complete and regular on its face;
    (b) who has acquired the instrument before it is over due or dishonored;
    (c) who has acquired the instrument for value (consideration); and
    (d) who has taken the instrument in good faith without notice of any title defect.

D.2 In commercial transactions, banks and other institutions are willing to discount drafts or cash cheques drawn on other banks or institutions with relatively little delay. Since they can acquire these instruments as holders in due course, they obtain a more secure entitlement. If the law did not provide protection, banks and commercial traders would be reluctant to purchase and hold negotiable instruments because of the exhaustive inquiry that would have to be made before a secure title could be obtained free of fraud, illegality, inadequate consideration, or duress.

D.3 When the holder of a negotiable instrument has direct dealings with the maker or endorser of the instrument (that is, the person who is liable), the two of them are immediate parties.

If the holder of the negotiable instrument has no direct dealings with the maker or endorser of the negotiable instrument then they are remote parties.

E.1   (a) The party liable under a negotiable instrument (whether maker or endorser) may have mere personal defenses available against a holder who is an immediate party.
(b) The party liable may have defenses that are good against all holders in due course, whether they are immediate parties or remote parties. These are termed real defenses.
(c) The party liable may acquire a defense against a holder whom, though a remote party, does not qualify as a holder in due course. These may be termed defect of title defenses.

E.2 Lack of consideration may be a personal defense available when a dispute is between immediate parties. If B sues A, A would have this personal defense available.

E.3 A holder's renunciation of his right to receive payment operates to discharge the instrument, and gives A a defense. However, the renunciation does not affect the rights of a holder in due course. Unless there is something on the face of the note, and the holder has no notice of the renunciation, C can enforce the obligation against A.

E.4   Real defenses are good against any holder, even a holder in due course, and include:
(a) incapacity because of infancy;
(b) cancellation;
(c) absence of delivery where the instrument is incomplete when taken;
(d) fraud as to the nature of the instrument;
(e) forgery;
(f) lack of authority by an agent signing on behalf of the responsible party; and
(g) cancellation.

Multiple-Choice Questions

1. Gower has drawn a time draft on Cohen, payable three months after sight to Jenkins. The draft is complete and regular with the possible exception of a clause that Cohen, the drawee, is "to pay the amount of this draft out of money due to me on December 31 for professional services rendered." If Cohen refuses to accept the draft, does he owe its amount in future to Gower or to Jenkins?

a) Jenkins because he is the named payee in the instrument.

b) Gower because Cohen did not accept the draft so it has no obligation to pay Jenkins.

c) Jenkins because Cohen did not accept the draft so it has no obligation to pay Gower.

d) Gower because the time draft may not cover the entire amount of due for services rendered.

e) Gower because the draft is not sum certain so it is not a negotiable instrument.

2. Janice is the maker of a note in which she undertakes to pay $500 to a moneylender on demand. Subsequently, Janice pays an installment of $200 to the moneylender on this liability. What steps should Janice take to ensure that she will not have to pay a further $500 at some later date?

a) Get a written letter or receipt from the moneylender for the partial payment.

b) Write cancel on the note and write a new note for $300.

c) Ensure that an endorsement is put on the note to acknowledge the partial payment.

d) Get the moneylender's oral acknowledgement that the payment has been made.

e) Do nothing.

3. Jason is a holder of a bill of exchange drawn by Richie on Ward, payable to Macdonald or order, accepted by Ward, and endorsed in blank by Macdonald. Upon presentation by Jason to Ward for payment, payment is refused. What steps should Jason take to protect his rights?

a) Promptly notify Macdonald of the dishonor.

b) Commence a lawsuit against Richie.

c) Promptly notify Richie, Ward and Macdonald.

d) Commence a lawsuit against Richie, Ward and Macdonald.

e) Do nothing.

4. What are the types of endorsement?

a) In writing, feature, restrictive, unconditional, unqualified and anomalous.

b) In blank, feature, open, unconditional, unqualified and anomalous.

c) In writing, special, open, conditional, qualified and ordinary.

d) In blank, special, restrictive, conditional, qualified and anomalous.

e) In blank, special, restrictive, unconditional, unqualified and ordinary.

5. Rebecca, a 16 year old, gives the local trendy clothing store a cheque to pay for some winter clothes that she has picked out. The clothes are necessary because none of her winter clothes from the previous year fit her this year. What is Rebecca's liability on the instrument?

a) Rebecca cannot be sued on the instrument, even if it was used to purchase necessities.

b) Rebecca can be sued on the instrument because it was used to purchase necessities.

c) Rebecca cannot be sued on the instrument, unless there is some irregularity with the instrument.

d) Rebecca can be sued on the instrument provided there are no irregularities and it was used to purchase necessities.

e) Rebecca can only be sued on the instrument by a holder in due course.

6. Paul drew a cheque for $100 in favor of Quinn. Paul has his account at the Really Big Bank. In drawing the cheque, Paul left a blank space before the words "one hundred" and Quinn added the words "two thousand and." The addition was in a different colored ink and was obviously in a different handwriting. The Bank paid Quinn $2100 and then Quinn left the country with the proceeds. May Paul insist that the Bank make good his loss of $2000?

a) No because the Bank had no way of knowing that the cheque had been altered.

b) Yes because the Bank paid out money on an altered cheque.

c) No because the Bank had an obligation to confirm a cheque of that size with Paul.

d) Yes because the loss was the Bank's fault.

e) No because Paul left the space that allowed the alteration.

7. Ayer drew a draft on Coole with the drawer named as payee. Coole accepted it, and Ayer then endorsed it to the order of Winter. Before Winter had endorsed it, the instrument was stolen and Winter's signature was forged by way of endorsement. The party guilt of the forgery succeeded in negotiating the bill to Frost who took it innocently and who in turn negotiated it to Holden. Who can Holden successfully sue to force payment of the draft?

a) Holden can force Ayer to pay the amount because Ayer is the drawer.

b) Holden can force Frost to pay the amount because Frost was the first endorser after the forgery.

c) Holden can force Winter to pay the amount because it was Winter's signature that was forged.

d) Holden can force the forger to pay the amount because he or she did the forgery.

e) Holden can force Coole to pay the amount because Coole accepted the draft.

8. Zeus delivered $50 000 worth of goods to Acme Limited and drew a draft on it for that amount payable in 90 days. Acme accepted and Zeus then discounted the draft at his bank for the sum of $49 200 credited to his account. Acme dishonored the draft at maturity. Who can the bank successfully sue for payment?

a) The bank can sue Zeus or Acme because it is a holder in due course.

b) The bank can sue Zeus because he drew up the draft and is owed the money.

c) The bank can sue Acme because Acme accepted the draft and has the goods.

d) The bank can sue Zeus or Acme because the bank is the innocent party so someone else must pay.

e) The bank cannot sue either Zeus nor Acme because the draft has been dishonored so is unenforceable.

9. On October 1, Martin made a note for $125 payable to the order of his son, Mark, as a birthday present. The note was due October 31. Mark misplaced the note and his father refused to pay its amount until it was found. Mark did not locate the note until January 2, by which time his father had died. Mark presented the note for payment to the executor of his father's estate, who refused to honor it. Can Mark successfully sue the estate for payment?

a) Yes because a note, unlike a cheque, cannot become stale dated.

b) No because a note, like a cheque, can become stale dated.

c) Yes because the note is a negotiable instrument that an estate is required to pay.

d) No because the note was gratuitous so it is not binding for a lack of consideration.

e) Yes because, although the note was gratuitous, it is binding even if it is given without consideration.

10. What is the distinction between a bill of exchange and a promissory note?

a) A bill of exchange is a written promise to pay a specified sum of money to a named party. A promissory note is a written order to pay a specified sum of money to the named party.

b) A bill of exchange is an oral promise to pay a specified sum of money to a named party. A promissory note is an oral order to pay a specified sum of money to the named party.

c) A bill of exchange is a written order to pay a specified sum of money to a named party. A promissory note is a written promise to pay a specified sum of money to the named party.

d) A bill of exchange is an oral order to pay a specified sum of money to a named party. A promissory note is an oral promise to pay a specified sum of money to the named party.

e) A bill of exchange is an oral order to pay a specified sum of money to a named party. A promissory note is a written promise to pay a specified sum of money to the named party.

11. What is the distinction between assignment of a contract and a negotiable instrument?

a) For a negotiable instrument: notice to non-changing party is required; an assignee cannot get a better right to sue than its predecessor; and a holder must sue in the original party's name.

b) For a negotiable instrument: notice to non-changing party is not required; an assignee cannot get a better right to sue than its predecessor; and a holder can sue in his or her own name.

c) For a negotiable instrument: notice to non-changing party is required; an assignee can get a better right to sue than its predecessor; and a holder must sue in the original party's name.

d) For a negotiable instrument: notice to non-changing party is not required; an assignee cannot get a better right to sue than its predecessor; and a holder must sue in the original party's name.

e) For a negotiable instrument: notice to non-changing party is not required; an assignee can get a better right to sue than its predecessor; and a holder can sue in his or her own name.

12. Ryanic Limited draws a bill of exchange on Clara Inc. payable to George. Clara Inc. refuses to accept the bill. Does Clara Inc. owe anything to George?

a) Yes because the written bill gives notice to Clara Inc. of its contents.
b) No because, without acceptance, there has been no notice as required by a proper contractual assignment.
c) Yes because the bill has been properly negotiated to Clara Inc.
d) No because the bill is not a negotiable instrument.
e) Yes because the bill has been properly drawn up.

13. What are the purposes of an endorsement?

a) Endorsement may be a means of transferring title, giving less security to a holder, identifying the party entitled to payment, or acknowledging full payment.
b) Endorsement may be a means of transferring possession, giving less security to a holder, identifying the party entitled to payment, or acknowledging a partial payment.
c) Endorsement may be a means of transferring title, giving increased security to a holder, identifying the party entitled to payment, or acknowledging full payment.
d) Endorsement may be a means of transferring possession, giving increased security to a holder, identifying the party entitled to payment, or acknowledging full payment.
e) Endorsement may be a means of transferring title, giving increased security to a holder, identifying the party entitled to payment, or acknowledging a partial payment.

14. Which of the following is part of the criteria for a holder in due course?

a) The instrument is taken complete and regular on its face.
b) The instrument is taken before it is overdue and without notice of any dishonor.
c) The instrument is taken in good faith and without notice of any defect in title.
d) The instrument is taken by someone, or through someone, who has given consideration for it.
e) All of the above.

15. Which defenses apply to which class of holder?

a) Immediate parties: mere personal, defect of title and real; remote parties: defect of title and real; holders in due course: real.
b) Immediate parties: mere personal and real; remote parties: real; holders in due course: defect of title and real.
c) Immediate parties: real; remote parties: defect of title and real; holders in due course: mere personal and real.
d) Immediate parties: mere personal and defect of title; remote parties: mere personal; holders in due course: defect of title and real.
e) Immediate parties: mere personal, defect of title and real; remote parties: defect of title and real; holders in due course: real.

16. Which of the following is/are accurate statements about negotiable instruments?
I. A negotiable instrument contains an express or implied promise made by one or more parties to pay the amount specified in the document.
II. A negotiable instrument cannot be assigned without giving notice to the maker of the instrument.
III. Until an instrument is delivered, its maker has no liability. Even after signing it, the maker may reconsider, not use the instrument and therefore create no rights in the payee.
a) I only
b) II only
c) III only
d) I and III only
e) I, II and III

17. Which of the following statements apply to a holder in due course of a negotiable instrument?

a) The holder must know the nature of the original transaction between the maker and the payee of the instrument if he is to participate in that agreement.
b) The holder must have given valuable consideration for the instrument in order to be a holder in due course.
c) The holder must have acquired the instrument after the due date in order to guarantee its maturity.
d) The holder may require the person from whom the instrument is received to endorse the instrument so that the holder can be protected by the endorser's liability if the instrument is dishonored.
e) The holder must take the instrument in good faith and without notice of any defect in the title of the person who negotiated it.

18. Magleby has given a certified cheque to Peterson in payment for goods purchased. Peterson has not cashed the cheque. Magleby is dissatisfied with the goods and orders the bank to "stop payment" of the cheque. Which of the following accurately reflects the consequences?

a) Peterson would have to give the cheque back immediately and sue Magleby for not paying for the goods.

b) The bank, as an agent of Peterson, could cash the cheque at any time because it is certified.

c) Peterson could use the cheque as legal tender to pay other debts.

d) The bank can make the cheque N.S.F. and return it to Peterson if he tries to cash it.

e) The bank will require that the cheque be returned to it for cancellation, or that Magleby must agree to indemnify the bank if the cheque is presented for payment, before the bank will honor the "stop payment."

Answers to Multiple-Choice Questions

1. b)
See page 445 for more information.

2. c)
See page 449 for more information.

3. a)
See pages 450–451 for more information.

4. d)
See page 448 for more information.

5. a)
See page 458 for more information

6. e)
See pages 462–463 for more information.

7. b)
See pages 449 and 460–462 for more information.

8. a)
See pages 452–453 for more information.

9. d)
See page 455 for more information.

10. c)
See page 442 for more information.

11. e)
See pages 445–446 for more information.

12. b)
See page 447 for more information.

13. e)
See page 449 for more information.

14. e)
See page 453 for more information.

15. a)
See pages 454, 455, 458 and 459 for more information.

16. d)
See pages 445–446 for more information.

17. b)
See page 453 for more information.

18. e)
See page 444 for more information.

True/False Questions

1. In Canada, negotiable instruments are within provincial jurisdiction.

2. The drawee of a bill of exchange becomes an acceptor when it indicates its willingness to comply with a demand for future payment of the bill by expressing that consent on the face of the bill with the word "accepted" and the date of the acceptance.

3. A promissory note involves two essential parties, rather than the three essential parties of a bill of exchange. A promissory note contains an express promise to pay from the outset and never undergoes presentment for acceptance.

4. A cheque is not a specialized form of a bill of exchange.

5. In order to be adequately negotiated, an order instrument does not have to be endorsed when delivered.

6. As long as the holder meets the proper criterion, the endorser becomes liable on the terms of the instrument even if the drawer's signature has been forged, or a prior endorsement is a forgery.

Answers to True/False Questions

1. False. In Canada, negotiable instruments are within federal jurisdiction.

2. True.

3. True.

4. False. A cheque is a specialized form of a bill of exchange. It is drawn against a bank and contains an implied promise by the drawer that the drawer has funds on deposit at the bank sufficient to meet the amount of the cheque. A cheque is also payable on demand.

5. False. An order instrument must be endorsed as well as delivered in order to be adequately negotiated. A party who purchases an order instrument without requiring proper endorsement acquires limited rights, probably limited to rights against the immediate transferor.

Endorsement is not necessary for a bearer instrument.

6. True.

22

Intellectual Property

Purpose and Significance

Trademarks, copyright, patents, and industrial design are examples of intellectual property. They are the product of mental effort and must be protected if the creators are to be encouraged. This chapter explores the nature of these and other forms of intellectual property and how the law protects such works.

Learning Objectives

A. Discuss the nature and kinds of intellectual property.

B. Consider the developing concept of confidential information.

Content Outline

I. The nature of intellectual property
    A. Industrial property and intellectual trademarks
    B. Should intellectual property be protected

II. Forms of intellectual property

III. Trademarks
    A. Passing-off
    B. Section 7 of the *Trade-marks Act*
    C. Business name
    D. Registered Trademarks
        1. Rights obtained by registration
        2. Duration
    E. Registration
        1. The mark
        2. Requirements for registration
        3. The owner
    F. Opposition proceedings
    G. Remedies for infringement
        1. Unauthorized use
        2. Action for infringement
    H. Assignment, licensing, and franchising

IV. Copyright
    A. Statutory origin
    B. International treaties
    C. Nature of copyright
    D. Limits to copyright
    E. Works in which copyright exists
        1. Literary works
        2. Computer software
        3. Dramatic works
        4. Musical works
        5. Artistic works
        6. Excluded works

Questions on Learning Objectives

Objective A: **Discuss the nature and kinds of intellectual property.**

A.1 What is "intellectual property"? (pp. 470–471)

A.2 List and describe four types of intellectual property. (pp. 471–472, 481, 489, 495)

A.3 What is the tort of "passing-off"? (p. 472)

A.4 Should one register a trademark? (pp. 475–576)

A.5 What remedies exist for infringement of intellectual property? (pp. 479–480)

A.6 List the basic rights of a copyright holder. (p. 482)

A.7 What elements must exist for an invention to be patentable? (p. 498)

Objective B: **Consider the developing concept of confidential information.**

B.1 What is confidential information? (p. 497)

B.2 How does the law protect confidential information? (p. 497)

Answers to Questions on Learning Objectives

A.1 Intellectual property is the term used to describe various types of property, which are the products of mental activity. Intellectual property is concerned with ideas or inventions of which individuality or originality is an essential feature. Moreover, the ideas, information or inventions must qualify as property in the eyes of law to amount to intellectual property.

A.2 The four common types of intellectual property are: trademarks, copyright, patents and industrial designs.

A trademark is a mark that is used for the purpose of distinguishing wares or services. It also refers to a certification mark or a distinguishing guise. It is generally accepted to refer to any visual characteristic of goods or their presentation that serves to distinguish them from goods that do not have the same trade connection.

Copyright is the right to restrain others from using rights that the owner or author has in every original literary, dramatic, musical or artistic work.

A patent is the exclusive property in an invention for a period of twenty years. The property comprises the exclusive right, privilege and liberty of making, constructing and using the invention and selling it to others to be used.

Industrial designs are features of shape, configuration, pattern or ornament that, in a finished article, appeal to the eye.

A.3 A tort of passing-off is misrepresentation of goods, services or a business in such a way as to deceive the public into believing that they are the goods, services or business of some other person and in so doing causes damage to that other person.

A.4 Trademarks are protected at common law through the tort of passing-off. However, registration of trademarks secures certain advantages including the exclusive right to its use throughout Canada so that the right of use is not restricted to the area in which its owner actually does business and has established a reputation. Trademarks that have been registered in Canada may be registered in other countries as well. The registration of the trademark creates the presumption that it is valid and distinctive and is indeed owned by the owner.

A.5 Remedies for infringement of intellectual property include damages, an accounting of profits and an injunction restraining the wrongdoer from further infringements. A court may also order the wrongdoer to allow the proper owner to search for and seize offending materials.

A.6 A copyright holder has the right to produce or reproduce the work in question or any part of it, the right to perform or deliver the work in public and the right to published and unpublished work. The copyright holder also has the right to translate the work, convert the work from one form to another, make a recording or film of a work, communicate the work by radio communication, exhibit the work and authorize any of these rights in others. Unassignable rights of a copyright holder are the right to the integrity of the work, the right to prevent its being distorted or mutilated, the right to prevent it from being used in association with some product, service, cause or institution and the right to be associated with the work and author.

A.7 For an invention to patentable it must be an art, process, machine, manufacturer, or composition of matter or an improvement to such; new; and useful.

B.1 Confidential information is any information that is valuable to people other than its owner. For example, a list of customers or clients may be important information. Similarly, trade secrets or know how are also information which, though not amounting to intellectual property, are valuable.

B.2 The law protects confidential information through the laws of licensing and by protecting covenants that stipulate that the buyer of the information will not divulge the secret to anyone else. Restrictive covenants that restrain an employee from making use of an employer's confidential information when she leaves are enforceable in the courts. Finally, employees, directors and officers of companies that stand in a fiduciary relationship to their employers may not misuse or divulge confidential information acquired in the course of the relationship.

Multiple-Choice Questions

1. Michael has just created a new computer program that he wants to market and make millions of dollars. He has even come up with a catchy name. Obviously, he does not want one of the big high-tech firms to steal his idea. What forms of intellectual property should he consider?

a) Copyright protection for the program and a patent for the name.
b) A patent for the computer program and copyright protection for the name.
c) A patent for the computer program and trademark protection for the name.
d) Copyright protection for the program and trademark protection for the name.
e) Trademark protection for the program and copyright protection for the name.

2. Gillian, a mad scientist, has just found a remedy for the common cold. The remedy requires a simple vaccination at the age of 6 months. After the vaccination, there is no need for further treatment and the person will never get a cold. Gillian has applied for a patent to protect her discovery. Is it possible for Gillian to obtain the patent?

a) No because the invention is a pharmaceutical product.
b) Yes because the invention is a pharmaceutical product.
c) No because the invention is a form of medical treatment.
d) Yes because the invention is a form of medical treatment.
e) No because the invention is not new.

3. Mark has a patent on an invention that makes cars run cleaner, thereby saving the environment. There is a large demand in Canada for such products, but Mark has little money to build and market his invention so it is not available to anyone. The Clean Car Company knows that the invention is not being marketed so, relying on the information filed with the Patent Office, has copied the invention and started to market it. Mark learns of the copying and asks his lawyer for advice. What would be that advice?

a) Sue the Company for patent infringement and win a big damage award.

b) A compulsory license based on abuse of patent rights would be issued if the Company asked the Commissioner of Patents for one.

c) Sue the Company for an injunction to prevent the Company from continuing to market the invention.

d) Ask the Company for a share of the profits.

e) Do nothing as the Company relied on public information.

4. Jennifer is an artist who draws and paints distinctive cartoon animals. Her paintings are mostly done on wooden furniture that is perfect for children. Due to the high demand for her work, Jennifer has decided to protect her works by intellectual property. Also, Jennifer is about to sign a contract with a furniture manufacturer who will reproduce pieces of furniture with her paintings after she creates the original. What forms of intellectual property should Jennifer consider?

a) Copyright protection for the original pieces, industrial design protection for the reproduced furniture, and trademark protection for any distinguishing logo or name.

b) Trademark protection for the original pieces, industrial design protection for the reproduced furniture, and copyright protection for any distinguishing logo or name.

c) Copyright protection for the original pieces, trademark protection for the reproduced furniture, and industrial design protection for any distinguishing logo or name.

d) Industrial design protection for the original pieces, trademark protection for the reproduced furniture, and copyright protection for any distinguishing logo or name.

e) Industrial design protection for the original pieces, copyright protection for the reproduced furniture, and trademark protection for any distinguishing logo or name.

5. Typical of a university student, Dillon has little money to buy textbooks. Instead he usually photocopies a textbook belonging to a friend in the same class. As a result, by the end of third year, Dillon has a large collection of photocopied textbooks. To raise some money to pay his tuition for fourth year, Dillon decides to sell his copied textbooks. In order to advertise the sale, Dillon posts a few pages from each book on a bulletin board to let other students know what books he is selling and what the quality is like. Unfortunately, the publisher of most of the textbooks gets wind of what Dillon is planning and sues him for copyright infringement. What rights has Dillon infringed?

a) The right to reproduce the book and the right to sell the book to the public.

b) The right to publish the book and the right to communicate the book to the public.

c) The right to deliver the book to the public and the right to sell the book to the public.

d) The right to reproduce the book and the right to exhibit the book in public.

e) The right to reproduce the book and the right to deliver the book to the public.

6. As is fairly common at university, Professor Smith prepared a textbook for his second-year class which contains numerous personal notes and articles, and a few articles and parts of chapters from other textbooks which were copied without permission of the authors. On the first day of class, Professor Smith tells his class that the textbook is available from the photocopy shop just down the street from the university. Unfortunately for the photocopy shop, an RCMP officer is a member of the class. After buying the textbook, the officer tells his commander about the book and the RCMP sues the photocopy shop for copyright infringement. What is the likely outcome of the case?

a) The photocopy shop has to pay damages to the RCMP.
b) The photocopy shop owner is given a prison sentence.
c) The photocopy shop wins the suit arguing that the use of the textbook is fair dealing, an exception under the Copyright Act.
d) The photocopy shop sues Professor Smith for putting it into the situation.
e) The photocopy shop has to pay damages to the authors whose work is reproduced in the textbook.

7. The Stones Company is a family-run business in Calgary owned by the Stone family. The Stone Company registered its name as a business name 25 years ago. Six years ago, Stone Limited expanded its business into Alberta, opening stores in Calgary and Edmonton. About the same time that Stone Limited expanded to Alberta, it applied for and obtained a trademark on its name. Both the Stones Company and Stone Limited are in the same line of business. Now Stone Limited has decided to bring a trademark infringement suit against the Stones Company. What is the likely outcome of the suit?

a) The Stones Company will have to change its name.
b) Stone Limited will lose its trademark and have to change its name.
c) The Stones Company will be allowed to continue to use its name, but will have to pay damages to Stone Limited for the six years of infringement.
d) The Stones Company will be allowed to continue to use its name provided it adds the line "not associated with Stone Limited" to the storefront and in all advertisements.
e) The Stones Company will be allowed to continue to use its name provided they move the store to Red Deer where Stone Limited has no store.

8. The Sheep Company, a company that makes all-wool sweaters, has applied for a trademark for their new corporate logo "ALLCOTON." The Horse Company, a company that also makes all-wool sweaters, wants to oppose the application since it is in a similar business and its logo is "ALLTON." On what ground may they oppose?

a) The logo is not distinctive.
b) The application form was not properly filed.
c) The Sheep Company is not the person entitled to registration.

d) The logo is not registrable because it is likely to be confused with a registered trademark

e) The logo is not registrable because it is deceptively misdescriptive of the character of the goods.

9. A sailboat company came up with the idea of a new kind of boat. It put a sail on a mast with a wishbone boom, put the mast on a surfboard and called it a Windsurfer. Before marketing the new boat, the company applied for a patent to protect its invention. Unbeknownst to the company, a 10-year-old in California had put a small sail on a surfboard and gone surfing in Malibu. For what reason did the patent office turn down the Windsurfer's application?

a) The Windsurfer is not a useful object.
b) The Windsurfer is not a new object.
c) The Windsurfer is not an improvement to an existing machine.
d) The Windsurfer is not an art, process, machine, manufacture or composition of matter.
e) The Windsurfer does not have an element of ingenuity in its invention.

10. Which of the following is a definition of goodwill?

a) The good feeling that the owner has for his business.
b) The name or logo associated with a business.
c) The market price that someone will pay for a business.
d) The good work that the owner does for the surrounding community.
e) The difference between the market value of a business as a going concern and its break-up value.

11. What is the geographic area covered by a registered trademark?

a) The city or town where the associated business is located.
b) The county where the associated business is located.
c) The province where the associated business is located.
d) Canada.
e) The whole world.

12. Which of the following are the moral rights under the Copyright Act?

a) The rights to integrity, to prevent its being distorted or mutilated, and to be associated with the work.
b) The rights to control reproduction, to prevent its being abused, and to be anonymous.
c) The rights to integrity, to prevent its being the subject of criticism, and to be associated with the work.
d) The rights to integrity, to prevent its being the subject of criticism, and to be anonymous.

e) The rights to control reproduction, to prevent its being distorted or mutilated, and to be associated with the work.

13. Generally, what is the duration of copyright protection in a book?

a) 50 years.
b) Life of the author.
c) Life of the author plus 50 years.
d) 99 years.
e) Life of the author plus 99 years.

14. What is the principal advantage of obtaining a patent for an invention?

a) The right to make the invention public.
b) The right to exclusive property in the invention for 17 years.
c) The right to make money off the invention.
d) The right to exclusive property in the invention for 20 years.
e) The right to exploit the invention indefinitely without any competition.

15. Of the various forms of intellectual property, which require formal registration and an examination process?

a) Copyright, trademark, patent and industrial design.
b) Copyright, patent and industrial design.
c) Trademark and industrial design.
d) Trademark, patent and industrial design.
e) Trademark and patent.

16. Which of the following are types of intellectual property?
I. Trademarks
II. Patents
III. Confidential information

a) I only
b) II only
c) III only
d) I and II only
e) I, II and III

17. All of the following statements about confidential information are true EXCEPT:

a) Confidential information is valuable.
b) Confidential information is protected at law on the basis of contractual and fiduciary relationships.
c) Confidential information is property.
d) Customer and client lists are examples of confidential information.

e) Misuse of confidential information may lead to an award of damages, an accounting for profits or the imposition of an injunction.

18. Which of the following statements accurately describes the remedies available for infringement of intellectual property?

a) Damages, account of profits, an injunction restraining further infringements and an order to deliver up or dispose of infringing materials are all available to owners of intellectual property for infringements.
b) Damages and an accounting of profits are available to the owner of intellectual property.
c) Damages, injunctions and statutory actions are available to owners of intellectual property.
d) Intellectual property is now governed by statute and the remedies available for infringement are those dictated by the particular statutes in question.
e) The remedies available for infringement include common law and statutory remedies.

Answers to Multiple-Choice Questions

1. d)
See pages 474 and 482 for more information.

2. b)
See page 491 for more information.

3. b)
See page 494 for more information.

4. a)
See page 496 for more information.

5. d)
See page 482 for more information

6. c)
See page 488 for more information.

7. d)
See pages 574–575 for more information.

8. e)
See pages 476–478 for more information.

9. b)
See pages 490–491 for more information.

10. e)
See page 472 for more information.

11. d)
See page 475 for more information.

12. a)
See page 482 for more information.

13. c)
See page 486 for more information.

14. d)
See page 490 for more information.

15. e)
See page 490 for more information.

16. d)
See page 471–472 for more information.

17. c)
See page 497 for more information.

18. a)
See page 479–480, 488–489, 492–493, 496–497 for more information.

True/False Questions

1. Intellectual property is concerned with ideas or contracts of which individuality or originality is an essential feature.

2. A tort of passing-off is misrepresentation of goods, services or a business in such a way as to deceive the public into believing that they are the goods, services or business of some other person and in so doing causes damage to that other person.

3. Trademarks are protected at common law through the tort of passing-off.

4. Registration of trademarks secures certain advantages including the exclusive right to its use throughout Canada so that the right of use is not restricted to the area in which its owner actually does business and has established a reputation

5. Trademarks have been registered in Canada cannot be registered in other countries.

6. The registration of the trademark creates an automatic right that it is valid and distinctive and is indeed owned by the owner.

7. A copyright holder has the right to produce or reproduce the work in question or any part of it, the right to perform or deliver the work in public and the right to publish and unpublished work.

8. The copyright holder also has the right to translate the work, convert the work from one form to another, make a recording or film the work and authorize any of these rights.

9. Unassignable rights of a copyright holder are the right to the integrity of the work, the right to prevent its being distorted or mutilated, the right to prevent it from being used in association with some product, service, cause or institution and the right to be associated with the work and author.

10. For an invention to be patentable it must not be an improvement of an art, process, machine, manufacture, or composition of matter.

11. The laws protects confidential information through the laws of licensing and by protecting covenants that stipulate that the buyer of the information will not divulge the secret to anyone else.

12. Restrictive covenants which restrain an employee from making use of an employer's confidential information when she leaves are enforceable in the courts.

13. Employees, directors and officers of companies that stand in fiduciary relationship to their employers may not misuse or divulge confidential information acquired in the course of the relationship.

Answers to True/False Questions

1. False. Intellectual property is the term used to describe various types of property which are the products of mental activity. Intellectual property is concerned with ideas or inventions of which individuality or originality is an essential feature. Moreover, the ideas, information or inventions must qualify as property in the eyes of the law to amount to intellectual property.

2. True.

3. True.

4. True.

5. False. Trademarks that have been registered in Canada may be registered in other Countries as well.

6. False. The registration of the trademark creates the presumption that it is valid and distinctive and is indeed owned by the owner.

7. True.

8. True.

9. True.

10. False. For an invention to be patentable it must be an art, process, machine, manufacture, or composition of matter or an improvement to such; new; and useful.

11. False. The law protects confidential information through the laws of licensing and by protecting covenants that stipulate that the buyer of the information will not divulge the secret to anyone.

12. True.

13. True.

23

Interests in Land and Their Transfer

Purpose and Significance

With an item of personal property, you either own it or have possession of it. There are really no other types of interests that exist in personal property. Real property is different. First, the meaning of real property is not readily apparent and is explored in this chapter. There is a variety of types of interest in real property. In this chapter, we go on to explore what interests may be created in real property and how one may own those interests. One particular type of interest that is explored is that obtained through adverse possession. Finally, we explore how you can obtain an interest in land.

Learning Objectives

A. Discuss property and land.

B. Discuss the types of interests that may be acquired in real property.

C. Explain co-ownership of real property.

D. Discover the meaning of adverse possession.

E. Describe how a person obtains an interest in land.

Content Outline

I. The nature of property of interests in land
  A. Real property
      1. The meaning of "Property"
      2. The meaning of "Real"
      3. The meaning of "Real Property"
  B. The definition of land
  C. Restrictions on the use of land
      1. Historical restrictions
      2. Nuisance
      3. Public regulation of land use
  D. The development of strict rules in land law

II. Estates in time
  A. Freehold estates
      1. Fee simple estates
      2. Life estate
      3. Rights in the matrimonial home
  B. Leasehold estates
  C. Concurrent interests in estates
      1. Tenancy in common
      2. Joint tenancy
      3. Severance
  D. Condominiums
      1. The nature of ownership in a condominium
      2. Responsibility for maintaining units
      3. Investment risks
      4. Maintenance and management of a condominium
      5. Financing and insurance
  E. Cooperative housing

III. Interests less than estates
    A. Easements
        1. At common law
        2. "Statutory Easements"
        3. Easements by prescription
    B. Covenants
        1. The consequences of a covenant
        2. Restrictive covenant
        3. Remedies for breach of a covenant
        4. Building-scheme covenants
    C. Other interests
        1. Oil, gas, and mineral leases
        2. Licenses

IV. Adverse possession
    A. The reasons for limitation periods
    B. Application of limitation periods to land
    C. Elements of adverse possession
    D. When the owner is presumed to be in possession

V. The transfer of interests in land
    A. On death of the owner
    B. By compulsory sale
    C. By a voluntary grant

VI. The recording of interests in land
    A. English system
    B. Systems in Canada and the United States
        1. Registry systems
        2. Land titles systems
        3. The two systems compared
    C. Claims that are not registered on title
        1. Adverse possession
        2. Arrears of taxes
        3. Creditor's claims
        4. Tenant in possession

Questions on Learning Objectives

Objective A: Discuss property and land.

A.1 What are two meanings of the word "property"? (p. 501)

A.2 What meaning does the word "land" have in the law of real property? (p. 502)

A.3 Describe two types of restrictions on the use of land. (p. 503)

Objective B: Discuss the types of interests that may be acquired in real property.

B.1 What is a fee simple? (p. 504)

B.2 Distinguish a life estate in real property from a leasehold estate. (p. 506)

B.3 List three disadvantages of a life estate. (p. 505)

B.4 What is an easement and how may one be acquired? (p. 511)

B.5 What is a restrictive covenant? Why might you want to extract one? (p. 513)

Objective C: Explain concurrent interests in real property.

C.1 What is co-ownership of land? (p. 507)

C.2 What does it mean to be a tenant in common? (p. 507)

C.3 How is a joint tenancy different from a tenancy in common? (p. 507)

C.4 What types of property interests do condominiums and co-operatives create? (pp. 507–508)

Objective D: **Discover the meaning of adverse possession.**

D.1 Discuss the law of limitations. (p. 515)

D.2 What is adverse possession? (p. 516)

D.3 How can an owner prevent a person from establishing adverse possession of her land? (p. 516)

Objective E: **Describe how a person obtains an interest in land.**

E.1 How may a person dispose of an interest in land during his lifetime? (p. 517)

E.2 What happens to an interest in land if its holder dies intestate? (p. 517)

E.3 Define the word "expropriation." (p. 517)

E.4 What is a reservation? (p. 518)

E.5 Describe the major difference between registration under the registry system and under the land titles system. (pp. 518–519)

Answers to Questions on Learning Objectives

A.1 The word property sometimes means everything that is capable of being owned or that has value. In this sense, property is the thing itself. Property, however, also refers to the legal interests that a person may have in a thing, the rights which the law will recognize and protect. In this sense it is synonymous with ownership. When property is used to mean ownership the word "title" is interchangeable with the words "property" and "ownership."

A.2 Land includes the surface (ground), the minerals beneath the surface, the air above the surface, all buildings affixed to the land, any other things permanently affixed to the surface such as trees and fences.

A.3 The use of land is limited by the government and by private individuals. The government has the power to regulate such things as dangerous activities on land and private individuals may restrain others from activities that interfere with the ordinary enjoyment of their land.

B.1 A fee simple estate is the most common type of land ownership interest in this country. It comes closest to the idea of complete ownership. A fee simple estate gives its owner the right to the land for an unlimited period of time and the power to dispose of the property during life or upon death.

B.2 If a person has the right to use property for a lifetime, her interest is considered a life estate. A life tenant may use the property but may not do anything that would permanently injure the property. Under a lease, the tenant may occupy and use the property for a definite period of time. The critical distinction between the two is that a life estate is for an indefinite period of time whereas a lease is for a definite length of time.

B.3 Disadvantages of the life estate are that it makes the land subject to a life estate difficult to sell, the life tenant is limited in her abilities to make changes on the land without the consent of the remainderman, and the life tenant cannot compel the remainderman (person entitled to the land after the life estate is over) to contribute anything to the cost of repairs and maintenance.

B.4 An easement is the right to enter land owned by another for a special purpose. One common example of an easement is a right of way. An easement may be created by express agreement. It can be sold, given or reserved by a property owner. An easement may be acquired by grant or by prescription. An easement acquired by prescription arises where an adjoining landowner continuously exercises a right openly, notoriously, without fraud or deceit, without use of force or threats against the owner of the land and does so continuously for at least twenty years.

B.5 A restrictive covenant is a promise to refrain from certain conduct on, or use of, land. Restrictive covenants run with the land. If you want to control or restrict the use of property when you sell it you might extract a restrictive covenant from the purchaser. For example, if you own a large lot and you sell a piece of the lot, you may want to ensure that the parcel is used only for residential purposes. In order to ensure that, you would require the purchaser to enter into a restrictive covenant in which she promises not to use the property for commercial purposes.

C.1 If two or more people own the same estate in land at the same time, they are concurrent holders of the estate. That is, they are co-owners. Co-owners have rights to the whole property but no separate rights to any particular part of the property.

C.2 Tenants in common hold shares simultaneously in an estate in land. That is, each tenant in common is entitled to possession of the whole of the property and to share in any income from the property. No tenant is entitled to exclusive use of any portion of the property. A tenant in common may transfer his interest to any third party without consent of the other co-owner. When a tenant in common dies his interest goes to his heir.

C.3 A joint tenancy is created when equal interests in real property are conveyed to two or more people by a single document, which specifies that they are to hold as joint tenants. Joint tenants have a right to survivorship. Thus, when one joint tenant dies, her interest passes to the surviving joint tenant and does not devolve on her estate. A tenant in common need not necessarily hold equal shares and there is no right of survivorship in tenants in common.

C.4 A condominium owner obtains title to a specific apartment or unit and also becomes a tenant in common of all common areas such as hallways. In a co-operative, a group or corporation owns the entire building. An individual buys stock in the corporation and takes an apartment or unit under a long-term lease.

D.1 The law of limitations is the law that stipulates when a person, who has a right of action against another, will lose that right if not pursued within a specified period of time.

D.2 A person may acquire title to land by adverse possession. To do so, he must stay in exclusive possession of the land, using it as an owner and ignoring the claims of other persons including the true owner. Possession must be open, notorious and continuous.

D.3 To prevent acquisitions by adverse possession, a property owner must take steps to interrupt the other's possession before the limitation period elapses. The most effective interruption is to have the possessor ejected from the land. Another is to demand and receive rent from the possessor in acknowledgement of the owner's rights to the land.

E.1 A person may dispose of interests in land during her lifetime by transferring them to another in a deed of conveyance. A deed, you will recall, is a document made under seal.

E.2 A person dies intestate when he dies without leaving a will. In the absence of a will, interests in land will pass according to the statutory rules of inheritance in the province in which the person resided.

E.3 Expropriation refers to compulsory transfer of land. Normally, it refers to acquisition of the land by the government. (Compensation must be paid for the land).

E.4 A reservation of land occurs when an owner conveys away her whole interest except for a part that she expressly reserves to herself.

E.5 When an interest in land is created by document under the registry system, you must register a copy of that document. Then, when the land is transferred, the new purchaser must search the documents at the registry house in order to determine what state title to the land is in. If you fail to register the document, then a purchaser who buys the land without knowledge of the unregistered claim buys free of that claim.

Under the land titles system, when a purchaser buys property, the Land Titles Office provides a document showing the state of the title and the purchaser is entitled to rely on the document. He doesn't need to got through all the pieces of paper that have been registered to try and understand the state of the title and the interests involved.

Multiple-Choice Questions

1. In his will, Chris left a piece of land to "Sarah for life and Bill thereafter." Bill receives an offer from Jane to buy the land for $50 000 with immediate possession. What is he entitled to do?

a) Bill could accept Jane's offer and transfer the land with immediate possession.
b) Bill could join with Sarah to accept Jane's offer and transfer the land with immediate possession.
c) Bill could sue Sarah in court to have the land divided between the two of them and then negotiate with Jane for his part of the land.
d) Bill could challenge the will in court to remove Sarah's interest in the land.
e) Bill could accept Jane's offer but stipulate that possession will not occur for 10 years.

2. Paul purchases a house from Vera, with possession in three months. The deed of conveyance describes only the land on which the house is situated and includes no description of the house. Which of the following is Vera entitled to do before the closing date of the sale of the land?

a) Vera may move the house from its foundation and have it delivered to another piece of land.
b) Vera may destroy the house because of hazardous chemicals within the walls.
c) Vera may remove all the built-in shelves and cupboards in the house.

d) Vera may do nothing to the house.

e) Vera may cut down the two old maple trees in the front yard.

3. Which of the following are the elements of an easement obtained by prescription?

a) Use of the land for 20 years, in a continuous, open and notorious manner, without fraud or deceit, and without using force or threats against the owner of the land.

b) Use of the land for 5 years, in an intermittent, open and notorious manner, without fraud or deceit, and without using force or threats against the owner of the land.

c) Use of the land for 20 years, in an intermittent manner, with fraud or deceit, and with force or threats against the owner of the land.

d) Use of the land for 5 years, in a continuous, open and notorious manner, without fraud or deceit, and without using force or threats against the owner of the land.

e) Use of the land for 20 years, in an intermittent, open and notorious manner, without fraud or deceit, and without using force or threats against the owner of the land.

4. Kerry's neighbours have parties every Friday night that last until 4 a.m. and make a lot of noise keeping Kerry awake. What should Kerry do to stop the noise?

a) Kerry should buy earplugs.

b) Kerry should ask the municipality to pass a by-law prohibiting noisy parties after 9 p.m.

c) Kerry should seek a court-ordered injunction under the tort of nuisance.

d) Kerry should ask a court to place a restrictive covenant on the deed for his neighbour's house.

e) Kerry should seek a court order of specific performance under the tort of nuisance.

5. Which of the following statements about adverse possession is correct?

a) A person has a right of action against another and must pursue it within a definite time period or lose it.

b) Ownership of the land in question is transferred in a deed of conveyance.

c) Equal interests in real property are conveyed to two or more people by a single document.

d) A person stays in exclusive possession of the land with the owner's consent.

e) A person stays in exclusive possession of the land openly, notoriously and continuously, and uses the land like an owner would.

6. Garner built a one-foot-thick stone wall at the edge of his property so that the edge of the wall closest to his house was exactly on the property line with his neighbour Jane. Jane objects to having the wall sit on her property. Can Jane successfully sue Garner over the wall?

a) Yes, based on the tort of trespass.
b) Yes, based on the tort of conversion.
c) Yes, based on the tort of nuisance.
d) No, Jane should simply ignore the wall and be thankful she is separated from her neighbour.
e) Yes, based on a breach of Jane's contract to purchase her house.

7. In 1976, Mark and Dean bought cottages on adjoining pieces of land. Both cottages had frontage on the lake, but only Dean's frontage was suitable for building a boat dock. Mark agreed to pay for half the cost of building the dock if Dean agreed to let Mark keep his boat tied up at the dock. Dean agreed, but nothing was ever written down. Through the years a firmly established path was created between Mark's cottage and the dock. In fact, Mark put gravel down on the path every spring to help limit the destruction of the surrounding forest. In 1997, Dean dies and the cottage is sold to Bill. The first thing Bill does is erect a fence on the property line with Mark, remove the gravel on the path and reseed the path. What would be Mark's best course of action?

a) Mark should ask a court to declare that the path is a public path so that Bill has to remove his fence.
b) Mark should tell Bill that Dean sold him the land under the path and sold him half the dock, but Mark had forgotten to register his interest.
c) Mark should sue Bill for the tort of nuisance for removing the gravel on his path.
d) Mark should ask a court to declare that the path is subject to an easement so Bill has to remove his fence.
e) Mark should tear down the fence, re-gravel the path and tell Bill that he owns half the dock.

8. In Nova Scotia, Donald buys a house from Michael after having his lawyer search title at the Land Registry Office. His lawyer missed a deed that was registered in 1971 in which Michael, the seller, had sold the property to his daughter Carol. Therefore, he no longer owns the property. Who can Donald sue over the missed deed?

a) Donald should sue his lawyer for negligence for missing the deed.
b) Donald should sue the government who guaranteed the accuracy of title shown on record.
c) Donald should sue Carol for possession of the property.
d) Donald should sue Michael for breaching the contract of sale with Carol.
e) Donald should sue nobody, as there is no possible lawsuit.

9. In Manitoba, Donald buys a house from Michael after having his lawyer search title at the Land Title Office. His lawyer missed a deed that was registered in 1971 in which Michael, the seller, had sold the property to his daughter Carol. Therefore, he no longer owns the property. Who can Donald sue over the missed deed?

a) Donald should sue his lawyer for negligence for missing the deed.
b) Donald should sue the government who has guaranteed the accuracy of title shown on record.
c) Donald should sue Carol for possession of the property.
d) Donald should sue Michael for breaching the contract of sale with Carol.
e) Donald should sue nobody, as there is no possible lawsuit.

10. The New Age Gas Company has acquired a mineral lease from Mr. Jones to look for oil on Mr. Jones's land. They find oil in a back corner of the 100-acre lot. The Company brings in the necessary equipment to pump the oil and builds an asphalt road across Mr. Jones's best wheat field to allow access to the site. Mr. Jones is angry and wants to object to the road. What would be Mr. Jones' best course of action?

a) Mr. Jones should sue the Company for the tort of nuisance.
b) Mr. Jones should bill the Company for the price of the wheat lost each year due to the road.
c) Mr. Jones should sue the Company for the tort of trespass.
d) Mr. Jones should rip up the lease and kick the Company off his land.
e) Mr. Jones should do nothing since the oil lease includes the right to travel back and forth over the land and the right to move equipment.

11. Which of the following are the ways in which interests in land may be transferred?

a) On the coming of age of the owner, by compulsory sale and by a voluntary grant.
b) On the death of the owner, by voluntary sale and by a compulsory grant.
c) On the death of the owner, by compulsory sale and by a voluntary grant.
d) On the coming of age of the owner, by compulsory sale and by a compulsory grant.
e) On the death of the owner, by voluntary sale and by a voluntary grant.

12. What quality must a restrictive covenant have in common with an easement if it is to be enforceable?

a) Be continuous for 20 years.
b) Have the equivalent of a dominant and servient tenement.
c) Have a negative effect on a neighbouring piece of land.
d) Be written into a deed of conveyance.
e) End when the land is transferred to a third person.

13. Which of the following is a definition of real property?

a) A legal interest in property other than land.
b) The surface of a piece of land.
c) A form of property that physically exists.
d) A legal interest in land.
e) The buildings attached to, but not including, a piece of land.

14. Which of the following describes the nature of ownership in a condominium?

a) Exclusive possession of a unit.
b) Exclusive possession of the common elements and an undivided part ownership, in common with other unit owners, of the units.
c) Exclusive possession of a unit and of the common elements.
d) An undivided part ownership, in common with other unit owners, of the entire building (i.e., units and common elements).
e) Exclusive possession of a unit and an undivided part ownership, in common with other unit owners, of the common elements.

15. Sarah, Caitlin and Emily own the family farm in fee simple as joint tenants and all three live on the farm with their husbands. Sarah and Caitlin die at the same time in a tragic car crash. Who owns the property now?

a) Sarah's estate, Caitlin's estate and Emily.
b) Sarah's estate and Caitlin's estate.
c) Emily.
d) Sarah's husband, Caitlin's husband and Emily.
e) Sarah's husband, Caitlin's husband and Emily's husband.

16. All of the following statements about co-ownership of land are correct EXCEPT:

a) Co-owners of land are entitled to simultaneous possession of the property.
b) Co-owners of land are not entitled to any particular part of the property.
c) Co-owners of land may leave their interests in the land to their heirs in a will.
d) Co-owners of land are entitled to possession of the whole of the land.
e) Co-owners of land may transfer their interests in land to third parties.

17. Which of the following statements is correct?

a) Adverse possession of land refers to the situation where a person has a right of action against another and must pursue it within a definite time period or lose the right.
b) Transferring the right in a deed of conveyance creates adverse possession of land.
c) Adverse possession of land is created when equal interests in real property are conveyed to two or more people by a single document.

d) Adverse possession of land refers to the situation where a person stays in exclusive possession of the land using it like an owner and the possession is open, notorious and continuous.

e) Adverse possession of land is created by possession of another's land.

18. Which of the following is/are restrictive covenants?

I. A promise to build a fence between your land and your neighbour's property.

II. A promise to keep your fence to a maximum height of 6 feet.

III. A promise to keep the fence in good repair.

a) I only

b) II only

c) III only

d) I and II only

e) I, II and III

Answers to Multiple-Choice Questions

1. b)
See pages 504–505 for more information.

2. d)
See page 502 for more information.

3. a)
See pages 512 for more information.

4. c)
See page 503 for more information.

5. e)
See page 516 for more information

6. c)
See page 503 for more information.

7. d)
See page 512 for more information.

8. a)
See pages 518–519 for more information.

9. b)
See pages 519–520 for more information.

10. e)
See page 514 for more information.

11. c)
See page 517 for more information.

12. b)
See page 513 for more information.

13. d)
See page 502 for more information.

14. e)
See page 508 for more information.

15. c)
See page 507 for more information.

16. c)
See page 507 for more information.

17. d)
See page 515 for more information.

18. b)
See page 513 for more information.

True/False Questions

1. The word property means possession.

2. The use of land is limited by the government and by private individuals. The government has the power to regulate such things as dangerous activities on land and private individuals may restrain others from activities that interfere with the ordinary enjoyment of their land.

3. If a person has the right to use property for a lifetime, her interest is considered a life estate. A life tenant may use the property but may not do anything that would permanently injure the property. Under a lease, the tenant may occupy and use the property for a definite period of time. The critical distinction between the two is that a life estate is for an indefinite period of time whereas a lease is for a definite length of time.

4. A joint tenancy is created when two equal interests in real property are conveyed to one party by a single document that specifies that they are only one tenant.

5. A person may acquire title to land by adverse possession. To do so, he must stay in exclusive possession of the land, using it as an owner and ignoring the claims of other persons including the true owner. Possession must be open, notorious and continuous.

6. Expropriation refers to voluntary transfer of land. Normally, it refers to acquisition of the land by the another party.

Answers to True/False Questions

1. False. The word property sometimes means everything that is capable of being owned or has value. In this sense, property is the thing itself. Property, however, also refers to the legal interests that a person may have in a thing — the rights that the law will recognize and protect. In this sense it is synonymous with ownership. When property is used to mean ownership the word "title" is interchangeable with the words "property" and "ownership."

2. True.

3. True.

4. False. A joint tenancy is created when equal interests in real property are conveyed to two or more people by a single document that specifies that they are to hold as joint tenants. Joint tenants have a right to survivorship. Thus, when one joint tenant dies, her interest passes to the surviving joint tenant and does not devolve on her estate. A tenant in common need not necessarily hold equal shares and there is no right of survivorship in tenants in common.

5. True.

6. False. Expropriation refers to compulsory transfer of land. Normally, it refers to acquisition of the land by the government. (Compensation must be paid for the land.)

24

Landlord and Tenant

Purpose and Significance

Most of us will rent accommodation at some point in our lives. When the rental is a lease, the rules of the game are different than in a contractual situation such as the rental of an evening's accommodation in a hotel.

In this chapter we will discover what a lease is. We will then look at the promises that a landlord and tenant exchange. If those promises are breached, remedies exist for both the landlord and tenant; those remedies will be discussed. As well, because it is important to note how to end a lease, we will examine termination. Finally, we will consider what happens when a tenant makes permanent alterations or additions to the leased premises.

Learning Objectives

A. Explain the nature of a lease.

B. Examine common covenants of landlords and tenants.

C. Discuss the remedies available to landlords and tenants.

D. Examine how a lease may be terminated.

E. Explore the concept of a fixture.

Content Outline

I. The nature of the relationship
    A. Exclusive possession
    B. Definite or ascertainable period

II. Classes of tenancies
    A. Term certain
    B. Periodic tenancy
    C. Tenancy at will
    D. Tenancy at sufferance

III. Covenants
    A. The price paid for a definite term
    B. The unqualified nature of the promise
    C. The limited range of relief from payment
    D. The landlord is also bound by the covenant
    E. Assignment and subletting
        1. Freedom to assign
        2. A term requiring the landlord's consent
        3. Withholding consent
        4. Subletting
    F. Restriction on use of premises
    G. Fitness for occupancy
    H. Repairs
        1. The general rule
        2. The landlord's duties in particular circumstances
        3. The tenant's duties in particular circumstances
        4. The usual covenants in the lease of an entire building
        5. The usual covenants in the lease of part of a building
    I. Quiet enjoyment
    J. Insurance
        1. Who takes responsibilities for obtaining insurance?

2. The consequences of severe damage to leased premises

3. Provision of services and payment of taxes

IV. Remedies of the landlord for breach of covenant
  A. Damages and rent at common law
    1. Relevance of the contract duty to mitigate
    2. Effect of bankruptcy and insolvency act
  B. Eviction
  C. Distress
  D. Injunction

V. Remedies of the tenant for breach of covenant
  A. Damages
  B. Injunction
  C. Termination of the lease

VI. Termination and renewal of a tenancy
  A. Surrender
  B. Forfeiture
  C. Termination by notice to quit
    1. Periodic tenancies
    2. Tenant that remains in possession after the expiration of a term certain
    3. Parties may set their own terms for notice
  D. Renewal

VII. Fixtures
  A. General rules for ownership of fixtures
  B. Determining whether an object is a fixture
  C. Tenant's fixtures
  D. Advantages of an express agreement about fixtures

VIII. Oral leases

IX. Transfer of the landlord's interest
  A. Relationship between a tenant and a purchaser of the landlord's interest
  B. Privity of contract with the former landlord
  C. Relationship between a tenant and the landlord's mortgagee
  D. The need to register a long-term lease

X. Leasebacks
  A. Long-term leases in the united kingdom
  B. The growth of long-term leases in North America
  C. Business incentives for the use of leasebacks
  D. Options to purchase in leasebacks

XI. Residential tenancies
- A. The changing needs of residential tenants
- B. Legislated protection for tenants
    1. Restrictions on security deposits
    2. Landlord's obligation to maintain premises
    3. Freeing a tenant from further performance after a landlord's breach
    4. Freeing a tenant from further performance by applying the doctrine of frustration
    5. Abolition of the remedy of distress
    6. Landlord's duty to mitigate
    7. Assignment, subletting, and termination by notice to quit
    8. Municipalities may establish mediation and arbitration

Questions on Learning Objectives

Objective A: Explain the nature of a lease.

A.1 Describe the two essential characteristics of a lease. (pp. 525–526)

A.2 What is the difference between a lease for an ascertained period and one for an ascertainable period? (p. 527)

A.3 What is the difference between a term certain and a periodic tenancy? (p. 527)

A.4 Distinguish a tenancy at will from a tenancy at sufferance. (pp. 527–528)

A.5 When must a lease be in writing to be enforceable? (p. 542)

Objective B: Examine common covenants of landlords and tenants.

B.1 List and describe two covenants that a tenant must fulfill. (pp. 528–529, 530–531)

B.2 Discuss how the covenant to make repairs and pay insurance may apply to either the landlord or the tenant. (pp. 531–532, 533–534)

B.3 Does the landlord have an obligation to ensure that the premises are fit for occupancy? (p. 531)

B.4 Distinguish a sublease from an assignment of a lease. (pp. 529–530)

B.5 Distinguish the obligations of a tenant who assigns his lease from a tenant who subleases. (p. 530)

Objective C: Discuss the remedies available to landlords and tenants.

C.1 Is a tenant liable to pay rent if he abandons the premises without giving proper notice to the landlord? (p. 535)

C.2 Describe the landlord's remedy of eviction. (p. 536)

C.3 What is a power of distress? (p. 536)

C.4 List and briefly explain the three remedies that a tenant has if a landlord breaches her covenants. (pp. 537–538)

Objective D: Examine how a lease may be terminated.

D.1 What is the difference between surrendering and forfeiting a lease? (pp. 538–539)

D.2 What length of notice is required to bring a tenancy to an end? (p. 539)

D.3 How may a tenant ensure that he has the right to renew a lease? (p. 540)

Objective E: Explore the concept of a fixture.

E.1 What is a fixture? (p. 541)

E.2 What is the legal result of an object becoming a fixture? (p. 541)

E.3 What fixtures may a tenant remove when he vacates the premises? (pp. 541–542)

Answers to Questions on Learning Objectives

A.1 The two key characteristics of a lease are that the interest in land is for a definite period of time and the tenant is entitled to exclusive possession. That is, the tenant controls the land and has the right to exclude all others, including the owner, for a fixed period.

A.2 If a lease is for an ascertained period its duration is specified. A lease for an ascertainable period does not have its duration specifically set but the duration can be calculated. For example, if the lease specifies a date on which the lease begins and the date on which it will end then the duration of the lease can be calculated. That is, its duration is ascertainable.

A.3 A lease for a term certain is a tenancy that expires on a specific day without further act of either party. A periodic tenancy, on the other hand, renews itself automatically on the last day of the term for a further term of the same duration unless either the landlord or the tenant serves notice to bring the tenancy to an end.

A.4 A tenancy at will is not really a leasehold interest at all because it does not last for a definite period nor does the tenant have the right to exclude the landlord. It refers to the situation where the tenant is allowed on premises at the landlord's will. The landlord may demand possession at any time without notice.

A tenancy at sufferance is also not a tenancy. It normally is a situation of an overholding tenant. An overholding tenant is one who was in possession rightly under a lease but stays in possession after the term of the lease expires.

A.5 A lease of three years or longer duration must be in writing in order to be enforceable. The Statute of Frauds requires this.

B.1 The tenant must pay rent to the landlord. As well, the tenant must abide by any restriction on use of premises stipulated by the landlord.

B.2 Neither the landlord nor the tenant has an obligation to make repairs to the premises unless one or the other expressly promises to do so. However, the tenant is not able to use the premises in a way that causes excessive wear nor is the tenant able to cause waste to the premises. There are economic and legal incentives for the landlord to keep the structure and common areas of the leased premises in a reasonable state of repair.

Again, in the absence of an express provision, neither the landlord nor the tenant must insure the premises.

B.3 The landlord does not have an obligation to ensure that the premises are fit for occupancy unless he expressly so promises to the tenant.

B.4 An assignment is a transfer of the whole of the balance of the tenant's term to a third party. A sublease is a transfer of part only of the tenant's term to a third party.

B.5 If an assignee of a lease performs all the covenants, the tenant has no further right or interest in the lease. In a sublease, the tenant remains liable to the lessor. In addition, the terms of the sublease may differ materially from the main lease. Under both an assignment and a sublease, the tenant remains liable to the landlord to perform all covenants in the main lease.

C.1 If the landlord gives notice to the tenant that he will sublet the premises and hold the tenant liable for any deficiency, then the tenant will be liable for that deficiency. However, if the landlord leaves the premises vacant, he may sue the tenant for all the rent that is owing over the period of inadequate notice.

C.2 Eviction is the landlord's right to re-enter the premises for the tenant's failure to pay rent.

C.3 Distress is the landlord's right to seize assets of the tenant of the leasehold premises and to sell them to pay for arrears of rent.

C.4 If a landlord breaches his promise to the tenant, the tenant may recover damages for breach, get an injunction to restrain the landlord from further breach or terminate the lease and vacate the premises.

D.1 When a lease expires, vacating the premises by the tenant is termed "surrender." Surrender may also take place during the term of the tenancy if the landlord and tenant so agree. Forfeiture, on the other hand, refers to the situation when the landlord evicts the tenant and causes the tenant to lose the lease.

D.2 The length of notice required to bring a tenancy to an end is normally now set by provincial legislation. Where the legislation does not set the period, the length of notice in a periodic tenancy is one clear period. If the parties wish to alter the period they may do so by an express term of the lease.

D.3 In order to ensure that a tenant has the right to renew a lease, she may obtain an option. Under an option the tenant pays a certain amount in order to obtain the space at the end of the leasehold period if she so wishes.

E.1 A fixture is an item of personal property that has become permanently affixed to the land or a building on the land.

E.2 Once an object becomes a fixture, it belongs to the owner of the land. A tenant cannot normally remove fixtures.

E.3 The only exception to the general rules against removing fixtures is when the fixtures become the tenant's. Tenant's fixtures are those that are attached for the convenience of the tenant or for the better enjoyment of the object or that are brought onto the premises for the purpose of carrying on some trade or business. A tenant may remove those trade fixtures before the end of the tenancy provided that in doing so the tenant does not do permanent damage to the structure and repairs whatever damage is done. If the tenant leaves without removing the fixtures and the term expires, the tenant loses the right to remove the fixtures.

Multiple-Choice Questions

1. Jay owns a warehouse, which he rents to Robin. The terms of the rental arrangement have been a series of leases, which always terminate on December 31. No written lease was entered for the current year although Jay continues to let Robin occupy the premises at the same rent as the previous year. On May 12, Jay sells the warehouse for a very favourable price, the closing date being May 31. On May 13, Jay tells Robin to make sure that he has moved out by May 31. Must Robin comply with the request to leave?

a) Yes because a tenant is required to follow all commands of his landlord.
b) No because one element of a lease is exclusive possession, even against a landlord.
c) Yes because an overholding tenant may be evicted at any time.

d) No because a minimum notice period of two months is required for terminating any lease.

e) Yes because the selling of the property always terminates all leases.

2. Alan found a house with a "For Rent" sign on it. Alan went to the landlord, Mr. Smith, and arranged to rent the house starting immediately. The lease, in writing and signed by both parties, stated that: i) The rent was $200 per month due on the first day of the month; ii) Alan was to be the only one with a key; iii) the rental arrangement would continue until Alan could afford to build his own house, or Mr. Smith needed the house for a family member, which ever came first. After being in the house for 2 months, Alan finds that the roof leaks badly every time it rains. Alan wants to get out of the lease. What advice should a lawyer give Alan?

a) There is no lease since the house is unfit for habitation.
b) Sue Mr. Smith to force him to repair the roof.
c) There is no lease since Alan was not given exclusive possession.
d) Sue Mr. Smith for breach of his duties as a landlord.
e) There is no lease since the term of the lease is not definite.

3. John found the house of his dreams and entered a two-year lease with Mr. Smith. Being interested in the law, John made sure all the necessary elements of a lease were present. After being in the house for 6 months, John learned he had been accepted to law school and given a full scholarship. The law school is 2000 miles away so John had to give up his house and move. John advertised in the local paper for a new tenant, and ended up assigning the remainder of the lease to Louise. After moving in, Louise decided she does not like the placement of the windows so cut new holes in the walls for windows. She also thought the rent was too high so only paid half the amount. Mr. Smith was furious. He never agreed to the assignment and wanted Louise out and the damages repaired. Who should Mr. Smith sue?

a) Sue John because the assignment was invalid since Louise did not pay the proper rent.
b) Sue Louise for the damage she has done to the house.
c) Sue John because he is still liable under the lease although he assigned his obligations.
d) Sue John and Louise since both are parties to the lease.
e) Sue John and Louise for breach of the terms of the lease.

4. Cathy has a two-year lease with John for a small house. A month after she moves in, Cathy is transferred out of the country for 18 months. She still adores the house so arranges an 18-month sublet with Alan. The terms of the sublet set the rent at three-quarters the rent that Cathy was paying. John is not notified of the sublet. For six months everything is fine, then Alan starts having loud noisy parties which result in numerous holes in the walls of the house. John drops by one day to fix a leaky faucet and discovers all the damage and that Cathy is out of

the country. Also, the rent has not been fully paid for the past six months. Who should John sue?

a) Sue Alan for the damage to the house.
b) Sue Cathy for the missing rent.
c) Sue Alan for the missing rent.
d) Sue Cathy for the missing rent, for the damage to the house and for breaching the lease by not informing him of the sublet.
e) Sue Alan and Cathy for the missing rent, for the damage to the house and for breaching the lease by not informing him of the sublet.

5. Stan rents the ground floor and basement of a building from Marilyn. The space has been a restaurant under various managers for the past ten years. Marilyn assumed that Stan would open a restaurant. Instead, Stan opens a nightclub that serves food and stays open until 3 a.m. 6 nights a week. Marilyn has an apartment on the upper floors of the building and is very bothered by the noise. What would be Marilyn's best course of action?

a) Sue Stan for breaching the lease for not opening a restaurant as she thought.
b) Evict Stan because of the noise level.
c) Sue Stan for noise pollution.
d) Sue Stan for not treating the premises in a tenant-like manner.
e) Do nothing because there is nothing a landlord can do about how the tenant uses the premises if there is no restriction in the lease.

6. Gale rents a space for an office and showroom from Keith. The rent is $400 per month plus five percent of the gross profits from the designer clothing business Gale intends to open in the space. For the first three months, Gale has no sales as she is still setting up the business so the rent is just $400. For the next six months, business is not good so there are no gross profits and Gale fails to pay the $400 per month. Keith becomes tired of his premises being used, but receiving no income. What would be Keith's best course of action?

a) Sue Gale for the missing rent or the right to distrain.
b) Evict Gale and sue for the right to distrain.
c) Sue Gale for the missing rent and an injunction.
d) Evict Gale and sue for an injunction.
e) Sue Gale for the missing rent, for the right to distrain and for an injunction and evict her.

7. Brian is looking for a building for his computer service business and where he can live in the back. He locates the perfect building on the main street of town, which has an area for a store on the main floor and an apartment on the second floor. He rents the building from Mr. Smith and opens his store. Four months after Brian moves in, Mr. Smith starts repairs on the front of the building. The work involves cleaning and repointing all the brickwork. The work requires that scaffolding be erected over the front of the building, completely blocking the

entrance to the store. The work will take 8 months. After 2 months, Brian discovers that his sales are down 70%. What would be Brian's best course of action?

a) Sue Mr. Smith for damages in the form of his lost profits.
b) Sue Mr. Smith for termination of the lease.
c) Sue Mr. Smith for an injunction to stop the work.
d) Sue Mr. Smith for a right of distress.
e) None of the above.

8. Bill rents the third floor of a three-storey building for his bookkeeping practice. He has been in the same location for fifteen years and all his clients are within walking distance of his office. Occasionally there has been a bit of flooding in the basement of the building when the snow melts in the spring, but it has never inconvenienced Bill. This year, however, the flooding has been very bad all over town and in Bill's building the water reached halfway up the walls of the first floor. It was predicted that it would take weeks for the water to subside and the building to be repaired. This meant Bill could not get to his office and it was tax time, the busiest time of year. What would be Bill's best course of action?

a) Sue the landlord for damages resulting from the building being closed for a month.
b) Sue the landlord for an injunction to prevent the landlord barring Bill from his office.
c) Sue the landlord for termination of the lease and vacate the premises.
d) Refuse to pay the landlord any rent.
e) Accept that there is nothing the landlord can do and try and arrange a way to get his records so he can work at home.

9. For twenty years, Joyce has run a children's book and toy store out of the same premises. Joyce has decided to move to a small town so she gives her landlord the appropriate notice of her departure. Because she intends to open another, smaller book and toy store in the new town, Joyce wants to take all the store's fixtures that she installed twenty years ago. The landlord has located a new tenant who wants to open a store at that location and who wants to use the existing fixtures. May Joyce legally remove the fixtures?

a) No because once an object is attached to a building it becomes part of the land so the fixtures now belong to the landlord.
b) Yes because she bought the fixtures.
c) No because the landlord has included the fixtures in the next tenant's lease.
d) Yes because, although they are fixtures, they are trade fixtures that may be removed when a tenant vacates.
e) Yes because, although they are fixtures, they were attached for their better enjoyment.

10. What are the classes of tenancies?

a) Term certain.
b) Periodic.
c) At will.
d) At sufferance.
e) All of the above.

11. In what ways may a lease be terminated?

a) By surrender, by forfeiture or by notice to quit.
b) By notice to quit.
c) By surrender or by eviction.
d) By forfeiture or by notice to quit.
e) By surrender, by forfeiture, by notice to quit or by eviction.

12. Gunz entered a term certain lease of a warehouse for five years. During the term of the lease the landlord, Brown, mortgaged the land to Sweetwater Mortgage Company. Since the mortgage gives Sweetwater title to the land, is Gunz's lease affected?

a) Yes because the landlord has now changed.
b) No because the lease interest was given first so the mortgage is subject to the lease.
c) Yes because Sweetwater now has the right to evict Gunz if Brown defaults on the mortgage.
d) No because the landlord has not changed.
e) Yes because Sweetwater can now increase the rent anytime that it wants.

13. What is a leaseback?

a) A situation where both the tenant and the landlord switch roles in relation to a different building.
b) A situation where the tenant constructed the building and then sold it to a financial institution before becoming the tenant.
c) A lease where the tenant has the right to give the premises back to the landlord at any time without notice.
d) A lease where the term is more than fifty years.
e) A situation where the lease covers premises which are out back of another building.

14. What are some of the differences that distinguish a residential tenancy from a commercial tenancy?

a) The landlord has a duty to mitigate, no remedy of distress, applicability of the doctrine of frustration and an obligation to maintain the premises.

b) The landlord has a duty to mitigate, a remedy of distress, applicability of the doctrine of frustration and no obligation to maintain the premises.

c) The landlord has no duty to mitigate, a remedy of distress, no applicability of the doctrine of frustration and no obligation to maintain the premises.

d) The landlord has a duty to mitigate, a remedy of distress, applicability of the doctrine of frustration and an obligation to maintain the premises.

e) The landlord has no duty to mitigate, no remedy of distress, no applicability of the doctrine of frustration and an obligation to maintain the premises.

15. What led to the distinction between commercial and residential tenancies?

a) The need for the government to control slum landlords.

b) The baby boom following World War II.

c) The inequality of bargaining positions between a landlord and a residential tenant.

d) The dramatic rise in the cost of housing and the influx of immigrants and rural Canadians to the cities.

e) None of the above.

16. What is a tenant's fixture?

a) It is an object permanently affixed to a building or real property.

b) It is an object that has been fastened to a building with the intention that it should become part of it.

c) It is an object attached to a building or to real property for the convenience of the tenant, the better enjoyment of the object, or the purpose of carrying on some trade or business.

d) It is the right of a tenant to sue her landlord for breach of a covenant in a lease.

e) It is the rights to restrain a landlord from breach of the covenant of quiet enjoyment.

17. Which of the following is/are remedies of the landlord for breach of covenant by the tenant?
I. Distress
II. Eviction
III. Injunction

a) I only
b) II only
c) III only
d) I and II only
e) I, II and III

18. All of the following statements are correct EXCEPT:

a) A lease is an interest in land.
b) A lease entitles the tenant to exclusive possession.

c) A lease is for a definite or ascertainable period of time.

d) A lease is the right to enter another's land.

e) A lease for more than three years duration must be in writing to be enforceable.

Answers to Multiple-Choice Questions

1. c)
See page 528 for more information.

2. e)
See pages 527–528 for more information.

3. c)
See pages 529–530 for more information.

4. d)
See page 530 for more information.

5. e)
See pages 530–531 for more information

6. a)
See page 536 for more information.

7. b)
See page 538 for more information.

8. e)
See page 538 for more information.

9. d)
See page 542 for more information.

10. e)
See pages 527–528 for more information.

11. a)
See pages 538–539 for more information.

12. b)
See page 543 for more information.

13. b)
See page 545 for more information.

14. a)

See pages 546–547 for more information.

15. d)

See page 546 for more information.

16. c)

See page 542 for more information.

17. e)

See page 534–537 for more information.

18. d)

See page 525–526 for more information.

True/False Questions

1. The two key characteristics of a lease are that the interest in land is for a definite period of time and the tenant is entitled to exclusive possession. That is, the tenant controls the land and has the right to exclude all others, including the owner, for a fixed period.

2. A lease of three years or longer duration does not be in writing in order to be enforceable.

3. The landlord does not have an obligation to ensure that the premises are fit for occupancy unless he expressly so promises to the tenant.

4. If an assignee of a lease performs all the covenants, the tenant has no further right or interest in the lease. In a sublease, the tenant remains liable to the lessor. In addition, the terms of the sublease may differ materially from the main lease. Under both an assignment and a sublease, the tenant remains liable to the landlord to perform all covenants in the main lease.

5. If a landlord breaches his promise to the tenant, the tenant may recover damages for tort in law.

6. In order to ensure that a tenant has the right to renew a lease, the tenant need to pay for an option.

Answers to True/False Questions

1. True.

2. False. A lease of three years or longer duration must be in writing in order to be enforceable. The Statute of Frauds requires this.

3. True.

4. True.

5. False. If a landlord breaches his promise to the tenant, the tenant may recover damages for breach, get an injunction to restrain the landlord from further breach or terminate the lease and vacate the premises.

6. False. In order to ensure that a tenant has the right to renew a lease, the tenant may obtain an option. Under an option the tenant pays a certain amount in order to obtain the space at the end of the leasehold period if she so wishes.

25

Mortgages of Land and Real Estate Transactions

Purpose and Significance

As Canadians, we enjoy a standard of living that makes owning a home possible. Few of us, however, can afford to buy our houses outright, so we rely on mortgages to provide the purchase money. As most of us will be involved with mortgages at some stage in our lives, it is important to have a basic understanding of the law relating to mortgages.

This chapter deals with mortgages as security for land. First we describe mortgages. Then we describe the major rights and remedies of the lender (mortgagee) and the borrower (mortgagor). Finally, we go through a typical real estate transaction step by step so that we better understand what happens when we buy a house.

Learning Objectives

A. Discuss the meaning and functions of a mortgage.

B. Describe the legal position of a mortgagee.

C. Describe the legal position of a mortgagor.

D. Discuss the typical real estate transaction.

Content Outline

I. The concept of the mortgage

II. The development of mortgage law
- A. Harshness of the common law
- B. The mortgagor's right to redeem
- C. The mortgagee's right to foreclose
    - 1. Need for the foreclosure remedy
    - 2. Why mortgagees rarely take possession
- D. The consequences of these developments

III. Rights of the mortgagee and mortgagor under common law and equity
- A. The mortgagee
- B. The mortgager

IV. The mortgagee's remedy of sale upon default
- A. Sale by the court
- B. Sale by the mortgagee

V. Sale by a mortgagor of his interest
- A. Financial arrangements
- B. Effect of default by the purchaser

VI. Second mortgages
- A. Uses of a second mortgage
- B. Rights of a second mortgage
- C. Risk for a second mortgage when the mortgagor defaults
- D. Subsequent mortgages after a second mortgage

VII. Mortgagee's rights compared with rights of other creditors

VIII. The mortgage as a contract and as a transfer of an interest in land
- A. The mortgage as transfer of an interest in land
- B. Assignment

C. Discharge of mortgages
    1. Effects of a discharge
    2. Arrangements for prepayment of mortgage debt
    3. Partial discharges
IX. Provincial variations
    A. The mortgagee's rights
    B. The mortgagor's rights

X. Reverse mortgages

XI. A typical real estate transaction
    A. The circumstances
    B. The offer to purchase
    C. Preparations for completing the transaction
        1. Accepting the offer
        2. Verifying title and possession
        3. Preparing the documents for closing
        4. Preparing the accounts for closing
    D. Closing
        1. Trading documents
        2. Delivering possession
    E. After closing
    F. The distinctiveness of each transaction

Questions on Learning Objectives

Objective A: Discuss the meaning and functions of a mortgage.

A.1 What is a mortgage? (pp. 553–554)

A.2 Describe the equity of redemption. (p. 555)

A.3 What does the term "foreclosure" mean and why was it necessary? (p. 555)

A.4 Describe the normal covenants of a mortgagor and a mortgagee in the mortgage contract. (p. 562–563)

A.5 A mortgage is a transfer of an interest in land as well as a contract. What terms are contained in the transfer that would not necessarily be contained in the contract? (pp. 562–563)

A.6 Explain the following terms in relation to mortgages: assignment, discharge, and open mortgage. (pp. 563–564)

Objective B: Describe the legal position of a mortgagee.

B.1 List five remedies a mortgagee has upon default by the mortgagor. (pp. 556–557)

B.2 How can a mortgagee recover the balance of the debt if he obtains the land? (pp. 557–558)

B.3 How is the legal position of the second mortgagee different than that of a first mortgagee? (pp. 559–561)

B.4 Compare the mortgagee's rights with those of a general creditor. (p. 561)

Objective C: Describe the legal position of a mortgagor.

C.1 What rights does a mortgagor have after he defaults on repayment of the mortgage? (p. 557)

C.2 If the owner of a mortgaged property sells it, does he maintain any liability for repayment of the mortgaged debt? Explain. (p. 558)

Objective D: Discuss the typical real estate transaction.

D.1 What essential terms should be included in an offer to purchase a piece of property? (pp. 567–568)

D.2 What is a statement of adjustments? (pp. 569–570)

D.3 What is a closing date? (pp. 559, 567–568)

Answers to Questions on Learning Objectives

A.1 At common law, a mortgage is a conveyance of an interest in land as security for a debt. If the debt is repaid as agreed upon, the conveyance becomes void and the interest in land reverts. If the debt is not repaid then the mortgagee owns the interest absolutely. The Land Registry system operates as the common law did.

However, under the Land Titles system, mortgages are not conveyances of the legal title. Rather they are liens upon the land and, if the mortgagor defaults, the mortgagee must enter into foreclosure proceedings to gain title to the land.

A.2 If a mortgagor defaults in repayment of the debt, the mortgagee is entitled to take the land. The equity of redemption is the period of grace that the courts allow the mortgagor. During that period of time, if the mortgagor tenders payment of the debt in full then the land will be reconveyed to the mortgagor.

A.3 As mortgagors became able to redeem their interest in land, mortgagees began to appeal to the courts for a declaration that the redemption period had expired and the mortgagor's right to redeem was forever "foreclosed." The mortgagee was then able to treat the land as his own. The meaning of the term "foreclosure" is the same today.

A.4 Normally, a mortgagor promises to repay the amount she borrowed plus interest at specified times, maintain adequate insurance on the land and buildings, pay the taxes and keep the buildings in a proper state of repair.

A mortgagee will promise to discharge the mortgage upon payment in full and allow the mortgagor quiet enjoyment of the land so long as she is in good standing.

A.5 Both the normal terms in a transfer of land are required: a description of the parties and the land being transferred. The form of transfer must be suitable for registration in the jurisdiction in which the land is located.

A.6 Assignment of a mortgage is the transfer of the land subject to the mortgage and the rights to the covenants made by the mortgagor to a third party.

If a mortgage is paid off, the mortgage is discharged or cancelled. It serves to reconvey the land to the mortgagor.

An open mortgage is one that allows repayment of the outstanding debt at any time.

B.1 If a mortgagor defaults, a mortgagee has the following remedies:
(i) he may sue the mortgagor on his personal covenant to repay,
(ii) he may dispossess the mortgagor and occupy the land himself,
(iii) he may sell the land,
(iv) he may foreclose on the property,
(v) in some jurisdictions, following foreclosure, the mortgagee may sue on the covenant to pay so long as he is willing and able to reconvey the land to the mortgagor.

B.2 If a mortgagee forecloses on land and sells it to a third party he may not sue the mortgagor for any outstanding balance. If, however, the land is sold the mortgagee may sue the mortgagor for any deficiency. This remedy is *not* available in all provinces.

B.3 The rights of a second mortgagee are similar to those of the first mortgagee except that he ranks behind the first mortgagee in priority of payment. In other words, where there is insufficient money to pay both the first and second mortgagee, the first mortgagee takes priority. If the land has to be sold to satisfy the mortgaged debts, again, the first mortgagee's debt is repaid first.

B.4 A general creditor who is unsecured has no claim to any particular assets of the debtor. Its security for repayment is solely the promise of the debtor. A mortgagee has security in the debtor's land. Failure to repay a debt entitles the mortgagee either to claim the land or to sell it and use the funds to cover the amounts outstanding.

C.1 Even if the mortgagor defaults he is entitled to certain rights at law. First, he may repay the full amount outstanding (i.e., the mortgage loan plus interest plus costs) and obtain a reconveyance of his land. Second, he may obtain an accounting of benefits received by the mortgagee and deduct those from the amount owing on redemption. Finally, if he is sued on his covenant to repay after foreclosure, he is entitled to demand that the mortgagee prove that it is ready and able to reconvey the land upon repayment.

C.2 The owner of a mortgaged property is entitled to sell it. However, it is important to remember that in some provinces the mortgagor will continue to be liable on the covenant to repay the debt even after assumption of the mortgage by a purchaser.

D.1 An offer to purchase must always include a total selling price and its composition, the date of closing, the names of the parties and description of the property and stipulate that risk remains with the vendor until closing, that all taxes, insurance, and normal expenses will be borne by the vendor up to and including the date of closing, how long the offer is open for and to whom acceptance must be communicated.

D.2 A statement of adjustments is a reconciliation of all amounts, both credits and debits, that must be adjusted between the parties in order to arrive at the amount that the purchaser is to pay on closing.

D.3 A closing date is the date set for the house sale to close. The vendor transfers title to the land to the purchaser and the purchase price is given to the vendor from the purchaser. Various other documents are also exchanged.

Multiple-Choice Questions

1. Bruce and Sean have just entered into a contract to buy a house. In order to finance the purchase, they signed a mortgage for $200 000 on May 1 with the local Property Bank that registered the mortgage on May 10. To furnish the house, they took out another mortgage with Up-Town Credit Union for $50 000. This mortgage was signed May 9 and registered the same day. Unknown to the other two lenders, Bruce and Sean took out a third mortgage with a friend, Rob, for $25 000 on May 5 which was registered on May 11. What is the order of priority of the mortgages?

a) Property Bank, Rob, and Up-Town Credit Union.
b) Up-Town Credit Union, Rob and Property Bank.
c) Rob, Property Bank, and Up-Town Credit Union.
d) Up-Town Credit Union, Property Bank and Rob.
e) Property Bank, Up-Town Credit Union and Rob.

2. Jane borrowed money from Jack who received a mortgage in return. Jack registered the mortgage. Jane then borrowed money from Jill and granted a mortgage to Jill who chose not to register it. Jane then borrowed money from Jerry to pay Jack and Jane so granted a mortgage to Jerry who also chose not to register his mortgage. The mortgage in favor of Jack was discharged. Jane, finding the need for more money, granted a further mortgage to Ernest who registered his mortgage. Jane failed to make the monthly payment to Ernest. Ernest commenced a foreclosure action. What is the order of priorities?

a) Jack, Jill, Jerry and Ernest.
b) Ernest, Jerry, Jill and Jack.
c) Jill, Jerry and Ernest.
d) Jerry, Ernest and Jill
e) Ernest, Jill and Jerry.

3. Barry has mortgaged his house to Matthew. Unfortunately, Barry has been unable to keep up with the mortgage payments, and Matthew has started foreclosure proceedings in court. Barry does not understand all the implications of

foreclosure, but he heard somewhere that the normal procedure is for a court to sell the house. Barry approaches Matthew about this, but Matthew says that Barry has no rights or interest in the sale since he defaulted on the mortgage. Barry approaches the court hearing the foreclosure action and requests a sale by the court instead. Is Barry likely to succeed?

a) No because Matthew is right, Barry has no rights once he defaults on the mortgage.
b) Yes because foreclosure is an old remedy that is no longer used.
c) No because it is the mortgagee who gets to decide how to proceed on default.
d) Yes because the order is the court's decision and the court will order sale when it believes that the land is worth more than the amount of the mortgage.
e) No because foreclosure is the only remedy available for default on a mortgage.

4. Jane borrowed money from Jack who received a mortgage in return. Jack registered the mortgage. Jane then borrowed money from Jill and granted a mortgage to Jill who chose not to register it. Jane then borrowed money from Jerry to pay Jack so granted a mortgage to Jerry who also chose not to register his mortgage. The mortgage in favor of Jack was discharged. Jane, finding the need for more money, granted a further mortgage to Ernest who registered his mortgage. Jane failed to make the monthly payment to Ernest. Ernest commenced a foreclosure action. What effect would a foreclosure order have on the other mortgagees?

a) The other mortgagees would lose their security and could only sue on the debt.
b) The other mortgagees would ask Jane to pay their mortgages in full immediately.
c) The other mortgagees would sue Jane on the outstanding debt.
d) The other mortgagees would sue Ernest for taking away their security.
e) The other mortgagees would appeal the order since their mortgages have priority.

5. Ida mortgaged her house to Randy in exchange for $50 000. When Ida discovered rot in the main wooden supports for the house and in the roof beams, she needed additional money to make necessary repairs. So, Ida entered a second mortgage with Nellie for $30 000 to cover the repairs. While Ida made all the required payments on the second mortgage, she missed a few on the first mortgage with Randy. As a result, Randy decides to ask a court to sell the house for default of his mortgage. What would be Nellie's best course of action?

a) Pay off Randy and then ask a court to sell the house for default on her mortgage.
b) Pray that there is enough surplus from the sale to cover her mortgage as well.
c) Pay off Randy and continue to accept payments on the total amount owed, $80 000.
d) Sue Ida on her outstanding debt with Nellie.
e) Do nothing as she is unaffected by Randy's actions.

6. Albert, the owner of Blackacre, mortgages it to Trust Co. for $50 000. Subsequently Albert sells Blackacre to Walter for $80 000. In what way may that sum be paid, considering the mortgage?

a) Pay $80 000 to Albert and obtain an undertaking that Albert will pay off the mortgage.
b) Pay $30 000 to Albert and $50 000 to Trust Co. to pay off the mortgage.
c) Pay $30 000 to Albert and accept Blackacre subject to the mortgage.
d) All of the above.
e) None of the above.

7. Victor offers Hillcroft for sale for $230 000 subject to a mortgage for $150 000 to Mickey Co. Ltd. Paul would like to buy Hillcroft, but he has only $55 000 in cash and needs another $25 000. Paul arranges to borrow $25 000 from a business associate and gives a second mortgage in exchange. Having made these arrangements, Paul accepts Victor's offer and a closing date is arranged. What should happen on the closing date?

a) Victor delivers a deed to Paul; Paul delivers a mortgage of Hillcroft to his associate; the associate gives $25 000 to Paul; Paul gives $80 000 to Victor and assumes the first mortgage.
b) The lawyers for Paul and Victor get together to discuss the title to the property and set a date to complete the transaction.
c) Either party can terminate the agreement of purchase and sale.
d) The two mortgagees get together to discuss the best method for liquidating Hillcroft.
e) The lawyers for Paul and Victor get together to discuss the necessary requisitions.

8. Mercy defaulted on the mortgage on her house. The mortgagee obtains an order to sell the property by public tender. The largest tender bid is for $110 000, $20 000 less than the outstanding amount of the mortgage. What would be the mortgagee's best course of action?

a) Accept the offer of $110 000 and sue Mercy for the remaining $20 000.
b) Accept the offer of $110 000 and accept the $20 000 loss.
c) Treat the public tender process as flawed, and extend the time for bids to permit a larger bid.
d) Reject the $110 000 and return to court asking for a new order of foreclosure.
e) None of the above.

9. Mercy has defaulted on both the first and second mortgages on her house. The first mortgage is for $75 000 and the second mortgage is for $50 000. The first mortgagee obtains an order to sell the property by public auction. The final bid is for $150 000. What happens to the $150 000?

a) The entire amount goes to the first mortgagee who obtained the court order of sale.

b) The first and second mortgagees split the $150 000 equally.

c) The first mortgagee gets $75 000, the second mortgagee gets $50 000 and the remaining $25 000 goes to Mercy.

d) The first and second mortgagees split the $150 000 on a pro rata basis.

e) The first mortgagee gets $75 000 and Mercy gets the remaining $75 000.

10. What are the remedies or rights of the mortgagor when he or she defaults on the mortgage?

a) He may bring the loan up to date and continue making required payments, and may obtain an accounting for any benefits obtained from the land by the mortgagee and deduct them from the amount owing.

b) He may repay the full amount of the loan, and may obtain an accounting for any benefits obtained from the land by the mortgagee and deduct them from the amount owing.

c) He may bring the loan up to date and continue making required payments, and may require the mortgagee to prove willing and able to reconvey the land on repayment.

d) He may repay the full amount of the loan, may obtain an accounting for any benefits obtained from the land by the mortgagee and deduct them from the amount owing, and may require the mortgagee to prove willing and able to reconvey the land on repayment.

e) He may repay the full amount of the loan.

11. How did equity mitigate the harshness of the common law by which a mortgagor lost his land and still owed the debt?

a) The mortgagee was given the choice of suing on the debt or taking possession of the land.

b) The mortgagee was restrained from taking possession of the land unless he came to court with clean hands.

c) The mortgagee was restrained from suing for the debt unless he agreed to reconvey the land to the mortgagor on payment of the full amount owing.

d) The mortgagee was restrained from taking possession of the land until a court gave him permission.

e) The mortgagee was given the choice of selling the land or taking possession.

12. How does subrogation play a role in the law of mortgages?

a) If someone undertakes to pay a mortgage, that person becomes subrogated to the mortgagor's rights.

b) If someone pays off a mortgage, that person becomes subrogated to the mortgagee's rights.

c) If someone buys the land from the mortgagor, that person becomes subrogated to the mortgagee's rights.

d) If someone takes an assignment of the mortgage from the mortgagee, that person becomes subrogated to the mortgagor's rights.
e) If someone pays off a mortgage, that person becomes subrogated to the mortgagor's rights.

13. What is the maximum number of mortgages that can be placed on one piece of land?

a) One.
b) Two.
c) Three.
d) Five.
e) Infinite.

14. What is a reverse mortgage?

a) A mortgage in which a financial institution borrows money from a client and gives a mortgage as security.
b) A mortgage in which no repayment is due until the mortgagor reaches the age of majority.
c) A mortgage given in return for a monthly payment where no repayment is due until the mortgagor sells or dies.
d) A mortgage given by someone over the age of seventy.
e) A mortgage in which the money received is used to pay off another mortgage.

15. What is the normal way to terminate a house mortgage?

a) Receive a partial discharge of the mortgage for each payment made.
b) Default on the mortgage and have the mortgagee seize or sell the property.
c) Have the mortgagor die and have his or her heirs pay the rest of the amount due.
d) Fully repay the loan and accept a discharge from the mortgagee.
e) Arrange to refinance the mortgage for another five years.

16. Which of the following is/are characteristics of a mortgage?
I. A mortgage is the right to reconveyance of land upon payment of all outstanding amounts against it.
II. A mortgage is a contract.
III. A mortgage is a conveyance of an interest in land.

a) I only
b) II only
c) III only
d) I, II and III
e) II and III only

17. Claus wishes to sell his office building, which has a mortgage against it. Olga purchases the building subject to the existing mortgage. She later defaults. All of the following are correct EXCEPT:

a) The mortgagee may foreclose on the mortgage.
b) The mortgagee may sue Claus for repayment of the debt.
c) The mortgagee may sue Olga for payment of the debt.
d) The mortgagee may sell the land.

18. Which of the following statements correctly describes the legal position of the holder of a second mortgage?

a) A second mortgagee holds land as security for the debt owed to him.
b) A second mortgagee ranks equally with the first mortgagee in priority of repayment.
c) A second mortgagee's interest is destroyed if the first mortgagee forecloses on the property.
d) A second mortgagee is liable to the first mortgagee if the mortgagor defaults.
e) A second mortgagee has identical rights to a first mortgage.

Answers to Multiple-Choice Questions

1. d)
See pages 561 for more information.

2. e)
See pages 561 for more information.

3. d)
See page 557 for more information.

4. a)
See page 560 for more information.

5. c)
See page 560 for more information

6. d)
See page 558 for more information.

7. a)
See pages 559–560 for more information.

8. a)
See page 557 for more information.

9. c)

See page 557 for more information.

10. d)

See page 557 for more information.

11. c)

See pages 554–555 for more information.

12. b)

See page 559 for more information.

13. e)

See page 559 for more information.

14. c)

See page 565 for more information.

15. d)

See pages 563–564 for more information.

16. e)

See page 554 for more information.

17. c)

See page 559 for more information.

18. c)

See page 559–561 for more information.

True/False Questions

1. At common law, a mortgage is a conveyance of an interest in land as security for a debt. If the debt is repaid as agreed upon, the conveyance becomes void and the interest in land reverts. If the debt is not repaid then the mortgagee owns the interest absolutely.

2. The Land Registry system operates as the civil law did.

3. Under the Land Titles system, mortgages are not conveyances of the legal title. Rather they are liens upon the land and, if the mortgagor defaults, the mortgagee must enter into foreclosure proceedings to gain title to the land.

4. As mortgagors became able to redeem their interest in land, mortgagees began to appeal to the courts for a declaration that the redemption period had expired

and the mortgagor's right to redeem was forever "foreclosed." The mortgagee was then able to treat the land as his own. The meaning of the term "foreclosure" is the same today.

5. If a mortgagor defaults, a mortgagee has the following remedies:
(i) he may sue the mortgagor on his personal covenant to repay
(ii) he may dispossess the mortgagor and occupy the land himself
(iii) he may sell the land
(iv) he may foreclose on the property
(v) in some jurisdictions, following foreclosure, the mortgagee may sue on the covenant to pay so long as he is willing and able to reconvey the land to the mortgagor.

6. The rights of a second mortgagee are similar to those of the first mortgagee

7. When the mortgagor defaults, he is entitled to no rights at law.

Answers to True/False Questions

1. True.

2. False. The Land Registry system operates as the common law did.

3. True.

4. True.

5. True.

6. False. The rights of a second mortgagee are similar to those of the first mortgagee except that he ranks behind the first mortgagee in priority of payment. In other words, where there is insufficient money to pay both the first and second mortgagee, the first mortgagee takes priority. If the land has to be sold to satisfy the mortgaged debts, again, the first mortgagee's debt is repaid first.

7. False. Even if the mortgagor defaults he is entitled to certain rights at law. First, he may repay the full amount outstanding (i.e., the mortgage loan plus interest plus costs) and obtain a reconveyance of his land. Second, he may obtain an accounting of benefits received by the mortgagee and deduct those from the amount owing on redemption. Finally, if he is sued on his covenant to repay after foreclosure, he is entitled to demand that the mortgagee prove that it is ready and able to reconvey the land upon repayment.

26

Partnership

Purpose and Significance

A business enterprise is an organized form of carrying out a profit-making activity. Most of us realize that starting a gardening business requires organization. That is, gardening tools have to be acquired, customers located, prices established and the like. In addition, legal matters, such as contracts and licenses, must be addressed.

One legal matter that must be addressed is the legal form the business is to take. The law offers a variety of choices for the legal organization of a business enterprise. The different forms of organization give rise to different legal results in the following matters:

a) the legal standing of business organization;
b) the relationship of the participants (partners, shareholders, etc.) to one another and to the business enterprise;
c) the relationship of the enterprise to third persons (customers, employees, lenders); and
d) the formalities of organization required by law.

Since the enterprise involves economic activity for gain the issues raised by each of these categories has to be considered from different perspectives. Who is legally responsible for debts and obligations of the business? Who is legally entitled to which portion of economic benefits?

This chapter and the next explore two types of business organization: partnerships and incorporation.

Learning Objectives

A. Discuss how and why a partnership might be created.

B. Explore the legal relationship that exists among members of a partnership.

C. Describe formal aspects affecting partnerships.

Content Outline

I. Choosing the appropriate form of business organization

II. Sole proprietorships

III. Partnerships
    A. Advantages and disadvantages
    B. The *Partnership Act*

IV. The nature of partnership
    A. The definition of partnership
    B. The partnership relationship
    C. The definition of partnership
        1. The partnership relationship
        2. The business nature of partnership
        3. The profit motive
    D. The legal nature of partnership
        1. Legal personality
        2. The continuing relationship between partners
        3. Partnership property
        4. Creditors of the firm
        5. Legal proceedings

V. The creation of a partnership
    A. The partnership agreement
    B. Drafting and effective agreement
    C. Registration

VI. The liability of a partner
    A. Contractual liability
        1. Agency principles
        2. Joint liability
        3. Apparent partners
    B. Tort and breach of trust
    C. Limited liability partnerships

VII. The relationship of partners to one another
    A. Implied terms
        1. Partnership property
        2. Financial arrangements
        3. Conduct of the business
        4. Membership
    B. Fiduciary duties
        1. Information
        2. Secret benefits
        3. Duty not to compete
VIII. Termination of partnership
    A. Express provision
    B. Implied statutory rules
        1. Termination by notice or expiry
        2. Termination on death or insolvency
    C. Dissolution by law
    D. Effects of dissolution

IX. Joint ventures

X. Limited partnerships

Questions on Learning Objectives

Objective A: Explore the differences and similarities between sole proprietorships and partnerships.

A.1 Distinguish between sole proprietorships and partnerships. (pp. 579–580)

A.2 Must the name of the sole proprietorship or of a partnership be registered? (p. 579)

Objective B: Discuss how and why a partnership might be created.

B.1 How is a partnership defined in law? (pp. 580–581)

B.2 Can two persons be partners in the absence of an agreement? (p. 581)

B.3 If two people decide to own property jointly, have they formed a partnership? (p. 581)

B.4 Does the fact that two business people share gross receipts or profits establish that they are partners? (p. 582)

B.5 Is a partnership a legal person like a corporation? (p. 582)

Objective C: **Explore the legal partnership, which exists among members of a partnership.**

C.1 Describe three types of liability a person incurs on becoming a member of a partnership. (pp. 585–587)

C.2 If a partnership owes a creditor $100,000, but the partnership only has $50,000 in assets, can the creditor sue the partners personally for the $50,000 that the business is unable to pay? (p. 586)

C.3 Is a partner liable for obligations incurred after she ceases to be a partner? (p. 587)

C.4 What is the difference between an implied term in a partnership contract and an express term? (p. 591)

C.5 Can a partner carry on a second business, which competes with the business of the partnership? (p. 594)

C.6 A partnership is in the business of selling hats. One of the partners pays for a shipment of merchandise out of her own pocket. Is she entitled to be reimbursed by the partnership? (p. 592)

C.7 There are five partners in the partnership. Three want to purchase a new piece of machinery, and the other two don't. How is the decision to be made? (p. 593)

C.8 There are five partners in the partnership. Three want to change the business from selling hats to selling fish and chips. Two don't want to change. How is the decision to be made? (p. 593)

C.9 Why can't a partner assign or mortgage his interest in the partnership? (p. 593)

C.10 How may a partnership end? (pp. 595–596)

Objective D: **Describe formal aspects affecting partnerships.**

D.1 Are the terms of a partnership contract binding on third parties that carry on business with the partnership? (pp. 583–584)

D.2 Does a partnership agreement have to be in written form? (p. 583)

D.3 What is the principal advantage of a written partnership agreement? (p. 583)

D.4 Is it necessary for a partnership to be registered or licensed? (p. 585)

D.5 What are the prerequisites for creating a limited partnership, which permits the liability of some partners to be limited to their capital contributions? (p. 597)

Answers to Questions on Learning Objectives

A.1 A partnership is formed by two or more persons who want to carry on a business with a view to profit, whereas a sole proprietorship is an unincorporated business owned by a single individual.

A.2 In most provinces, statutes require that the name of the sole proprietorship or of a partnership must be registered except if it is the actual name of the owner.

B.1 A partnership is a joint business enterprise carried on for profit. It does not refer to joint enterprises for non-profit purposes, such as charities or public boards. The definition in the *Partnership Act* is: "Partnership is the relation which subsists between persons carrying on a business in common with a view of profit."

B.2 It is possible if they have acted as if they were partners, even though they have not expressly agreed to be partners. The courts will look at the substantial facts of the relationship, and will not be guided by what the parties choose to call it.

B.3 Not necessarily. A partnership has to involve carrying on a business. The bare owning of property does not necessarily amount to carrying on a business. In order to constitute a business, more than simple profit-taking must be involved. It is sometimes said that a business must include a "trade, occupation, or profession."

B.4 Sharing of gross receipts does not, generally speaking, establish the existence of a partnership. If a farmer rented his farm and received 30% of the crop as a rental payment, that fact alone would not indicate a partnership.

According to the *Partnership Act*, the sharing of profits does not by itself prove that a partnership exists. However, in connection with any other facts (such as contribution of property or labour to the enterprise, or taking part in management decisions), it is a basic element in proving partnership.

B.5 No, a partnership is not a legal person. In common law tradition, it has no separate existence from the members of the partnership. However, under some modern legislation, partnerships are given a semi-separate existence.

C.1 A partner is personally liable for:
(i) debts and obligations of the partnership incurred while he is a partner;
(ii) negligence and other torts perpetrated by any of the partners acting in the ordinary course of the partnership business;
(iii) a misapplication of trust funds placed in the care of the partnership.

C.2 Each partner is jointly liable with all other partners for the unpaid debts of the enterprise. The creditor can seize the personal assets of each of the partners until the debt is fully paid.

C.3 In principle a partner is only liable for obligations created by the firm while she is a member. However, if the retiring partner gives people dealing with the firm cause to believe that she is still a member of the firm, and those people advance credit on the basis of the understanding, then the retiring partner can be held liable as a partner.

C.4 An implied term is one that the law will assume describes the agreement between the partners, unless the partners can prove that they had specifically agreed to something else. For example, the *Partnership Act* (s. 27(a)) provides that all partners can show they expressly agreed to permit one of the partners to receive 70% of the profits. Then the implied term does not apply.

C.5 If a partner carries on another business in competition with the partnership business he must "account to the firm for any benefit derived by him without the consent of the other partners" (s. 33). An accounting means that his profits from the competing business can be taken by the partnership. The errant partner will, thus, have to share that profit with his fellow partners under the partnership agreement.

C.6 If the expenditure is made "in the ordinary and proper conduct of the business" the firm must indemnify for such expenditures, unless the parties have agreed otherwise. (s. 27(b))

C.7 Unless the parties have agreed otherwise, "any difference arising as to ordinary matters connected with the partnership business may be decided by the majority of the partners." (s. 27(h))

C.8 Unless the parties have agreed otherwise, no fundamental change can be made to the business of the partnership without the agreement of all partners. (s. 27(h))

C.9 A partnership is a personal relationship that is entered into because the partners are acquainted with the qualities and contributions of the other members of the partnership. Members of the partnership are entitled to be protected from being put into partnership with others unknown to them.

C.10 If no fixed term is agreed upon for the duration of the partnership, it ends upon one partner giving notice to the others (s. 29). It is also dissolved by the death, bankruptcy or insolvency of any partner unless otherwise provided for (s. 36(1)). It can be dissolved if one partner charges or assigns his interest in the partnership (s. 36(2)), becomes incompetent or incapable (ss. 38(b), (c)), conducts himself in a manner prejudicial to the business (s. 39(c)), willfully commits breaches of the partnership agreement (s. 38(d)), or whenever the court finds it just and equitable to dissolve the partnership (s. 38(e)). The parties can also terminate by agreement.

D.1 The significance of the agreement lies only in the relations of the partners among themselves, unless a third party has actual knowledge of the contents of the agreement.

The partnership is bound for obligations made to third parties, provided the partner or employee who made the obligation was acting within the scope of usual authority. Unless the third party actually knows about the contents of the partnership agreement, the third party's rights are not limited by the agreement.

D.2 No. A partnership agreement can be created orally or it can be implied from the conduct of the partners.

D.3 Misunderstanding and mistrust, bred by a failure to foresee and address important issues, are often the causes of partnership breakdown. Using proper professional assistance, most partnerships can foresee and deal with the task of clearly stating business objectives, partners' responsibility, capital contribution, shares of profits and losses, terms of dissolution, and other important matters relating to the conduct of the partnership. A clearly stated agreement reduces the prospect of ambiguity and misunderstanding and, even in the event of dissolution, provides an efficient, peaceful and economical course of procedure.

D.4 Almost all provinces require registration. The penalties for failure to register are a fine and disallowance of any court action on a contract made in connection with the partnership business. The fine is almost never levied, however, and court action can be taken even when the registration occurs after the contract is made or a lawsuit started. However, there is considerable advantage to public notice of the existence of the partnership and, in the appropriate time, of its dissolution.

D.5   (a) There are strict registration requirements.
    (b) Provision must be made for at least one partner to be a "general partner" whose liability is not limited.
    (c) The "limited partner" is prohibited from taking any active role in the management of the partnership business.

Multiple-Choice Questions

1. Stacey and William had a partnership for the purpose of carrying on a landscape business during the summer vacation. Their agreement expressly stated that the partnership would end when school re-opened in September. However, they continued the business without any changes to the agreement until the snow started to fall in November. What type of partnership did Stacey and William have after September?

a) A partnership by estoppel.
b) A partnership by agreement.
c) A limited partnership.
d) A partnership at will.
e) No partnership at all.

2. Lyle and Skip were partners in the operation of a bed and breakfast that they sold to Jeff. One of the assets sold in the transaction was a boiler. Skip had made a fraudulent misrepresentation about the boiler that induced Jeff to enter into the contract for its purchase. Although Skip knew that what he said was false, Lyle was not aware of what was said or that there was any problem with the boiler.

Shortly after Jeff's purchase, the boiler broke down and had to be replaced. What would be Jeff's best course of action?

a) Sue only Skip for the replacement cost.
b) Sue only Lyle for the replacement cost.
c) Sue both Lyle and Skip for the replacement cost.
d) Do nothing and accept the replacement cost as a cost of doing business.
e) None of the above.

3. Susan, Lucy and Christine have decided to set up a landscaping business. Lucy and Christine are excellent gardeners and will be the labour for the business, in addition to other employees. Lucy also has extensive experience in running a business and in marketing. Both Lucy and Christine will contribute $20 000 to the start-up costs. Susan's contribution will be all the gardening equipment needed for the business. Susan is not interested in becoming involved in the day-to-day operations because she has another full-time job with a salary of $60 000, but would like to share in the profits. The business will need to borrow $50 000 to cover all the start-up costs and the daily expenses until sufficient clientele can be developed. What kind of a business organization would be possible?

a) Partnership.
b) Limited Partnership.
c) Incorporation.
d) All of the above.
e) None of the above.

4. Smith Jones is a limited partnership with three general partners, namely Beck, Carling and Oland, and one limited partner, Macdonald. Although a limited partner, Macdonald constantly interfered with the management and control of the partnership. Daisy wants to sue the partnership for outstanding debts. Who should be listed as the parties to the lawsuit?

a) Smith Jones, a partnership, and Macdonald.
b) Beck, Carling and Oland.
c) Beck, Carling, Oland and Macdonald.
d) Smith Jones, a partnership; Beck; Carling; Oland and Macdonald.
e) Carling, Oland and Macdonald.

5. Jack and Jill, two university students, decide to earn money in the summer by doing landscaping work. They both own their own gardening equipment and plan to work independently. They decide to pool their funds to buy the necessary supplies, such as grass seed and fertilizer. The proceeds from any jobs would be deposited in the pool. Jack, with Jill's approval, places an order for 200 pounds of grass seed. After the grass seed had been delivered and Jack had seeded five lawns, Jack informed Jill that he had decided to return home to save on living expenses. Jack gave the remaining grass seed to Jill and asked for his share of the

profits to date. The grass seed had not yet been paid for. What is the nature of the relationship between Jack and Jill?

a) Just friends who do similar work.
b) Partners as there is a sharing of profits, jointly contributed capital and shared management.
c) Independent contractors who co-ordinate jobs.
d) Two sole proprietors.
e) One sole proprietor, Jill, and one unemployed student, Jack.

6. Maggie and Jennifer have formed a partnership to make and market natural baby food. They persuade Maggie's grandmother and Jennifer's uncle to contribute $30 000 each as limited partners. Maggie's grandmother, a retired accountant, occasionally gives them free financial advice and has pension assets worth $800 000. Jennifer' s uncle, a businessman, advises them on the management of the business and has personal assets worth $200 000. The partnership has assets worth $50 000 and Maggie and Jennifer each have personal assets worth $5000. If a customer wants to sue the partnership for $2 million, what assets would be available to satisfy any judgement?

a) Partnership assets, Maggie's and Jennifer's personal assets, Maggie's grandmother's pension assets and Jennifer's uncle's personal assets.
b) Partnership assets, Maggie's and Jennifer's personal assets.
c) Partnership assets, Maggie's grandmother's pension assets and Jennifer's uncle's personal assets.
d) Partnership assets, Maggie's and Jennifer's personal assets and Jennifer's uncle's personal assets.
e) Maggie's and Jennifer's personal assets, Maggie's grandmother's pension assets and Jennifer's uncle's personal assets.

7. A group of persons, including Kamex Ltd., joined together to purchase a piece of development property with a view to reselling it at a profit. One of the co-owners, March, entered into an exclusive listing agreement with a real estate agent without the agreement of his co-owners. The group sold the property on its own and the real estate agent sued the members of the group for her commission. The agent claimed that the group had formed a partnership and that they were consequently jointly liable on the contract made by March. Who was liable for the commission?

a) March alone.
b) The group as a partnership.
c) The group, other than March.
d) Kamex Ltd. as a corporation.
e) No one is liable for the commission, as the agent was not involved in the sale.

8. Fred, George and Rufus have carried on business as a partnership for many years. Rufus, being considerably older than Fred and George, has decided to retire

on December 31. The partnership informs the government of the retirement, but no one else. In January and February of the following year, Fred and George decide to expand the business and incur large debts with existing creditors as a result. When the debt is not repaid, whom may the creditors sue?

a) Fred, George and Rufus.
b) Fred and George.
c) Fred and Rufus.
d) George and Rufus.
e) Rufus.

9. Fred, George and Rufus have carried on business as a partnership for many years. Rufus, an avid skydiver, dies on Friday, July 13. The partnership informs the government of the death, but no one else. In August and September following the death, Fred and George decide to expand the business and incur large debts as a result. When the debt is not repaid, whom may the creditors sue?

a) Fred, George and Rufus' estate.
b) Fred and George.
c) Fred and Rufus' estate.
d) George and Rufus' estate.
e) Rufus' estate.

10. Which of the following is a reason for forming a partnership?

a) Low start-up costs.
b) Two or more persons are involved.
c) Shared liability.
d) Pooling of knowledge, skills and financial resources.
e) All of the above.

11. Which of the following is a characteristic of a sole proprietorship?

a) One owner.
b) No separation between the business and the proprietor.
c) No government formalities are required except name registration if the business is carried on under a name other than the name of the proprietor.
d) Profit from the business is claimed as part of the proprietor's personal income taxes.
e) All of the above.

12. What are the fiduciary duties of partners?

a) Duty not to compete.
b) Duty to bind the other partners in contracts and duty to pass on information.
c) Duty not to keep secret benefits and duty to run a competing business.

d) Duty to pass on information, duty not to keep secret benefits and duty not to compete.

e) Duty to assist in the management of the partnership, duty to pass on information, duty not to keep secret benefits and duty not to compete.

13. A court can order the dissolution of a partnership where a partner is found to be mentally incompetent. Under what other circumstances can a court order the dissolution of a partnership?

a) Where a partner has been declared bankrupt, where a partner has died and where a partner becomes permanently incapable of performing his part of the agreement.

b) Where a partner becomes permanently incapable of performing his part of the agreement, where a partner has been guilty of conduct likely to prejudicially affect the business, and where it is just and equitable that the partnership be dissolved.

c) Where a partner has entered into contract on behalf of the partnership, where a partner has been guilty of conduct likely to prejudicially affect the business, and where it is just and equitable that the partnership be dissolved.

d) Where a partner becomes incapable of performing his part of the agreement, where a partner has been guilty of conduct likely to prejudicially affect the business, and where a partner has no obligation to participate in the management of the business.

e) None of the above.

14. A joint venture is a business venture undertaken jointly by two or more parties. What is the distinction between a contractual joint venture and an equity joint venture?

a) Whether common law or the law of equity governs the relationship among the participants.

b) Whether there is a written, signed agreement or an oral agreement among the participants.

c) Whether there is a contractual relationship among the participants for a specific undertaking or a separate corporation incorporated for the venture with each participant holding shares.

d) Whether the relationship among the participants is governed by contract law or tort law.

e) Whether the joint venture is for the purposes of profit or for the purposes of charity.

15. For what reason is a written partnership agreement usually drafted?

a) Because it is required by the *Partnership Act* to create the partnership.

b) Because the partners have perfect memories as to the terms of their agreements.

c) Because it is the only way to adopt the implied terms in the *Partnership Act*.
d) Because it helps avoid future misunderstandings and varies the implied terms in the *Partnership Act*.
e) Because it is the only way to have a successful business.

16. All of the following statements about partnerships are correct EXCEPT:

a) A partnership involves the operation of a business by two or more persons.
b) A partnership is a separate legal entity.
c) Each partner is personally liable for the debts incurred by the business during the time she is a partner.
d) Each partner is liable for torts committed by any of the partners while acting on behalf of the partnership.
e) A partnership can be created expressly or through course of conduct.

17. A fundamental change to the business that a partnership operates can be made by:

a) A majority of the partners.
b) Any one of the partners.
c) Agreement of all of the partners.
d) A minority of the partners.
e) The partner who has invested the most capital in the business.

18. Which of the following is/are advantages of using a partnership agreement?
I. It can set out business objectives.
II. It can provide an efficient, peaceful method of dissolution.
III. It forces the partners to come to grips with important matters.

a) I only
b) II only
c) III only
d) I and II only
e) I, II and III

Answers to Multiple-Choice Questions

1. d)
See page 595 for more information.

2. c)
See page 588 for more information.

3. d)
See pages 580, 597 for more information.

4. d)
See page 598 for more information.

5. b)
See pages 580–582 for more information

6. d)
See pages 586, 598 for more information.

7. a)
See pages 581–582 for more information.

8. a)
See pages 587–588 for more information.

9. b)
See page 587 for more information.

10. e)
See page 580 for more information.

11. e)
See page 579 for more information.

12. d)
See pages 593–594 for more information.

13. b)
See page 596 for more information.

14. c)
See page 597 for more information.

15. d)
See pages 583–584 for more information.

16. b)
See page 580–581 for more information.

17. c)
See page 590–595 for more information.

18. e)
See page 583–585 for more information.

True/False Questions

1. A sole proprietorship is a business that is carried on by one individual. No formalities are necessary in its creation. There is no distinct body of law relating to sole proprietorships.

2. A partnership is a business carried on by two or more persons. There are no formalities required in the creation of a partnership, but a well-developed body of law governs the affairs of a partnership.

3. A partnership is a legal person.

4. In principle, a partner is only liable for obligations created by the firm while she is a member. However, if the retiring partner gives people dealing with the firm cause to believe that she is still a member of the firm, and those people advance credit on the basis of that understanding, then the retiring partner can be held liable as a partner.

5. A partnership is a personal relationship that is entered into because the partners are acquainted with the qualities and contributions of the other members of the partnership. Members of the partnership are entitled to be protected from being put into partnership with others unknown to them.

6. A partnership agreement cannot be created orally.

Answers to True/False Questions

1. True.

2. True.

3. False. A partnership is not a legal person. In common law tradition, it has no separate existence from the members of the partnership. However, under some modern legislation, partnerships are given a semi-separate existence.

4. True.

5. True.

6. False. A partnership agreement can be created orally or it can be implied from the conduct of the partners.

27

The Nature of a Corporation and Its Formation

Purpose and Significance

No legal form of organization is more important to our business world than the corporation. Corporations are so much a part of the business world that the two have become almost synonymous. It is common for people to talk about "incorporating a business" and to suppose that someone who owns the corporation also owns the business. This is not an accurate understanding. The corporation is a legal "person," and as such may own a business in the same way that a human being may own a business.

Even though a person may be a shareholder of the corporation, that shareholding does not give the person a legal interest in the property or business that the corporation owns.

The purpose of this chapter is to provide you with an understanding of the nature of a corporation. In order to do so, it is necessary to outline how a corporation is created and governed and to know the effects on legal and business relationships that the corporation as a form of business organization has.

Learning Objectives

A. Examine the implications of a corporation's separate legal existence.

B. Describe the means of creating corporations under Canadian law.

C. Describe some important types of enterprise organizations.

D. Discuss the impact of the corporate constitution on participants in the corporate enterprise.

E. Describe the nature of corporate securities.

Content Outline

I. The nature of a corporation

II. 2. Characteristics of corporations and partnerships
    A. Liability
    B. Transfer of ownership
    C. Management
    D. Duty of good faith
    E. Continuity

III. Consequences of separate corporate personality
    A. Capacity
    B. Separate existence
        1. *Salomon*'s case
        2. Implications of Salomon's case
    C. Limitations on the principle of separate corporate existence
        1. Exceptions to limited liability
        2. Other statutory provisions
        3. Lifting the corporate veil

IV. Methods of incorporation
    A. Early methods of incorporation
    B. Incorporation statutes
        1. The memorandum and letters patent systems
        2. The articles of incorporation system
    C. The choice of jurisdiction

V. The constitution of a corporation
    A. Articles of incorporation
    B. By-laws
        1. Nature of by-laws

2. Content

3. Authorization to directors

VI. Widely held and closely held corporations

    A. Public and private corporations

    B. Widely held corporations

    C. Closely held corporations

VII. Corporate capital

    A. Equity and debt

        1. Share capital

        2. Par value

VIII. Corporate securities

    A. The distinction between shares and bonds

    B. Rights and privileges of security holders

        1. Bondholders

        2. Common shareholders

        3. Preferred shareholders

        4. Class rights

IX. The transfer of corporate securities

    A. Negotiability

    B. Restrictions on share transfer

Questions on Learning Objectives

Objective A: Examine the implications of a corporation's separate legal existence.

A.1 What difference does the separate existence of a corporation make to the liability of participants in a corporate enterprise, as compared to the liability of members of a partnership? (pp. 601–602)

A.2 Does a shareholder have the same ability to bind a corporation to a contract as a partner does to bind a partnership to a contract? (p. 603)

A.3 How do the stated objects of a corporation limit its capacity to perform acts and enter into legal obligations? (p. 604)

A.4 What effect did the *Salomon* case have on the law of corporations? (pp. 605–606)

A.5 Is the corporation a legal person separate from its shareholders under the Canadian *Income Tax Act*? (p. 664)

Objective B: **Describe the means of creating corporations under Canadian law.**

B.1 In which provinces is incorporation accomplished by the issuance of letters patent by a government agency as a representative of the Crown? (p. 609)

B.2 Describe incorporation by articles and where it is used in Canada. (p. 609)

Objective C: **Discuss the impact of the corporate constitution on participants in the corporate enterprise.**

C.1 What information is contained in a corporate charter? (p. 611)

C.2 Can a corporate charter be amended? (p. 611)

C.3 How do by-laws and articles of association differ? (p. 611)

C.4 What are the two main categories of by-laws? (p. 612)

Objective D: **Describe some important types of enterprise organizations.**

D.1 Is there a legal difference in Canada between broadly-held corporations and closely-held corporations? (pp. 613–614)

D.2 Is a closely-held corporation always small? (p. 614)

D.3 What is the difference between "authorized capital" and "issued" or "paid-up capital"? (pp. 614–615)

D.4 Does a share have to have a par value? Does the par value set the market value of the share? (p. 615)

Objective E: **Describe the nature of corporate securities.**

E.1 What is the difference between a share and a bond? (pp. 615–616)

E.2 Are stocks and bonds negotiable instruments? (p. 617–618)

E.3 Is there a difference between interest paid to a bondholder and dividends paid to a shareholder? (pp. 615–616)

E.4 If a company is wound up, all creditors paid, capital returned to preferred shareholders and common shareholders, and there is still a surplus sum of money, do the preferred shareholders share it with the common shareholders? (p. 617)

Answers to Questions on Learning Objectives

A.1 A corporation, as a separate legal person, is liable for its own debts. Shareholders liability is limited to their capital contribution.

Each partner is liable for debts for the partnership to the limit of his personal assets.

A.2 No, a shareholder has no authority to bind his corporation to contractual obligations. Only officers and employees of the company may do so.

A.3 In memorandum jurisdictions other than British Columbia, the doctrine of *ultra vires* nullifies the effect of any legal action undertaken by a corporation that does not fit within its stated objects.

Some specially-constituted corporations, such as municipal corporations, are also limited in the range of action permitted by their statutory creation.

However, certificate jurisdictions do not require a corporation to state objects in its charter. And if the incorporation chooses to state objects, it does not limit corporate action under the *ultra vires* doctrine. Rather, an aggrieved shareholder can enforce compliance with the objects by bringing an action against the controllers of the corporation who are causing it to act beyond its intended scope.

A.4 The *Salomon* case succeeded in assuring the separation of the company from its shareholders in terms of legal responsibilities and entitlements. A shareholder, as Salomon found out, could become a mortgagee of company property and have priority over other creditors.

However, courts later decided that a shareholder has no insurable interest in property that belongs to the corporation, even if the shareholder owns one hundred per cent of the shares. (A recent Ontario decision has modified this result.)

A.5 Yes, a corporation is a separate taxpayer and corporation as taxpayers are taxed in the same manner as other business owners except that special rates of tax are applied to corporations.

In order to avoid abuse of the special corporate tax provisions, the *Income Tax Act* makes special provision for "looking through the corporate veil;" for example, where associated corporations try to multiply the tax advantage of the small business deduction.

B.1 Only in Quebec and Prince Edward Island are letters patent still used. However, the letters patent system was used elsewhere in Canada before the present statutory schemes were adopted.

B.2 Ontario, Manitoba, Saskatchewan, New Brunswick, Alberta, Newfoundland and the federal Parliament all permit incorporations by articles. To so incorporate, those persons wishing to form a corporation sign and deliver articles of incorporation to a government office which, in turn, issues a certificate of incorporation.

C.1 Information that is central to the corporation such as name, registered office, and restrictions on business, shares and transfers of shares are contained in the charter. The incorporators may include arrangements and agreements that are otherwise considered essential to the corporate enterprise and organization.

C.2 Yes, but a special amending procedure dictated by the statute must be followed.

C.3 They are substantially similar in that both contain the corporation's operating rules. By- laws are used by letters patents and certificate of incorporation companies. Articles of association are used by memorandum companies.

Though they have similar content and effect, by-laws are generally more flexible and more easily introduced and amended.

C.4 The first category consists of general by-laws that provide the basic operating rules of the company. These are quite long and detail such things as the number and terms of directors, quorums necessary for meetings, the categories and duties of executive officers, voting rules and so forth.

The second category of by-laws includes those passed to give directors or officers authority from the shareholders to carry out specific transactions which require by-laws approval under terms of the statute or the charter.

D.1 In all Canadian jurisdictions, no matter how many shareholders or how large the corporation is, it will be incorporated under the same statutory requirements. In most provinces, no statutory distinction is drawn for corporate purposes between broadly-held or closely-held corporations.

However, in British Columbia, Prince Edward Island and Nova Scotia, the *Companies Act* permit the formation of private companies. These companies must maintain three characteristics to retain the status:
(i) the right to transfer shares must be restricted in some manner;
(ii) the number of shareholders is limited to 50; and
(iii) no invitation to buy shares can be made to the public.

D.2 Often it is. "Closely-held" refers to the number of shareholders. However, many very large corporations are closely-held. For example, the Canadian subsidiary or a large foreign parent company is often closely-held because the parent is the sole or principal shareholder.

D.3 Authorized capital is set out in the charter and stipulates the terms and limits under which directors can cause shares to be issued to shareholders. Shares can be authorized in different classes with different par values, voting rights and dividend rights. Also, the authorized capital can create an upper limit on the number of shares.

In certificate of incorporation jurisdictions other than Manitoba, the requirement of authorized capital has been removed.

Issued or paid-up capital is the result of a series of contracts between the company and its shareholders. Shares issued by the directors are sold to or acquired by shareholders. That holding, expressed in the "stated capital account" which constitutes consideration paid for the shares, constitutes the issued or paid-up capital.

D.4 In a very few jurisdictions shares must have a par value, though the par value may be stated as a very small amount. However, in most jurisdictions it is not necessary for shares to have a par value and no par value shares may be issued.

Par value does not measure the actual value of the share and, except in one circumstance, it does not measure either the maximum or the minimum value of a share.

Directors can sell newly-issued shares for any price above par value. They may not issue shares for less than par value. Thereafter, shareholders trading in shares that have been acquired from the company may trade them at any value, above or below the par value.

E.1 In the business world today, the distinction between a share and a bond or debenture is often blurred because features attached to corporate securities are broadly mixed.

At the most basic level, a share is a proportionate ownership of the company. It is called an "equity" holding because it reflects entitlement to a portion of the corporate enterprise. Thus, unless special conditions are attached to the share (as might be the case with some preferred shares) the shareholders' investment is not secured or guaranteed but is dictated by the success of the enterprise.

A bond or debenture is a document evidencing a debtor/creditor relationship. The company is the debtor and the bondholder is the creditor. A registered lien or mortgage against the property of the company usually secures the debt under bond or debenture.

E.2 They can be. Bonds in bearer form were considered a type of negotiable instrument at common law. Certificate of incorporation statutes expressly treat share certificate in bearer form as a type of negotiable instrument.

E.3 Interest due to a bondholder is a debt against a company. It can be paid whether or not the corporation has a profit and is usually deductible as a business expense in measuring corporate income for tax purposes.

Shareholders have no entitlement to dividends until the directors have declared them. Directors cannot declare a dividend unless the corporation has been profitable. Dividends paid are not deductible as an expense for income tax purposes.

Preferred shareholders are in an intermediate position, and the effect of payments made to them will depend on how the substance of their preferred shares is construed.

E.4 The answer depends firstly on whether the corporate charter clearly describes the rights of the shareholder to a surplus on winding up. A properly prepared corporate charter would address the issue. Where the charter is not specific, the courts must decide the issue. In 1947, the Supreme Court of Canada held that preferred shareholders would share in a surplus with common shareholders in such a case. But in 1949, the House of Lords decided that the preferred shareholders exhausted their rights in their stated preference.

In 1950, the Supreme Court of Canada became our ultimate court of appeal, replacing the House of Lords. It is unclear how a future case involving this issue will be decided.

Multiple-Choice Questions

1. Kelly, a Toronto lawyer, had incorporated a real estate company, Rockwell, of which he effectively owned all the shares. Rockwell became involved in a contractual dispute with another corporation, Newtonbrook, and eventually brought an action against Newtonbrook for specific performance of the contract. Rockwell lost the action and Newtonbrook was awarded costs of $4800. When Newtonbrook sought to recover the costs, it found that Rockwell's entire assets consisted of $31.85 in its bank account. What would be Newtonbrook's best course of action?

a) Sue Kelly to recover the rest of the costs.
b) Accept the loss and do nothing.
c) Petition Rockwell into bankruptcy.
d) File a complaint with the government that incorporated Rockwell.
e) None of the above.

2. Resource Corp., a large holding corporation, had five subsidiaries. Resource Corp. and four of the subsidiaries were in serious financial difficulties. The remaining subsidiary, Gold Mine Inc., averaged annual profits of $500 million. Should the profits of Gold Mine Inc. be used to pay the creditors of the other related corporations?

a) No because the corporations are all separate entities.
b) Yes because they are all controlled by the same entity.
c) No because it is not Gold Mine's fault the others are in financial difficulty.
d) Yes because it is fair and equitable for the creditors.
e) Yes because they are associated corporations under the Income Tax Act.

3. James and John have decided to go into business for themselves. Since the business is in the high-tech sector and could be quite risky, they have decided to incorporate. The headquarters of the business will be in Ontario with the factories in Quebec and British Columbia. Which of the following methods of incorporation could be used for the business?

a) Articles of incorporation under the Canada Business Corporations Act.
b) Letters patent under the Quebec Civil Code.
c) Articles of incorporation under the Ontario Business Corporations Act.

d) Memorandum of association under the British Columbia Company Act.
e) All of the above.

4. Albert, Benny and Charles want to set up an Internet access business. Albert is the marketing wizard, Benny is the computer expert, and Charles the business management guru. Albert has $10 000 in savings to invest as well as an on-going annual income of $50 000 from consulting contracts with other companies. Benny only has $1 000, but has $12 000 worth of computer equipment that the business can use. Charles is flat broke from his last get-rich-quick scheme that resulted in his being declared bankrupt. Only last week was he released from bankruptcy. Another $150 000 capital will be needed as well as a $50 000 line of credit to cover daily expenses. What kind of business organization would be advisable for Albert, Benny and Charles?

a) Sole proprietorship.
b) Limited Partnership.
c) Incorporation.
d) All of the above.
e) None of the above.

5. Pliable Plastics Inc. was incorporated under an article of incorporation system. Its articles contained no restriction on the total number of shares that may be issued and its shares have no par value. Initially, the corporation issued 50 000 shares at $100, giving it a stated capital of $5 000 000. The directors wish to raise a further $3 000 000. All the shares are to be issued on the same day. On the day of the announcement, the market price of the shares is $10. On the day of actual issue, the market price is $60. How many shares need to be issued to raise the $3 000 000?

a) 30 000.
b) 300 000.
c) 50 000.
d) 25 000.
e) None of the above.

6. Pliable Plastics Inc. was created under a memorandum of association system with an authorized share capital of $10 000 000, divided into 100 000 shares of $100 nominal value. Initially, the corporation issued 50 000 shares at the par value of $100, giving it an issued and paid-up capital of $5 000 000. The directors wish to raise a further $3 000 000. All the shares are to be issued on the same day. On the day of the announcement, the market price of the shares is $10. On the day of actual issue, the market price is $60. How many shares need to be issued to raise the $3 000 000?

a) 30 000.
b) 300 000.
c) 50 000.

d) 25 000.
e) None of the above.

7. New Age Inc., a high-tech company, has been marketing a new word-processing package, but it is not selling very well. As a result, the corporation is in debt for $500 000. New Age only has three shareholders, each of whom own a third of the shares. Sarah is also a director and has personal assets worth $5000. Caitlin has no involvement in the management of the corporation and has personal assets of $3 million. Emily is a junior employee of the company and has personal assets of $30 000. A creditor, who is owed $300 000, wants to sue the company. Who should be listed as parties to the action?

a) New Age Inc., Sarah, Caitlin and Emily.
b) New Age Inc., Sarah and Emily.
c) New Age Inc. and Sarah.
d) New Age Inc., Sarah and Caitlin.
e) New Age Inc.

8. Considering the harshness of the weather in recent years and the resulting number of natural disasters, Stacey and William decide to set up a non-profit business to provide disaster relief. The business will fundraise for money and supplies that can be used when an emergency arises. To reduce administrative costs, Stacey and William want the simplest structure that is possible. What business organization should they consider?

a) Sole proprietorship.
b) Partnership.
c) Limited partnership.
d) Incorporation.
e) None of the above.

9. What conditions must be present for a court to lift the corporate veil?

a) A majority shareholder must control the corporation to the exclusion of other shareholders; the control must have been exercised to commit a fraud, wrong, or breach of duty; the misconduct must be the cause of the plaintiff's injury.
b) An individual must control the corporation and the control must be the cause of the plaintiff's injury.
c) A majority shareholder must control the corporation to the exclusion of other shareholders, and it is just and equitable for the court to lift the corporate veil.
d) An individual must control the corporation, the control must have been exercised to commit a fraud, wrong, or breach of duty, and the misconduct must be the cause of the plaintiff's injury.
e) A majority shareholder must control the corporation to the exclusion of other shareholders, the majority shareholder uses the corporation for his own purposes, and the corporation must have caused the plaintiff's injury.

10. What are the minimum restrictions for a private or closely held corporation?

a) Fewer than 50 shareholders, the right to transfer shares is restricted in some manner, and any invitation to the public to buy shares must be governed by a securities commission.
b) Blood or marriage must relate all the shareholders and the right to transfer shares is restricted in some manner.
c) Fewer than 50 shareholders, all the shareholders must be related by blood or marriage and invitations to the public to buy shares are prohibited.
d) Fewer than 50 shareholders, the right to transfer shares is restricted in some manner and any invitation to the public to buy shares is prohibited.
e) Fewer than 50 shareholders and any invitation to the public to buy shares is prohibited.

11. What factors influence a corporation's choice between issuing shares and bonds?

a) Preference of paying interest, which is a business expense or paying dividends.
b) Preference of making payments in before- or after-tax dollars.
c) Preference of having a choice whether or not to make payments.
d) Preference of subjecting the corporation's assets to further security.
e) All of the above.

12. What are the main purposes of by-laws?

a) Provide the detailed operating rules for a corporation's day-to-day affairs.
b) Provide the detailed operating rules for a corporation's long-term future.
c) Provide the detailed framework for the corporation's establishment.
d) Provide the detailed operating rules for the subsidiaries of the corporation.
e) Provide the detailed rules for the structure of the corporation.

13. Which of the following distinguish a corporation from a partnership?

a) Separation of ownership and management.
b) Limited liability.
c) Indefinite existence.
d) Ease of transfer of ownership.
e) All of the above.

14. Which of the following are exceptions to the limited liability principle of corporations?

a) Personal guarantees to creditors; improper distribution of corporate assets, such as a dividend; personal liability of directors and senior officers; and shareholder liability for acts of the directors.
b) Personal guarantees to creditors; improper distribution of corporate assets, such as a dividend; and personal liability of directors and senior officers.

c) Personal guarantees to creditors; and improper distribution of corporate assets, such as a dividend; and shareholder liability for acts of the directors.
d) Personal guarantees to creditors; and personal liability of directors and senior officers.
e) Improper distribution of corporate assets, such as a dividend; personal liability of directors and senior officers; and shareholder liability for acts of the directors.

15. What are the special rights that normally attach to preferred shares?

a) A preferential right to receive dividends.
b) A preferential right to receive dividends, a preferential right to notice of shareholder meetings and a preferential right to be redeemed on the dissolution of the corporation.
c) A preferential right to receive dividends and a preferential right to be redeemed on the dissolution of the corporation.
d) A preferential right to receive dividends, a preferential right to redemption at any time of the corporation's choosing and a preferential right to be redeemed on the dissolution of the corporation.
e) A preferential right to be redeemed on the dissolution of the corporation.

16. In which of the following situations is a joint venture appropriate?
I. Capital in excess of that which one person alone can afford is required.
II. Expertise of several persons is required for a business venture.
III. Risk sharing in a business venture is desired.

a) I only
b) II only
c) III only
d) I and II only
e) I, II and III

17. All of the following statements are correct EXCEPT:

a) Shares are a proportionate ownership of a corporation.
b) Shares are equity in a corporation.
c) Shareholders are in a debtor/creditor relationship with a corporation.
d) Shareholders are entitled to dividends only when the corporation makes a profit and the directors declare that dividends shall be paid.
e) On a winding-up of a company, shareholders are repaid after creditors.

18. Authorized capital is:

a) The kind and number of shares that can be issued in a corporation.
b) The number of shares actually issued by a corporation.
c) The document that sets out the terms of incorporation.
d) The document containing the basic operating rules of a corporation.

e) The document giving the directors and officers of a corporation authority to carry out certain activities.

Answers to Multiple-Choice Questions

1. b)
See page 605 for more information.

2. a)
See page 606 for more information.

3. e)
See pages 609–610 for more information.

4. c)
See pages 602–603 for more information.

5. c)
See page 615 for more information

6. a)
See page 614 for more information.

7. e)
See page 602 for more information.

8. d)
See page 602 for more information.

9. d)
See page 608 for more information.

10. d)
See page 613 for more information.

11. e)
See page 616 for more information.

12. a)
See page 611 for more information.

13. e)
See pages 602–604 for more information.

14. b)
See page 607 for more information.

15. c)
See page 617 for more information.

16. e)
See page 597 for more information.

17. c)
See pages 614–618 for more information.

18. a)
See page 614 for more information.

True/False Questions

1. A corporation, as a separate legal person, is liable for its own debts. Shareholders' liability is limited to their capital contribution.

2. Each partner in a partnership is liable for the debts of the partnership to the limit of his personal assets.

3. The *Salomon* case succeeded in assuring the separation of the company from its shareholders in terms of legal responsibilities and entitlements. A shareholder, as Salomon found out, could become a mortgagee of company property and have priority over other creditors.

However, courts later decided that a shareholder has no insurable interest in property that belongs to the corporation, even if the shareholder owns one hundred per cent of the shares.

4. Ontario, Manitoba, Saskatchewan, New Brunswick, Alberta, Newfoundland and the federal Parliament all permit incorporations by articles. To so incorporate, those persons wishing to form a corporation sign and deliver articles of incorporation to a government office which, in turn, issues a certificate of incorporation.

5. In all Canadian jurisdictions, no matter how many shareholders or how large the corporation is, it will be incorporated under the same statutory requirements.

6. In all provinces, there is a statutory distinction for corporate purposes between broadly held or closely held corporations.

7. In the business world today, there is no distinction between a share and a bond or debenture because features attached to corporate securities are broadly mixed.

Answers to True/False Questions

1. True.

2. True.

3. True.

4. True.

5. True.

6. False. In most provinces, no statutory distinction is drawn for corporate purposes between broadly held or closely held corporations.

However, in British Columbia, Prince Edward Island and Nova Scotia, the Companies Acts permit the formation of private companies. These companies must maintain three characteristics to retain the status:
(i) the right to transfer shares must be restricted in some manner;
(ii) the number of shareholders is limited to 50; and
(iii) no invitation to buy shares can be made to the public.

7. False. In the business world today, the distinction between a share and a bond or debenture is often blurred because features attached to corporate securities are broadly mixed.

At the most basic level, a share is a proportionate ownership of the company. It is called an "equity" holding because it reflects entitlement to a portion of the corporate enterprise. Thus, unless special conditions are attached to the share (as might be the case with some preferred shares) the shareholders' investment is not secured or guaranteed but is dictated by the success of the enterprise.

A bond or debenture is a document evidencing a debtor/creditor relationship. The company is the debtor and the bondholder is the creditor. The debt under bond or debenture is usually secured by a registered lien or mortgage against the property of the company.

28

The Internal Affairs of Corporations

Purpose and Significance

The directors and shareholders are important players in the life of a corporation. The role of directors is to manage the business and affairs of the corporation. Along with this role come certain duties. The shareholders are those holding shares in the corporation. They have invested money in the corporation, but have no say in the day-to-day operation of the corporation. However, shareholders possess certain rights, such as the right to attend at annual meetings. Minority shareholders are given certain rights in order to prevent oppression by other shareholders.

In this chapter we discuss the authority and responsibilities of directors in the operation and management of the corporation, the rights of shareholders and the protection of minority shareholders.

Learning Objectives

A. Examine the business, affairs and structure of the modern business corporation.

B. Describe the role and duties of directors of a corporation.

C. Examine the rights of shareholders, including the means of protection available to minority shareholders.

Content Outline

I. Business and affairs of a corporation

II. The structure of the modern business corporation

III. Directors
    A. The role of the directors
    B. The appointment and removal of directors

IV. Duties of directors
    A. To whom are directors' duties owed?
        1. To the corporation
        2. To the shareholders
        3. To the public
    B. Duties of care and skill
        1. Negligence
        2. Strict liability
    C. Fiduciary duties
        1. Contracts with the corporations
        2. Interception of corporate opportunity
        3. The director's mandate
        4. Corporate information
        5. Competing with the corporation
        6. Consequences of a breach of fiduciary duty
    D. Insider trading

V. Rights of shareholders
    A. The role of shareholders
        1. In widely held corporations
        2. In closely held corporations
    B. Rights attached to shares
    C. Voting: A voice in the affairs of the corporation
        1. Notice and attendance at meetings
        2. The right to requisition meetings
        3. The right to vote

Questions on Learning Objectives

Objective A: Discuss the business, affairs and structure of a modern business corporation.

A.1 Distinguish the "affairs" from the "business" of a corporation, which was incorporated under the *Canadian Business Corporations Act* or a corresponding provincial statute. (pp. 621–622)

A.2 What are the two essential organs common to all corporations? (p. 622)

Objective B: Describe the duties of directors of a corporation.

B.1 List the four most important powers conferred on directors by the *Canadian Business Corporations Act*. (p. 623)

B.2 How is the board of directors of a corporation chosen? (p. 624)

B.3 Must the directors of a corporation inform the shareholders of a takeover offer? (pp. 625–626)

B.4 Can a director of a corporation contract with the corporation? (p. 627)

B.5 If a director is sent by the corporation to buy a piece of property, can she buy the property for herself instead? (p. 628)

B.6 What is insider trading, and who is an "insider" for the purposes of the legislation? (pp. 630–631)

Objective C: Examine the rights of shareholders, including the means of protection available to minority shareholders.

C.1 What is meant by the terms "locked in" and "frozen out" when applied to minority shareholders? (p. 632)

C.2 Do shareholders have a right to examine the books of account of the corporation? (p. 638)

C.3 How often must a corporation hold a shareholders' general meeting? (p. 633)

C.4 What is a proxy? (p. 634)

C.5 Do Canadian courts recognize the pre-emptive rights of a shareholder? (pp. 636–637)

C.6 How does a corporation determine when to pay a dividend, and how much to give to each shareholder? (p. 636)

C.7 What is a derivative action? (pp. 641–642)

C.8 Discuss the ways in which a contract between shareholders of a corporation can be used to protect their interests. (pp. 643–644)

Answers to Questions on Learning Objectives

A.1 The affairs of a corporation are the internal arrangements among the corporation, shareholders, directors and officers. The business of a corporation is the external relations between the corporation and those who deal with it as a business enterprise (for example, the customers and suppliers of the corporation).

A.2 The two basic organs common to all corporations are the shareholders and the board of directors.

B.1 The most important powers conferred on directors by the *Canadian Business Corporations Act* are:
(i) to issue shares;
(ii) to declare dividends;
(iii) to adopt by-laws governing the day-to-day affairs of the corporation; and
(iv) to call meetings of shareholders.

B.2 The shareholders elect the board of directors of a corporation.

B.3 Unless there is a statutory duty, the directors are under no legal duty to forward a takeover offer to the shareholders. Under common law, directors owe general duties to the corporation, but not to the shareholders.

Securities legislation enacted in several provinces can make specific changes in the duties of directors and, in the case of takeover bids, can attempt to ensure fair treatment of shareholders.

B.4 A set of rules has evolved in Canada, in court decisions and legislation, to deal with this problem. In general, the rule works on the following principles. A director who has contracted with the corporation, or who has any interest in a contract, must disclose such interest at the meeting of the board of directors considering the contract. He must not vote on the contract. If, after learning of this interest, the remaining directors wish to vote approval of the contract, it becomes a binding contract.

Failure by the director to disclose his interest gives the corporation the right to rescind the contract upon learning of his interest in it. Alternatively, it may affirm the contract on the terms on which it was made.

B.5 The position of a director who acquires an interest in property while under a duty to the corporation is the same as that of an agent who acquires an interest in property on behalf of her principal. Although the director has formal or legal ownership of the property, she holds it for the benefit of the corporation (or principal).

B.6 Insider trading is the buying or selling of a corporation's shares by an "insider" in the corporation who makes use of confidential inside information in order to make a profit or avoid a loss. For the purposes of the legislation, an "insider" is a director or officer, an employee, any shareholder who holds more than 10 percent of the corporation's securities, and a person who knowingly receives confidential information from an insider.

C.1 In theory, a shareholder who is dissatisfied with the management of the corporation can sell her shares to get out of the unfortunate situation. In fact, many closely-held corporations have restrictions on the free transfer of shares, which make a sale complicated and difficult. In addition, shares in a small or badly-run corporation might not be worth very much in a free market. The result is that a minority shareholder can be "locked in," unable to sell or liquidate a bad investment.

Alternatively, if the holders of the majority of shares wish to "freeze out" a minority shareholder, they can use their voting power to exclude the minority shareholder from participation in the running of the business or from sharing the profits.

C.2 Only the auditor, as representative of the shareholders, and the directors have a right to examine the books of account.

C.3 A corporation is required by statute to hold at least one annual general meeting. Other general meetings may be called, however.

C.4 All corporation law statutes permit a shareholder who will not be present at a general meeting to assign his voting right to any shareholder who will be present. This is done by signing a proxy form. The proxy form may give the voting shareholder full freedom in how to use the assigned vote, or it may direct that the voting shareholder vote in the manner dictated by the absent shareholder.

C.5 United States courts have declared that shareholders have pre-emptive right to continue to hold their percentage of the shareholding even when the number of total shares changes.

Canadian courts do not recognize full pre-emptive rights. As long as the directors are acting for the purpose of raising capital they have full discretion to issue shares to whomever they wish upon payment of a fair price. But if the directors distribute shares not to benefit the corporation but to change the voting control, they may be stopped.

C.6 The declaring of dividends is a matter entirely in the discretion of the board of directors. Once declared, however, there can be no discrimination between shareholders owning the same class of shares; each is entitled to a share of the dividend in proportion to the number of shares that class held.

Preferred shareholders, as permitted by the corporate charter, may have dividend rights which are special or different from the dividend rights of other classes of shares.

C.7 A corporation has its own legal rights and may sue to affirm them. The decision about whether to sue is ordinarily made by the officers or board of directors. If the officers or directors are wrong-doers, it is unlikely that they will cause the corporation to sue. Provision has been made by common law and statute for a shareholder or shareholders to begin an action on behalf of the corporation in such a circumstance. Such an action is usually called a derivative action.

C.8 The value of a shareholder agreement is limited only by the imagination and foresight of its parties. Experience has demonstrated that it is most useful to include terms on the right to employment, right to participate in management, and right to a fair price on the liquidation of share interest.

Multiple-Choice Questions

1. Market Inc., a corporation, carries on the business of retailing clothing. The company has two directors, Jane and Alice, each of whom hold 45% of the shares. The remaining 10% of the shares is held by David, an unrelated investor. In 1996 the company realized its first profit — a very good profit — and looks forward to further profits through additional expansion. However, due to its earlier precarious financial position, the company by resolution in 1995 decided not to acquire the rights to a retail shoe franchise which would have complimented its clothing operation. Six months ago, the shoe franchise was still available so Jane and Alice formed a company that acquired the franchise. In the last six months, the franchise has been very profitable. On what basis can David sue Jane and Alice?

a) Breach of their duty to do what is in the best interests of the shareholders.
b) Breach of their duty of conflict of interest.
c) Breach of their duty not to compete with the corporation.
d) Breach of their duty to abstain from abusing a corporate opportunity.
e) Breach of their duty of care and skill.

2. Donald, Michael and Geoff are in the construction business using a corporation. Donald has learned about a property with large potential for gold mining. Without the knowledge of Michael and Geoff, Donald invests excess funds of the company in the property and sets up a gold mining business. When the gold business begins to make profits, Donald claims the profits for himself. These investments in no way interfered with the company's operations, and the funds taken have been replaced. On what basis can Michael and Geoff sue Donald?

a) Breach of his duty of conflict of interest.
b) Breach of his duty to abstain from abusing a corporate opportunity.
c) Breach of his duty of care and skill.
d) Breach of his duty to do what is in the best interests of the shareholders.
e) Breach of his duty not to compete with the corporation.

3. Donald, Michael and Geoff are in the construction business using a corporation. Donald has learned about a property with large potential for gold mining. Without the knowledge of Michael and Geoff, Donald invests excess funds of the company in the property and sets up a gold mining business. When the gold business begins to make profits, Donald claims the profits for himself. These investments in no way interfered with the company's operations, and the funds taken have been replaced. If the corporation was to sue Donald, what would be their preferred remedy?

a) An estimate of the damages incurred by the construction business.
b) A specific performance order to force Donald to perform according to his duties as a director.
c) All the profits of the gold business.
d) An injunction to stop Donald from breaching his duties as a director.
e) None of the above.

4. Monty is a shareholder in ABC Corporation. He is a passive investor, in that he lent $1 million to the corporation for a specific land development project and took back shares in return. Lancaster and Degrasse are the only other shareholders and the only directors of ABC. They manage the day-to-day affairs of the business. ABC purchased a piece of land from Lancaster and Degrasse for $1 million. Monty learns that the land is only worth $500 000 and wants to take some action against the corporation as well as against Lancaster and Degrasse. On what basis can Monty sue Lancaster and Degrasse?

a) Breach of their duty of conflict of interest.
b) Breach of their duty to abstain from abusing a corporate opportunity.

c) Breach of their duty of care and skill.

d) Breach of their duty to do what is in the best interests of the shareholders.

e) Breach of their duty not to compete with the corporation.

5. Lars PB Corp. is in negotiations to purchase land on Baffin Island to set up a resort. This land is low on Lars PB's priority list, and negotiations have stalled. Bea, a director of Lars PB, approached the owner of the land and bought it for her own company, Sunshine Resorts Inc. The land turned out to be perfect for a resort, and Sunshine made a profit of $1 million in its first year of operation. On what basis can Lars PB sue Bea?

a) Breach of her duty not to compete with the corporation.

b) Breach of her duty of conflict of interest.

c) Breach of her duty to abstain from abusing a corporate opportunity.

d) Breach of her duty to do what is in the best interests of the shareholders.

e) Breach of her duty of care and skill.

6. Lars PB is also having problems with a director. Walrus is one of the three directors of Lars PB and has recently become friends with a vice president of a competing firm. They often go away on weekend fishing trips, and frequently play snow golf together. The other directors are unhappy about Walrus's contact with a competitor and the possibility of his leaking confidential business plans and information. Walrus maintains that it is none of Lars PB's business, since it is part of his personal life. The other directors want to remove Walrus from his position on the board of directors. On what grounds can they base their action for removal?

a) Care and skill.

b) Conflict of interest.

c) Doctrine of corporate opportunity.

d) Personal liability.

e) None of the above.

7. As vice-president of marketing, Jack was involved in all marketing and media communications for the corporation. In preparation for releasing the latest quarterly reports, Jack learned that the reports would show a $50 million loss for the corporation. Before the information was made public, Jack sold all his shares in the corporation thereby avoiding a large loss when the share price dropped. What should Jack be concerned about?

a) He should be concerned about how to invest all the money he just made.

b) He should be concerned about being charged with insider trading.

c) He should be concerned about being accused of breaching his duty of conflict of interest.

d) He should have no concerns.

e) He should be concerned about being accused of breaching his duty not to abuse corporate opportunity.

8. Concentric Circle Limited, a manufacturer of light bulbs, wants to expand the business and get into the manufacture of other round objects, such as tires. At a shareholders' meeting called to discuss the expansion, a majority of shareholders approved the expansion. Keith, a very conservative investor, does not like the idea of the expansion and voted against it. Since the expansion was approved, what would be Keith's best course of action?

a) Commence a derivative action.
b) Commence an oppression action.
c) Use the appraisal remedy.
d) Commence an action to wind up the corporation.
e) Do nothing and accept the majority's decision.

9. Sixty percent of the shares of Figaro Limited are held by Almaviva Inc., a large public corporation, and forty percent are held by its original founder Suzanna. Following a disagreement over company policy with Suzanna, Almaviva uses its majority voting power to appoint three of its own directors to be directors of Figaro. The new directors subsequently sell an important piece of Figaro's property to Bartolo Limited, a corporation wholly controlled by Almaviva. The sale is at a grossly undervalued price. What is Suzanna's best course of action?

a) Commence a derivative action.
b) Commence an oppression action.
c) Use the appraisal remedy.
d) Commence an action to wind up the corporation.
e) Do nothing.

10. The shares in Jenufa Limited are held in equal proportions by Stephanie, her husband Mark, and his two children by a previous marriage, Gillian and Michael. All had been directors until recently. After an acrimonious divorce, Mark, Gillian and Michael use their majority voting power to remove Stephanie from the board. Subsequently, they greatly increase their own salaries as full-time officers of the corporation, which consequently reduces the corporation's profits. Instead of distributing the remaining profits as dividends, they decide to reinvest the profits in a fund to provide for the long-term capital needs of the corporation. They also refuse to consent to Stephanie transferring her shares to any third party. What would be Stephanie's best course of action?

a) Commence a derivative action.
b) Commence an oppression action.
c) Use the appraisal remedy.
d) Commence an action to wind up the corporation.
e) Do nothing and accept the majority's decision.

11. What is meant by a derivative action?

a) A court action brought concerning derivatives.
b) A court action brought by a shareholder concerning a director's breach of duty.
c) A court action brought by a director concerning a shareholder's breach of duty.
d) A court action brought by a shareholder in the name of the corporation.
e) A court action brought by the corporation concerning a director's breach of duty.

12. Who is an insider?

a) The directors.
b) Any shareholder who owns more than ten percent of the outstanding shares.
c) Any person who receives confidential information.
d) The senior officers.
e) All of the above.

13. The right to appoint a proxy is considered one of the important rights of shareholders. Why is a proxy so important?

a) It allows shareholders entrance to a shareholders' meeting.
b) It allows shareholders to instruct the directors on certain issues.
c) It allows shareholders who cannot attend a shareholders' meeting to express their point of view and to vote.
d) It allows shareholders to control the day-to-day affairs of the corporation.
e) It allows the shareholders to have access to the corporate records.

14. What are rights of the shareholders?

a) Right to notice of shareholders' and directors' meetings; right to requisition shareholders' and directors' meetings; right to vote; right of access to the documents of record and the record of insider trading.
b) Right to notice of shareholders' meetings; right to requisition shareholders' meetings; right to audited financial statements.
c) Right to notice of directors' meetings; right to requisition directors' meetings; right to vote; right to audited financial statements.
d) Right to notice of shareholders' and directors' meetings; right to requisition shareholders' and directors' meetings; right to audited financial statements.
e) Right to notice of shareholders' meetings; right to requisition shareholders' meetings; right to vote; right to audited financial statements; right of access to the documents of record and the record of insider trading.

15. What is the advantage of a shareholder's right to attend a shareholders' meeting?

a) Opportunity to voice concerns about the day-to-day management, question directors and make criticisms about the overall management.

b) Opportunity to replace the directors.
c) Opportunity to meet the directors and other shareholders.
d) Opportunity to review the audited financial statements.
e) All of the above.

16. Which of the following statements correctly describe the legal position of a corporate director?

a) The director of a corporation is not entitled to examine the books of account of the corporation.
b) If the director of a corporation sells property to that corporation through an agent and doesn't disclose his ownership of the property, the corporation may rescind the contract.
c) A director cannot rely on the information given to her by the officers of the corporation, but must investigate all things on her own and discover the truth or she can be sued by the shareholders.
d) If a director learns of a business opportunity that is appropriate for the corporation, the director is not in breach of duty if she takes advantage of the opportunity without giving the corporation first chance.
e) A director is elected by the shareholders of the corporation, and owes a fiduciary duty to those shareholders.

17. Which of the following would describe protections that a minority shareholder might take against possible oppression by the majority?
I. A minority shareholder can make a binding contract with other shareholders to mutually agree to elect one another to the board of directors.
II. If there is one class of shares, a minority shareholder is entitled to sue the corporation for his shares of the profits of the corporation.
III. If the directors are abusing their office and cheating the corporation, the shareholder probably cannot sue in his own name but may be able to sue on behalf of the corporation in a representative or derivative action.

a) I, II and III
b) I and III only
c) II only
d) III only
e) II and III only

18. Which of the following statements accurately describe what is permitted by law in arranging the financial status of a corporation?

a) Shares with a par value can never be sold for less or more than par value.
b) If a corporation becomes insolvent, the shareholders are entitled to a return of their investment before any creditors are paid.
c) Before a corporation can sell shares to the public it must receive permission under the Securities Act in the province where it sells, usually by filing a prospectus.

d) All shareholders must receive the same dividend rights. No shareholders, even if they have preferred shares, are entitled to larger dividends than other shareholders.

e) If a corporation has no profit or surplus, it may still pay a dividend to shareholders, but it must continue to pay interest to bondholders.

Answers to Multiple-Choice Questions

1. d)
See pages 628–629 for more information.

2. b)
See pages 628–629 for more information.

3. c)
See page 630 for more information.

4. a)
See page 627 for more information.

5. c)
See page 628 for more information

6. e)
See pages 627–630 for more information.

7. b)
See pages 630–631 for more information.

8. c)
See page 641 for more information.

9. a)
See page 641 for more information.

10. b)
See page 642 for more information.

11. d)
See pages 641–642 for more information.

12. e)
See page 630 for more information.

13. c)
See page 634 for more information.

14. e)
See pages 632–639 for more information.

15. a)
See page 633 for more information.

16. a)
See pages 623–631 for more information.

17. b)
See pages 640–643 for more information.

18. c)
See pages 631–640 for more information.

True/False Questions

1. The affairs of a corporation are the internal arrangements among the corporation, shareholders, directors and officers. The business of a corporation is the external relations between the corporation and those who deal with it as a business enterprise (for example, the customers and suppliers of the corporation).

2. The most important powers conferred on directors by the Canadian Business Corporations Act are:
(i) to issue shares
(ii) to declare dividends
(iii) to adopt by-laws governing the day-to-day affairs of the corporation
(iv) to call meetings of shareholders.

3. Unless there is a statutory duty, the directors are under no legal duty to forward a takeover offer to the shareholders. Under common law, directors owe general duties to the corporation, but not to the shareholders.

4. Securities legislation enacted in several provinces does not allow specific changes in the duties of directors and, in the case of takeover bids, can attempt to ensure fair treatment of shareholders.

5. The position of a director who acquires an interest in property while under a duty to the corporation is the same as that of an agent who acquires an interest in property on behalf of her principal. Although the director has formal or legal ownership of the property, he holds it for the benefit of the corporation (or principal).

6. Only the auditor, as representative of the shareholders, has a right to examine the books of account.

7. United States courts have declared that shareholders have pre-emptive right to continue to hold their percentage of the shareholding even when the number of total shares changes.

8. Canadian courts also recognize full pre-emptive rights.

Answers to True/False Questions

1. True.

2. True.

3. True.

4. False. Securities legislation enacted in several provinces can make specific changes in the duties of directors and, in the case of takeover bids, can attempt to ensure fair treatment of shareholders.

5. True.

6. False. Only the auditor, as representative of the shareholders, and the directors have a right to examine the books of account.

7. True.

8. False. Canadian courts do not recognize full pre-emptive rights. As long as the directors are acting for the purpose of raising capital they have full discretion to issue shares to whomever they wish upon payment of a fair price. But if the directors distribute shares not to benefit the corporation but to change the voting control, they may be stopped.

29

The External Responsibilities of a Corporation

Purpose and Significance

Though the law can make a corporation a legal person, it cannot give a corporation the characteristics of a person. Because it does not have its own hand or its own mind, a corporation will have to act through human agents.

Since shareholders of corporations have limited liability, the law provides certain protections for creditors and current and prospective investors.

Because the corporation is an independent legal entity, it can be found liable of certain offences at law. As well, directors and senior officers of a corporation can be held personally liable for certain actions.

In this chapter we discuss the authority and responsibilities of corporate agents in the operation and management of the corporation, the protection given to creditors and investors, and the potential liability of corporations and their directors and officers.

Learning Objectives

A. Discuss the liability of a corporation for the acts of its agents.

B. Examine the means of protecting third party interests, such as those claimed by creditors and investors, through public regulation of corporations.

C. Discuss the liability that may be imposed on corporations, their directors and officers.

Content Outline

I. The changing nature of business responsibilities

II. Liability of a corporation for acts of its agents

III. Pre-incorporation contracts

IV. Protection of creditors
    A. Implications of limited liability
    B. Minimum capital requirement
    C. Preservation of capital
    D. Protection of capital under the CBCA
    E. The solvency test
    F. The maintenance of capital test
        1. Dividends
        2. Return of capital
        3. Loans to shareholders, directors, and employees

V. Protection of investors
    A. Securities Legislation
        1. Objectives of securities legislation
        2. Licensing
        3. Prospectuses
        4. Continuing disclosure
        5. Takeovers and reorganizations

VI. Protection of the public interest

VII. The nature of corporate liability
    A. Regulatory offences
        1. The requirement of fault
        2. The presumption of fault
        3. Absolute liability

B. Liability of corporations
      1. Can corporations commit crimes?
      2. The "Directing Mind" principle
C. Personal liability of directors and senior officers

VIII. The basis for liability imposed on enterprises and their human agents: Environmental legislation
    A. What standard of skill and care must be met?
      1. The expertise required of directors and senior officers
      2. A uniform standard
    B. Who should be found liable?
      1. Those in charge of an activity?
      2. Outside directors?
      3. The difficulty in determining responsibility
    C. What should be punishment?
    D. The business consequences

Questions on Learning Objectives

Objective A: Discuss the liability of a corporation for the acts of its agents.

A.1 What is the indoor management rule? (p. 650)

A.2 Is a corporation bound by a contract made in its name before it was legally incorporated? (pp. 651–652)

Objective B: Explain the means of protecting third party interests, such as those claimed by creditors and investors, through public regulation of corporations.

B.1 Can directors ever be held liable for the outstanding debts of their corporations? (p. 652)

B.2 What is the maintenance of capital test? (pp. 654–655)

B.3 Can a corporation buy its own shares? (p. 655)

B.4 In Canada, what level of government governs the public trading of corporate securities? (p. 655)

B.5 What devices are used in Canadian securities legislation to achieve its purposes? (pp. 655–656)

Objective C: Discuss the liability that may be imposed on corporations, their directors and officers.

C.1 Distinguish between civil liability and criminal liability. Which of these two does liability imposed by government regulation more closely resemble? (p. 658)

C.2 In general, what must be proved for an accused to be guilty of an offence? (p. 658)

C.3 What is a regulatory offence? (pp. 658–659)

C.4 Into what three classes did the Supreme Court of Canada, in a 1978 case, divide criminal offences? (p. 659)

C.5 Explain the significance of the *Lennard's Carrying Company* case. (pp. 660–661)

C.6 What argument can be made that certain individuals associated with the corporation, and not just the corporation, should be held liable and punished for certain offences? (pp. 661–662)

C.7 Why is it sometimes difficult to prosecute individuals in addition to the corporation? (pp. 661–662)

C.8 What tests have our legislatures enacted to determine whether an individual is liable? (pp. 664–665)

C.9 Explain the significance of the *R.* v. *Bata Industries Ltd.* case. (p. 666)

C.10 What defence can be raised by a corporation or an individual to overcome the presumption of negligence? (p. 663)

C.11 What factors did the court in *R.* v. *Varnicolor Chemical Ltd.* say should be used in determining the severity of the sentence for an environmental offence? (p. 667)

Answers to Questions on Learning Objectives

A.1 The indoor management rule was set out in the English case of *Royal British Bank* v. *Turquand*, and has been applied in Canada. Under the rule it has been held that in the absence of notice of irregularity or suspicious circumstances, everything in the operation of a corporation that appears to be properly done may be relied on by an outsider and will bind the company.

A corporation cannot ratify a contract made in its name before the date of its incorporation. Such a contract is a nullity.

In some provinces, legislation has made it possible for the corporation to ratify a pre-incorporation contract.

B.1 The directors might become liable for debts of their corporation if they misuse the corporate assets in the payment of dividends, or in the redemption or re-purchase of corporate shares, and if the transactions result in the insolvency of the corporation.

The test is created by a number of provisions in the *Corporation Act*. It is designed to insure that the capital fund, made up of the assets paid into the corporation by shareholders, will be available to absorb business losses that cannot be met out of the corporation's ongoing business earnings.

B.3 Under the common law a corporation could not purchase its own shares. Under Canadian certificate of incorporation statutes, it is now possible for corporations created by those statutes to purchase their own shares for a number of specified reasons subject to certain statutory limitations.

B.4 Securities legislation is substantially within provincial jurisdiction. Each province has a *Securities Act* or *Securities Fraud Prevention Act*.

B.5 There are two principal devices: (a) Registering and licensing those engaged in the securities business, including stock exchanges, stockbrokers and securities salesmen. (b) Requiring a corporation that issues securities for sale to the public to file a prospectus. A prospectus is designed to fully reveal the business and financial affairs of a corporation so that a prospective investor is able to judge accurately the nature of this investment.

C.1 Civil liability is liability to a plaintiff, often to pay damages for harm resulting from commission of a tort or breach of a contract. Criminal liability arises out of a conviction for an offence, and is typically punished by payment of a fine or imprisonment. Liability imposed under government regulatory schemes more closely resembles criminal liability in that the schemes prohibit certain conduct and punish those who ignore such prohibitions.

C.2 In general, the prosecution must prove (beyond a reasonable doubt) that the accused committed the act or omission that is the subject of the offence, but also that the accused had *mens rea* (a guilty mind).

C.3 A regulatory offence is an offence with a broader definition of *mens rea* than the traditional criminal offences. To establish liability under a regulatory offence, it may be sufficient to show that the accused *should have* known that his conduct would result in the commission of the offence.

C.4 The Supreme Court of Canada in the *R.* v. *Sault Ste. Marie* case, divided criminal offences into the following three classes: (i) *Mens rea* offences where a "guilty mind" must be shown; (ii) Offences of *strict liability* where the accused can avoid liability by showing he took all reasonable care; and (iii) Offences of *absolute liability* where the mere doing of the act makes the accused guilty of the offence.

C.5 The *Lennard's Carrying Company* case stands for the proposition that a corporation can, in some circumstances, commit an act requiring a guilty mind.

C.6 A large corporation might consider a fine for the commission of an offence to be a mere cost of doing business. Also, a corporation may be merely a "shell" allowing those who control it to walk away from it and start up a new corporation where the original corporation has insufficient assets to pay a fine. Thus, effective deterrence may require the individuals responsible for the offence to be punished directly.

In large corporations, quite often it is difficult to sufficiently identify the individual who is responsible for the act.

C.8 Canadian legislatures have tended to used two phrases to describe the test for liability: the first makes liable those who "cause or permit" a hazardous substance to be discharged; the second makes liable any officer, director or agent who "directed, authorized, assented to, acquiesced in or participated in the commission of an offence."

C.9 In *R.* v. *Bata Industries Ltd.*, charges were laid against three directors of the corporation. The significance of the case is that the court looked at the individual involvement of each of the three directors in the event which brought on the charges to determine whether or not each director was guilty.

C.10 When a corporation or individual is charged with an offence, there is a presumption that the activity in question was carried out negligently. An accused can overcome the presumption by showing they used "due diligence" in carrying out their duties.

C.11 The court found that the following factors should be considered in determining the severity of the sentence:
(i) the nature of the environment affected;
(ii) the extent of the damage actually inflicted: and
(iii) the deliberateness of the offence.

Multiple-Choice Questions

1. A corporation's premises contained a large, toxic chemical waste storage site with many decaying, rusting and uncovered containers. Soil samples revealed concentrations of various dangerous chemicals. Against who should the prosecution lay charges?

a) The corporation.
b) The directors.
c) The local environmental association.
d) The corporation, the directors and the local environmental association.
e) The corporation and the directors.

2. A corporation disposed of industrial wastes. Unfortunately, waste materials escaped from its toxic disposal site into the ground water and moved towards a river that was a source of drinking water for communities. Of the three vice-presidents, Jason was responsible for the disposal site. Margot, another vice-president, reviewed reports about the site, but had no control over the site. The remaining vice-president, Justin, had no connection with the site. The board of directors received annual reports on all the operations of the corporation, but no mention was made of the escaped waste materials. When the corporation took no action to clean up the spill, the Ministry of the Environment did the clean-up at a cost of $2.5 million. Who should the Ministry sue to get its money back?

a) The corporation.
b) The corporation and the directors.
c) The corporation, the directors and the officers.
d) The corporation, Jason and Margot.
e) The corporation, Jason and the directors.

3. Gerald entered into contract negotiations with the Alpha Corp. to sell steel bars. The value of the contract was $200 000. At the end of the negotiations, a formal written contract was drawn up and signed by Gerald and Thomas, a vice-president of Alpha. Unbeknownst to Gerald, the by-laws of Alpha specified that two officers must sign any contract over $50 000. After the first delivery of steel bars, Alpha refused to pay, arguing that the contract was not valid due to the lack of a second signature. Who can Gerald sue?

a) Sue Alpha for breach of contract relying on the indoor management rule.
b) Sue Thomas for breach of warranty of authority.
c) Sue Alpha for breach of contract relying on the *Statute of Frauds*.
d) Sue Thomas for breach of his duties as an officer of Alpha.
e) Sue nobody, as Alpha is correct.

4. The Sigma Corporation has been found guilty of improperly disposing of hazardous biological waste. The three directors of the corporation are also being investigated. To avoid liability, the directors have to show that they acted with due diligence. What is involved in due diligence?

a) Establishing rules prohibiting the dumping of hazardous materials.
b) Providing training to employees on how to properly dispose of hazardous materials.
c) Establishing, monitoring and improving a system to prevent the dumping of hazardous materials.
d) Doing anything that would have prevented the dumping of hazardous materials.
e) Using the latest technology in establishing systems to prevent the dumping of hazardous materials.

5. SAD Limited has 10 000 outstanding shares with a share capital of $50 000. It is the practice of the corporation to declare a dividend each year to reward shareholders. In the past year, however, business has not been good and the corporation has suffered a significant loss. In calculating the financial statements it is learned that the net assets of the corporation are now $30 000. Can the corporation still declare a dividend?

a) Yes because the corporation is not insolvent.
b) No because there has been a significant loss so there is no profit to give shareholders.
c) Yes because it is the practice of the corporation.
d) No because the maintenance of capital test would not permit it.
e) Yes as long as the stated capital of the corporation is reduced.

6. SAD Limited has 10 000 outstanding shares with a share capital of $50 000. It is the practice of the corporation to declare a dividend each year to reward shareholders. In the past year, however, business has been slow so the corporation has made a very small profit. In calculating the financial statements it is learned that, while the assets of the corporation exceed liabilities, the corporation is not able to pay all its debts as they become due. Can the corporation still declare a dividend?

a) Yes because the corporation made a profit.
b) No because the corporation is insolvent.
c) Yes because the maintenance of capital test can be passed.
d) No because the small profit should be reinvested into the business.
e) No because the corporation is going to be petitioned into bankruptcy.

7. What is the distinction between a reduction of stated capital and an actual return of capital?

a) In a reduction of stated capital, a corporation buys back its shares. An actual return of capital is the payment of money, such as through a dividend, to the shareholders.
b) A reduction of stated capital recognizes a state of affairs in the financial statements. In an actual return of capital, shareholders pay additional money into the corporation.
c) A reduction of stated capital recognizes a state of affairs in the financial statements. An actual return of capital is the payment of money, such as through a dividend, to the shareholders.
d) In a reduction of stated capital, a corporation buys back its shares. In an actual return of capital, shareholders pay additional money into the corporation.
e) In a reduction of stated capital, the auditor changes the stated capital line on the financial statements. In an actual return of capital assets are credited to the stated capital account.

8. Jerry owns a 2000-acre lot in the middle of northern Ontario. The land is not worth much since it is mostly rock and scrub trees and Jerry is not using it for anything. Jerry decides that the best way he could earn money with his land is to make it available as a hazardous waste disposal site, particularly as there are lots of caves available on the land to shelter material from the elements. About five years after the disposal site is opened, people in the neighbouring area start getting sick. It turns out that the ground water for 100 miles around Jerry's land is contaminated with many different chemicals. Jerry claims that it is not his fault, but the government charges him anyway. It seems that storing hazardous waste involves a number of absolute liability offences. What would be Jerry's best course of action?

a) Defend the charge on the basis that he did not know what the law said.
b) Defend the charge on the basis that storage was the responsibility of his clients, he only provided the land.

c) Defend the charge on the basis that the Crown cannot prove that the chemicals on his land caused the problem.

d) Defend the charge on the basis that he did not intend to cause any problem so he does not have a guilty mind.

e) Provide no defence, as no excuse is acceptable.

9. What special problems are there when prosecuting corporations?

a) It is difficult to determine if the directors of the corporation caused the problem, and there is no way to fine a director.

b) It is difficult to determine whether a corporation can actually carry out an act, it is difficult to determine if a legal person could have a guilty mind, and it is difficult to determine how to punish a corporation.

c) It is difficult to determine if a corporation carried out the act and had a guilty mind, and it is difficult to determine how to punish a corporation.

d) It is difficult to determine if a corporation carried out the act and had a guilty mind, and there is no way to fine a corporation.

e) It is difficult to determine whether a corporation can actually carry out an act, it is difficult to determine if a legal person could have a guilty mind, and there is no way to imprison a corporation.

10. Can an agent enter into a contract on behalf of a corporation before the corporation comes into existence?

a) Yes because of a rule in the corporate legislation.

b) No because of the rule of agency law that states that the principal must be in existence at the time the contract is entered into.

c) Yes because of the rules of agency law concerning ratification of contracts.

d) No because a corporation lacks contractual capacity until it is incorporated.

e) Yes because the contract can be listed as part of the incorporation documents.

11. What is the definition of insolvent for the solvency test?

a) When assets exceed liabilities.

b) When liabilities exceed assets.

c) When debts cannot be paid as they become due.

d) When assets exceed liabilities or when debts cannot be paid as they become due.

e) When liabilities exceed assets or when debts cannot be paid as they become due.

12. What is the maintenance of capital test?

a) Another name for the insolvency test.

b) A test to ensure that the stated capital account is maintained for creditors.

c) A test to ensure the periodic payment of dividends to shareholders.

d) Another name for the accounting test.

e) A test to ensure that shareholders receive periodic payments of stated capital.

13. What are the objectives of securities legislation?

a) To prevent and punish insider trading and to require full disclosure of financial information to perspective buyers of shares and bonds offered for the first time to the public.
b) To prevent and punish fraudulent practices in the securities industry, to license people working in the securities industry, and to require full disclosure of corporate financial statements to the public.
c) To prevent and punish fraudulent practices in the securities industry and to require full disclosure of financial information to perspective buyers of shares and bonds offered for the first time to the public.
d) To license people working in the securities industry and to require full disclosure of corporate financial statements to the public.
e) To prevent and punish insider trading and to require full disclosure of corporate financial statements to the public.

14. What types of things does securities legislation require in order to fulfil its objectives?

a) Licensing or registering those engaged in the securities business and disclosure of information such as annual financial statements.
b) Requiring the issuer of securities to the public to file a prospectus with the securities commission and disclosure of information such as annual financial statements.
c) Licensing or registering those engaged in the securities business and requiring the issuer of securities to the public to file a prospectus with the securities commission.
d) Licensing or registering those engaged in the securities business, requiring the issuer of securities to the public to file a prospectus with the securities commission, and continuing disclosure of information such as annual financial statements.
e) Disclosure of any information concerning a corporation which may be of interest to prospective shareholders.

15. What is the distinction between a regular criminal offence and a strict liability offence?

a) The length of the prison sentence which is possible.
b) Whether the directors of the corporation can also be charged.
c) The opportunity for the accused to provide an excuse or a defence.
d) The requirement of the accused having to prove themselves innocent.
e) The element of *mens rea*.

16. All of the following statements are true EXCEPT:

a) An officer of a corporation acting within his or her usual authority but without express authority may bind the corporation to contracts made with third parties.
b) A corporation may not ratify acts made by unauthorized agents on its behalf.
c) An innocent third party may rely on the regularity of a corporate act.
d) At common law, a corporation cannot ratify a contract made on its behalf before it comes into existence.
e) Articles of incorporation statutes provide that a corporation may, within a reasonable time after it comes into existence, adopt a written contract made in its name or on its behalf before it came into existence.

17. Which of the following statements correctly describes the position of a creditor of a limited company when that company becomes insolvent?
I. The creditor may seize the personal assets of the shareholders.
II. The creditor may seize the personal assets of the directors.
III. If the assets held by the corporation are inadequate, the creditor has no further remedy against the shareholders.

a) I only.
b) II only.
c) III only.
d) I and II only.
e) II and III only.

18. Which of the following statements accurately describe the potential liability of a corporation and/or its directors and officers for an offence?

a) An outside director will always be treated the same as an inside director.
b) Only one individual can be the "directing mind" of a corporation.
c) Directors and officers of a corporation, as well as the corporation itself, can be punished under the criminal law, even where a "guilty mind" is required.
d) A corporation as well as any of its directors and officers, charged with an offence such as improper disposal of hazardous wastes, are presumed to have acted with due diligence.
e) The standard of care and skill required of officers and directors varies depending on their expertise.

Answers to Multiple-Choice Questions

1. e)
See page 666 for more information.

2. d)
See page 666 for more information.

3. a)
See page 650 for more information.

4. c)
See page 663 for more information.

5. d)
See page 654 for more information

6. b)
See page 653 for more information.

7. c)
See page 655 for more information.

8. c)
See pages 659–660 for more information.

9. e)
See pages 660–661 for more information.

10. a)
See page 651 for more information.

11. e)
See pages 653–654 for more information.

12. b)
See page 654 for more information.

13. c)
See pages 655–656 for more information.

14. d)
See pages 656–657 for more information.

15. e)
See page 659 for more information.

16. b)
See pages 650–651 for more information.

17. c)
See page 652 for more information.

18. c)
See page 658–667 for more information.

True/False Questions

1. The indoor management rule was set out in the English case of *Royal British Bank* v. *Turquand*, but has not been applied in Canada.

2. The directors will not become liable for debts of their corporation if they misuse the corporate assets in the payment of dividends or in the redemption or re-purchase of corporate shares, and if the transactions result in the insolvency of the corporation.

3. Under the common law, a corporation could not purchase its own shares. Under Canadian certificate of incorporation statutes, it is now possible for corporations created by those statutes to purchase their own shares for a number of specified reasons subject to certain statutory limitations.

4. A prospectus is designed to fully reveal the business and financial affairs of a corporation so that a prospective investor is able to judge accurately the nature of this investment.

5. A regulatory offence is an offence with a wider definition of *mens rea* than the traditional criminal offences.

6. A large corporation might consider a fine for the commission of an offence a high cost of doing business.

Answers to True/False Questions

1. False. The indoor management rule was set out in the English case of *Royal British Bank* v. *Turquand*, and has been applied in Canada. Under the rule it has been held that in the absence of notice of irregularity or suspicious circumstances, everything in the operation of a corporation that appears to be properly done may be relied on by an outsider and will bind the company.

2. False. The directors might become liable for debts of their corporation if they misuse the corporate assets in the payment of dividends or in the redemption or re-purchase of corporate shares, and if the transactions result in the insolvency of the corporation.

The test is created by a number of provisions in the *Corporation Act*. It is designed to ensure that the capital fund, made up of the assets paid into the corporation by shareholders, will be available to absorb business losses that cannot be met out of the corporation's ongoing business earnings.

3. True.

4. True.

5. False. A regulatory offence is an offence with a broader definition of *mens rea* than the traditional criminal offences. To establish liability under a regulatory offence, it may be sufficient to show that the accused should have known that his conduct would result in the commission of the offence.

6. False. A large corporation might consider a fine for the commission of an offence to be merely a cost of doing business. Also, a corporation may be merely a "shell," allowing those who control it to walk away from it and start up a new corporation when the original corporation has insufficient assets to pay a fine. Thus, effective deterrence may require that the individuals responsible for the offence be punished directly. In large corporations, it is often difficult to sufficiently identify the individual who is responsible for the act.

30

Legal Devices for Securing Credit

Purpose and Significance

Debt transactions are the most fundamental form of legal transaction in commercial life. They arise in two basic contexts:
1. A lender gives money to a debtor, and the debtor promises to repay the money to the lender.
2. A seller gives goods to the buyer, and the buyer promises to pay for the goods.

In each event, the debtor/purchaser must pay money to the lender/seller as provided in contractual terms. If the debtor/purchaser does not pay as agreed, then the lender/seller can use the law to enforce payment.

However, the law can enforce payment only if the debtor/purchaser has money or property from which to pay. To avoid loss, the lender/seller might attempt to secure payment by other means. A pawnbroker, for example, lends money but requires the borrower to leave property that can be sold for repayment of the debt if the borrower does not meet the agreed terms. A seller of goods might keep the goods in storage until the sale price is received. These are the most direct forms of secured transactions.

Land mortgages are widely used to secure loan transactions and to permit land to be productively traded in transactions, which provide for future payment of the purchase price. This chapter deals with secured transactions involving only chattels, that is, property other than land. It outlines the most common legislative devices used throughout Canada to facilitate such security arrangements.

We should be careful to note that, except for security interests taken by banks, Canadian legislation relating to security interests is under provincial jurisdiction. Therefore, each province has its own particular law. While the various forms of legislation have a great deal in common, there are significant differences. In particular, there is a marked difference between those provinces that have recently adopted comprehensive personal property security legislation and those provinces that still provide a variety of traditional devices (chattel mortgages, conditional sales, etc.). We should take into account these differences and inquire about the specific laws of your province.

Learning Objectives

A. Discuss the role of collateral security as a means of security credit.

B. Outline the types, uses and differences among legislative devices that create security interests in chattels.

C. Compare the position of a security holder with that of innocent third parties.

D. Compare the position of a security holder with that of general creditors.

E. Discuss the personal property security legislation.

F. Review special security provisions for bank loans.

Content Outline

I. The meaning of "Security"
   A. Types of security interest
   B. Security practices
   C. Rights of a secured creditor

II. Methods of securing credit
   A. Credit devices previously considered
      1. Mortgages
      2. Leases
      3. Consignments
      4. Other credit devices
   B. Conditional sales
      1. Nature of the security
      2. Obligations of a conditional buyer
      3. Remedies of a conditional seller
      4. Rights of the conditional buyer
      5. Assignment of the conditional seller's interest
   C. Chattel Mortgages
      1. Nature of a chattel mortgage
      2. Business uses of a chattel mortgage
      3. The security
      4. Remedies of a chattel mortgagee
      5. Bills of sale
   D. Floating charges

III. Personal property security legislation
   A. Jurisdiction and application
   B. Purpose of PPSA legislation

C. Uniform treatment of security interests
    1. Financing statement
    2. Leases and consignments as security interests
    3. After-acquired property
D. Registration
E. Competing Interests

IV. Effect of security interests on purchasers
    A. Separation of possession and ownership
    B. Effect of registration
    C. The mercantile agency rule
    D. Registration practice

V. Effect of security interests on other creditors
    A. Assignment of book debts
    B. Priorities

VI. Security for bank loans
    A. Loans under the bank act
    B. Rights of a lending bank
    C. Other forms of collateral security for bank loans
    D. Conflicts between the bank act and personal property security acts

Questions on Learning Objectives

Objective A: Discuss collateral security as a means of securing credit.

A.1 What is collateral security? (pp. 674–675)

A.2 Distinguish an unsecured creditor from a secured one. (p. 675)

A.3 Briefly describe the advantages and disadvantages of requiring security when extending credit. (p. 675)

A.4 Explain how a consignment amounts to an indirect type of security. (p. 677)

Objective B: Outline the types, uses and differences among legislative devices that create security interests in chattels.

B.1 Describe a conditional sales contract. (p. 677)

B.2 What remedies does a seller have under a conditional sales contract if the buyer defaults? (p. 678)

B.3 What rights does a buyer under a conditional sales contract have? (p. 678)

B.4 What rights does an assignee of the seller under a conditional sales contract acquire? (p. 679)

B.5 How does a chattel mortgage differ from a conditional sale? (pp. 679–680)

B.6 Describe two common business uses of a chattel mortgage. (p. 680)

B.7 What is the effect of a floating charge? (p. 682)

B.8 Why might a creditor wish to take a floating charge in addition to a mortgage of real property? (p. 682)

Objective C: Discuss the personal property security legislation.

C.1 What purposes does personal property security legislation fulfill? (pp. 683–684)

C.2 What two requirements must be met to create a valid security interest under personal property security legislation? (pp. 686–687)

Chapter 30

C.3 How does such legislation deal with competing priority claims in the same asset? (p. 687)

Objective D: Compare the position of a security holder with that of innocent third parties.

D.1 How might a security arrangement over chattels affect third parties that deal with them? (p. 688)

D.2 A third party buys goods that a seller appears to own, but because of a security arrangement, does not. Under the common law, what rights does the third party have? (p. 688)

D.3 Where legislation requires registration of a security interest, what happens if a secured creditor fails to register its interest? (pp. 689–690)

Objective E: Compare the position of a security holder with that of general creditors.

E.1 Can a financially troubled debtor prefer one creditor over another? (p. 691)

E.2 Outline three common situations in which security interests are required. (pp. 690)

E.3 Describe the effect of an assignment of book debts on general creditors. (p. 691)

Objective F: Review special security provisions for bank loans.

F.1 To whom may chartered banks lend? (p. 692)

F.2 What terms are generally found in section 178 borrowing agreements? (pp. 692–693)

F.3 Name four types of collateral security that a bank may acquire. (p. 693)

426

Answers to Questions on Learning Objectives

A.1 Collateral security is an interest in personal or real property given in addition to the bare promise of repayment. Typically, it refers to the right to take possession of and to sell or resell specified assets of the debtor in satisfaction of the debt.

A.2 An unsecured creditor is one who exchanges goods, services, or money for the bare promise of a debtor to pay. A secured creditor is one who, in exchange for goods, services or money, takes from the debtor a security interest or lien on some of the debtor's property.

An unsecured creditor is a general creditor with no security interest in any of the debtor's assets. An unsecured creditor may eventually acquire some interest in a debtor's property through going to court and obtaining a judgement in the amount of the debt. After obtaining judgement the creditor may obtain an execution order authorizing seizure and sale of certain of the debtor's assets. Secured creditors needn't invoke court proceedings in order to enforce rights over the security. Moreover, security interests provide a creditor with an interest in a specific asset whereas an unsecured judgement creditor has no right to seize any particular asset.

A.3 Disadvantages in acquiring security are that it is more complex and expensive to obtain. It may also alienate customers. However, it minimizes risk to the creditor.

A.4 In a sense, a consignment amounts to a type of secured credit. Under a consignment contract, the consignee holds the goods for sale but does not take title to them. Thus, in the event that the consignee goes bankrupt, the consignor may recover the inventory because it has never actually become part of the consignee's goods.

B.1 Under a conditional sales contract, title is not transferred to the buyer until he has completed a series of scheduled installment payments. In the meantime, the buyer obtains possession of the goods but the seller retains ownership of the goods and thus full security for payment of the purchase price.

B.2 If a buyer defaults under a conditional sales contract, the seller may sue the buyer for the unpaid balance of the debt. He may also repossess the goods. He may resell the goods once he has taken possession of them. In many provinces, the seller may also sue the buyer for any deficiency due because the amount owed exceeds the amount realized on resale.

B.3 The rights of a buyer under a conditional sales contract vary from province to province. In some provinces the buyer may redeem repossessed goods within a specified period so long as he pays all the arrears plus the interest and costs. Others entitle the buyer to receive any surplus realized by the seller upon repossession and resale of the goods.

B.4 An assignee of a seller under a conditional sales contract gets the same rights as the seller. Thus, if a buyer had rights against the original seller he will have them against any assignee of the seller. For example, he may have right to offset amounts due based on defects in the goods.

B.5 In a conditional sale, the security is represented by the very goods themselves. In a chattel mortgage, the debtor may give security over a variety of personal property and even in property acquired after the chattel mortgage has been executed.

B.6 Chattel mortgages are frequently used in the sale of business where office equipment, machinery or vehicles are included in the transaction. Where the purchaser does not have sufficient cash to buy the business outright the vendor may take a chattel mortgage on the specific equipment or machinery as security. Another use of the chattel mortgage arises on sale of a building with equipment. Again, the vendor may take, as security, a chattel mortgage on equipment in the building such as refrigerators and stoves in apartment blocks.

B.7 A floating charge refers to a security interest taken over all assets not otherwise mortgaged or pledged. It places the holder of the floating charge ahead of unsecured creditors.

B.8 A creditor might take a floating charge in addition to a mortgage because it provides security over all the assets of the business. It also generally provides for the placement of a receiver-manager who operates the business if the debtor defaults. As a business is often most lucrative when it is operating, this is a distinct advantage over a mortgage.

C.1 Personal property security legislation was passed to try to reconcile the conflicting security interests in goods. It creates a single system of registration for all secured interests, defines the secured parties, gives remedies against the debtor and defines priorities between various secured parties and third party purchasers or general creditors.

C.2 To create a valid security interest, the security interest must attach and be perfected. Attachment occurs upon performance of the agreement by both parties. Perfection occurs when the secured party either takes possession or files an appropriate financing statement within the registration system.

C.3 Competing priority claims to the same asset in the system are resolved by assigning priority to the creditor who first perfects its interest.

D.1 Possession of goods creates an appearance of ownership. Hence, when a security holder has an interest in the chattel, but the debtor has possession, an innocent third person might think the debtor has full entitlement to sell, mortgage or use the goods.

D.2 A seller cannot give better title to goods than he himself has, thus the third party will not acquire title. The original owner may repossess them from him.

D.3 The rules about registration of security interests vary from province to province. Normally, if registration of a security interest is required, failure to do so means that third parties may acquire interests that prevail over the secured creditor. The interest is valid but it may not have priority over other claimants.

E.1 If a debtor is in danger of insolvency or bankruptcy and protects one creditor by conniving in the creation of a preferred security interest, the transaction would be a fraudulent preference. Such a transaction can be struck down under both federal law and provincial law.

The registration of some security interests requires the filing of an affidavit of *bona fides* to prevent the use of improper preferences.

E.2   (a) The sale of goods on credit.
            (b) Borrowing money to purchase goods.
            (c) An existing creditor requires additional security as a condition for leaving the loan outstanding.

E.3 Where a debtor defaults, the holder of the assignment of book debts may give notice and realize directly on the book debts owed in priority to the general creditors.

F.1 Chartered banks may lend to wholesalers and purchasers in the areas of agriculture, forest, mines, wares and merchandise. They may also lend to manufacturers, farmers, fishermen and forestry producers.

F.2 When a person borrows money from a bank under a section 178 agreement, he promises to keep the property insured and free from claims, account to the bank for proceeds of sales, give the bank possession in the event of default, grant a power of attorney to the bank and consent to the sale of security if he defaults. Money received from the sale of goods included under the section 178 agreement must be deposited into a separate account and be used for reduction of the loan.

F.3   (a) An assignment of warehouse receipts, book debts or cash surrender value of an insurance policy.
            (b) A chattel mortgage.
            (c) A guarantee.

Multiple-Choice Questions

1. Car Technologies Inc. makes electrical systems for cars. It wants to borrow $200 000 to buy new equipment for expansion and has approached Capital Inc. for a loan. Capital Inc. has reviewed the business plan and history of Car Technologies, and has decided it is a good investment. Which of the following forms of security should Capital Inc. consider?

a) Section 178/427 of the *Bank Act*.
b) Chattel mortgage.
c) Conditional sales agreement.
d) Lease.
e) All of the above.

2. Frankie, a cod and lobster fisherman, needs to buy new nets and lobster traps for his boat. The weather over the past year has been very bad and most of his traps and nets have been lost or severely damaged. Frankie has approached the local bank for a loan to cover the new nets and traps. Which of the following forms of security should Frankie expect the bank to consider?

a) Section 178/427 of the *Bank Act*.
b) Assignment of book debts.
c) Conditional sales agreement.
d) Floating charge.
e) All of the above.

3. Fred and Charlie have decided to go into business for themselves. As part of setting up the new business, which will manufacture and export specialty widgets, they need to borrow money from the bank. Which of the following forms of security should Fred and Charlie expect the bank to consider?

a) Section 178/427 of the *Bank Act*.
b) Chattel mortgage.
c) Assignment of book debts.
d) Personal guarantees.
e) All of the above.

4. Fred and Charlie have decided to go into business for themselves. As part of setting up the new business, which will manufacture and export specialty widgets, they need start-up money. After having considered and rejected the idea of a bank loan, Fred and Charlie decided to seek money from other sources. Which of the following would be the preferred option?

a) Section 178/427 of the *Bank Act*.
b) Conditional sales agreement.
c) Corporate debentures.
d) Real estate mortgage.
e) Chattel mortgage.

5. Cindy, a university student, desperately wanted a car to get around town. One day on campus, she saw a notice for a car for sale on a bulletin board. The car, a 1969 red Mustang, was being offered for $3000. Taking a friend, who was a licensed car mechanic, Cindy went to check out the car and, with her friend's approval, agreed to the price. She immediately wrote a cheque for the price and received the signed registration in return. Two weeks later, a collection agency came to Cindy's apartment and demanded the car because there was a registered chattel mortgage on the car for $10 000 which had not been paid for six months. What should Cindy do?

a) Slam the apartment door in the agency's face and hide the car at a friend's house.
b) Give the agency the car and sue the seller for the $3000.
c) Pay the $10 000 and accept that the car cost $13 000, not $3000.
d) Keep the car and tell the agency where to find the seller.
e) Give the agency the car and call the police to report a stolen car.

6. Herb's Car Sales sold cars on behalf of a number of car manufacturers. Because of the large cost of buying inventory, most of the cars were purchased under a wholesale conditional sales contract. Unfortunately, Herb failed to keep up to date with his installment payments to the manufacturers so they repossessed all his inventory. However, before the repossession could take place, Herb sold a car to Clare. The appropriate manufacturer asked Clare to return the car. What should Clare do?

a) Give the manufacturer the car and sue Herb.
b) Keep the car hidden at a friend's house.
c) Give the manufacturer the car and accept that the money is gone.
d) Keep the car and tell the manufacturer to go away.
e) Give the manufacturer the car and assign the associated chattel mortgage to the manufacturer.

7. Jane has won the Lotto 6/49 three times so she has lots of money. Being a kind friend, Jane enters into loan agreements with her friends to assist them in funding their education. The agreements include various forms of security devices depending on the assets of each friend. Jane decides not to register the devices under the provincial personal property security legislation. Is the non-registration a problem for Jane?

a) Yes because Jane commits a criminal offence if she does not register the devices.
b) No because registration is not mandatory, but she takes a risk of losing the security.
c) Yes because Jane will have no security for the loans if she does not register the devices.

d) No because signing the credit devices is enough to perfect her security.
e) Yes because her friends do not have to repay the loans if she does not register the devices.

8. George has just finished his Christmas shopping and put all the purchases on his bank credit card. After his family has unwrapped his gifts, it is discovered that two of the gifts are broken and cannot be fixed. Both gifts came from the same store that says they do not take returns. George is furious and refuses to pay that charge on his credit card bill. Is George correct in taking this course of action?

a) Yes because the bank has taken an assignment of the store's accounts receivable.
b) No because it is the store that will not take the goods back.
c) Yes because if George does not pay the bank, the bank will simply not pay the store.
d) No because the store has already been paid and the bill simply represents a loan with the bank.
e) Yes because any complaint that might be raised with the store can be raised with the bank.

9. Can a lease be a security device?

a) No because a lease only deals with transfer of possession, not title.
b) Yes because a lease can deal with chattels similar to a chattel mortgage.
c) No because a lease, like bailment, requires the chattel to be returned at the end of the contract.
d) Yes because rental payments can be used towards the purchase price, if the lessee has the option to buy the chattel at the end of the lease.
e) No because rental payments are a cost of doing business and are deductible under the *Income Tax Act*.

10. Which of the following is a step under the personal property security legislation?

a) Sign a security device.
b) Registration.
c) Attachment.
d) Perfection.
e) All of the above.

11. What is a floating charge?

a) A security interest taken over all the assets of the debtor that have not otherwise been mortgaged or pledged.
b) A charge over inventory.
c) The withholding of title from the buyer until he has completed a series of scheduled installment payments.

d) The right to repossess and resell goods upon failure of a debtor to pay.
e) A preferred security interest over goods.

12. Which type(s) of creditor has the right to seize and sell assets of the debtor?

a) Secured creditor.
b) Preferred creditor.
c) Unsecured creditor.
d) General creditor.
e) All of the above.

13. When a debtor defaults under a conditional sales contract, it is normal for the debtor to have to pay the entire amount still owing, not just the arrears, to avoid the creditor seizing and selling the goods subject to the contract. What is the name of the clause in the conditional sales contract that causes this?

a) Pay-off clause.
b) Remedy clause.
c) Cutout clause.
d) Acceleration clause.
e) Recourse financing clause.

14. Security under section 178/427 of the *Bank Act* can be distinguished from other forms of security in what manner?

a) It is covered by federal legislation.
b) The bank does not acquire title.
c) It can be described as a short-term self-liquidating loan.
d) It is not covered by personal property security legislation.
e) All of the above.

15. Priority of payments is always an important issue for creditors since it determines the order in which creditors will be paid. What is it called when a secret security interest is created in a scheme by a debtor to deprive general creditors of assets?

a) Purchase money security interest.
b) Fraudulent preference.
c) Improper repossession.
d) Fraudulent misrepresentation.
e) Absconding with funds.

16. Which of the following is/are security interests in chattels?
I. Chattel mortgages
II. Conditional sales
III. Floating charges

a) I only
b) II only
c) III only
d) I and II only
e) I, II and III

17. All of the following statements about an unsecured creditor are correct EXCEPT:

a) An unsecured creditor exchanges goods, services or money for the bare promise of repayment.
b) An unsecured creditor is a general creditor.
c) An unpaid, unsecured creditor may acquire an interest in a debtor's assets through court action.
d) An unsecured creditor need not invoke court proceedings in order to obtain rights over a debtor's property.
e) An unsecured creditor has more risk of non-payment than does a secured creditor.

18. A floating charge is:

a) A security interest taken over all assets of a debtor that have not otherwise been mortgaged or pledged.
b) A charge over inventory.
c) The withholding of title from the buyer until he has completed a series of scheduled installment payments.
d) The right to repossess and resell goods upon failure of a debtor to pay.
e) A preferred security interest over goods.

Answers to Multiple-Choice Questions

1. b)
See page 680 for more information.

2. a)
See pages 691–692 for more information.

3. e)
See pages 680, 690 and 691 for more information.

4. c)

See page 682 for more information.

5. b)

See page 688 for more information

6. d)

See page 688 for more information.

7. b)

See pages 689–690 for more information.

8. d)

See page 693 for more information.

9. d)

See page 676 for more information.

10. e)

See pages 686–687 for more information.

11. a)

See page 682 for more information.

12. a)

See page 675 for more information.

13. d)

See page 678 for more information.

14. e)

See pages 691–692 for more information.

15. b)

See pages 691 and 707 for more information.

16. e)

See page 676–683 for more information.

17. d)

See pages 675 and 691 for more information.

18. a)

See page 682 for more information.

True/False Questions

1. Collateral security is an interest in personal or real property given in addition to the bare promise of repayment. Typically, it refers to the right to take possession of and to sell or resell specified assets of the debtor in satisfaction of the debt.

2. Under a conditional sales contract, title is not transferred to the buyer until he has completed a series of scheduled installment payments. In the meantime, the buyer obtains possession of the goods but the seller retains ownership of the goods and thus full security for payment of the purchase price.

3. An assignee of a seller under a conditional sales contract does not get the same rights as the seller.

4. A creditor does not take a floating charge in addition to a mortgage because it provides insecurity over all the assets of the business.

5. To create a valid security interest, the security interest must attach and be perfected. Attachment occurs upon performance of the agreement by both parties.

6. Perfection occurs when the secured party either takes possession or files an appropriate financing statement within the registration system.

Answers to True/False Questions

1. True.

2. True.

3. False. An assignee of a seller under a conditional sales contract gets the same rights as the seller. Thus, if a buyer had rights against the original seller he will have them against any assignee of the seller. For example, he may have the right to offset amounts due based on defects in the goods.

4. False. A creditor might take a floating charge in addition to a mortgage because it provides security over all the assets of the business. It also generally provides for the placement of a receiver-manager who operates the business if the debtor defaults. As a business is often most lucrative when it is operating, this is a distinct advantage over a mortgage.

5. True.

6. True.

31

Creditors' Rights

Purpose and Significance

Many creditors take steps to protect themselves against the risk of default. Often, however, creditors in the normal course of business cannot afford the time or expense of securing debt against the property of the debtor.

The merchant who sells seed grain to farmers or who provides building materials to contractors might find it difficult, costly and time-consuming to secure every customer. Some attempts have been made by our legal system to protect the reasonable expectations of general creditors from abusive and fraudulent practices. This chapter outlines three statutory schemes intended to protect legitimate creditors' rights.

Learning Objectives

A. Discuss the history and policy of bankruptcy legislation in Canada.

B. Examine the purposes and procedures of bulk sales legislation.

C. Examine the purposes and procedures of mechanics' lien legislation.

D. Discuss the effect of limitations statutes on creditors' rights.

Content Outline

I. Statutory arrangements for the protection of creditors

II. The *Bankruptcy and Insolvency Act*
- A. Background
- B. Policy issues
- C. Government supervision
- D. Persons to whom the act applies
    - 1. Bankrupts and insolvency persons
    - 2. Consumer debtors
    - 3. Corporations

III. Procedures under the act
- A. Proposals
    - 1. Commercial proposals
    - 2. Consumer proposals
- B. Assignments
- C. Receiving orders
- D. Acts of bankruptcy

IV. Administration of a bankrupt's affairs
- A. Powers and duties of the trustee
- B. Recovery of property
- C. Settlements
- D. Preferences
- E. Reviewable transactions
- F. Payment of claims
    - 1. Unpaid sellers
    - 2. Secured creditors
    - 3. Preferred creditors
    - 4. General creditors
- G. Proving Debts
- H. Duties of the bankrupt debtor
- I. Bankruptcy offences
- J. Discharge of the bankrupt debtor

Questions on Learning Objectives

Objective A: Discuss the history and policy of bankruptcy legislation in Canada.

A.1 What is the meaning of "insolvency"? (p. 701)

A.2 Outline the four tasks that the *Bankruptcy and Insolvency Act* performs. (p. 699)

A.3 Describe who administers a bankrupt's estate. (p. 700)

A.4 What is the difference between a bankrupt and an insolvent person? (p. 701)

A.5 Describe three procedures under the Act and when each is applicable. (p. 702)

A.6 What constitutes an "act of bankruptcy"? (pp. 704–705)

A.7 List three potential sources of abuse by debtors. (pp. 706–707)

A.8 What is the difference between secured creditors, preferred creditors and general creditors in a bankruptcy proceeding? (pp. 709–710)

A.9 What is the effect of discharging a bankrupt debtor? (p. 711)

Objective B: Examine the purposes and procedures of bulk sales legislation.

B.1 What interest does a general creditor have in the bulk sale of a debtor's business assets? (pp. 719–720)

B.2 How does a *Bulk Sales Act* protect general creditors? (pp. 719–720)

B.3 Describe the operation of the Ontario *Bulk Sales Act*. (pp. 719–720)

Objective C: Examine the purposes and procedures of mechanics' lien legislation.

C.1 What is a "mechanics' lien"? (p. 714)

C.2 What types of creditors can claim a mechanics' lien? (pp. 714–715)

C.3 What is the legal effect of registering a mechanics' lien? (p. 716–717)

C.4 What is a "statutory holdback"? (p. 715)

Objective D: Discuss the effect of limitations statutes on creditors' rights.

D.1 What is the limitation period applicable to an action for breach of contract in the common law provinces? (p. 721)

D.2 Is there anything a debtor might do which will extend the limitation period for action to be brought against him on the contractual debt? (pp. 721–722)

Answers to Questions on Learning Objectives

A.1 A person is insolvent when he is unable to meet his debts to his creditors as they fall due, or when his liabilities exceed his realisable assets.

A.2   (a) It establishes a uniform practice in bankruptcy proceedings throughout the country.
(b) It provides for an equitable distribution of a debtor's assets among creditors.
(c) It provides a framework for preserving and reorganizing the bankrupt's affairs by working out an arrangement with the creditors.
(d) It provides for the release of an honest but unfortunate debtor and permits a fresh start.

A.3 The highest trial court in each province is the designated court for bankruptcy proceedings. It names a licensed trustee to administer the debtor's affairs. The creditors appoint inspectors to instruct the trustee and review the actions of the trustee.

A.4 A bankrupt is a person who has made an assignment or against whom a receiving order has been made; a formal step must be taken in order to declare a person bankrupt.

An insolvent person is defined, under the Act, as a person who is not bankrupt, whose liabilities to creditors amount to $1,000 and who is unable to meet his obligations as they generally become due, has ceased paying his current obligations in the ordinary course of business as they generally become due or has debts due and accruing due, the aggregate of which exceed the realizable value of his assets.

A.5 A proposal is a procedure to avoid formal liquidation of the debtor's estate by allowing the debtor time to attempt to re-organize her affairs.

An assignment is a voluntary application by a debtor to institute bankruptcy proceedings.

A "receiving order" is initiated by the creditors to have the debtor declared bankrupt by the court and has the effect of vesting the bankrupt's property in the trustee appointed by the court to administer the estate.

A.6 In order to have a debtor adjudged bankrupt, creditors must prove that an act of bankruptcy has been committed. Acts of bankruptcy include:
(i) assignment of assets to a trustee,
(ii) a fraudulent transfer of assets,
(iii) a fraudulent preference,
(iv) an attempt by the debtor to abscond or hide property,
(v) failure to redeem goods seized under execution, and
(vi) disclosure of insolvency, including refusal or failure to meet liabilities as they become due.

A.7 The debtor may make gifts of property before becoming bankrupt. Second, the debtor may attempt to favour certain creditors; she may make a payment of money or transfer of property, which amounts to a fraudulent preference if made within three months preceding bankruptcy. Third, the debtor may enter into transactions that are not at "arm's length."

A.8 Holders of security interests in property of the bankrupt estate (e.g., mortgagees) have first priority to the value of the security against the property of the bankrupt. They are called *secured creditors*.

Preferred creditors have first claim on free assets after secured claims have been satisfied. The preference is defined by the *Act* and the order of priority amongst preferred creditors is established.

General creditors (or unsecured creditors) are paid a proportionate share of the funds remaining after secured and preferred creditors have been satisfied.

A.9 The discharge of a bankrupt debtor usually cancels the unpaid portion of debts remaining after the trustee has liquidated the debtor's assets and distributed the proceeds. The debtor has a clean slate and can start business again.

A discharge is given in the court's discretion when it thinks that it is proper to do so. If a bankrupt debtor attempts to carry on business before a discharge is received he must disclose that he is an undischarged bankrupt or he will be liable to criminal penalties.

B.1 A general unsecured creditor appraises the financial circumstances of the debtor and extends credit by assessing and anticipating a cash flow that can reasonably be anticipated from the debtor's gross assets. If the debtor sells his gross assets (stock-in-trade and business fixtures) then the cash flow will be impaired.

B.2 Bulk sales legislation establishes a procedure, which makes it difficult for the owner of a business to dispose of stock-in-trade outside the normal business course without the payment or concurrence of trade creditors.

B.3 Application can be made to a court to exempt the bulk sale from the *Bulk Sales Act*. The court must be satisfied that the sale will not impair the ability of the debtor/seller to pay his creditors in full.

Alternatively, the purchaser may pay the seller/debtor and obtain valid title by obtaining one of the following:
(a) a detached statement of creditors showing that aggregate claims of secured and unsecured creditors do not exceed $2,500; or
(b) an affidavit from the seller assuring that before the sale all creditors have either paid fully or been given security for payment.

C.1 Persons who have extended credit in the form of goods and services to improve land have a statutory right to record a security claim against the land that they have improved. The lien is created statutorily in each province of Canada.

If the claim of the lienholder is not paid, the lienholder might eventually be able to cause the land to be sold and can receive payment from the proceeds of the sale.

C.2 A mechanics' lien is available, under most provincial acts, only to creditors that participate directly as workers or supply material for use directly in construction.

Courts have held that an architect who prepares building plans is entitled to a lien. Some statutes qualify a lessor of equipment used in construction for entitlement. Suppliers of material used in the construction are also entitled to file a mechanics' lien. But a creditor who sells tools or machinery to a contractor is not so entitled.

C.3 Registration provides public notice of the lienholder's claim and establishes the lienholder's priority over unsecured creditors of the owner of the property, subsequent mortgages and subsequent purchasers. The effect of registering is also to provide a fixed period of time within which the lienholder must commence legal action on the debt.

The effect of not registering within the statutory time period is that the lien ceases to exist.

C.4 A principal contractor can achieve protection against the owner of land under the *Mechanics' Lien Act*. The Act also provides a mechanism to ensure that the principal contractor meets obligations to subcontractors.

If a subcontractor is unpaid by the contractor, the subcontractor can file a mechanic's lien and the burden of the debt falls on the owner of the land rather than on the debtor/contractor.

To protect himself in such a circumstance, the owner is permitted by statute to retain or "hold back" a portion of payment due to the contractor. If liens are registered by subcontractors the owner can pay the holdback into court and have the liens removed.

D.1 In common law provinces the remedy for breach of ordinary contracts is barred when six years have elapsed from the time the right of action arose.

D.2 The limitation period for an action for breach of contract starts over again if the debtor makes a part payment or delivers a written promise to pay. The creditor will have six years in which to bring the action from the time of the part payment or the delivery of the written promise.

Multiple-Choice Questions

1. The McInnis Company is a large multinational that has been buying up lots of other businesses. However, with a downturn in the stock market, its shares have dropped in value and it is having difficulty with cash flow. With its liabilities being more than double its assets, the Company is in real trouble. However, if the Company is declared bankrupt, thousands of people will be out of work. What is McInnis Company's best course of action?

a) Voluntarily assign itself into bankruptcy.
b) Ask the government for a bailout.
c) Explain the problem to the Superintendent of Bankruptcies and ask for assistance.
d) Make a proposal to creditors to restructure the company and its finances.
e) Wait for a creditor to request a receiving order.

2. Mr. and Mrs. Jones own a large collection of paintings done by the Group of Seven and have four bank accounts in the Cayman Islands. Unfortunately, the Jones are very much in debt in Canada. Realizing that a couple of their creditors are about to petition them into bankruptcy, Mr. Jones arranges for ten of the most

valuable paintings to be given to his brother in the Cayman Islands. After being appointed, what should the trustee in bankruptcy do?

a) Only deal with the assets in Canada, as there is no access to assets in the Cayman Islands.
b) Use what cash exists in Canadian bank accounts to pay creditors and then arrange for the Jones to be discharged from bankruptcy.
c) Try to reclaim the paintings from the brother, as the transfer was a settlement.
d) Sell the remaining paintings and use the money to pay general creditors first.
e) Treat the brother as a creditor and claim the paintings as a preference.

3. Roland, a farmer, supplies the Green Grocer with fresh vegetables. Harold, a dealer in garden supplies, sold some bags of fertilizer to the Green Grocer. Neither Roland nor Harold has been paid. Within 30 days of delivery, Roland and Harold learn that the Green Grocer has become bankrupt. They immediately demand the return of their goods. The vegetables delivered by Roland have already been sold, but there are similar vegetables still in the store. The fertilizer is also still in the store. Can both Roland and Harold get their goods back?

a) Both Roland and Harold can get their goods back under the unpaid seller rule.
b) Roland can get his goods back but Harold cannot, under the unpaid seller rule.
c) Harold can get his goods back but Roland cannot, under the unpaid seller rule.
d) Neither Roland nor Harold can get their goods back under the unpaid seller rule.
e) Both Roland and Harold should claim to be secured creditors under bankruptcy law.

4. After retrieving all the property and assets of a bankrupt, the trustee in bankruptcy is ready to pay the creditors. The list of preferred creditors includes: the trustee's expenses, arrears of rent, municipal taxes and funeral expenses. In what order will the preferred creditors be paid?

a) Trustee's expenses, arrears of rent, municipal taxes, and funeral expenses.
b) Funeral expenses, trustee's expenses, municipal taxes and arrears of rent.
c) Trustee's expenses, funeral expenses, arrears of rent and municipal taxes.
d) Arrears of rent, municipal taxes, trustee's expenses, and funeral expenses.
e) Municipal taxes, trustee's expenses, funeral expenses and arrears of rent.

5. Joanna has agreed to buy Sandy's business and the entire inventory that the business currently owns. Sandy is ready to retire so is looking for sufficient money to create a pension. The creditors of the business learn of the sale and are concerned that they will not be paid since all their contracts are with Sandy, not Joanna. A couple of creditors are considering petitioning the business into bankruptcy. What is Joanna's best course of action to appease the creditors?

a) Joanna should make a proposal to the creditors before the sale goes through.
b) Joanna should back out of the deal.

c) Joanna should ask Sandy to assign the business into bankruptcy.
d) Joanna should renegotiate the deal to get a lower price.
e) Joanna should follow the requirements of the Bulk Sales Act.

6. As part of his business, David buys whole crops of vegetables from farmers and then sells them to grocery wholesalers. As a result, David's list of assets goes from no chattels and lots of money in the bank to lots of assets and no money in the bank depending on whether David has just bought or sold a crop. While David's list of creditors consists of only one bank loan with the assets as security, the bank is concerned about the constantly changing assets. What would be the Bank's best course of action?

a) The bank should challenge each sale of assets under the Bulk Sales Act.
b) The bank should petition the business into bankruptcy.
c) The bank should seize and sell each crop until the loan is paid off.
d) The bank should demand payment on the loan.
e) The bank should do nothing.

7. Wood Supply Co. makes and delivers 100 sheets of plywood to a construction site on a weekly basis for 5 weeks. The total cost of the wood is $10 000. When Wood Supply Co. has not been paid a month after the last delivery, what would be the company's best course of action to secure its loan?

a) Sue the builder for breach of contract.
b) Petition the builder into bankruptcy.
c) Register a lien under the Mechanics' Lien Act.
d) Sue the owner of the property for breach of contract.
e) Register a real property mortgage against the construction site.

8. Bart hired Houses-R-Us to build a house on his property. The contract price was $80 000. Houses-R-Us entered contracts with: a) Fitzgerald Plumbing for $20,000 with a finish date of March 1; b) Henry's Electrical for $10,000 with a finish date of March 15; and c) Ralph's Roofing for $15,000 with a finish date of February 15. On April 7 the house was finished and Bart moved in. He also made the final payment for the full contract price. On April 14 Fitzgerald Plumbing registers a mechanics' lien on the house for non-payment. Immediately Henry's Electrical and Ralph's Roofing also register mechanics' liens. Bart is concerned about these mechanics' lien claims. Assuming the house is located in Ontario, which of the mechanics' liens are valid?

a) Fitzgerald Plumbing, Henry's Electrical and Ralph's Roofing.
b) Henry's Electrical and Ralph's Roofing.
c) Fitzgerald Plumbing.
d) Fitzgerald Plumbing and Henry's Electrical.
e) Ralph's Roofing.

9. Big Contractor Company is building a set of luxury condominiums. Ace Plumbing Company is supplying the entire bathroom plumbing fixtures for the building. The contract says that payment for the fixtures would be in two installments due at the start of delivery, which is October 1, and on completion, which is March 31. The first installment was paid, but the second is now long overdue. Assuming the condominiums are located in Ontario, what steps, in order, should Ace Plumbing Company take to secure payment of its outstanding account?

a) Register a mechanics' lien within 45 days of completion, commence a court action within 90 days of completion, and register a certificate stating that the action has been started.
b) Register a mechanics' lien within 15 days of completion, commence a court action within 15 days of registering the mechanics' lien, and register a certificate stating that the action has been started.
c) Commence a court action within 90 days of completion, register a certificate stating that the action has been started, and register a mechanics' lien within 45 days of commencing the court action.
d) Register a certificate stating that a court action will be commenced within 45 days, and commence a court action within 45 days of registering the certificate.
e) Register a certificate and a mechanics' lien stating that a court action will be commenced within 45 days, and commence a court action within 45 days of registering the certificate.

10. What is the difference between a receiving order and an assignment under the *Bankruptcy and Insolvency Act*?

a) A receiving order is an order of a court while an assignment is a voluntary act.
b) All the creditors seek a receiving order while an insolvent person does an assignment.
c) A receiving order is issued after the trustee in bankruptcy receives all the bankrupt's assets while an assignment is done before the insolvent person is declared bankrupt.
d) A receiving order can be issued if the person is not insolvent while an insolvent person does an assignment.
e) All of the above.

11. Which of the following are acts of bankruptcy?

a) A fraudulent transfer which is a transfer of property by a debtor, usually to a related person, with the intention of putting that property out of the reach of creditors.
b) An attempt by the debtor to abscond, with intent to defraud creditors.
c) Notice to any creditors that the debtor is suspending payment of his debts.
d) A default in any proposal that the debtor has previously persuaded the creditors to accept as a means of forestalling bankruptcy proceedings.
e) All of the above.

12. What is the order of payment to creditors?

a) General creditors, preferred creditors, and secured creditors.
b) Preferred creditors, unsecured creditors and secured creditors.
c) Secured creditors, general creditors and preferred creditors.
d) Secured creditors, preferred creditors and unsecured creditors.
e) Secured creditors, general creditors and unsecured creditors.

13. What is the effect of the *Statute of Limitations* on a breach of contract situation?

a) The injured party loses the right to bring a court action after the time period in the statute has passed.
b) The injured party cannot bring a court action until the time period in the statute has passed.
c) The injured party loses title in the property that is the subject matter of the contract.
d) The injured party's damages are limited to the amount specified in the statute.
e) The injured party must have discovered his injuries by the end of the time period in the statute.

14. What is the definition of holdback?

a) The amount which subcontractors may withhold from each delivery of materials.
b) The amount that the landowner may withhold from payments made to the principal contractor.
c) The amount that the principal contractor may withhold from payments made to subcontractors.
d) The amount that the landowner may withhold from payments made to subcontractors.
e) The amount which the principal contractor must pay extra to the subcontractors.

15. Why is it important for a buyer in a bulk sale to comply with the *Bulk Sales Act*?

a) Otherwise the sale is invalid.
b) To prevent the creditors suing the seller.
c) Otherwise the sale would require court approval.
d) The sale may be voidable at the creditors' request.
e) To prevent the seller suing the buyer.

16. All of the following statements about a bankrupt debtor are true EXCEPT:

a) The discharge of a bankrupt debtor usually cancels the unpaid portion of his debts and gives the debtor a clean slate with which to start business again.

b) An insolvent person may make proposals to his creditors with a view to avoiding bankruptcy and if a resulting arrangement is made it provides an alternative to bankruptcy proceeding.

c) A bankrupt debtor is the same as an insolvent person in the *Bankruptcy and Insolvency Act.*

d) A debtor may voluntarily institute bankruptcy proceedings by applying to the official receiver to have a trustee in bankruptcy appointed.

e) A transfer of property by a debtor in anticipation of bankruptcy in order to withhold assets from other creditors is a fraudulent transfer and may be declared void.

17. Which of the following is/are the result of the application of the Ontario *Bulk Sales Act* to a specific bulk sale?

I. Unsecured creditors of the seller are not entitled to notice of a bulk sale.

II. A seller who has made a bulk sale must pay all of his unsecured creditors before the sale can pass effective title to the buyer.

III. A court can exempt the seller from the provisions of the *Bulk Sales Act* if it is satisfied that the seller's ability to pay his creditors will be unimpaired.

a) I only
b) II only
c) III only
d) I and II only
e) I, II and III

18. Which of the following statements accurately describe the effect of the *Mechanics' Lien Act* on a contractor who provides work or materials for a construction project?

a) The contractor can take personal possession of the lands and building and sell them to realize her claim.

b) The contractor may file a lien anytime before he receives payment for his claim.

c) If the contractor does work for a tenant on a building erected on leased land, the contractor can file a lien against the landlord's property interest.

d) The Mechanics' Lien Act is a federal Act in Canada, and liens must be filed with the federal government.

e) If the property against which the lien is registered is sold to satisfy creditors, the mechanics' lienholder has a claim against the proceeds of sale that ranks after municipal tax, mortgagees with prior registered mortgages and wage claimants.

Answers to Multiple-Choice Questions

1. d)
See page 702 for more information.

2. c)
See page 706 for more information.

3. c)
See pages 708–709 for more information.

4. b)
See page 710 for more information.

5. e)
See page 719 for more information.

6. e)
See page 719 for more information.

7. c)
See pages 716–717 for more information.

8. d)
See pages 716–717 for more information.

9. a)
See page 716 for more information.

10. a)
See pages 703–704 for more information.

11. e)
See pages 704–705 for more information.

12. d)
See pages 709–710 for more information.

13. a)
See pages 721–722 for more information.

14. b)
See page 715 for more information.

15. d)
See pages 719–720 for more information.

16. c)
See pages 701 and 711 for more information.

17. c)
See page 719 for more information.

18. e)
See pages 714–718 for more information.

True/False Questions

1. A person is insolvent when he is unable to meet his debts to his creditors as they fall due, or when his liabilities exceed his realisable assets.

2. A proposal is a procedure to avoid formal liquidation of the debtor's estate by allowing the debtor time to attempt to re-organise.

3. An assignment is a voluntary application by a debtor to institute bankruptcy proceedings.

4. A "receiving order" is initiated by the creditors to have the debtor declared bankrupt by the court and has the effect of vesting the bankrupt's property in the trustee appointed by the court to administer the estate.

5. Holders of security interests in property of the bankrupt estate (e.g., mortgagees) have second priority to the value of the security against the property of the bankrupt.

6. Preferred creditors have second claim on free assets after secured claims have been satisfied.

7. General creditors (or unsecured creditors) are paid a fixed share of the funds remaining after secured and preferred creditors have been satisfied.

8. Bulk sales legislation establishes a procedure that makes it difficult for the owner of a business to dispose of stock-in-trade outside the normal business course without the payment or concurrence of trade creditors.

9. A mechanics' lien is available, under most provincial acts, only to creditors that participate directly as workers or supply material for use directly in construction.

10. Courts have held that an architect who prepares building plans is not entitled to a lien.

11. Suppliers of material used in the construction are also entitled to file a mechanics' lien. But a creditor who sells tools or machinery to a contractor is not so entitled.

12. In common law provinces, the remedy for breach of ordinary contracts is barred when three years have elapsed from the time the right of action arose.

Answers to True/False Questions

1. True.

2. True.

3. True.

4. True.

5. False. Holders of security interests in property of the bankrupt estate (e.g., mortgagees) have first priority to the value of the security against the property of the bankrupt. They are called secured creditors.

6. False. Preferred creditors have first claim on free assets after secured claims have been satisfied. The preference is defined by the Act and the order of priority amongst preferred creditors is established.

7. False. General creditors (or unsecured creditors) are paid a proportionate share of the funds remaining after secured and preferred creditors have been satisfied.

8. True.

9. True.

10. False. Courts have held that an architect who prepares building plans is entitled to a lien. Some statutes qualify a lessor of equipment used in construction for entitlement.

11. True.

12. False. In common law provinces the remedy for breach of ordinary contracts is barred when six years have elapsed from the time the right of action arose.

32

Government Regulation of Business

Purpose and Significance

In this chapter we examine the regulatory framework in which Canadian businesses must operate. Such an examination begins with a survey of the legal environment, specifically, the powers granted to federal and provincial governments and their application to the regulation of business.

Regulation may occur in a variety of ways — from establishing quotas to setting prices and restricting activities that are deemed socially or economically disruptive. Both provincial and federal legislation has been enacted to set minimal standards that must be met by business. Legislation that we will look at in this section concerns the protection of consumers and the environment, and competition of business.

Consumer protection legislation has been developed to address the inability of consumers to adequately test the quality of products before purchase. The maxim "buyer beware" demonstrates the onus that has traditionally been placed on the purchaser with respect to purchases. Increasing complexity of products has made consumers' responsibility to test them impractical and, in many cases, impossible. Legislation in this area has given consumers greater bargaining power thus inducing businesses to maintain a higher standard of production and conduct.

The *Competition Act* has been introduced to ensure that businesses maintain an acceptable standard of competition. The intention is to ensure that various sectors do not become dominated by a handful of businesses. It has been recognized that competition promotes efficiency and low prices as well as quality and value. The *Competition Act* exists to restrict activity that may otherwise disrupt a competitive market.

Environmental protection legislation is an important tool with which to ensure that air, water, plant and animal life are sustained. Legislation in this field has played a role in encouraging business to diminish its output of environmentally harmful products.

Learning Objectives

A. Describe the legislative framework for government regulation of business.

B. Discuss the general nature of consumer protection legislation.

C. Discuss the general nature of the *Competition Act*.

D. Discuss the general nature of environmental protection legislation.

Content Outline

I. The legal framework for doing business in Canada

II. The power to regulate business
    A. Division of powers under the Constitution
    B. Restrictions on government powers: The *Canadian Charter of Rights and Freedoms*

III. Regulation of various business sectors

IV. Judicial review of government regulations

V. Consumer protection
    A. Background
    B. Modern Developments
    C. Principal types of consumer legislation
    D. Misleading advertising and other representations of sellers
    E. Regulation of labelling, product safety, and performance standards
    F. Regulation of business conduct towards consumers
        1. Pressure selling
        2. Unsolicited goods
        3. Telemarketing
        4. Repossession
        5. Financing arrangements
    G. Disclosure of the true cost of credit
    H. Regulation of business by licensing, bonding, and inspection

VI. Competition
    A. Background
    B. The common law
    C. The *Competition Act*
        1. Exemptions
        2. Enforcement

Questions on Learning Objectives

Objective A: Describe the source of power that enables government to regulate business.

A.1 What is federal paramountcy? When might it arise in the business context? (pp. 729–730)

A.2 Describe the grounds upon which an administrative act or decision may be challenged. (pp. 732–733)

Objective B: Examine the nature of consumer protection legislation.

B.1 What is consumer protection legislation? (p. 733)

B.2 Is consumer protection legislation necessary? Explain. (pp. 733–734)

B.3 List five classes of consumer protection legislation. (pp. 734–735)

B.4 Describe five business practices prohibited by the *Competition Act*. (pp. 740–745)

B.5 What is a cooling-off period? (p. 738)

B.6 Describe the effect of consumer protection legislation on unsolicited goods. (p. 738)

B.7 Explain the disclosure requirements for credit sales. (p. 739)

B.8 What happens if a credit sale is made but the actual cost is not disclosed? (p. 739)

Objective C: Discuss the general nature of regulation of competition.

C.1 What are the main features of the *Competition Act*. (pp. 741–747)

C.2 How does "conscious parallelism" differ from an agreement with respect to pricing? (pp. 742–743)

C.3 Distinguish discriminatory pricing, predatory pricing and regional price discrimination. (pp. 744–745)

C.4 What factors should be considered when examining whether a merger would threaten competition? (p. 747)

Objective D: Explore the general nature of environmental protection legislation.

D.1 What is the scope of the *Canadian Environmental Protection Act*? (p. 749)

D.2 What is the potential liability of a polluter? (p. 750)

Answers to Questions on Learning Objectives

A.1 Powers are granted to the federal government in the *Constitution Act 1867*. Federal powers are set out in section 91; provincial powers are described in section 92. The breadth of these powers may be problematic at times. In a business context, Parliament's jurisdiction over "the regulation of trade and commerce" may conflict with a given province's jurisdiction over "property and civil rights." When this happens, federal powers prevail over provincial powers. This priority of federal legislation is called the principle of federal paramountcy.

A.2 Administrative acts or decisions may be challenged on any or all of the following: constitutional grounds; lack of authority of the party who made the decision; procedural irregularity; and procedural unfairness.

B.1 Consumer protection legislation is legislation that protects individuals from losses due to receiving less than fair value for their money.

B.2 While common law remedies were sufficient to protect consumers in the 19th and early 20th century, modern developments make such remedies inadequate. First, litigation is expensive and people cannot always afford the time or money to go to court to remedy wrongs. Second, there is now a concentration of business in a number of enterprises, which leads to an inequality in bargaining power between the individual and the corporate seller. As well, some goods are now so complicated that it is difficult to detect defects even if examination is possible. Moreover, mass advertising may induce customers to buy things that do not conform to their expectations. The legislatures have had to develop statutes to deal with these problems as they arose.

B.3 The five classes of consumer protection legislation are; (a) regulation of advertising and selling practices, (b) regulation of standards affecting the safety and performance of goods and services, (c) regulation of business conduct towards consumers, (d) regulation requiring disclosure of the cost of credit, and (e) supervision of the businesses that deal with the public through licensing, bonding and inspection.

B.4 The *Competition Act* prohibits misleading representations made for the purpose of promoting the use of a product or concerning the regular price of a product. It also prohibits publication about a product that cannot be corroborated. It prohibits advertising a product at a bargain price when the seller does not supply reasonable quantities. It further prohibits pyramid selling, referral selling and the advertising of an article or service at a lower price than it is actually being sold for.

B.5 A cooling-off period is the period of grace given to a buyer after she purchases goods from a door-to-door salesperson. During that period, the buyer may terminate the contract by giving written notice to the seller. After doing so, she has no obligation under the contract and may recover any money that has already been paid.

B.6 A consumer who receives unsolicited goods may use them without becoming liable for their price. This legislation attempts to discourage sellers from sending unsolicited goods to customers.

B.7 In a credit sale, the contract must set out the actual cost of credit in both dollar amounts and percentage rates.

B.8 If the credit sale is made without such disclosure, the customer is not bound by the contract.

C.1 The *Competition Act* prohibits certain activities that would lessen competition. The following may be considered to be anti-competitive behaviour: conspiracy between two or more parties to lessen competition; creating or ensuring a continued monopoly in a market; and mergers of organizations, which would substantially effect competition. The threshold that is required to find that an activity is anti-competitive is that competition would be lessened unduly. This seems to suggest that a moderate reduction in competition is acceptable. However, a serious or significant reduction in competition will likely trigger application of the *Act*.

C.2 An "agreement" or "conspiracy" between parties regarding pricing strategies may be seen as anti-competitive and subject to the *Competition Act*. This may be distinguished from "conscious parallelism" which appears upon the surface to be a concerted effort to set prices but is actually a result of market forces. Competitors often must raise or drop prices in response to competitors pricing practices to simply retain market share.

C.3 Section 50 of the *Competition Act* prohibits three pricing practices as they are seen, in the eyes of the law, to lessen competition. Discriminatory pricing occurs where goods are sold at different prices to purchasers who are in competition with one another without a commercially reasonable explanation. This practice is distinguished from predatory pricing in which goods are sold to competing purchasers at an excessively low price. The reduced price, when compared to that which the seller and the seller's competitors would normally charge, is viewed to have been implemented in order to lessen competition. Regional price discrimination is apparent when a seller makes goods available to purchasers in one region for a substantially different price than purchasers in other regions. This activity may force competitors in the affected region to drop their price, greatly impacting competitors whose operations are confined to the particular region. A prolonged price reduction may substantially affect revenues and force these companies out of the market.

C.4 Section 93 of the *Competition Act* suggests that the following factors be considered: whether a reduction of competition in Canada will have adverse consequences due to the existence of foreign competition; whether the target company would otherwise have been likely to continue its operations; whether there are acceptable substitutes for the goods affected; whether barriers to entry into the market exist; whether effective competition will remain after the merger; and whether the merger would eliminate a vigorous, effective, and innovative competitor.

D.1 The *Canadian Environmental Protection Act* applies to air, water, atomic energy, organic and inorganic matter, living organisms, and transportation of dangerous goods. Guidelines and codes of practice have been created by the Minister of the Environment to deal with these matters. Recycling, storage, disposal, and conservation regulations must be complied with by organizations that have dealings that fall within these categories.

D.2 Companies may face liability for various infractions prescribed by statute. Under common law liability may be founded in tort or nuisance. Also, violation of a statute may support a finding of negligence. Injunctions may be issued to prevent or force certain actions; damages may be awarded for clean-up costs; prison sentences may be ordered; and fines may be issued under the statutory scheme.

Multiple-Choice Questions

1. The Acme Light Company manufacturers light bulbs in Manitoba and ships the bulbs for sale all over the country. The federal government passed a statute that regulates the importation and transportation of light bulbs. The provincial governments argue that the statute is not within the jurisdiction of the federal government so pass their own, different laws concerning the transportation of light bulbs. Which law should the Acme Lighting Company be concerned with when transporting its light bulbs?

a) The federal statute because Acme transports the bulbs across provincial boundaries.
b) The Manitoba law because the bulbs are manufactured in Manitoba.

c) Every province through which the bulbs are transported because each law applies while the bulbs are in that province.
d) The federal statute and all the provincial statutes to the extent that the laws do not conflict.
e) No law because the transportation of light bulbs is not a hazardous activity.

2. What is meant by the principle of "paramountcy"?

a) Federal and provincial laws never conflict but are always concurrent.
b) A provincial law prevails over a contrary federal law.
c) A federal law prevails over a contrary provincial law.
d) A provincial law of a province that entered confederation first prevails over a contrary provincial law of a province that entered confederation second.
e) A court must interpret overlapping provincial and federal laws to avoid conflicts.

3. A firm was criminally prosecuted for opening its store on a Sunday, contrary to the federal *Lord's Day Act*. In its defence, the firm claimed that the law was unconstitutional both with respect to jurisdiction and the *Canadian Charter of Rights and Freedoms*. Is the law unconstitutional?

a) Yes because the regulation of business is within the provincial powers, but it is not contrary to the *Canadian Charter of Rights and Freedoms*.
b) No because criminal laws preserving the sanctity of the Christian Sabbath are within the federal powers and are not contrary to the *Canadian Charter of Rights and Freedoms*.
c) Yes because the regulation of business is within the provincial powers and the law discriminates based on religion.
d) Yes because, although criminal laws preserving the sanctity of the Christian Sabbath are within the federal powers, the law discriminates based on religion.
e) No because the subject of the law is within both the federal and provincial powers and the law is not contrary to the *Canadian Charter of Rights and Freedoms*.

4. The Canadian Radio and Telecommunication Commission ("CRTC"), in its infinite wisdom, has decided to establish strict regulations for the broadcasting of educational programming. Each television station must show six hours of educational television each day between the hours of 9 a.m. and noon, and 2 p.m. and 5 p.m. The television stations object to these regulations and have asked a court to review the decision to impose the restrictions. On what grounds can a court review this decision?

a) On constitutional grounds if the CRTC's decision is within a provincial sphere of power, such as education.
b) On a lack of authority if the legislation which established the CRTC did not allow it to regulate this aspect of television programming.

c) On a procedural irregularity if the CRTC did not make its decision using appropriate procedures.
d) On procedural unfairness if the CRTC made an arbitrary decision.
e) All of the above.

5. New Age Medicines Inc. is marketing a new product as an all-natural medicine that can cure the common cold. When a lab tests the product, it finds three manufactured chemicals as part of the ingredients. Can the lab do anything about the product?

a) Yes because no medicine can cure the common cold.
b) No because natural products are not regulated by the government.
c) Yes because the product is not all natural so it is not labelled accurately as required by the *Food and Drug Act*.
d) No because manufactured chemicals can still be considered natural.
e) Yes because the product guarantees its effectiveness that is contrary to the *Competition Act*.

6. The Cheap Stereo and Television Store places an advertisement in the Saturday paper stating "For one day only, the 20-inch Special Television is $200, instead of its regular price of $400." When Joe goes to the store ten minutes after it opens, he finds that all the Special Televisions have been sold, but the store has another unadvertised special: a 20-inch television for sale at $350 instead of $450. Joe thinks there is a problem with this situation. Is he correct?

a) No, this is normal business practice.
b) Yes, it is called bait and switch and is contrary to the *Competition Act*.
c) Yes, it is called double ticketing and is contrary to the *Competition Act*.
d) Yes, it is called referral selling and is contrary to the *Competition Act*.
e) No, the store had an adequate supply of the Special Televisions, but they sold out in ten minutes.

7. Sean finds that there is little food in his kitchen and he is hungry. Being sick of pizza and Chinese food, Sean decides to try a different approach and goes grocery shopping. Sean picks up six cans of soup and finds that all six have two price tags on them. At the checkout, the cashier rings in the higher price. Sean thinks there is a problem with this situation. Is he correct?

a) No, the store obviously just upped the price and the person putting on the labels did not make sure that the new label was directly over the old label.
b) Yes, it is called bait and switch and is contrary to the *Competition Act*.
c) Yes, it is called double ticketing and is contrary to the *Competition Act*.
d) Yes, it is called referral selling and is contrary to the *Competition Act*.
e) No, the store has a choice of which price tag to use.

8. Diane has developed a new software package that makes connecting to, and using, the Internet much simpler. There are so many other similar packages on the market that Diane decides to mail out 3000 copies of her package to businesses hoping that the businesses will like the software and purchase additional copies. Because of the cost of producing the 3000 copies, the diskette with the package is sealed in a pouch with a label stating "Opening this package indicates acceptance of the offer to purchase this software package and you now owe the seller $50 for the copy." After Bill opens and tries out his copy of the software package, Diane sends a letter demanding payment of $50. Does Bill have to pay?

a) Yes because opening the package indicated acceptance of the offer to sell.
b) No because the goods were unsolicited under the provincial business practices acts.
c) Yes because Bill did not just open the pouch, he used the software package.
d) No because the *Competition Act* would prevent Diane collecting the $50.
e) No because the provincial business practices acts require a cooling-off period.

9. Mac has noticed that every time the price of gas goes up 5¢ at one station, the price goes up at every other station in town within an hour. Mac thinks there is something wrong with this. Is he correct?

a) No, it is likely just an example of commercial parallelism.
b) Yes, it must be collusion for this to happen and collusion is contrary to the *Competition Act*.
c) Yes, it must be a conspiracy for this to happen and pricing conspiracies are contrary to the *Competition Act*.
d) Yes, even if it is just an example of a normal practice in the gas industry.
e) No, the price of gas reflects the international price of petroleum and all stations have to deal with international price changes at the same time.

10. Which of the following is an example of restrictive practices that may be prohibited by section 45 of the *Competition Act*?

a) An activity that places any limits on facilities for transporting, producing, or dealing in any product.
b) An activity that places any limits on the manufacture or production of a product.
c) An activity that places any limits on competition in the production, or the supply of a product.
d) An activity that places any limits on any other form of competition.
e) None of the above.

11. Why is a horizontal merger more significant than other forms of merger?

a) Because one business takes over a competitor thereby lessening competition.
b) Because one business takes over a subsidiary thereby consolidating its market share.

c) Because one business takes over a company in another industry thereby diversifying its operations.
d) Because one business takes over a competitor thereby increasing competition.
e) Because one business takes over a subsidiary thereby expanding its market share.

12. What are the distinctions between horizontal, vertical and diversification mergers?

a) In a horizontal merger, a business takes over another unrelated business. In a vertical merger, a business takes over a supplier or customer. In a diversification merger, a business takes over a competitor.
b) In a horizontal merger, a business takes over a supplier or customer. In a vertical merger, a business takes over another unrelated business. In a diversification merger, a business takes over a competitor.
c) In a horizontal merger, a business takes over a competitor. In a vertical merger, a business takes over a supplier or customer. In a diversification merger, a business takes over another unrelated business.
d) In a horizontal merger, a business takes over a competitor. In a vertical merger, a business takes over another unrelated business. In a diversification merger, a business takes over a supplier or customer.
e) In a horizontal merger, a business takes over a supplier or customer. In a vertical merger, a business takes over a competitor. In a diversification merger, a business takes over another unrelated business.

13. A factory is releasing so much smoke into the atmosphere that the area around the factory is constantly covered in ash. The neighbours cannot spend time in their backyards due to problems breathing. Is there anything the factory's neighbours can do to solve the problem?

a) The neighbours can sue the factory for breach of contract and ask the court for an injunction.
b) The neighbours can sue the factory for damages under nuisance, but the court cannot order the factory to stop polluting.
c) The neighbours can sue the factory for breach of contract and ask the court to force the factory to buy their houses.
d) The neighbours can sue the factory for damages under nuisance and the court can order the factory to stop polluting.
e) There is nothing the neighbours can do.

14. What is the purpose of an environmental impact assessment review?

a) To review major projects after they have been constructed to see if they are having an effect on the environment.
b) To review proposed major projects before they are constructed to prepare the construction company to deal with the environmental impacts.

c) To review major projects after they have been constructed to determine the amount of damages that the construction company owes to the surrounding neighbours to compensate for environmental injuries.
d) To review proposed major projects that are likely to have an impact on the environment in an effort to better prevent injury to the environment.
e) To review major projects both before and after construction to see the effect the project is having on the environment.

15. What types of orders are possible when there is public enforcement of environmental laws?

a) Orders to refrain from harmful activities, to remedy existing situations and to pay for the cost of clean-up.
b) Orders to refrain from doing any further activities in connection with the environmental problem.
c) Orders to imprison the corporation responsible for the environmental problem.
d) Orders to refrain from harmful activities, to refrain from doing any further activities in connection with the environmental problem and to imprison the corporation responsible for the environmental problem.
e) Orders to remedy existing situations, to pay for the cost of clean-up and to imprison the corporation responsible for the environmental problem.

16. Which of the following contracts may be affected by consumer protection legislation?
I. Purchase of a regularly priced item of clothing from a department store.
II. Goods sent to you in the mail on a 30-day trial basis.
III. Purchase of a car over time.

a) I only
b) II only
c) III only
d) II and III only
e) I, II and III

17. Which of the following acts is *not* an offence under the *Competition Act*?

a) An agreement between companies to limit production of goods.
b) Refusal to supply a particular customer.
c) Stipulating the price at which a product must be resold to consumers.
d) Competing firm agreeing with another that they will not submit a tender for a contract.

18. Which is true of environmental protection legislation?
I. It is intended to force business to actively "clean-up" the environment.
II. It governs waste management.
III. It has been enforced rigorously and consistently since its 19th century beginnings.

a) I only
b) II only
c) III only
d) I and II
e) I and III

Answers to Multiple-Choice Questions

1. a)
See pages 729–730 for more information.

2. c)
See page 730 for more information.

3. d)
See page 730 for more information.

4. e)
See pages 731–733 for more information.

5. c)
See page 735 for more information

6. b)
See page 736 for more information.

7. c)
See page 736 for more information.

8. b)
See page 738 for more information.

9. a)
See page 743 for more information.

10. e)
See page 742 for more information.

11. a)
See page 747 for more information.

12. c)
See page 747 for more information.

13. b)
See pages 748–749 for more information.

14. d)
See page 750 for more information.

15. a)
See page 750 for more information.

16. d)
See pages 733–740 for more information.

17. b)
See pages 740–748 for more information.

18. b)
See pages 748–751 for more information.

True/False Questions

1. Powers are granted to the federal government in the *Constitution Act 1867*. Federal powers are set out in section 92; provincial powers are described in section 91.

2. Consumer protection legislation is legislation that protects corporations from losses due to receiving less than fair value for their money.

3. The five classes of consumer protection legislation are (a) regulation of advertising and selling practices, (b) regulation of standards affecting the safety and performance of goods and services, (c) regulation of business conduct towards consumers, (d) regulation requiring disclosure of the cost of credit, and (e) supervision of the businesses that deal with the public through licensing, bonding and inspection.

4. A consumer who receives unsolicited goods cannot use them without becoming liable for their price.

5. An "agreement" or "conspiracy" between parties regarding pricing strategies is normal business practices.

6. The *Canadian Environmental Protection Act* applies to the protection of goods and services across Canada.

Answers to True/False Questions

1. False. Powers are granted to the federal government in the *Constitution Act 1867*. Federal powers are set out in section 91; provincial powers are described in section 92. The breadth of these powers may be problematic at times. In a business context, Parliament's jurisdiction over "the regulation of trade and commerce" may conflict with a given province's jurisdiction over "property and civil rights." When this happens, federal powers prevail over provincial powers. This priority of federal legislation is called the principle of federal paramountcy.

2. True.

3. True.

4. False. A consumer who receives unsolicited goods may use them without becoming liable for their price. This legislation attempts to discourage sellers from sending unsolicited goods to customers.

5. False. An "agreement" or "conspiracy" between parties regarding pricing strategies may be seen as anti-competitive and subject to the *Competition Act*. This may be distinguished from "conscious parallelism" which appears upon the surface to be a concerted effort to set prices but is actually a result of market forces. Competitors often must raise or drop prices in response to competitors pricing practices to simply retain market share.

6. False. The *Canadian Environmental Protection Act* applies to air, water, atomic energy, organic and inorganic matter, living organisms, and transportation of dangerous goods. Guidelines and codes of practice have been created by the Minister of the Environment to deal with these matters. Recycling, storage, disposal, and conservation regulations must be complied with by organizations that have dealings that fall within these categories.

33

International Business Transactions

Purpose and Significance

The days when businesses operated locally and nationally are long gone. Today, Canadian business is frequently global.

The legal consequences of operating outside our national boundaries can fall into two areas: private law and public law. The private law questions relate to the dealings between private individuals. When two parties to a transaction are from different countries, the laws of which country should govern? The public law element arises because governments are involved in the regulation of foreign trade and investment. There will often be questions about the government activities, which impinge upon foreign trade and investment such as export controls, import duties, and bilateral and multilateral agreements between governments.

In this chapter, we examine some of the legal questions that arise in connection with foreign trade and investment from both the private and the public law perspectives. The chapter concludes with a discussion of the mechanisms for resolving international business disputes.

Learning Objectives

A. Examine export contracts from a legal perspective.

B. Discuss government regulation of international trade.

C. Identify the key elements of foreign investment.

D. Discuss the ways in which international business disputes can be resolved.

Content Outline

I. Canadian business in a global economy

II. Law and international business

III. Foreign trade
    A. Export contracts
        1. The contract of sale
        2. The proper law of the contract
        3. Contractual terms
        4. The documentation
        5. Shipment and insurance
        6. Payment
        7. Financing
        8. Countertrade
        9. Export of services
    B. Government regulation of international trade
        1. Export promotion
        2. Export controls
        3. Import duties
        4. Import restrictions
        5. Dumping and subsidies
    C. The international law of trade
        1. The GATT and World Trade Organization
        2. North America Free Trade

IV. Foreign investment
    A. Forms of foreign investment
    B. Government regulation of foreign investment
    C. Foreign investment and international law

V. The resolution of international business disputes
    A. Judicial proceedings
        1. Jurisdiction
        2. Standing
        3. Choice of law
        4. Enforcement of foreign judgements
    B. Commercial Arbitration
    C. Inter-nation disputes
    D. The GATT and WTO
    E. The NAFTA

Questions on Learning Objectives

Objective A: Examine export contracts from a legal perspective.

A.1 The international sale of goods is the most common type of export transaction. What is the best method to use to determine which country's laws govern the transaction? (pp. 755–756)

A.2 What four documents are routinely required for an export sale? (p. 757)

A.3 Shipping arrangements are a vital aspect of an export sale. List four standard forms of shipping and explain what each means. (pp. 757–758)

Objective B: Discuss government regulation of international trade.

B.1 Briefly describe the meaning of the following forms of government regulation of foreign trade: export controls, import duties, import restrictions, and dumping and subsidies. (pp. 760–762)

B.2 What is GATT? What are its most important functions? (pp. 762–763)

B.3 What is NAFTA? How is NAFTA different from GATT? (p. 764)

Objective C: **Identify the key elements of foreign investment.**

C.1 What is foreign direct investment? How is it conducted? (p. 765)

C.2 What role, if any, does a government play in regulating foreign investment? (pp. 765–766)

Objective D: **Discuss the ways in which international business disputes can be resolved.**

D.1 If a dispute arises over an international transaction, is a party free to take the matter to any court that it wishes? (pp. 769–770)

D.2 What problems arise if judgement is obtained against a foreign person? (p. 770)

D.3 What is commercial arbitration and what are its advantages over court action? (p. 771)

D.4 How are disputes involving alleged breaches of GATT and NAFTA resolved? (pp. 772–773)

Answers to Questions on Learning Objectives

A.1 The clearest and best method is for the parties to expressly agree upon which country's laws are to govern the transaction. If they fail to make express provision, it will be up to the courts to decide "the proper law of the contract" by attempting to determine what the intention of the parties was in that regard.

A.2 An export sale normally requires the contract of sale, the bill of lading, the insurance policy or certificate and the invoice.

A.3 Four standard shipping arrangements are: ex works; free on board; cost, insurance and freight; and, delivery duty paid.

In Ex Works' contracts, the seller's responsibility is only to make the goods available to the buyer at the seller's own works or warehouse. The buyer bears the cost, and the risk, of transportation, though the seller is obliged to furnish the necessary invoice and to provide all reasonable assistance to obtain any export license or other authorization necessary for exporting the goods.

Under the Free on Board contract, the buyer arranges shipment and the seller's obligation is to deliver the goods to the carrier named by the buyer. The seller's responsibility ends when the goods are safely on board the ship or aircraft.

A Cost, Insurance and Freight contract represents a major extension of the seller's obligations as the seller has the responsibility for shipping the goods. Thus, the seller is responsible for insuring the goods as well as shipping.

The Delivery Duty Paid contract extends the seller's responsibility even further as the seller bears the risks and costs of transporting the goods and paying the import duties.

B.1 Export controls refer to the restrictions, placed by governments, upon exports. The restrictions may be upon the type of goods that can be exported, the amount of a particular type of good that can be exported or licensing arrangements to govern goods to be exported.

An import duty is a tax placed by governments upon goods coming into a country. Import restrictions, on the other hand, are limits on goods that may be imported into a country.

Dumping and export subsidies are two practices that are regarded as undesirable. Dumping occurs where a firm sells goods abroad at prices lower than those at which similar goods sell in the domestic market. The effect is for a company to use profit on domestic sales to subsidize its exports so that it can undercut the competition. Subsidization occurs where the government of a country provides special benefits, financial or otherwise, to its producers in order to assist them to export.

B.2 The General Agreement of Tariffs and Trade (GATT) is the principal instrument that lays down rules for international trade. GATT is important as a forum for negotiations and the resolution of trade disputes, harmonizing customs tariffs and establishing a body of rules governing trade between contracting states.

B.3 GATT permits the creation of regional free-trade areas. One such area consists of Canada, Mexico and the United States of America through the North American Free Trade Agreement (NAFTA). Although NAFTA is like GATT, it goes further in liberalizing trade and investment. All tariffs on goods among the three countries are to be eliminated by the year 2008. It streamlines customs procedures and eliminates user fees. NAFTA is not restricted to trade goods and services; it also contains provisions relating to investment.

C.1 Foreign direct investment occurs as part of active business operations and refers to investment made to acquire a lasting interest in an enterprise where the investor's purpose is to have an effective voice in the management of the enterprise.

C.2 A firm wishing to carry on business in another country must comply with the laws of that country. Different countries exert different degrees and levels of regulation over foreign investment.

D.1 A party may attempt to take the dispute to whatever court is wishes; however, a court will only consent to hear disputes over which it feels it has jurisdiction. To find jurisdiction, a court will insist on a litigant demonstrating a connecting factor with the country and perhaps even demonstrating that the court is in the country with the strongest connection to the dispute.

D.2 Even if a court takes jurisdiction and awards judgement, if the defendant has no assets in the jurisdiction, it will be difficult to realize on the judgement. In that case, the plaintiff will have to go to the courts of the country in which the defendant has assets and convince the foreign courts to recognize the plaintiff's judgement and allow the plaintiff to use the mechanisms available in the foreign country to realize on the judgement.

D.3 Commercial arbitration is the arrangement made by parties to have binding arbitration resolve disputes that arise as opposed to going through the courts.

The advantages of commercial arbitration include that fact that the arbitrators normally have greater experience in matters of international commerce, the proceedings are more confidential, costs are usually lower and decisions rendered more quickly. As well, arbitration awards are more easily enforced because of the consensual nature of the arbitration process.

D.4 Treaties normally contain their own procedures for the resolution of disputes. GATT contains two types of proceedings: consultation and, if necessary, conciliation; alternatively, a Panel may be appointed to adjudicate and make recommendations.

NAFTA provides similar dispute resolution mechanisms to GATT.

Multiple-Choice Questions

1. William, a Canadian citizen residing in France, entered into an agreement with Ian, a citizen of the United Kingdom residing in Japan, under the terms of which William was to supply certain goods to Ian. After delivery of the goods, Ian refused to pay for them. In which court should William take action?

a) In Canada as William is a citizen.
b) In France as William is resident there.
c) In the United Kingdom as Ian is a citizen.
d) In Japan as Ian is resident there.
e) In the country which has the closest ties to the contract.

2. The Book Company of the U.S. has printed too many copies of a book that was on the New York Times best seller list for eight weeks. In an attempt to get some of their money back, the Book Company decides to sell the extra copies to a discount book chain in Canada for $1.00 a book even though the book cost $25.00 to buy in the U.S. The discount book chain will sell the books for $2.50. The various regular book chains in Canada complain to the federal government about these books and the government decides to impose a charge on the books crossing the border. What would such a charge be called?

a) A countervailing duty.
b) An export subsidy.
c) An anti-dumping duty.
d) An administrative surcharge.
e) A non-tariff barrier.

3. Canada has decided to support its Pacific fishing industry by imposing new duties on salmon coming into Canada from other countries. The main countries affected are the U.S., the United Kingdom, Norway, Sweden and Russia, all of which are members of the World Trade Organization. The new duties are different based on the country of origin of the salmon, with the U.S. being required to pay the highest duty. The U.S. has filed a complaint with the World Trade Organization. Which of the following would be the basis of the U.S. main argument?

a) Most-favoured-nation treatment.
b) National treatment.
c) Unfair treatment.
d) Acceptable treatment.
e) Equitable treatment.

4. Canada has decided to support its Pacific fishing industry by imposing new duties on salmon coming into Canada from other countries. The main countries affected are the U.S., the United Kingdom, Norway, Sweden and Russia, all of which are members of the World Trade Organization. Following an order from the

World Trade Organization, the new duties are identical for all foreign countries. However, with the duties in place, the wholesale cost of Canadian salmon is one-quarter the price of imported salmon. The U.S. has filed a complaint with the World Trade Organization. Which of the following would be the basis of the U.S. main argument?

a) Most-favoured-nation treatment.
b) National treatment.
c) Unfair treatment.
d) Acceptable treatment.
e) Equitable treatment.

5. Knowing that the U.S. will object to a dispute resolution panel under the World Trade Organization or the North American Free Trade Agreement if Canada imposes a new duty on magazines, Canada decides to pass a law that magazines sold in Canada with 75% of the articles written by Canadians are entitled to tax breaks on income. The result is that while magazines that do not meet the Canadian content rule must pay 50% tax on profit, those that do meet the rule pay 15% tax. The American magazine industry objects and files a complaint with the World Trade Organization. How would the American magazine industry classify the new tax rules?

a) An indirect duty.
b) A rule contract to national treatment.
c) A non-tariff barrier.
d) A cultural subsidy.
e) An import duty.

6. Axel Inc. does extensive trade with foreign countries, such as the U.S. and Germany. Usually, Axel is required to make payments in the appropriate foreign currency. Due to the constantly fluctuating Canadian dollar, Axel is finding that it is losing money on some deals, but making money on others. What would be Axel's best course of action?

a) Axel should conclude all its deals in U.S. dollars and move the company to the U.S.
b) Axel should stop making deals with companies in other countries.
c) Axel should buy or sell foreign currency when the exchange rate is good, not necessarily when Axel needs to make a payment.
d) Axel should conclude all its deals in Canadian dollars and let its opponents deal with the currency problems.
e) Axel should do nothing and hope that the overall result is in its favour.

7. An American manufacturer sells goods stored in Mexico to a French customer. The goods will be shipped by a Canadian ship and insured by a British insurance company, and a Swiss bank will finance the transaction. The contract, concluded in the U.S., states that any arbitration will follow the international arbitration rules

established in Switzerland, and the American courts may settle disputes. Which of the following countries is the proper law of the contract?

a) Canada.
b) The United Kingdom.
c) Mexico.
d) The United States.
e) France.

8. A Canadian company agrees to sell goods to a wholesaler in Egypt. The Canadian company is responsible for delivering the goods to the wholesaler. It is standard practice for customs officers in Egypt to require an importer to pay a bribe before allowing goods to be cleared for entry into the country. What should the Canadian company do?

a) Refuse to pay the bribe because to do so is an offence under Canadian law.
b) Pay the bribe and count it as a business expense for tax purposes.
c) Tell the Egyptian government that the customs official asked for a bribe.
d) Tell the Organization for Economic Co-operation and Development (OECD) that Egyptian government officials are asking for bribes.
e) Refuse to deliver the goods to Egypt.

9. How are disputes resolved under the North American Free Trade Agreement?

a) Through the court system of the United States in all cases.
b) Through consultations, the Free Trade Commission, and an arbitration panel if necessary.
c) Through the court system of the country making the complaint.
d) Through the international court of justice.
e) Through arbitration with Mexico choosing the arbitrator.

10. In order to support the Canadian economy, which of the following should the Canadian government do?

a) Restrict exports and restrict imports.
b) Restrict exports and support imports.
c) Support exports and restrict imports.
d) Support exports and support imports.
e) Do nothing and let the Canadian economy take care of itself.

11. What is the main distinction between direct investment and portfolio investment?

a) Portfolio investment is investment in mutual funds whereas direct investment is investment in shares.
b) Portfolio investment is investment in active business operations whereas direct investment is passive investment.

c) Portfolio investment is investment with cash whereas direct investment is investment with chattels and/or property.

d) Portfolio investment is passive investment whereas direct investment is investment in active business operations.

e) Portfolio investment is investment by buying chattels and/or property whereas direct investment is investment by buying bonds and securities.

12. What are some of the ways to finance an international sale?

a) Bill of promise, collection arrangement or letter of credit.

b) Bill of exchange, collection agency or letter of credit.

c) Bill of exchange, collection arrangement or letter of promise.

d) Bill of exchange, collection arrangement or letter of credit.

e) Bill of promise, collection agency or letter of promise.

13. What is the role of Investment Canada?

a) To authorize all investments in foreign firms by Canadian companies.

b) To authorize all investment in Canadian companies by foreign firms.

c) To authorize the acquisition of larger existing Canadian businesses by foreign firms.

d) To authorize all investments made by the federal government.

e) To authorize all investments made by the federal government.

14. What is countertrade?

a) Exports of goods to a country that imports goods to Canada.

b) A trade of black-market goods.

c) Goods that are sold over the counter.

d) A trade consisting of an exchange of chattels or services, not cash, within a country.

e) Exports of goods by a firm to Canada in exchange for import of goods by the firm in a country such as Cuba.

15. What are the main advantages of commercial arbitration, as opposed to litigating disputes in the courts?

a) A neutral body to settle the dispute; greater experience of arbitrators; a non-public forum; awards that are easier to enforce.

b) A neutral body to settle the dispute; greater experience of arbitrators; a public forum; awards that are easier to enforce.

c) A neutral body to settle the dispute; greater experience of arbitrators; a non-public forum; awards that are more difficult to enforce.

d) A home court advantage for one party; greater experience of arbitrators; a non-public forum; awards that are easier to enforce.

e) A neutral body to settle the dispute; arbitrators with little experience; a non-public forum; awards that are easier to enforce.

16. Which of the following terms may commonly be found in a well drafted export contract?
I. The proper law of the contract
II. Provision for binding arbitration
III. A description of the shipping and insurance obligations of the parties

a) I only
b) II only
c) III only
d) I and III only
e) I, II and III

17. All of the following statements are correct EXCEPT:

a) Governments regulate foreign trade by controlling exports and imports.
b) Governmental policy is generally directed towards encouraging exports and discouraging imports.
c) Governments attempt to prevent dumping and export subsidization.
d) Governments enter into treaties like GATT and NAFTA in order to regulate international trade.
e) Governments will normally regulate foreign investment in their countries.

18. Xavier, a Canadian citizen, entered into an agreement with Yolanda, a citizen of the United Kingdom, under the terms of which Xavier was to supply certain goods. Xavier supplied the goods and Yolanda has refused to pay for them. Xavier is unsure whether he can take action in a Canadian court. The correct statement of his position is:

a) As a Canadian citizen, Xavier has the right to take action against Yolanda in a Canadian court.
b) Xavier has his choice: he can sue Yolanda here or in the English courts.
c) Xavier may take action in the country in which he is normally resident.
d) Xavier must take action in the country where the strongest connection is found to exist with the contract.
e) If the agreement stipulates which country's laws are to govern, Xavier must take action according to its terms. If there is no stipulation, Xavier must establish a connecting factor with the Canadian courts in order to have it heard here and he may even have to establish that the strongest connection exists between Canada and the contract.

Answers to Multiple-Choice Questions

1. d)
See page 756 for more information.

2. c)
See page 762 for more information.

3. a)
See page 763 for more information.

4. b)
See page 763 for more information.

5. c)
See page 761 for more information

6. c)
See page 759 for more information.

7. d)
See page 756 for more information.

8. d)
See page 764 for more information.

9. b)
See page 773 for more information.

10. c)
See page 760 for more information.

11. d)
See page 765 for more information.

12. d)
See page 759 for more information.

13. c)
See page 766 for more information.

14. e)
See page 759 for more information.

15. a)
See page 771 for more information.

16. e)
See pages 755–760 for more information.

17. c)
See pages 760–764 for more information.

18. e)
See pages 769–773 for more information.

True/False Questions

1. The clearest and best method for contracting is for the parties to expressly agree upon which country's laws are to govern the transaction. If they fail to make express provision, it will be up to the courts to decide "the proper law of the contract" by attempting to determine what the intention of the parties was in that regard.

2. Four standard shipping arrangements are ex works; free on board; cost, insurance and freight; and delivery duty paid.

In Ex Works' contracts, the seller's responsibility is only to make the goods available to the buyer at the seller's own works or warehouse. The buyer bears the cost, and the risk, of transportation, though the seller is obliged to furnish the necessary invoice and to provide all reasonable assistance to obtain any export license or other authorization necessary for exporting the goods.

Under the Free on Board contract, the buyer arranges shipment and the seller's obligation is to deliver the goods to the carrier named by the buyer. The seller's responsibility ends when the goods are safely on board the ship or aircraft.

A Cost, Insurance and Freight contract represents a major extension of the seller's obligations as the seller has the responsibility for shipping the goods. Thus, the seller is responsible for insuring the goods as well as shipping.

The Delivery Duty Paid contract extends the seller's responsibility even further as the seller bears the risks and costs of transporting the goods and paying the import duties.

3. The General Agreement of Tariffs and Trade (GATT) is the principal instrument that lays down rules for international trade. GATT is important as a forum for negotiations and the resolution of trade disputes, harmonizing customs tariffs and establishing a body of rules governing trade between contracting states.

4. Foreign direct investment occurs as part of active business operations and refers to a merger made with a competitor.

5. A party cannot attempt to take the dispute to whatever court it wishes; the party is subject to residence rules.

6. Commercial arbitration is the arrangement made by parties to have negotiations to resolve disputes that arise.

Answers to True/False Questions

1. True.

2. True.

3. True.

4. False. Foreign direct investment occurs as part of active business operations and refers to investment made to acquire a lasting interest in an enterprise where the investor's purpose is to have an effective voice in the management of the enterprise.

5. False. A party may attempt to take the dispute to whatever court it wishes; however, a court will only consent to hear disputes over which it feels it has jurisdiction. To find jurisdiction, a court will insist on a litigant demonstrating a connecting factor with the country and perhaps even demonstrating that the court is in the country with the strongest connection to the dispute.

6. False. Commercial arbitration is the arrangement made by parties to have binding arbitration resolve disputes that arise, as opposed to going through the courts.

The advantages of commercial arbitration include that fact that the arbitrators normally have greater experience in matters of international commerce, the proceedings are more confidential, costs are usually lower and decisions rendered more quickly. As well, arbitration awards are more easily enforced because of the consensual nature of the arbitration process.

34

Electronic Commerce

Purpose and Significance

This chapter provides a background on the growing business field of electronic commerce, a field that raises new legal issues. These issues will be examined in light of existing legal principles. We will try to explain how these principles can be used or adapted to meet the challenges of electronic commerce.

We need to understand what e-commerce is and how contracts are made on the Internet. This will guide us in understanding what laws govern the contracts. Consumers of e-products, as well as businesses, need to be protected. This requires that we understand how trademark and copyright laws apply to the Internet.

Finally, we will examine how the role of the government in regulating e-commerce.

Learning Objectives

A. Define e-commerce.

B. Describe the business of e-commerce.

C. Outline how e-commerce should be regulated.

Content Outline

I. The Growing Importance of Electronic Commerce

II. What is E-Commerce?
    A. The Internet
    B. Electronic retailing
    C. Business-to-business transactions
    D. Electronic transfer of funds
    E. Other business uses of the internet
    F. The potential benefits of e-commerce

III. Establishing an Online Business

IV. E-Commerce and the Law
    A. Contract law
        1. Formation of contracts
        2. The law governing the contract
        3. Formal requirements
    B. "Commercial Paper"
        1. Bills of lading
        2. Negotiable instruments
    C. Intellectual property
        1. Trademarks
        2. Domain names
        3. Copyright
    D. Jurisdiction

V. Regulating E-Commerce
    A. The power to regulate
    B. The application and adaptation of existing laws
        1. Consumer protection
        2. Privacy
        3. Illegal activities
        4. Taxation

VI. International Aspects of E-Commerce

Questions on Learning Objectives

Objective A: Define e-commerce.

A.1 Define e-commerce. (p. 777)

A.2 What is the Internet? (p. 777)

A.3 What is the most obvious form of e-commerce? (p. 778)

A.4 What is a "Web-wrap agreement"? (p. 779)

Objective B: Describe the business of e-commerce.

B.1 The law of contracts may be used to determine what elements in e-commerce contracts? (p. 781)

B.2 What are the precautions to take when establishing an e-commerce site? (p.783)

B.3 What is electronic data interchange? (p. 783)

Objective C: Outline how e-commerce should be regulated.

C.1 How is it possible for a domain name to infringe on someone's trademark? (pp. 784–785)

C.2 What is "cybersquatting"? (p. 787)

C.3 What is the "level of interactivity" test? (p. 789)

C.4 What are the main initiatives being taken, at the international level, to harmonize laws applicable to e-commerce? (pp. 793–794)

Answers to Questions on Learning Objectives

A.1 Electronic commerce can be broadly defined as "the delivery of information, products, services, or payments by telephone, computer or other automated media." It encompasses a number of types of commercial activity, with the common feature that all make use of the Internet or a similar method of communication.

A.2 Internet is the interconnected logical networks that link millions of computers worldwide. The key to the technological revolution introduced by the Internet is the process known as "digitization" — the process of converting information into a sequence of numbers. The information may take the form of writing, pictures or diagrams, speech, or music. Once converted, the information can be sent instantaneously anywhere in the world and can be converted by the recipient into its original form.

A.3 The most obvious form of e-commerce is retailing through the Internet. Electronic retailing can be divided into three categories: supplies of tangible goods, supplies of "electronic goods," and supplies of services.

A.4 A "Web-wrap agreement," also known as a "click-wrap agreement," is a Web site document setting out contractual terms, the acceptance of which is indicated by "clicking" on the appropriate icon.

B.1 The law of the contact may determine: the capacity of the parties to contract; the legality of the contract; the formal requirements governing the contract; any terms that are to be implied; the effects of, and remedies for, breach of contract; and the applicability of consumer protection legislation.

B.2 The precautions should be:
1) to become familiar with the laws of other countries in which it intends to do business;
2) where necessary, to customize contract terms for each country;
3) to design the Web site so that the terms of the contract are brought to the attention of customers before any contract is concluded;
4) to state clearly which law and jurisdiction applies to any contract formed
5) to avoid giving customers too much freedom to amend terms (i.e., use yes/no, or accept/decline options wherever possible)
6) to maintain full back-ups of all contracts made via Web pages.

B.3 Electronic data interchange (EDI) is the exchange of business information from one computer to another.

C.1 While a domain name — a registered internet address of a Web site — does not constitute a trademark, it is common for a domain name to consist of a trademark or trade name and, therefore, may amount to the infringement of another's trademark.

C.2 Cybersquatting happens when a person registers a domain name that includes a well-known trademark or brand name, and then offers to sell the domain name to the owner of the mark or brand. Such action is almost certainly constitutes a trademark infringement and may have serious consequences for the infringer, who may be ordered to relinquish the domain name and pay court costs.

C.3 In *Zippo Manufacturing Co.* v. *Zippo Dot Com, Inc.*, the U.S. court ruled that three types of jurisdictional situations existed:
(1) where the out-of-state defendant is carrying on substantial business within the jurisdiction;
(2) where the defendant maintains an interactive site; and
(3) where the defendant's site provides purely passive advertising.

The court held that it had jurisdiction in case (1), did not have jurisdiction in case (3), and case (2) remains uncertain.

C.4 The main initiatives being taken at the international level to harmonize laws applicable to e-commerce are the "Model Law on Electronic Commerce" drafted by UNCITRAL, and the OECD conferences on e-commerce. At the OECD conferences, a program of work was proposed to: initiate work on defining and measuring e-commerce, develop guidelines for consumer protection, work on the practical implementation of the 1980 OECD Privacy Guidelines, and set up specific technical advisory groups with business to address taxation issues.

Multiple-Choice Questions

1. The rapid growth of e-commerce has been promoted by which of the following factors:

a) Technical advances have greatly increased the speed of transmission and have increased the potential of the Internet to deliver goods and services online.
b) The reduction in the cost of computer hardware.
c) The increase in access to the Internet.
d) The increased regulation of the telecommunications sector.
e) The increase of business failures.

2. The key to the technological revolution introduced by the Internet is the process known as:

a) Internet service provider.
b) Logical infrastructure.
c) Information superhighway.
d) Digitization.
e) Transmission of information.

3. One of the most obvious forms of e-commerce is:

a) Government on-line.
b) Access to information.
c) Privacy information.
d) Supplies of services and goods
e) Contract negotiation.

4. E-cash is:

a) A software that manages money.
b) A software used in calculating the value of the stock market.
c) Cash used for payments of e-commerce purchases.
d) A software payment system that allows anonymous transfer of money over the Internet.
e) A software payment system that allows transfer of money over the Internet without anonymity.

5. Which of the following is a potential benefit of e-commerce?

a) Enables vast amounts of information to be transmitted in a fraction of a second.
b) Allows businesses to increase their efficiency and productivity.
c) Allows access to new markets.
d) Inventories are reduced by adopting "just-in-time" production methods.
e) All of the above.

6. Establishing an on-line business requires:

a) Negotiating a website development agreement.
b) Negotiating a website hosting agreement.
c) Negotiating an Internet access agreement.
d) Registering a domain name.
e) All of the above.

7. The law of a contract regarding e-commerce may determine which of the following:

a) The capacity of the parties to contract.
b) The legality of the contract.

c) The formal requirements governing the contract.
d) The applicability of consumer protection legislation.
e) All of the above.

8. When establishing an e-commerce site, we should take the following precautions:

a) Hire a legal counsel.
b) Hire an accountant.
c) Avoid determining the appropriate jurisdiction to allow more flexibility.
d) State clearly which law and jurisdiction applies to any contracts formed.
e) Provide customers with freedom to amend terms.

9. EDI is:

a) The exchange of business information in paper format.
b) The exchange of business information from one computer to another.
c) The exchange of business information by fax.
d) The exchange of information between individuals.
e) None of the above.

10. Trademark infringement often results from:

a) The close similarity of Internet addresses.
b) The close similarity of domain names.
c) The legitimate owners of the trademark had registered domain names but the infringers had been able to establish the website.
d) A and B.
e) A, B, and C.

11. Registering generic domain names in Canada is done by:

a) Government of Canada.
b) Parliament of Canada.
c) ICANN.
d) Local governments including municipalities.
e) None of the above.

12. Cybersquatting involves:

a) A person registering a new domain name.
b) A person registering a new brand name.
c) A person registering a new trademark.
d) A person registering a domain name containing the trademark of another with the intention of selling the domain to the owner of the mark.
e) A person registering a domain name containing the trademark of another with the intention of using the domain name.

13. The principles by which the courts determine whether they have jurisdiction to hear a particular dispute involves:

a) Knowing the origin of an e-mail.
b) Knowing the ISP.
c) Knowing the content of the message.
d) Knowing if the out-of-state defendant is carrying on substantial business within the jurisdiction.
e) Knowing if the defendant's site provides purely passive advertising.

14. The "level of interactivity" test involves:

a) The defendant's site providing purely passive advertising.
b) The out-of-state defendant carrying on substantial business within the jurisdiction.
c) The defendant maintaining an interactive site.
d) The defendant living in the jurisdiction.
e) The defendant carrying on substantial business in the jurisdiction.

15. Which of the following is a concern of tax administrators regarding e-commerce:

a) Individuals will pay too much in the way of taxes.
b) Sales taxes will be paid twice.
c) Sales taxes and customs duties are easy to evade in e-commerce transactions, especially where goods or services are delivered electronically.
d) E-commerce does not involve taxation issues.
e) There is no transfer of money since payment is done by credit cards.

Answers to Multiple-Choice Questions

1. a)
See page 777 for more information.

2. d)
See page 777 for more information.

3. d)
See pages 778–779 for more information.

4. d)
See page 779 for more information.

5. e)
See pages 779 for more information